The Bryce 5 Handbook

Shamms Mortier

The Bryce 5 Handbook

Shamms Mortier

CHARLES RIVER MEDIA, INC.

Hingham, Massachusetts

Publisher: Jenifer Niles
Production: Publishers' Design & Production Services, Inc.
Cover Design: The Printed Image
Cover Image: Shamms Mortier

CHARLES RIVER MEDIA, INC.
10 Downer Ave.
Hingham, Massachusetts 02043
781-740-0400
781-740-8816 (FAX)
info@charlesriver.com
www.charlesriver.com

This book is printed on acid-free paper.

Shamms Mortier. *The Bryce 5 Handbook.*
ISBN: 1-58450-217-7

Library of Congress Cataloging-in-Publication Data

Mortier, R. Shamms.
The Bryce 5 handbook / R. Shamms Mortier.
p. cm.
ISBN 1-58450-217-7 (paperback : acid-free paper)
1. Computer graphics. 2. KPT Bryce. 3. Computer animation.
4. Computer games—Programming. I. Title.
T385 .M6688 2002
006.6'869—dc21

2002003865

Printed in the United States of America
04 7 6 5 4 3 2

CHARLES RIVER MEDIA titles are available for site license or bulk purchase by institutions, user groups, corporations, etc. For additional information, please contact the Special Sales Department at 781-740-0400.

Requests for replacement of a defective CD-ROM must be accompanied by the original disc, your mailing address, telephone number, date of purchase, and purchase price. Please state the nature of the problem, and send the information to CHARLES RIVER MEDIA, INC., 10 Downer Ave., Hingham, MA. 02043. CRM's sole obligation to the purchaser is to replace the disc, based on defective materials or faulty workmanship, but not on the operation or functionality of the product.

DEDICATION

This book is dedicated to the memory of Tom Hayes.

Contents

Foreword

Since its inception in 1994, Bryce® has captured the hearts and minds of 3D artists everywhere. Its following of devoted users is a testament to the product's incredible versatility and power.

With perhaps the most innovative and captivating user interface of any 3D application, Bryce has always encouraged exploration and interaction. More than just software, it has become a way of life for many of its users. Using Bryce is as much about the experience as the end result—and few applications can match that experience.

Most companies dream of a group of users as fiercely loyal as Bryce customers are. The popularity and success of this product are due in great part to the vast network of users from virtually every corner of the globe—and we owe a great deal of thanks to them.

If you're a long-time Bryce user, you'll love what we've done with Bryce 5. If you're new to Bryce, welcome to the club. You're going to love it here!

The Bryce Team

Acknowledgments

Thanks are sent out to the following people for their assistance and guidance in creating this book:

To Jenifer Niles and Dave Pallai at Charles River Media, my esteemed publishers.

To David and Maureen at Waterside Productions.

To all of the helpful folks at Corel, especially Larry Raubach, and all of the developers of the other applications mentioned in the book.

Introduction

Bryce is a "fractal scenery" generator that you can use to create worlds to investigate and explore. Exactly what is a fractal scenery generator? To know the answer to this question is to have some understanding of the term *fractal* itself.

A fractal is a shape that has more than two but less than three dimensions. As opposed to two-dimensional (2D) objects whose perimeters can be finitely measured (e.g., squares, circles, and other shapes), fractal perimeters are infinite. That sounds very confusing, since we are accustomed to dimensions existing only in whole numbers. A 2D object, for instance, has length and width, but no depth. A planar surface, described by any collection of three points in space, fits this description quite well. A 3D surface, on the other hand, has height, width, and depth. Our perceptual world is filled with 3D objects, from those in nature, to objects we create with our own hands and minds. Fractal dimensions, however, allow for objects that have parameters or boundaries that are new to our understanding, boundaries that prove infinite under investigation.

The science of fractals is only a little more than a quarter of a century old. Although many investigators have contributed to the science of fractal geometry, Benoit Mandelbrot is usually credited with collecting, conceptualizing, and publicizing the language and importance of fractals. His work, done while he was a mathematician at IBM, resulted in a new language and a new paradigm of nature. This new language makes it possible to visualize fractal geometry, even with no prior mathematical background. Corel Bryce is a direct outgrowth of these investigations.

Corel Bryce has something that few other software applications have: a large and dedicated (dare I say obsessed?) user base. It is this user base that drives Bryce development and upgrades, by both its presence and attention to detail. When software developers heed the requests of their user base, users become even more excited. Bryce was originally designed to provide instant high-quality images and animations to the novice user, as well as to provide higher-end tools and capabilities to the CG professional. Bryce has continued its development with the full spectrum of potential users in mind.

Bryce is an open-ended creative system. You can create the awesome power and variety of nature with ease very quickly, or take weeks to fine-tune an immense and fantastic personal landscape. When completed, the results can be printed on paper or other media for gallery work, or sent to videotape, CDs, or DVDs as animated productions, to share with a wider community.

HOW THIS BOOK IS STRUCTURED

This book was designed to take you from the Bryce basics to levels of personal Bryce mastery, not that you will ever run out of new ways to use Bryce. Even after you have explored all of the material presented here, you will always be able to push your Bryce artwork explorations further, in direct proportion to the time you put in while taking creative risks.

CHAPTER 1: BRYCE BASICS

If you are brand new to Bryce, you'll want to make sure to read this chapter thoroughly. It's all about navigating the Bryce interface, and knowing where tools, controls, and menu items are located, and what they do. More advanced users can just skim this chapter and move on to the next.

CHAPTER 2: PRIMITIVES

This chapter details the use of standard Bryce Primitive objects in scenes and in the creation of more complex composited objects. Both Tree objects and Metaballs are passed over, since they are covered separately in following chapters.

CHAPTER 3: TREES

New to Bryce from version 5 and later is the addition of a full-featured Tree modeler. Being able to create trees and associated objects within

Bryce allows you to populate your otherwise barren worlds with all manner of vegetation.

CHAPTER 4: METABALL MODELS

Also added to Bryce modeling options in version 5 is Metaball modeling. If the concept of creating with Metaballs is new to you, be sure to read this chapter to understand it.

CHAPTER 5: BOOLEANS

Booleans offer you yet another way to create models inside of Bryce. This chapter details that process.

CHAPTER 6: TERRAIN MODELS

Since Bryce was conceived to allow you to create worlds with believable vistas, it had to address the creation of various types of terrain to make your worlds look like more than flat, endless planes. This chapter walks you through the terrain generation process.

CHAPTER 7: TERRAIN OBJECTS

Terrain objects are an extension of Terrains. Terrain objects can be used to emulate structures and contrivances of many types. This chapter details the processes involved.

CHAPTER 8: 2D PICTURE OBJECTS

2D Picture Objects allow you to load a scene with very complex content, while at the same time being kinder and gentler to the size and storage requirements of the resulting scene file.

CHAPTER 9: MATERIAL PRESETS

The first step in applying materials to a Bryce object is to know how to use the preset materials.

CHAPTER 10: THE MATERIALS LAB

After you become familiar with using the Materials Presets, you'll want to tweak them in the Materials Lab.

CHAPTER 11: THE DEEP TEXTURE EDITOR

When you really want to explore developing materials at the root level, you'll want to explore the Deep Texture Editor.

CHAPTER 12: INFINITE PLANES

Bryce's infinite planes are in large part responsible for the observed realism in a Bryce world, extending far beyond your screen view in all directions. This chapter covers their theory and use.

CHAPTER 13: ATMOSPHERICS

When you need to configure the clouds in a sky or apply fog and haze, this chapter tells you how.

CHAPTER 14: LIGHTS

You can place a series of different light types in any Bryce scene, and apply some interesting properties to them in the Light Lab.

CHAPTER 15: THE CAMERA

The Camera is your eye, with a number of special parameter controls.

CHAPTER 16: ANIMATION BASICS

Bryce animation centers on the understanding and use of the Timeline.

CHAPTER 17: EARTH, AIR, WATER, AND FIRE

Here's how to create special animated environmental effects.

CHAPTER 18: OBJECT ANIMATION

There are a number of things to keep in mind when you want to animate objects in a Bryce world.

CHAPTER 19: ADVANCED MOTION LAB

Using the Advanced Motion Lab, you can tweak all of the animated elements in a scene.

CHAPTER 20: ADVANCED ANIMATION TECHNIQUES

This chapter shows you more ways to think about generating animations in Bryce.

CHAPTER 21: TWO PROJECTS

Two project tutorials are included in this chapter.

The Color Gallery

The Color Gallery of the book displays a selection of eight full pages of images created and rendered in Bryce.

End Matter (Appendices and Index)

APPENDIX A: WHAT'S ON THE CD-ROM?

Here are the details of what is contained on the folders on the CD-ROM that accompanies this book.

APPENDIX B: VENDOR INFORMATION

Look in this appendix for developer contact information.

APPENDIX C: BRYCE SECRETS REVEALED!

Discover some of the undocumented features in Bryce.

APPENDIX D: HELPFUL HANDSHAKING

Where to find other software that can enhance your Bryce work.

The CD-ROM

Appendix A details the contents of the CD-ROM. Suffice it to say that the CD-ROM contains a large amount of value-added content useful to Bryce creators.

HOW TO USE THIS BOOK

How you use this book depends on who you are, what you are looking to do with your knowledge, and your previous experience with Bryce and/or other 3D software.

Bryce Users

If you are a new Bryce user, read and work through this book in its entirety. If you are already an experienced Bryce user, you might want to pay special attention to the new features of Bryce, and take a peek at Appendix D, "Helpful Handshaking," and the project tutorials at the end. Use the rest of the book as needed for a reference.

Computer Artists and Animators Who Are Not Bryce Enabled

First, purchase Bryce, and read and work through the documentation. Since the book details techniques that can be translated and used with the majority of 3D software applications on the market, read and work through the entire book. If you have experience with other 3D applications, your learning will obviously progress much faster in Bryce.

Game Designers, Moviemakers, Set Designers, and Film f/x People

Read and work through the entire book, paying special attention to those sections that seem to best address your specific needs.

Traditional Artists and Animators

Bryce is an excellent choice for your first exploration of 3D computer graphics and animation. Read the book in its entirety after purchasing Bryce, but thoroughly study the Bryce documentation first.

Schools and Colleges

If you are a student or a teacher at an academic institution that offers computer graphics and animation courses, think about using the tutorials and other data in the book as the basis for classroom work.

OK. Time to start your engines!

CHAPTER

1 Bryce Basics

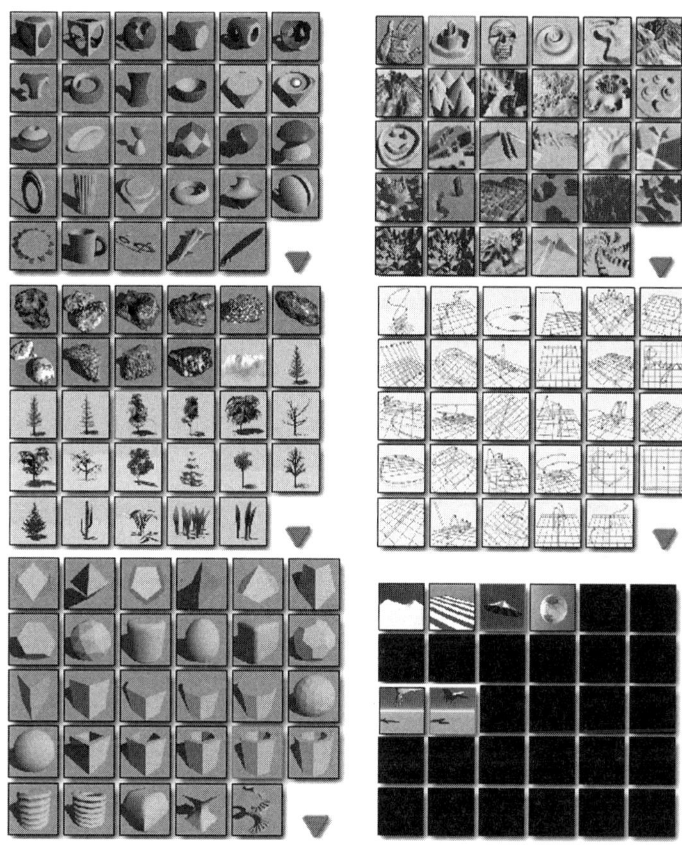

If you are new to Bryce, your first impression of the interface and tools might be a bit daunting. Even if you've had experience with other 3D software, the Bryce interface design (GUI, or graphic user interface) is unlike that of any other 3D software on the market. Our aim in this first chapter is to guide you through the Bryce maze. We'll pay special attention to the location and purpose of the tools and menu items, and how to optimize their use. When necessary, other chapters in the book will be referenced for your enhanced study. If you are already a seasoned Bryce user, you might want to just skim this chapter to locate any items you might have overlooked. In order to get the most out of this chapter as a new Bryce user, it is necessary that you already know the following:

- You should already have installed the Bryce software, following the directions that came with your software purchase.
- How to start your computer and open the Bryce program. As a reminder, just double-click your mouse button (Left Mouse Button, or LMB, for Windows users) on either the icon for the Bryce program in the folder in which you installed it, or its Shortcut (Windows) or Alias (Mac) to wherever you located it.
- How to interact with the mouse to initiate actions on the screen. Specific mouse instructions will be pointed out in this text when needed.

When Bryce first opens, you are presented with its GUI (see Figure 1.1).

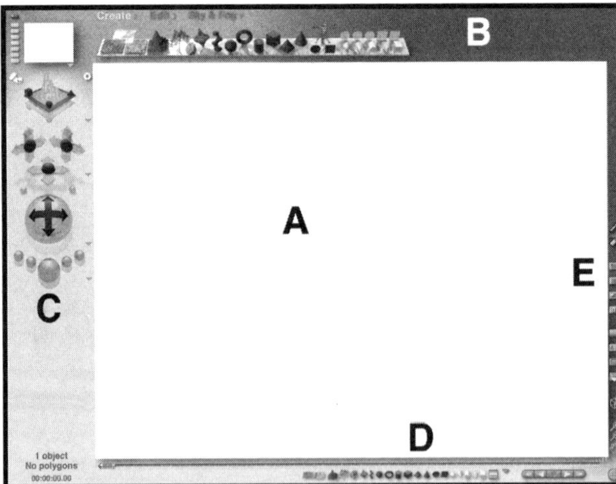

FIGURE 1.1 The Bryce GUI. (A) The Document Space. This is where your 3D content is placed and moved around. As we'll see later in this chapter, you can view the items in the Document Space from several different camera views. (B) The top toolbar. (C) The left toolbar. (D) The bottom toolbar. (E) The right toolbar. We will look at the items located in the toolbars in detail as this chapter progresses.

Throughout this book, you will find instructions such as File>Save, terms separated by the symbol indicated. In this case, the instruction asks you to go to the File *menu to locate the* Save *command. Where is the File menu located, or any menu for that matter? Well, Bryce is a bit tricky when it comes to locating and using various menus. Menus are typically located at the very top of any software's interface. Bryce menus are located here too, but they are invisible. In order to make them visible, just slide the mouse to the top of the screen (do not click it), and* voilà! *The menu names magically appear for you to select and interact with.*

DOCUMENT SETUP

The first thing you'll want to do when you have a little experience in Bryce is to get into the habit of configuring items in the Setup screen first. The Setup screen can be accessed from two places: File>Document Setup, or the downward-pointing arrow at the bottom of the left-hand toolbar. Try it now (see Figure 1.2).

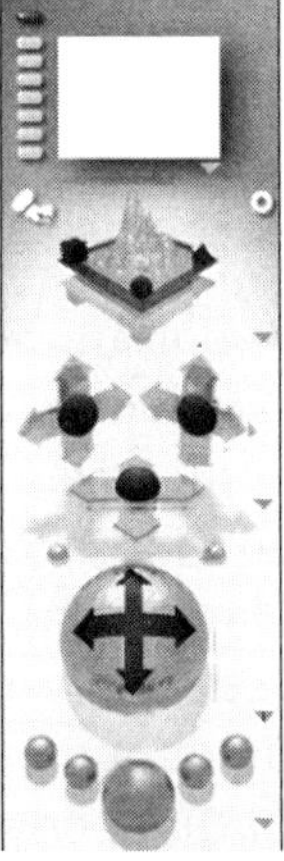

FIGURE 1.2 You can access the Document Setup screen from two places in Bryce: either from the File menu (File/Document Setup), or by left-mouse clicking (clicking and holding on the Mac) on the bottom-most downward-pointing arrow in the left-hand toolbar, as shown here.

Setting your screen size to the highest size possible is usually a good idea for getting the best initial overview of your Bryce world.

The layout of the Document Setup screen's dialog is easier to navigate when it is accessed from the File menu, although accessing the listing from the arrow in the toolbar is a little quicker. Either way, the options listed are the same. When you access this dialog from the File menu, either on a Mac or Windows system, the dialog appears as shown in Figure 1.3.

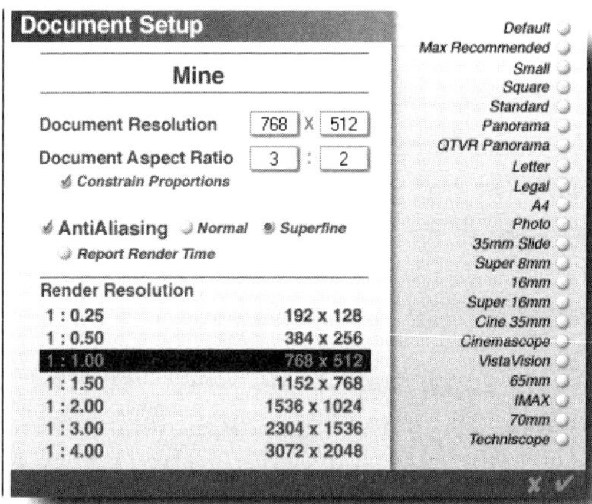

FIGURE 1.3 The Documentation Setup screen as it appears when accessed from the File menu, showing the selectable options.

Document Resolution/Aspect Ratio versus Render Resolution

The most important configuration in the Document Setup screen dialog is how you configure the Document Resolution and the Aspect Ratio. Why? The Document Resolution sets up your Bryce scene as it appears on your monitor. If your monitor cannot display this resolution because of its own limitations, the setting will not take place on the Bryce interface. Along the right-hand side of this dialog is a listing of common sizes for a variety of output options, ranging from standard settings, to multimedia, to a number of film sizes. Clicking on any one of these options changes your Document Space to match that choice. For example, selecting the 35mm Slide option changes the Document Resolution to 480 × 320 pixels, and the Aspect Ratio to 3 × 2. In the Render Resolution list in Table 1.1 below are various multiples of that resolution. At a Render Resolution of 1, the rendering will be the same as the Document Resolution, or 480 × 320 pixels. At a Render Resolution of 4 (four times larger than the Document Resolution), the setting is for 1920 × 1280 pixels. This means that you are working on the Document Resolution screen at 480 × 320, but that your rendering will be four times as fine as the working screen. Larger renderings take more time, but allow for much clearer output. Your selections depend on how and where your Bryce renderings are to be used. Refer to Table 1.1 for some examples.

Table 1.1 Bryce Settings for Output Options

OUTPUT PURPOSE	BRYCE SETTING	CONSTRAINED RATIO	RENDERING SUGGESTIONS
Multimedia (CD-ROM)	Standard	4 × 3	Render at 320 × 240, or one-half of the standard 640 × 480 setting. Antialiasing can be set to None.
Video and television	Photo	3 × 2 (Note that digital TV sizes are still in debate, with a likelihood that 4 × 3 or even 5 × 3 might be the best fit.)	Render at a ratio of 1: 1 or 768 × 512. This will result in some necessary bleed at the borders of your renders, about 25 pixels on each side and top and bottom, places where the image will not be shown on-screen. Make allowances for this when designing the scene and animating. Antialiasing should be set to Normal.
Web display	Standard Another option is either Panorama or QTVR (QuickTime VR) Panorama, for interactive virtual reality sites.	4 × 3 Panorama is 8 × 3, and QTVR Panorama is 13 × 4.	Render at 1:0.25, or 160 × 120 pixels. If your intended browsers are QuickTime enabled, render as a QuickTime movie. If you are going to need a GIF animation, render as single frames, and translate to a GIF movie in a suitable translation application. Antialiasing should be set to None.
Print media	Selection is determined by the maximum output of the printer or printing press being addressed, with common choices including: Square, letter, legal, and A4.	Determined by Bryce settings at left.	Render at the highest resolution needed by the medium you are addressing. Antialiasing should be set to Normal or Superfine.
Photographic slide (output to a suitable film recorder)	35mm slide	3 × 2	Render at the 4X setting as a bare minimum for clarity: 1920 × 1280. Antialiasing should be set to Normal.
High-end recorder for motion picture film	Selection is determined by the needs of the display medium being addressed, with common choices including Super 8mm, 16mm, Super 16mm, Cine 35mm, Cinemascope, VistaVision, 65mm, IMAX, 70mm, and Techniscope.	Determined by Bryce settings at left.	Render at the highest resolution needed by the medium you are addressing. Antialiasing should be set to Superfine.

Common Display Conventions

Unless you are using Bryce for high-end film work, you will probably select to output to multimedia (CD-ROM), television (NTSC or PAL), digital TV formats, or to print media sizes. Table 1.1 lists which Bryce formats to select for various output mediums.

Rendering Larger Sizes versus Antialiasing

In the Document Setup screen dialog is series of *Antialiasing* options . Antialiasing gets rid of the jaggies in a rendering, places where the angles of a rendered element are too severe to allow for a smooth look. However, antialiasing comes at a time cost in any 3D application. You have four options here under Quality: "Default" (No AA), "Regular" (Normal AA), "Super" (Fine Art AA), and "Premium" (Effect AA). Regular antialiasing can add anywhere from a few minutes to double the total rendering time to a Bryce animation or rendered picture, depending on the objects and their materials. Premium antialiasing, except for very high-end film or print work, should be avoided. It can easily quadruple the rendering time needed for a picture or for each frame in an animation.

Another option for making your output look clearer and crisper is to double the size of your rendered image or animation frame beyond what is required, and then reduce the size later in a suitable editing application. This is really an old trick, used by print media artists since the turn of the century. It might have first come into practice by the Sunday comics artists, who usually worked at four to 10 times the needed output size, allowing the camera to reduce the size later for the finished printing plate. In the case of digital work, all you need is a post-production application that will do the reduction for you. The most common applications used in this respect are Adobe Premier (Mac and Windows), Adobe After Effects (Mac and Windows), Strata Videoshop (Mac and Windows), and Ulead's Media Studio Pro (Windows). You can find other suitable commercial or shareware applications that also allow for these post-production operations.

Always work at the maximum screen size possible, even when the output rendering is set for one-half or one-fourth of that size. This makes it easier to see what you are doing so your "actors" (models and other elements) can be manipulated clearly, especially when the scene becomes very complex.

Constrain Proportions

Usually, you will leave this option checked (on), since it allows you to put in one dimension, while the computer automatically configures the other dimension according to the Aspect Ratio that is set. There are times, however, when you want direct control over both the width and height of the screen and the rendering, perhaps for a special print size for a calendar or a graphic in a magazine. If that happens, turn Constrain off (uncheck it), and enter the exact dimension for both height and width.

Report Render Time

This option is useful for your first test renderings, but after that, it can be turned off. There is no need to get a report on render times with each test render you do, since you will do many test renders in an involved scene to get lights and camera angles the way you want them. If necessary, you can toggle this item on again at various points in the scene development process. Unless you start to apply many transparent textures in your scene, or make other radical changes, the render time first reported will remain about the same. Rendering times start to differ from one frame to the next when the camera moves to encompass an entirely new perspective, one that might involve new rendering challenges. Other than that, render time reports are only approximate at best (see Figure 1.4).

Render Report

Untitled

Total Render Time:	01:20	Per Pixel
Pixels Rendered:	172800	
Pixels AntiAliased:	0	
Primary Rays:	172800	1.00
Shadow Rays:	90511	0.52
Total Rays:	263311	1.52
Ray Hits:	147282	0.85
Ray Misses:	257503	1.49
Total Intersect Attempts:	404785	2.34

FIGURE 1.4 The Render Time Report lists the rendered pixels in the scene, and all the information you might want to know concerning the raytracing used in the rendering.

Edit>Preferences

The Preferences item under the Edit menu brings up a small dialog that has a few very valuable options from which to choose when setting up a

Bryce project. This can help you optimize Bryce further, shaping it to the way in which you work. There are four options listed in this dialog (see Figure 1.5).

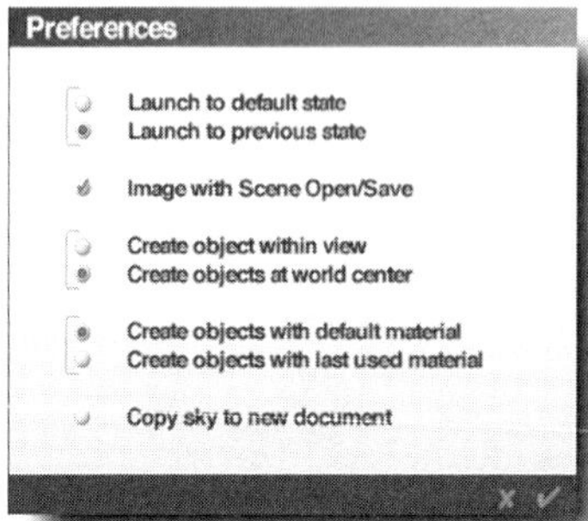

FIGURE 1.5 The Preferences dialog, found under the Edit menu, lists four options that can optimize your work.

LAUNCH TO DEFAULT OR PREVIOUS STATE

If you have a favorite resolution you prefer working in, then check "launch to Previous State." Each time Bryce opens a new file, your Resolution Prefs from the last session will be applied. If you would rather set the resolution each time, click the Default State item.

IMAGE WITH SCENE OPEN/SAVE

It is suggested that you leave this item checked. When checked, each time you save a Bryce file, the last rendering you did is saved as a PICT (Mac) or BMP (Windows) graphic.

When saving a Bryce project file on the Mac, include the Bryce extension required by Bryce on Windows. That way, you can always port your creations back and forth from either platform. Bryce on Windows adds this extension automatically, while the Mac does not normally require any extension to be added to filenames.

CREATE OBJECT WITHIN VIEW OR AT WORLD CENTER

This is a very important option. We suggest that you select to create new objects Within View rather than at the World Center. This allows you to see the object on-screen immediately, no matter where the camera is pointing at the moment, and to place new objects very close to where you want them with less movement required. When a scene gets very complex, as can happen fairly quickly in Bryce, you can move to an empty part of the scene, far from any other objects. Having selected the Within View option, you can create and texture your object in a space free of the confusion of other objects. If necessary to move it into the more cluttered part of a scene, this can be accomplished afterward.

CREATE OBJECTS WITH DEFAULT OR LAST USED MATERIAL

As you'll see when you begin to explore Bryce Materials, making a choice between these two options can save you time. For example, if you were to model and place a series of 3D models in your scene that appear as if they were made from the same material, checking Last Used Material here will prevent you having to manually place the same material on each model all over again.

COPY SKY TO NEW DOCUMENT

Turn this option on when the new document will be woven together with the one you just completed. Skies can be time consuming to configure. Although they can be saved, this option can be used to make the flow of your work run more smoothly. It is usually left off, since new Bryce scenes are more commonly not connected to each other. Every situation is different, however, and it's nice to have this option when needed.

THE LEFT-HAND TOOLBAR

These are the tools you will access most in Bryce as you build your scene (see Figure 1.6).

A. Memory Dots

Clicking on a Memory Dot forces Bryce to remember the camera position of the current scene. This allows you to return to the saved camera position after you've moved the camera to a new place and angle. Exactly when you use the Memory Dots depends on your work habits. Most users constantly switch to different views when composing a scene in Bryce. Clicking on a Memory Dot at any time to recall a saved camera view saves you a tremendous amount of time and headaches.

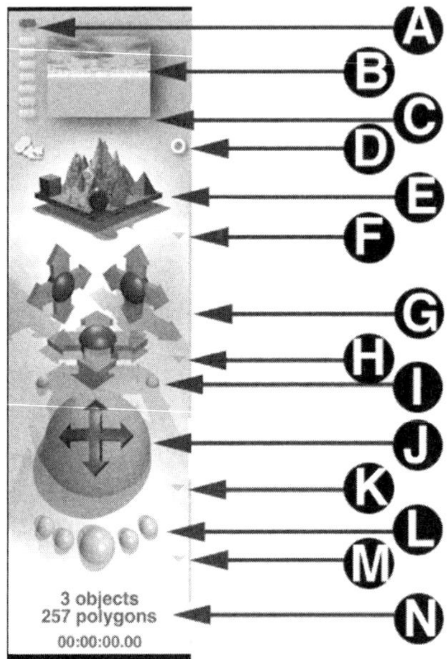

FIGURE 1.6 The left-hand toolbar with keyletter identifiers.

B. Nano Preview

The Nano Preview screen gives you a rough look at the way the scene will look when rendered. Although you can turn Auto Update on in the Nano Preview List (opened by clicking on the downward-pointing triangle next to the Nano Preview), we suggest that you select Fast Preview. As the Nano Preview is rendering, other operations come to a halt, which prevents you from continuing your creative pursuits. It's also advisable to remember that clicking anywhere on a blank portion of the Document Space halts the Nano Preview render. This is helpful when you have seen enough, even though the edit is only partially complete.

C. Nano Options List

This list of options appears when you click on the downward-pointing triangle next to the Nano Preview. In addition to the view selections already covered are three additional choices you have for Nano Rendering: Sky Only, Full Scene, and Wireframe. Click on Sky Only when you are designing a sky, and don't need to preview anything else in the scene. Full Scene should be chosen 99 percent of the time. Selecting Wireframe is fairly useless, as the view is far too small to do you any good.

D. Flyaround

You might think that this is meant for nothing but getting a cheap thrill by watching your scene spin in 3D space. You can, however, make use of this feature by noticing what global camera angles might prove interesting when it comes time to render the scene. This feature spins the scene so you get a global view of the placement and proximity of all of the components.

E. View Control

Clicking on the icon itself marches you through the view options in sequential order, and holding the mouse down while dragging on the icon flips through the various views. You can also access the View Options list by clicking on the downward-pointing triangle next to this icon, and selecting whatever view you would like to use from the list (see the next section, *F. View Control List*).

F. View Control List

Use this list, or the View Control tool, when a Memory Dot does not yet hold your selected view, or when the Memory Dots are full.

G. Camera Cross Controls

These controls represent Bryce's virtual 3D joystick, which can be used to fine-tune your needed camera view. These can't be used when you are in anything but the Camera view or the Director's view. Practice before using them in a project. Try them now by clicking and dragging on any of the associated icons.

The Director's view option (accessed by clicking on the downward-pointing triangle next to the Camera Cross Controls) allows you to work in another perspective view other than the Camera view. Note the choices in the View Options list marked "Camera to Director" *and* "Director to Camera." *These options allow you to snap the Director's view to the Camera view, and vice versa, so that whatever manipulations you carry out while in the Director's view can be forced to be transferred to the Camera view. This is important because it allows you to move the camera into place with the additional freedom offered while working in the Director's view. You can think of the Director's view as an exploratory perspective window. Until you commit your alterations to the Camera view (by selecting* Camera to Director*), nothing you do will affect the Camera view. The Director's view can always be reset to the present camera default position by selecting* Director to Camera. *See the text in the section* H. Camera Cross Control Option.

H. Camera Cross Control Option

There are three other important options that can be accessed in the Options list in addition to the *Camera to Director* and *Director to Camera* items we covered previously. It's easy to get lost in a Bryce world when scenes become overly complex. You might want to get a specific object in view, and find it time-consuming to zoom and move the camera to the needed position. When this happens, use one of the following options in this list:

- **Center Scene.** Use this command to reset the scene's center at the center of your working screen. It's a great option when you have been working far off in the distance and want to get back to ground zero.
- **Center Selection.** Use this command to center your working screen on any selected object or object group. This is a vital command when you want to do additional editing on an object or its material.
- **Eye Level Camera.** Use this setting to drop the camera to the ground, especially when you need to bring it back to a default location.

Editing the Current Camera

With the Camera view selected, the *Edit Current Camera* command brings up a dialog with three tabs: *General, Linking,* and *Animation*. We will cover Linking and Animation later in the book (Chapters 16 through 20), so let's focus on the controls and parameters in the General Edit tab for the Camera (see Figure 1.7).

You can tell if you are in Camera view if the only Camera Mode option available to you in the left column is Free. You should always leave

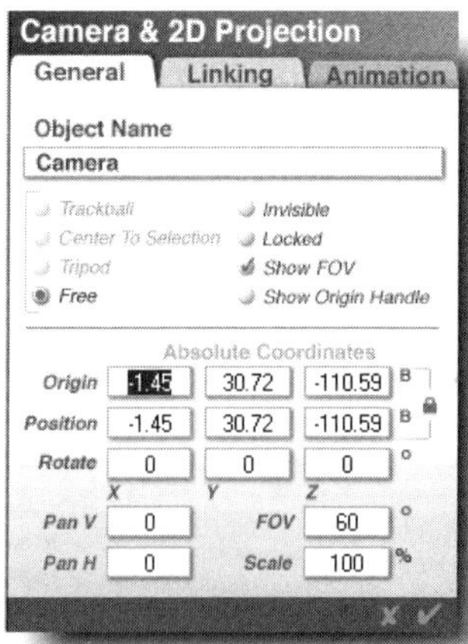

FIGURE 1.7 The General tab in the Current Camera Edit dialog, with the Camera view selected.

two items in the right-hand column checked: *Show FOV* and *Show Origin Handle*. FOV (Field of View) must be checked so that you can manipulate the FOV cone in the Document Space. The Origin Handle determines the point that is the fulcrum for camera rotations, and so should be made visible at all times. It appears as a red dot in the Camera's icon when the camera is visible in any non-Camera and Director's view.

I. Bank and Zoom

Just under and to either side of the XZ Cross Control are two small buttons. They are not paid much attention in the Bryce documentation, but they can be extremely important to your Bryce work. The one on the left is a *Banking Control*, and the one on the right controls the *Camera Zoom*. These controls work by dragging the mouse over them (left and right), and they are only accessible in either the Director's or Camera view. Bank is very important for simulating flight. Banking an aircraft as it turns creates a far more realistic feeling of flying. Zooming in on an element of interest can be vital for customizing its details.

J. Camera Trackball

Manipulate the Trackball by clicking and dragging the mouse button (Windows LMB). See the Trackball option in the Camera Modes list in the section *K. Camera Modes List*.

K. Camera Modes List

Only in the Director's view mode is it possible to access all of the Camera modes, emphasizing the importance of the Director's View. The only option allowed in Camera view is Free Camera, while working in the Director's view allows three more important camera options for optimizing your work:

- **Trackball.** This is the item to choose when you want to move the camera in a way that is similar to the Flyaround option discussed previously. The Trackball option aims the camera so that it is focused on the global center of the scene, allowing you to orbit the scene at its global center by using the Trackball controller. Set this option while in the Director's view.
- **Center to Selection.** This is the option to choose when you want to aim the camera at a selected object in the scene. It locates the camera so that it is focused on the selected object, allowing you to orbit the

object by using the Trackball controller. You could, for example, use this option to orbit one selected building in a cityscape. Set this option while in the Director's view.

- **Tripod.** This is the item to choose when you want to simulate a camera attached to a tripod. It locates the camera so that it is securely fastened to a tripod, allowing you to view the scene from that vantage point by using the Trackball to rotate (but not move) the camera in 3D space. The Tripod option is best used in conjunction with the *Eye Level Camera* selection in the Camera Cross Control Options list (detailed previously).

L. Render Controls

This grouped array of five buttons controls single-picture rendering (rendering an animation is controlled by selecting the Render Animation command from the File menu). From left to right, the spheres are *Texture Toggle* (see Chapters 9 through 11 for information on materials), *Fast Preview Toggle*, *Render*, *Resume Render*, and *Clear and Render*. Some tips for uses include:

- Use the first button on the left to turn textures off when you need to see how light placement is affecting the objects in your scene without the placement of any textures on objects. The rendering is faster, and you can see how shadows and light cones overlap much clearer.
- If you have complex textures in your scene, and need a preview render, selecting the *Fast Preview Render* button doesn't make much sense. It gives you a poorer idea of what the textures look like, and still takes its time to show you the results. If you need to preview the look of textures, use the center Render button (the large spherical one).
- Use the *Resume Render* button after you have partially rendered a scene and have decided to stop the render by clicking anywhere on the screen. Resume Render will start where you left off, as long as you haven't tinkered with any scene elements in the rendering break.
- *Clear and Render* is of dubious use. It's easier to click the center Render button again when a complete re-rendering is called for.

M. Document Setup List

If you are using a monitor setting less than 600 × 800, you might not be able to see this list. In that case, simply bring up the Setup options from the

File menu (File>Document Setup). We covered the Document Setup parameters previously when we detailed Document Setup (see Figure 1.2).

N. Data Display Area

The Data Display Area provides important information concerning the difference in rendering times involved when various rendering options are activated. It also keeps track of the number of polygons in any selected objects, or in the entire scene when no objects are selected. The more polygons, the larger the disk space needed to store the scene.

THE TOP TOOLBARS

There are three toolbars that you can toggle among at the top of the Bryce interface by clicking on their names: *Create*, *Edit*, and *Sky & Fog*. We will cover the uses of the tools located in each of these toolbars in later chapters, but here are some additional items about each that you will want to take note of (see Figure 1.8).

FIGURE 1.8 The Create toolbar allows you instant access to Bryce object creation. From left to right: Water, Sky, and Ground Planes; Terrain, Tree, Rock, Symmetrical Lattice (Mirrored Terrain), Metaball, Sphere, Torus, Cylinder, Cube, Tetrahedrons, Cones, Flat Planes, 2D Picture Object, Disk and Rectangular Planes, and Lights.

The Create Toolbar

Clicking on any of the icons in the Create toolbar places that object in your scene. Here are some things to explore and keep in mind concerning the Create toolbar items. See all of the following chapters in this book for specific details concerning each of the objects and object types represented by icons in the Create toolbar. The following hints should be revisited after you have had a chance to explore Bryce more thoroughly, so mark this page:

- Terrains are added to a scene by clicking on the icon that looks like a mountain. Use the same Terrain object for background mountain ranges—just duplicate and rotate, and possibly resize the original. You'll be surprised by how different a single Terrain object can appear when rotated just a few degrees.

- If you need to build a cityscape from these *Primitive* objects (sphere, cube, pyramid, etc.), make sure the cityscape contains more than just rectangular or cubic objects. This is especially true if your urban environment is supposed to emulate a city of the future. Use a variety of object forms, and stack non-blocky primitives on top of cubic ones. Bryce primitives can offer you a myriad of optional looks if you spend some time exploring the possibilities.
- Use a flat disk in the distant sky to emulate a sun or planet. Although Bryce allows you to configure the sun and moon, these Sky objects are confined to earth parameters and laws. It's much quicker to use a flat disk most of the time, and you can customize the texture easily. See Chapter 13, "Atmospherics," for more details.

THE OBJECT LIBRARIES IN THE CREATE TOOLBAR

The downward-pointing arrow next to the word *Create* allows you to access the Object Libraries. Clicking on any object and then on the check mark at the bottom-right of a library places the selected item in your Bryce Document Space (see Figure 1.9).

Here are some important tips when working with the Object Libraries:

- Use Boolean objects sparingly. They are impossible to see in detail in Bryce until rendered, and some increase rendering time dramatically.
- Terrain objects also contain many polygons, so if you are working with a limited amount of memory, try not to use too many.
- Be wary of using too many Tree objects, since they are constructed by using materials with various transparency settings. This costs you in rendering time. Some of the Tree objects are also Booleans, so use the newer Tree objects in the Create toolbar instead to create needed vegetation.
- There are a number of primitive forms in Bryce's Imported Objects Library. They render quickly, take textures without a hitch, and can be used to extend your composite creations. Use them as often as you like.
- You can save your own 3D models to a Bryce library folder. In no time, you will amass your own customized model libraries.

The Edit Toolbar

The Edit Toolbar contains all of the tools that allow you to customize and transform your selected 3D models (see Figure 1.10).

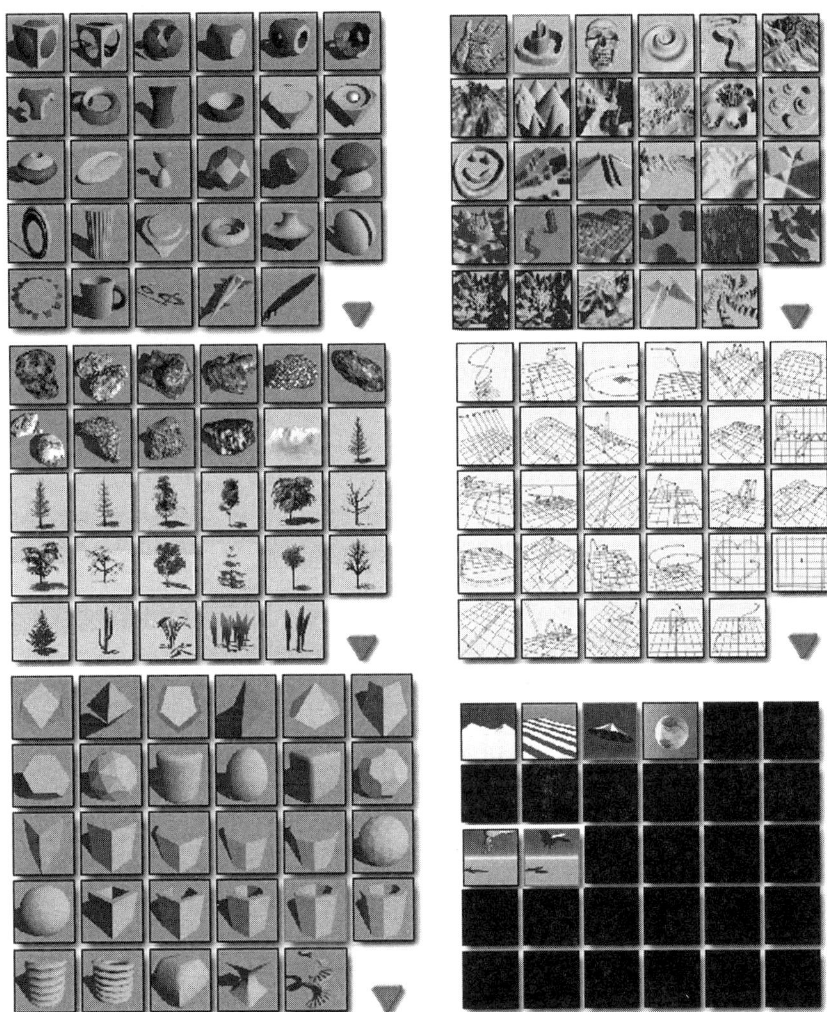

FIGURE 1.9 The Object Libraries contain a number of diverse object resources, and you can always add your own. Bryce ships with hundreds of objects to start your world-creating tasks. Included are Booleans, Mountains, Rocks and Trees, Paths, Imported Objects, and spaces for your own saved creations.

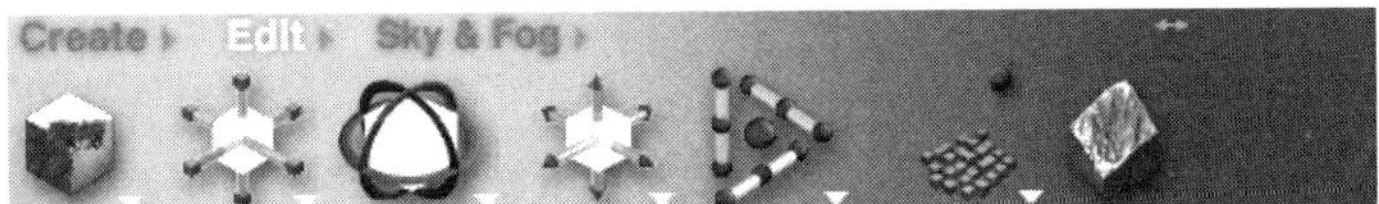

FIGURE 1.10 The Edit toolbar has seven icons: Materials Lab, Resize, Rotate, Reposition, Align, Disperse, and the Editor. The almost invisible double arrows at the top right of this same toolbar access object substitution options.

USING THE EDIT TOOLS

If you are new to Bryce, do the following exercise to become working familiar with the tools in the Edit toolbar:

1. First, click on the Cube object in the Create Toolbar to place a Cube in the scene. Click on the Camera Options triangle on the right of the XZ Camera Control icon in the left-hand toolbar, and choose Center Selection from the list that appears. Your Cube (which appears as a red wireframe object) is now centered in the Document Space on the screen.
2. Go to the Edit toolbar by clicking on the word *Edit* at the top of the Bryce interface. You are going to explore what the second through fourth tools in the Edit row do (Resize, Rotate, and Reposition), and how they alter any selected object.
3. Place your mouse pointer over the Resize tool. Note that by placing the mouse in the center of the tool, the data readout at the bottom left reads *Resize XYZ*, and that placing the mouse pointer over any of the separate cubic faces of this icon causes the data readout to be *Resize X*, *Resize Y*, or *Resize Z*. Click and drag the mouse over each of these options in turn, and watch how your actions affect the cube you placed in the Document Space. This is how to edit the dimensions of any selected object in Bryce.
4. Place your mouse pointer over the Rotate tool. Note that by placing the mouse in the center of the tool, the data readout at the bottom left does not respond. That's because it is impossible to rotate a selected object on all of its axes at the same time. Now, place the mouse pointer over any of the three rings that encircle this icon, causing the data readout to change to *Rotate X*, *Rotate Y*, or *Rotate Z*. Click and drag the mouse over each of these options in turn, and watch how your actions affect the cube you placed in the Document Space. This is how to edit the rotation angle of any selected object in Bryce.
5. Place your mouse pointer over the Reposition tool. Note that by placing the mouse in the center of the tool, the data readout at the bottom left shows no data. That's because you cannot move any object in 3D space in all directions at the same time with this tool. Now, place the mouse pointer over any one of the six directional arrows that extend from this icon, causing the data readout to be *Reposition X*, *Reposition Y*, or *Reposition Z*. Click and drag the mouse over each of these options in turn, and watch how your actions affect the cube you placed in the Document Space. This is how to move any selected object in Bryce along one of its three axes.

If you click and drag on any selected object in the Document Space, no matter what view you are in, you can reposition it along any axis or multiple axes addressed by the view you are in. If you click and drag on any of the dots that are displayed on the XYZ dimensions of any selected object's wireframe in the Document Space, you can manually alter its scale along that axis.

When you use Resizing, Rotation, and Repositioning on an object from one of these respective icons in the Edit toolbar, you can apply the alteration in any one of three spatial modes: *Object Space*, *World Space*, or *Camera Space*. You can choose one of these modes by opening the list accessed by clicking on the downward-pointing triangle to the bottom-right of each icon. The Default is *World Space*.

Object Space centers the rotation axis on the object's original rotation parameters. If it's an imported object, the axis can sometimes differ from the axis of Bryce objects. Object Space is a good alternative when you notice an object skewing under World Space, and is usually a better choice when the object is to be animated (see Chapters 16 through 20).

World Space is the best choice for aligning objects to their global environment, as when placing Terrain objects on the ground plane. In general, use World Space as a default.

Camera Space can be used after you have explored camera banking. Selecting *Camera Space* moves all selected objects in relation to whatever the altered camera angles are. This is the trickiest of the three options, and needs the most exploration and experimentation.

Here are some additional things to explore and keep in mind when working with the Edit toolbar items:

- The quickest way to resize an object that needs customized resizing is to globally resize it first, followed by shortening or elongating any singular axis.
- Resize objects before you rotate them, or *skewing* might result. Skewing can be prevented in many cases by selecting Object Space instead of Global Space.
- Smaller components in your scene can seem farther away from the camera. You can place objects fairly close to the camera, and by making them smaller, create the illusion of distance.
- It is advisable to *stick to one rotation mode* whenever possible (Object Space, World Space, or Camera Space). Confusion here is the mother of frustration and weirdness.
- Use the Reposition options when the selected object is either or both small and/or in the midst of a confusing array of other objects, and

manual movement (clicking and dragging on the actual object in the Document Space) is tricky. The Repositioning tools are best used to move objects "out of the way" so they can be edited or moved to a clearer space. Whenever repositioning an object with the mouse leads to constant selection of the wrong object, use the Repositioning tool as an alternative.

- *Snap to Land* can be used to move an object to any layer of a stack of objects beneath that object. Using Snap to Land after you have reached the bottom-most object will then snap the object to the invisible Ground Plane. Snap to Land, when a plane or object is beneath an invisible Ground boundary, will not work. Snap to Land is activated by clicking on the downward-pointing arrow that appears in any selected object's Attributes icons at the right of a selected object. It is the bottom-most icon (see Figure 1.11).

FIGURE 1.11 The downward-pointing arrowhead will snap the object down to the top of the object underneath it. If the arrowhead points upward, the Snap will occur in an upward direction.

Randomize

The Randomize tool and its options are located to the left of the Editor icon in the Edit toolbar (see Figure 1.12).

Randomizing is meant to be applied to a collection of selected objects, normally more than two. It is used to make objects look less similar to

FIGURE 1.12 The icon and arrowhead list selector for the Randomize tool and options.

each other, and can affect rotation, size, and position. Do the following exercise to explore Randomization effects:

1. Click the Cube in the Create toolbar six times to place six Cubes in a scene. They will all be placed on top of each other, so you'll see only one.
2. In the Document Space, click and drag the mouse (LMB for Windows users) so that you draw an imaginary rectangle over what appears to be one Cube, but is in reality several Cubes that occupy the same space. Use any view.
3. With all of the Cubes now selected, select the 3D Disperse Size/Rotate item from the Randomize list. A check will appear next to your selection. Now, click and dragthe mouse button (LMB) over the Randomize icon. Watch the Cubes as they are randomized according to your selection in the list, and release the mouse button when the effect pleases you (see Figure 1.13).

   - Use **3D Disperse Size** to make multiple selected objects random sizes.
   - Use **3D Dispersions** to simulate randomized objects being moved by an unseen force, such as rocks being ejected from a volcano.
   - Use **Dispersion Effects** to create unique members of a self-similar group, such as fish in a school.

Align

The Align tools are between the Reposition and Randomize tools in the Edit toolbar (see Figure 1.14).

FIGURE 1.13 Randomization adds variety to an otherwise monotonous collection of forms.

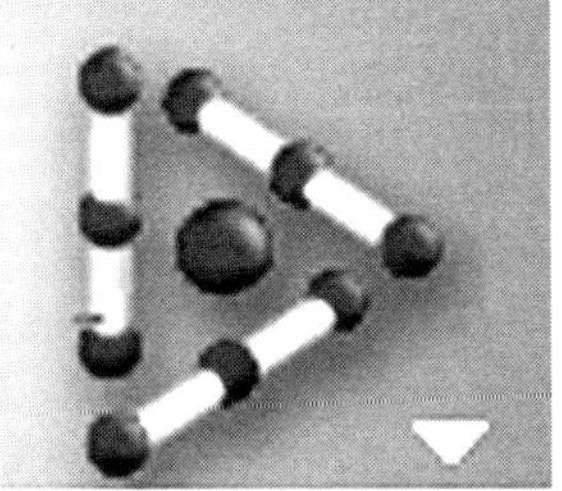

FIGURE 1.14 The Align tools.

The Align tools consist of three elongated cylinders and a spherical button at the center. Each of the cylinders has three separate buttons for causing alignments to occur from the center or ends of selected objects: Align Y Center/Top/Bottom, Align X Center/Right/Left, and Align Z Center/Front/Back. Clicking on the central spherical button will align all selected objects at their respective centers. You have to explore the use of these operations to get the hang of what this means, so do the following:

1. Place four Cubes in the scene, and move each so that they are all randomized in position from each other, with space in between. Select all of the Cubes.
2. With all four cubes selected, click one of the Randomize buttons and see what happens. Use Edit>Undo to delete the action, and repeat with another of the Align options. As you will see, Align actions can save you a lot of time compared to manually attempting to align a selection of objects.

Convert Selection To...

This is a Bryce option that we have never found in any other 3D software, and it's very handy. It's accessed from the tiny bidirectional arrow at the very top right of the Edit toolbar. Clicking and holding the mouse (LMB for Windows users) reveals a very small set of icons that mimic those found in the Create toolbar. Here's how to explore the use of the *Convert Selection To* operation:

1. Place four Cubes in the scene, and move each so that they are all randomized in position from each other, with space in between. Select all of the Cubes by clicking and dragging a Rectangular marquee around them in the view you are in.
2. With all four Cubes selected, click and hold on the *Convert Selection To* arrow. Without releasing the mouse button, move to one of the non-Cube icons. Release the mouse button. All of your selected cubes are transformed into the 3D object you selected. Use Edit>Undo to delete the action, and repeat with another one of the options. Neat, huh?

Preset Materials

To the right of the word *Edit* at the top of the Bryce interface is a downward-pointing triangle that accesses the Preset Materials Libraries. Clicking on this triangle opens the Materials Library preset selections (see Figure 1.15).

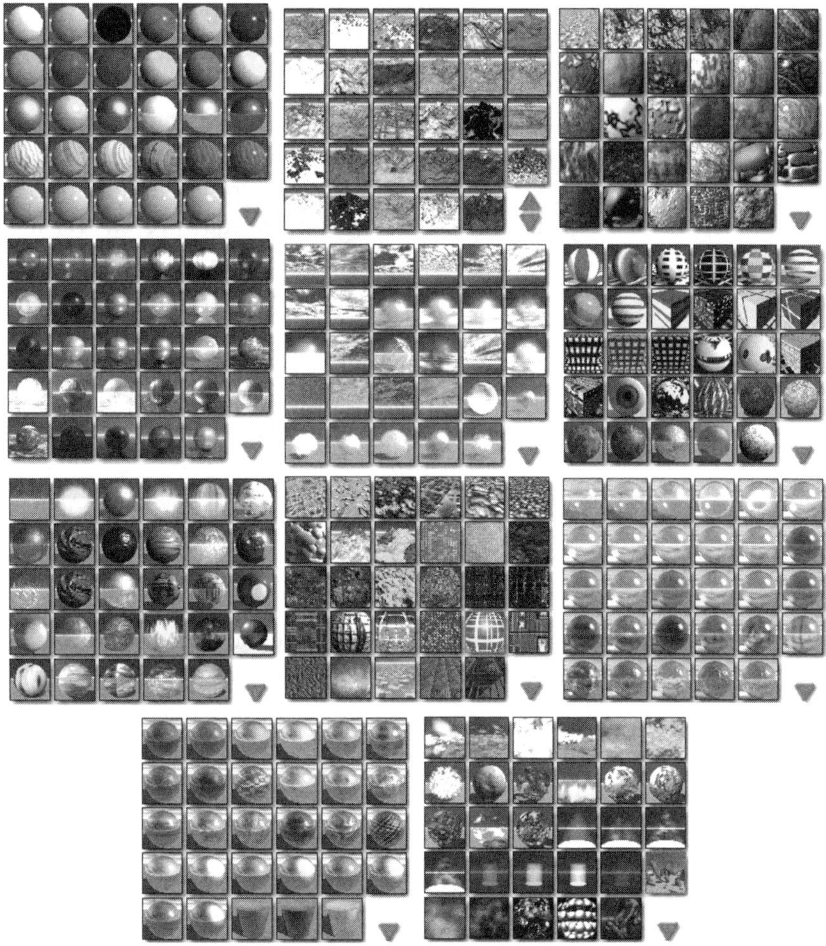

FIGURE 1.15 Bryce Materials Presets are used to apply textures to objects.

APPLYING PRESET MATERIALS

The Bryce novice will find preset materials very easy and intuitive to apply, while the seasoned Bryce user realizes that preset materials are also infinitely customizable. Applying materials to an object gives the object personality. A glass ball has a different personality, and different expectations on its performance in a scene, than does a ball made of stone or metal. A great deal of the allure of computer graphics has to do with creating objects seemingly made of different material. To apply a preset material to an object, do the following:

1. Select the object to which you want to apply a preset material.
2. Open the Preset Libraries, and select one of the Materials Library types.
3. Click on one of the presets in the selected library, and read its description. If you want to apply it, simply click on the check mark at the bottom of the Library Preset window. That's it! When you render the object(s) targeted for that preset, the material you selected is what it will appear to be made of.

Bryce sometimes makes a distinction between materials *and* textures, *although the two terms are used interchangeably in much of the industry at large. Materials, in Bryce, are generally based on algorithmic (mathematical) formulas, while textures are bitmap graphics wrapped on the object. There is an ambiguous middle ground, however, since some "materials" can also be created by layering algorithmic materials and bitmaps together in numerous ways.*

Never be afraid to assign an "unreal" material to an object. A mountain can look interesting when made of glass, and an apple can take on a unique personality when seemingly constructed of wood. There's a lot more to Materials than just presets. See Chapters 9 through 11 for a more detailed look at how to use and customize Materials.

The Editor

Clicking on the Editor icon at the far right of the Edit toolbar brings up Editing mode. The look of the Editing modes differs, depending on what object type you are editing. Editing is a topic that has to be approached in detail, and you will find that detailed coverage in Chapters 3, 6, 7, and 8.

The Sky & Fog Toolbar

The Sky & Fog toolbar is the third place where Bryce content is created (see Figure 1.16).

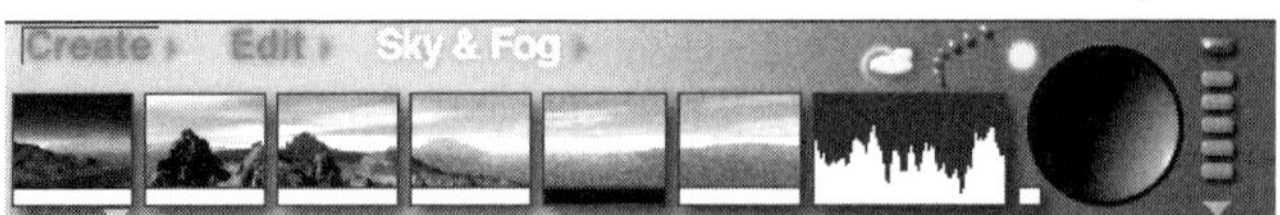

FIGURE 1.16 The Sky & Fog toolbar contains icons for (left to right) Sky Modes, Shadows, Fog, Haze, Cloud Height, Cloud Cover, Cloud Frequency and Amplitude, the Sun Control Trackball, and the Sky Memory Dots.

A detailed look at the inner workings of Sky & Fog options is provided in Chapter 13. For Bryce newbies, here's a quick way to appreciate Bryce skies. Do the following:

1. Go to the Sky & Fog toolbar by clicking on its name at the top of the Bryce interface.
2. Click on the downward-pointing triangle at the right of the Sky & Fog name. This brings up the Sky Presets Library (see Figure 1.17).

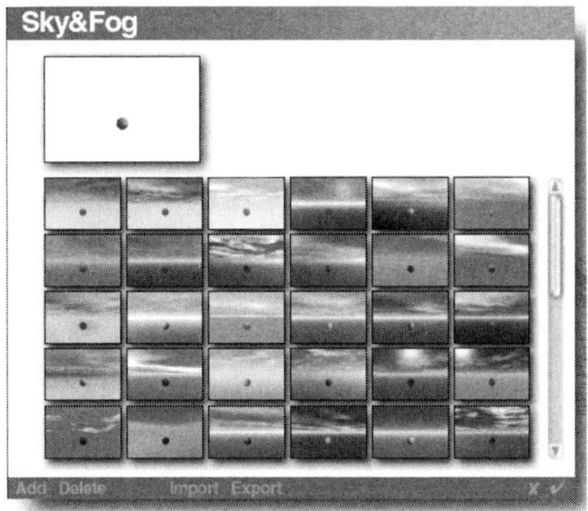

FIGURE 1.17 The Sky Presets Library pops up.

3. Click on any Sky Preset that you like, which places it in the Document Space.
4. Skies are only viewable in the Nano Preview or after you render. Click on the large Rendering button to see your Preset Sky in all its majesty.

See Chapter 13 to learn much more about creating skies and other atmospheric effects.

Here are a few general Sky & Fog suggestions that might help you work with some of the other tools in the Sky & Fog toolbar you read Chapter 13:

- **Sky Modes.** Use the *Atmosphere Off* setting (found in the list that expands out from the first icon on the left of the toolbar)when you need to render objects against a solid color background. Just select the color from the Palette bar attached to this icon—the horizontal strip at the bottom of the icon—to select a color from the palette that appears. *Custom Sky* is the option to choose when you have the clouds you want, but the colors aren't satisfactory.

- **Shadows.** Altering the shadow color to a darker hue can add more drama to a scene. A shadow's color is set by selecting a color from the palette just below the Shadow icon in the toolbar (the second icon from the left).
- **Fog.** The best fog effects are those that show objects only partially viewable, allowing the viewer the mystery of figuring out exactly what the object is. Monster movies make great use of fog, with unpleasant beings suddenly appearing and disappearing into it. Click and drag the mouse button (LMB for Windows users) over the Fog icon to set Fog density and depth. Watch the Nano Preview, or do a render to preview your Fog creation.
- **Haze.** Haze can be the thickness associated with a humid afternoon, or the poisonous, smoggy aftereffects of an atmosphere gone astray. Haze in Bryce has another major purpose: to mask the horizon line where the land (or water) meets the sky. The most important thing to remember when using haze to mask this too-blatant edge is the color that is used. If you select a color that is not related to either the sky or the ground (or water plane), the hazed edge will look as disquieting as a hard edge with no haze. Use a color that blends the two planes into one, most commonly a color from the sky at the point where it touches the horizon. Set Haze density by click-dragging the mouse button (LMB for Windows users) over the Haze icon (the fourth icon from the left in the toolbar).
- **Cloud Height.** Set Cloud Height by clicking and dragging the mouse button (LMB for Windows users) over the Cloud Height icon (the fifth icon from the left in this toolbar). Explore various height settings with each new sky you design. Realize that altering the color in the palette attached to the Cloud Height tool (*Sky Dome Color*) will also colorize the ground, as if there was a colorized filter over your world.
- **Cloud Cover.** Click and drag the mouse over the Cloud Cover icon (the sixth icon from the left in this toolbar) to set the amount of cloud cover for your world. Altering the color in the palette attached to the Cloud Cover will colorize the clouds, but will have no effect on the coloring of the rest of your world.
- **Cloud Frequency and Amplitude**. Experiment with the cloud types this tool produces, and preview the results in the Nano Preview screen or in a rendering. Click and drag the mouse over the Cloud Frequency and Amplitude icon (the seventh icon from the left in this toolbar) to set the parameters.
- **Sun Control Trackball.** The most important thing to remember when using this tool is that the "Moon" is directly opposite the "Sun." To either see the sun or moon on the horizon, you have to

place them just on the very edge of the Trackball's perimeter, which takes some practice. Also remember that colorizing the Sun affects the colors in the whole scene, so opt for subtle pastels rather than primary colors, unless a truly alien look is your goal. Click and drag in the Trackball to adjust the time-of-day effects.

- **Sky Memory Dots.** At the very right of the Sky and Fog toolbar is a stack of Memory Dots meant to store your favorite sky designs. The skies stored in the Memory Dots are saved for the present work session only. Once your computer is shut off, the Memory Dots are emptied. If you save your skies in the Sky Presets library, they are available (unless deleted) every time you use Bryce (see Chapter 13).
- **Randomize Buttons.** No matter how much creativity you were born with, everyone runs low on ideas once in a while. When that occurs during a Bryce world-building session, and you can't seem to find a sky that looks unique, try clicking on one of the Randomize buttons just to the left of the Sun icon in this toolbar. You'll march through a random set of Sky parameters.

The best place to save your own sky creations is to a separate library on your hard drive, or on removable media. That way, you can share your customized Sky Library creations with friends and associates. Note that Bryce 5 has added a new icon for accessing the Sky Lab (which we'll cover later in Chapter 13). It is the cloud-shaped icon at the top right of the toolbar. How to save a custom sky:

1. Create your sky by manipulating the necessary Sky & Fog Toolbar controls mentioned previously. Bring up the Sky Presets library, and click Export.
2. Select a name and a destination, preferably in a folder with a name that relates to the new sky contents.
3. Save your customized sky.

Later, if you want to use it again, just click on the Import command in the Sky Presets Library. Locate the saved preset and load it.

THE RIGHT-HAND TOOLBAR

Sliding your mouse to the right, across the border of your Bryce editing screen, makes the icons in the right-hand toolbar visible (see Figure 1.18).

Tips on Using the Right-Hand Toolbar Options

Here are some tips to guide your use of the tools in the right-hand toolbar.

FIGURE 1.18 The toolbar on the right side of the screen contains icons for (top to bottom): Demo Marker, Spray Rendering, Display Max/Min, Background Paper, Nano Editor On/Off, Plop Renderer On/Off, Wireframe Depth Cue On/Off, Wireframe Shadows On/Off, Wireframe Underground On/Off, Wireframe Resolution On/Off, Display Modes, Zoom in/out, Pan, and the Time/Selection Palette Toggle.

- **Demo Marker.** This tool is meant for production houses, where a creative team might be working on a Bryce project together. The marker is used like a pencil, and leaves a bright red trail, useful when production managers and art directors call attention to needed details in a Bryce scene. It works on any part of the Bryce interface, so it can be used to call attention to tools as well as elements in a scene. Pressing any key on the keyboard erases the mark(s).
- **Spray Rendering Tool.** The icon for this tool is shaped like a can of spray paint. Clicking and dragging the mouse button (LMB for Windows users) renders the scene where the spray is directed. Interesting abstract graphics can result from the use of this tool by rendering only what is targeted and leaving the rest as a wireframe in the Document Space. You can also use it to preview any part of a scene.
- **Display Max/Min.** One click and your display is either maximized or minimized. It's the fastest way to get more elbow room in Bryce.
- **Background Paper.** Clicking on this tool opens a list of background options, from colors to a grid and other choices. This is a background for the Document Space Wireframe view only, and not for the rendered scene. Try it.

- **Nano Editor On/Off.** This is a small edit screen window, useful when quick editing is needed. It appears as an overlay on top of the Camera Controls. It is interesting, but saves little time.
- **Plop Renderer On/Off.** Plop Rendering is initiated by clicking this tool on (it turns red), and then by click-dragging out a framed area in a rendered image. This allows you to render selected parts of an image that has been altered, as opposed to rendering the entire scene. Use this control to turn the Plop Render frame off after a render is completed, so you can see the newly rendered section. Try it after placing some objects in your scene to get a feel for how it works. Do the following:

  1. Place some objects in a scene, and do a render.
  2. After the render is complete, return to the Wireframe view and place another object in the scene.
  3. Return to the rendered image, and click-drag out a Plop Render frame around the area where the new object is located.
  4. Use the Render button on the Plop Render frame to render only the selected area.

Be careful when applying Plop Renders to a picture with different antialiasing settings involved. The Plop Renderer works within rectangular borders, so whatever appears inside of the border has to blend completely with the part of the picture over which the Plop Rendering is placed. Doing a Plop Render on something sitting on a cloudy sky and turning on antialiasing, when the rest of the cloudy sky was not antialiased, will result in a distinct and observable difference between the Plop Rendered area and the rest of the picture. Therefore, look closely at the section of the image you are Plop Rendering, and pay attention to that portion where the Plop Render borders meet the rest of the image.

- **Wireframe Depth Cue On/Off.** Leave the Wireframe Depth Cue on, so you can get a better 3D idea of where objects are placed in a scene when working in Wireframe view.
- **Wireframe Shadows On/Off.** This tool should also be left on, so you can appreciate where an object is placed on the Y (height) World axis. Shadows will be visible in Wireframe view.
- **Wireframe Underground On/Off.** *Underground* is an invisible plane. When objects in a scene are placed lower than the Underground, the part below the Underground disappears. As you become more familiar with Bryce, you'll find there are times when you'll want to switch Underground on, and other times when you'll want to switch it off.

- **Wireframe Resolution.** There are three Wireframe resolutions involved here: *Motion, Static,* and *Selected.* They are revealed when you click on this icon and the options list appears with the three choices: *Motion Resolution, Static Resolution,* and *Selected Resolution.* Each of these choices has its own set of enumerated choices. The higher value set for a resolution, the clearer the object will appear in Wireframe view, but the slower the system might function.

  Motion: Motion Resolution refers to the on-screen resolution of objects in motion. Explore setting this as high as possible (dependent on the speed of your system), so you can get the best idea of exactly how objects will appear in an animation. On slower systems, setting this too high will adversely affect preview playback speed.

  Static: Static resolution refers to the on-screen resolution of unselected objects at rest in your scene. You can usually keep this setting to medium, and choose to heighten the resolution of your selected items.

  Selected: Selected Resolution is the on-screen resolution of selected objects. This should usually be set as high as possible on systems with lots of RAM in order to allow you to see object elements more clearly for editing purposes.

- **Display Modes.** You will use this control often during the design phase of a Bryce world. Of its three options (Wireframe, Wireframe/Render composite, and Render), the Wireframe/Render composite is extremely useful in the placement of objects. It allows you to work as you would in the Edit screen with wireframe proxies of objects, except that you see the wireframe against the last-rendered picture. Clicking on this icon cycles you through the three choices.
- **Zoom in/out, and Pan:** The Plus and Minus Magnifier icons and the Hand icon represent these tools. Zooms will always center on any presently selected object. If no object is selected, the zooms will be centered globally. Click and drag on any one of these three icons to perform the operation. Place some objects in a scene and explore these tools now.

THE BOTTOM TOOLBAR

The Time/Selection Toggle is shaped like a wireframe globe. Clicking on it alternates between the Time (animation) tools and the Selection tools.

The Time Palette

These tools and controls are grouped in what is called the *Time Palette*. The Time Palette is also referred to as the Animation toolbar, and it's where all of your keyframing activities take place. Read and work through Chapters 16 through 20 for details on configuring Bryce animations (see Figure 1.19).

FIGURE 1.19 The Time Palette has VCR-like tools for navigating through your animation and setting keyframes. See Chapters 16 through 20 for detailed data and tutorials.

Here is the general roadmap to the Time Palette tools and controls:

- **Timeline.** The Timeline is the long horizontal bar at the bottom of the Document Space window. When you click and drag the *Timeline Indicator* (the lozenge-shaped tool that sits on the Timeline), you indicate the place on the Timeline that represents a specific time and frame of an animation. Read Chapters 16 through 20 for animation concept details. Simply put, however, Bryce animations are for the most part created by moving the Timeline Indicator to a new frame on the Timeline, and then moving, resizing, or rotating a selected object.
- **Timeline Scaler.** This tool is almost invisible. It is at the upper right of the Timeline, represented by a series of rectangular dots. Clicking and dragging over this icon shortens or lengthens the amount of time represented on the Timeline.
- **Keyframe Memory Dots.** Use these dots to move quickly from one frame to another on the Timeline. As your animation becomes more involved, you can substitute needed frames for others already listed in any Memory Dot.
- **VCR Controls.** These buttons work similar to VCR controls, with some alterations. Represented are First Keyframe, Previous Keyframe, Stop, Play, Next Keyframe, and Last Keyframe. Clicking on any one of these controls moves the Time Indicator along the Timeline after the animation is underway.
- **Keyframe Controls.** These are the Plus and Minus icons. The Key is just a symbol that calls attention to the Plus and Minus controls. The icons represent Add Keyframe (Plus) and Delete Keyframe (Minus).
- **The Keyframe Options Menu.** When you click and hold on the Keyframe Plus button, the Keyframe Options menu appears (see Figure 1.20).

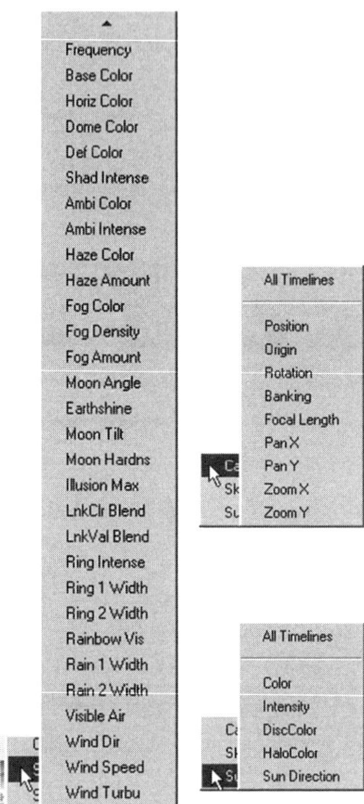

FIGURE 1.20 There are itemized listings in the Keyframe Options menu for keyframing every aspect of the Camera, Sky, Sun, or the selected object(s).These options are for advanced Bryce users.

- **Options Menu.** This menu of options is accessed by clicking on the downward-pointing triangle at the far right of the toolbar. The most important command in this menu is whether *Auto-Key* is turned on (checked) or off (unchecked). Auto-Key should normally be on at the start of your animation edits, and then unchecked when it comes time to fine-tune your work. The same menu allows you to set what the tick marks indicate as far as time increments on the Timeline. When Auto-Key is off, Bryce allows you to keyframe each discreet aspect of the Camera, Sky, and Sun manually (see Figure 1.21).

The Selection Palette

The Selection Palette's purpose is to allow you easy access to any object and object type in your Bryce scene (see Figure 1.22).

Bryce knows what tools you need to locate and select any object in your scene, no matter how complex things get. It makes no difference

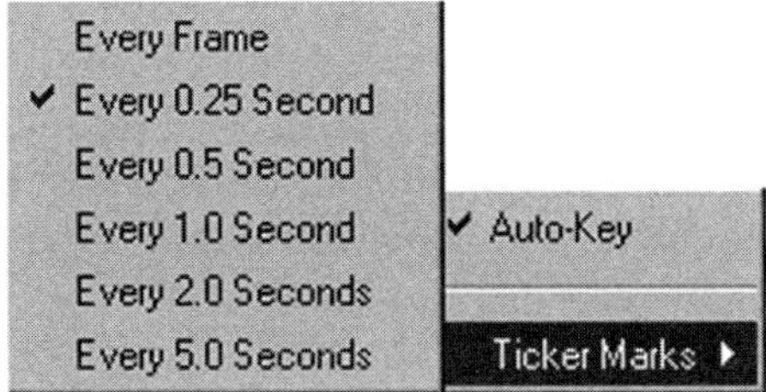

FIGURE 1.21 Knowing when to use the Auto-Key function is the secret to worry-free animating in Bryce. This is something learned through experience.

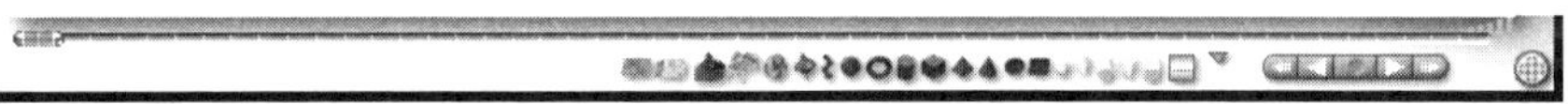

FIGURE 1.22 The Selection Palette.

how hidden in the mix your specific object might be. The *Selection Palette* is Bryce's answer to every computer artist's and animator's search-and-locate dream.

Icons for every Bryce object type are included in the Selection palette, while separate options are listed in the associated Selection menu for imported objects and grouped items in the scene. For Bryce objects in the scene, click and hold on any one of the specific icons that represent that object type, and a pop-up list appears with every member of that object type in the scene. Select the specific object from the list.

Alternatively, you can use the VCR control arrows at the right to march through the objects in the scene, either by type, or in the sequential order they were created (by making sure that Alternate VCR Mode is selected in the Selection menu) (see Figure 1.23).

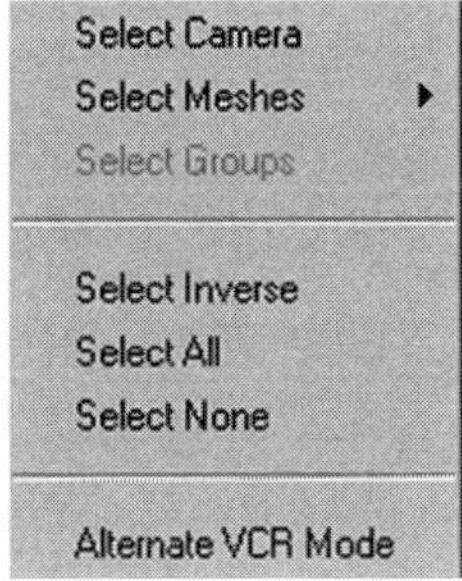

FIGURE 1.23 The Alternate VCR Mode option should be checked in the Selection menu when you want to step through each of the objects in the scene sequentially.

IMPORTANT MENU OPTIONS FOR OPTIMIZING YOUR WORK

The top menu bar contains the *File, Edit, Objects, Links,* and *Help* menus. Several of the options and commands in these menus are covered in the more detailed chapters that follow, but here is a basic rundown for Bryce newbies that we haven't mentioned before:

File>Save/Save As

Save, Save, Save! Save your work every 20 to 30 minutes, unless you enjoy seeing it all disappear in an instant. It's not that Bryce crashes that often, but that other elements of your computer might intervene (like not enough RAM allocated to Bryce) to cause a crash. Save both the Project file and any associated rendered images that need to be saved separately.

File>Merge

Keep merging in mind for developing large scenarios. With merge, you can prepare a scene by developing separate scenes that focus on individual complex elements, and merge them together with other saved scenes at the end. The only caution is to make sure that you have enough RAM to handle the size of the merged final scene.

Edit>Copy/Paste Material

Copying and pasting materials can allow you to create scenes with similar textures much faster. You can load in a few terrains, followed by a number of rocks and a ground plane, and assign the same material to each element in this fashion by clicking on one item and selecting Edit>Copy Material, and then on the other objects to Paste>Material. See Chapters 9 through 11 for details about Materials.

Edit>Copy/Paste Matrix

Copy/Paste matrix is a time-saving shortcut when you need to apply resizing/position/rotation parameters to an object so it matches another object's size/position/rotation. Duplicate and Replicate commands offer you new opportunities for object design alternatives. See Chapters 2 through 8 for possible places where you might use these commands.

Edit>Objects

The Edit>Object command alters the faceted look of an imported object and smoothes it out. Just click on either Faceted or Smooth after selecting the object, and Bryce does the job (see Figure 1.23).

Link

If your system is connected to the Internet, use one of the selections in the Link menu to quickly connect to one of the listed Bryce Web sites. By accessing the directions on how to do so at the bottom of this menu, you can add your own links.

Help

Always look at the topics in the Help menu when you are starting to learn any application. The material included is usually more detailed than the paper documentation, and most times includes a number of last-minute additions and help content files.

MOVING ON

In this chapter, we provided you with all of the needed locations and terminology for starting your Bryce adventures. The chapters that follow look at Bryce creations in much more detail

CHAPTER

2 Primitives

ENTER, THE ACTORS

The 3D Models in your Bryce world are the actors on your stage. Their movements give life to a scene, and their animated interactions with each other and their environment are interpreted as meaningful acts by the onlooker. Your models are alive, whether they represent organic creatures or mechanical constructs. The moment that an object moves, it is assumed to have some form of intent and purpose. Even cars, planes, and rockets seem to be breathing on their own as they fly through the world on their assigned paths. In the world of computer graphics, it is possible that at any moment, a tree might dance, or a car might sneeze.

Two general types of objects (actors) bring a Bryce scene to life: *2D Picture Planes* and *3D Models*. This chapter focuses on the differences and similarities amongst various types of 3D models, and how a variety of them can be constructed from Bryce Primitives.

Primitive Modeling Elements

What do we mean when we say "primitive" in a 3D application? A primitive is a 3D object that can be brought into a scene by clicking on its icon, or selected from a menu of options. Different 3D applications have varying numbers and types of primitives. The common 3D primitives shared by all are the cube, sphere, cone, and cylinder. Bryce goes beyond that, by adding other primitives. The Bryce primitives can be seen and activated by clicking on their associated icons in the Create toolbar (see Figure 2.1).

FIGURE 2.1 The Bryce Create toolbar displays various non-terrain primitive objects. From left to right: the Sphere, Torus, Cylinder, Cube, Pyramid, and Cone.

Transformation Tools

Any object that is added to a Bryce scene, whether primitive or imported, displays its own *Transformation menu* once it is selected. Each tool in this menu is important to explore before you start creating complex elements in a scene. Click on the Sphere in the Create menu, which places a Sphere in your workspace. The Sphere is selected by default, and its associated transformation menu is displayed alongside it (see Figure 2.2).

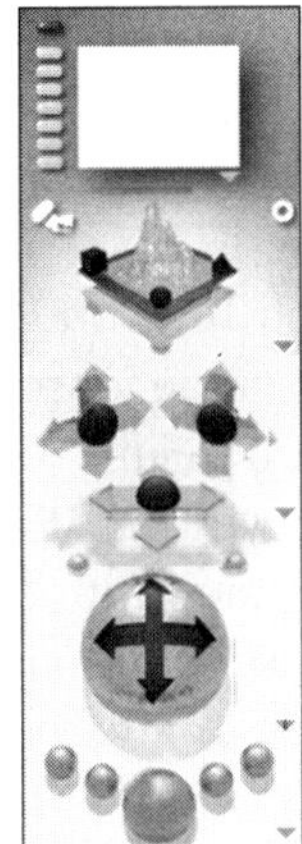

FIGURE 2.2 An object's Transformation tools are displayed in a vertical menu alongside of the object when it is selected.

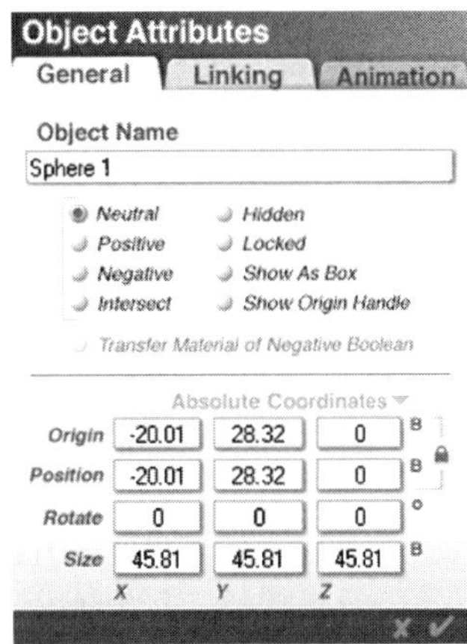

FIGURE 2.3 The General tab in the Object Attributes dialog is revealed after you click on the "A."

From top to bottom, the icons in the Transformation menu list represent Object Attributes dialog, "Family" color palette, Link icon, Target icon, Materials icon, and Gravity drop arrow. You have to familiarize yourself with these tools in order to have a working knowledge of Bryce. It's especially important that you become familiar with the use of the Object Attributes icon (represented by the letter "A" at the very top of the Transformation menu), and with the options contained in the *General* tab of the window that opens up when you click on the "A" (see Figure 2.3).

Although we will return to the use of items in the General tab at different points in the coming chapters, here are a couple of important tips:

- To change the name of a selected object, just type in a new name in the top input area.
- Lock/Unlock a selected object by checking or unchecking the Lock option. Locked objects cannot be moved or otherwise manipulated.

CITYSCAPE

By combining selected 3D objects in the Create toolbar (see Figure 2.1), you can construct an infinite number of recognizable objects, as well as use these primitives on their own as objects in a scene. The Torus, for example, can become a bagel or a car tire, while the Sphere can be transformed into a planet, a beach ball, or a dome in a cityscape. In fact, a cityscape is a good place to begin exploring the use of primitives as standalone objects.

Prim City

We are going to use primitives to construct a futuristic cityscape as our first project. Here's how to do it:

1. First, go to the right-hand toolbar and turn on the Grid in the Background Paper display. This gives you a guide for placing objects in proximity to each other. Remove the Ground Plane for now, by selecting it and pressing the Delete key on your keyboard. Work in the Top view.
2. Click on various object primitives to place your structures in the city. Click on them one by one, and move them into place on the grid. Use more than just rectangular primitives to give your cityscape a more interesting look. Resize some of the primitives from the Top view to vary the buildings (see Chapter 1, "Bryce Basics," for directions on using the Resize tool) (see Figure 2.4).

Spherical primitives contain more polygons than other objects, so to cut down on storage space for the file, use spheres sparsely if you are RAM-memory challenged.

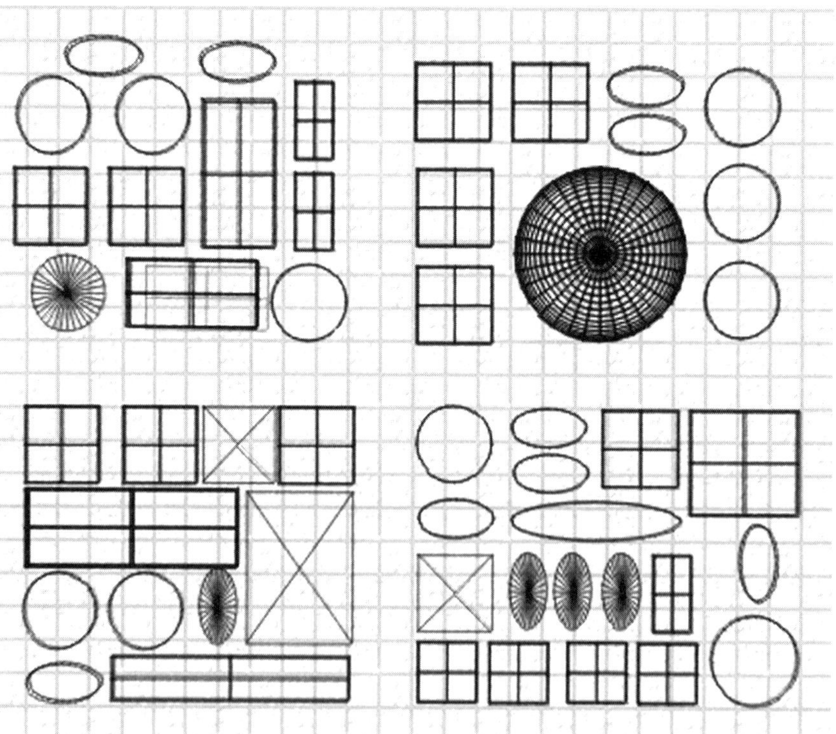

FIGURE 2.4 Use the grid as a guide in the Top view to move your primitive components into place.

3. Apply a solid color material to all of the objects (simple and fast—Blue metal) by opening the Materials Presets Library and clicking on the material with the object(s) selected. Create a Ground Plane mapped with Planes and Terrains: *Mud and Snow* material. Take a look at it from a perspective camera view (see Figure 2.5).

FIGURE 2.5 When seen in perspective, the cityscape begins to take on a more believable appearance. The city so far has only 1219 polygons, and because it has a simple material mapping, it renders very fast.

4. The cityscape could stop here, or we might want to tweak it a bit to make it more interesting—let's do that. First, select any spheres you have in the scene and move them down so that they show only their top half, like geodesic domes.
5. Next, edit the sizes of some of your similar shapes (cubes, for example) so they give more variety to the scene. Make some taller, and some shorter. Use the Resize tool in the Edit toolbar.
6. Add a few more primitive forms on top of some of the buildings. Especially effective is the addition of smaller customized cubes on top of larger ones, and pyramidal shapes on top of cubes. Experiment. Render a preview to judge your efforts thus far (see Figure 2.6).
7. After you have adjusted all of your buildings so they seem right for the scene, there's one more step: cities have roadways. For our roads, we'll simply add a few rectangles, squashed so they're close to the

FIGURE 2.6 By varying the buildings even more, we create a more interesting space.

FIGURE 2.7 With the addition of roads, this simple cityscape looks more complete.

ground and elongated beyond the city's borders, coloring the roads with a simple and fast *Black* material (see Figures 2.7 and 2.8).

The cityscape shown in Figure 2.8 has less than 1400 polygons, and renders in less than two minutes with minimal antialiasing on a 750 MHz Pentium III system.

FIGURE 2.8 Rendered against a cloudy sky from a head-on view, with a Haze setting of 60, gives us another appreciation on this simple cityscape.

The Great Pyramid

Just to show you that creating a startling graphic in Bryce is as simple as it can be, let's create a virtual view of the great Pyramid on the planes of Giza. This project should take just a few minutes to design, and should render very quickly. Here's how to proceed:

1. Place three Pyramid primitives (tetrahedrons) from the Top view as shown in Figure 2.9.
2. Create a sky from one of the sky presets, and add suitable materials to the pyramids from the Materials Presets. Although this is a very simple composition, it can still be very effective (see Figure 2.10).

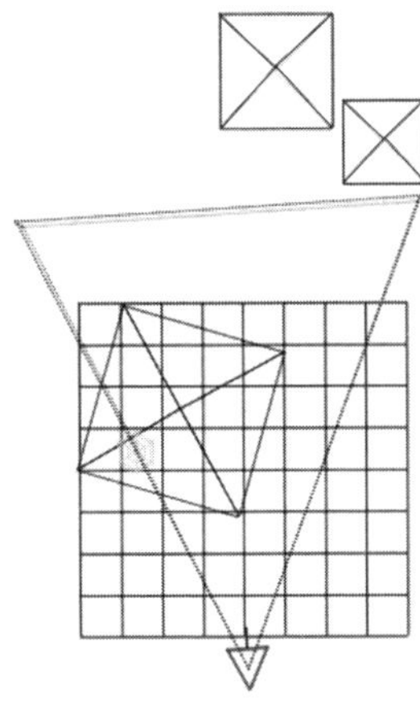

FIGURE 2.9 Place the tetrahedrons as shown in this Top view, with the camera located as you see it here.

FIGURE 2.10 The finished rendering, created from three basic primitive objects set against a sky.

A Basic Table

You can create a million variations on this theme, but this is the general way to go about it. This table is created entirely from Bryce primitive objects.

1. Go to the Right view, and place a cube in the scene. Place it as indicated above the ground, and adjust its height so that it looks similar to Figure 2.11.
2. Place an elongated cube and a tetrahedron in the scene. Resize them as shown in Figure 2.12, and place them as shown in this Right view. Select both of them and group them together by going to Objects>Group.

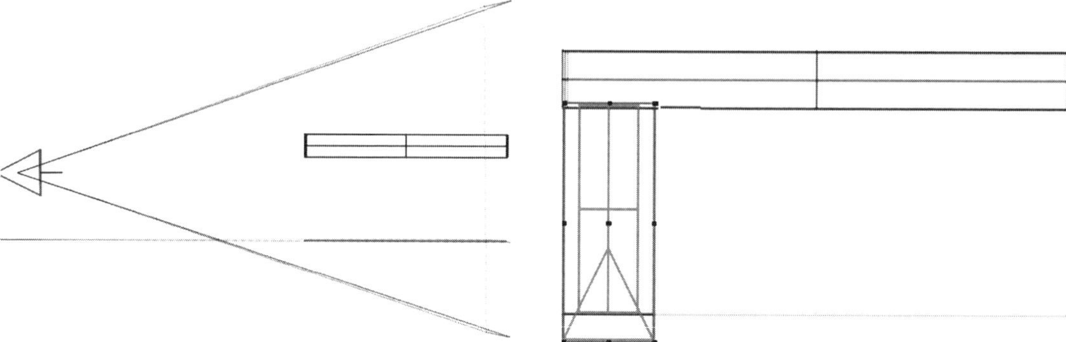

FIGURE 2.11 A resized cube is the start of the table.

FIGURE 2.12 The first leg is added to the table, and placed in position in the Right view.

3. From the Top view, Edit>Duplicate the table leg to generate the other three legs (refer to Figure 2.13).
4. Texture with whatever material presets you prefer, and save to disk (see Figure 2.14).

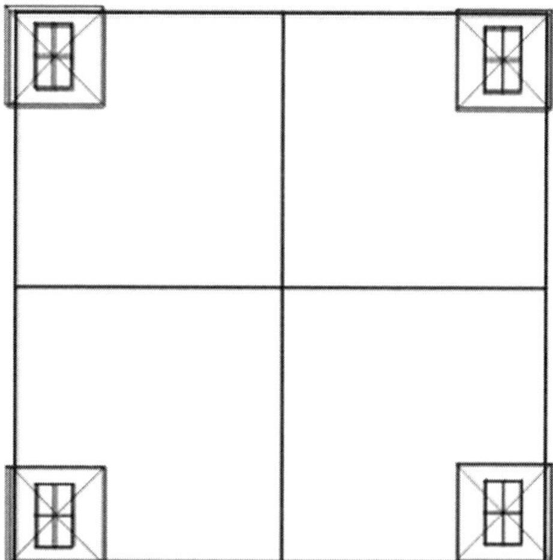

FIGURE 2.13 The legs are duplicated and placed in position in the Top view.

FIGURE 2.14 The finished and rendered table, made with primitive objects.

House

Remember the houses you used to draw in second grade? They were probably created by placing a triangle on top of a square, with perhaps a chimney added. We can do this same thing by using a cube and a tetrahedron in Bryce, but we'll push our creative efforts a little farther than that. Here's how:

1. Go to the Front view. Just for fun, let's start with the basic second-grade form, placing a red squashed tetrahedron on top of a cube. Group the cube and tetrahedron. Duplicate the group, and move the duplicated element away from the original (see Figure 2.15).
2. Next, we'll add some resized cubes colored black for a series of windows and a door. You're free to experiment here (refer to Figure 2.16).

FIGURE 2.15 The first step is to create these two duplicate forms, made from a grouped cube and squashed tetrahedron.

FIGURE 2.16 Windows and the door are simple cubes colored black.

3. Now add the main house, simply by adding another cube-tetrahedron group to the scene. Populate it with cubic windows and doors. If you like, add a porch with columns made from primitive cylinders. Add the ground and sky, and render for preview (refer to Figure 2.17).

FIGURE 2.17 By adding more primitive elements, our house can become a veritable mansion in a matter of seconds.

Robot

Although creating organic forms with primitive objects presents a problem when it comes to curved shapes, we can do the next best thing and build a robotic figure. Explore by using any primitives you think appropriate, and place them in position (see Figure 2.22 as a reference) (see Figure 2.18).

The primitives used in the construction of this robot are mostly spheres and distorted spheres. This gives us a more humanoid robot than if it were constructed from cubic forms. There's no doubt that it's still a robot, but we are made to feel that we might be able to reason with it if push comes to shove (see Figure 2.19).

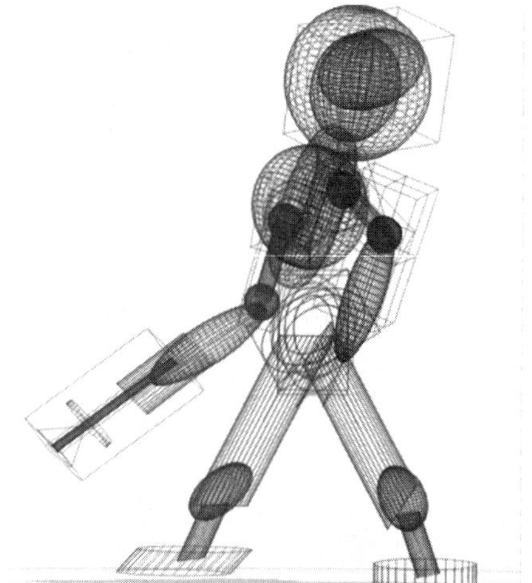

FIGURE 2.18 Notice that our robot is entirely constructed from primitive objects.

FIGURE 2.19 Here's a rendering of the robot, from both the Side and Front views.

IMPORTED MODELING ELEMENTS

Bryce allows for the import of 3D objects created in external applications in many 3D formats. You might be thinking, "Wait a minute! I thought this chapter was about Bryce internal primitives!" Don't be upset. To some degree, imported objects can also be described as primitives, in that they appear in Bryce as one unified form, and are many times also strung together to create a larger and more complex Bryce composite form.

Bryce has a minimum of modeling tools and options for creating complex 3D modeled elements internally. Other professional 3D modeling applications offer many more choices for creating objects of every description, due to expanded tool sets. The only question that remains, is "does the external 3D application I have export objects in a format compatible with Bryce?" If the answer is yes, then you have all you need to create infinite object content to place in Bryce worlds.

There is another reason for selecting imported objects to augment Bryce primitives. Bryce primitives tend to distort and skew sometimes, which can be a big problem in an animation. Imported objects and object elements are much less prone to this anomaly, and the resulting animations look cleaner and more professional.

The general rule is to use primitive objects to construct background elements in Bryce, or composite objects whose parts are grouped.

There are also dozens of CD-ROM libraries with a variety of 3D objects in a number formats available for purchase. Many of these libraries contain objects suitable for your Bryce work (see Figure 2.20).

FIGURE 2.20 Here is a selection of 3DS and DXF objects, imported and rendered in Bryce.

MULTIPLE REPLICATION ARRAY MODELING

One of Bryce's most interesting modeling tools can be found in the Edit menu at the top of the Bryce interface (normally hidden until you move

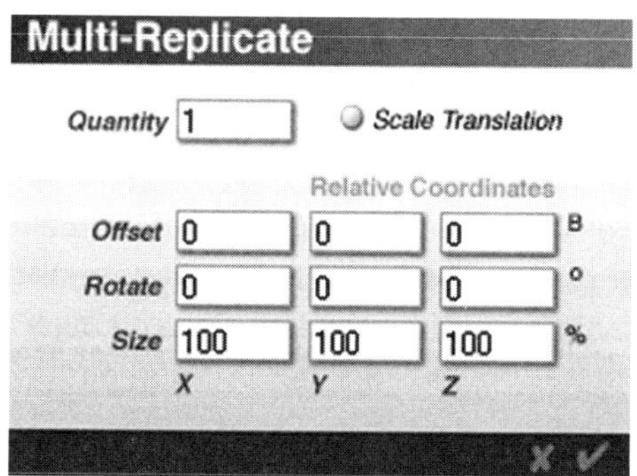

FIGURE 2.21 The Multi-Replicate dialog in the Edit menu allows you to apply offsets, resizes, and rotations to each succeeding object in an array, according to the parameters you set.

FIGURE 2.22 These spiral stairs were create by multi-replicating an elongated and squashed cube with an Offset of 12 on the Y-axis, and a Rotation of 12 degrees on the Y-axis.

the mouse up to the top of the screen): the Multi-Replicate tool. With this tool, you can create as many clones of an object as you like (as long as you have enough RAM). You can determine how each object in the array is separated from other objects by offsets on the XYZ axes, as well as rotation and sizing. Each object in the array will continue the progression of offsets, resizing, and rotations. All of the members of the array can be grouped as one object, or acted upon separately. Just select the object and open the Multi-Replicate dialog to set the values (see Figures 2.21 through 2.30).

FIGURE 2.23 This Toroid Tunnel was created by multi-replicating a front-facing Torus. Offsets were 0, –26, 0, and Resize was 85, 85, 85, causing each succeeding torus to be 85% of the last one. When standing on the large torus, this makes a great futuristic building in the background (3328 polygons).

FIGURE 2.24 This object is based on a multi-replicated group of squashed cylinders. Quantity was set to 12, Offset to 0, 7, 0, and Rotation to 0, 30, 0. Size was set to 90 on all axes. It was grouped, and multi-replicated again four times, with an Offset of 40 on the Y-axis. The result was a denuded treelike structure (6240 polygons). The object was then duplicated and rendered in a Bryce scene.

The Cubic Matrix

This array is a cubic structure that consists of separate cubic elements. It can be used to create a mesmerizing animation, with almost illusionary results, as the camera flies through the rows of cubes. Here's how to create the matrix:

1. Place one cube in your workspace. Select the Multi-Replicate command, and enter the following in the Offset row: 0, 0, 35. Set the Quantity to 6. Click on the check mark. An array of seven cubes now stretches into the Z direction.
2. Group all of the cubes. Select Multi-Replicate again, and this time enter the following in the Offset row: 0, 35, 0. Set the Quantity to 6. Click on the check mark. Now you have a wall of 49 cubes, with seven rows and seven columns. Group everything.
3. Repeat the Multi-Replicate operation one more time. This time, enter the following in the Offset row: 35, 0, 0. Set the Quantity to 6. Click on the check mark. Now you have a cubic array with 7 × 7 × 7 cubes (343 cubes). Group all of the cubes as one object. Save the object to disk as a possible animation project.

Create a similar array with spheres or toruses, or perhaps do it with an imported object that doesn't contain too many polygons (since you'll be multiplying the polygons by 343!) (see Figure 2.25).

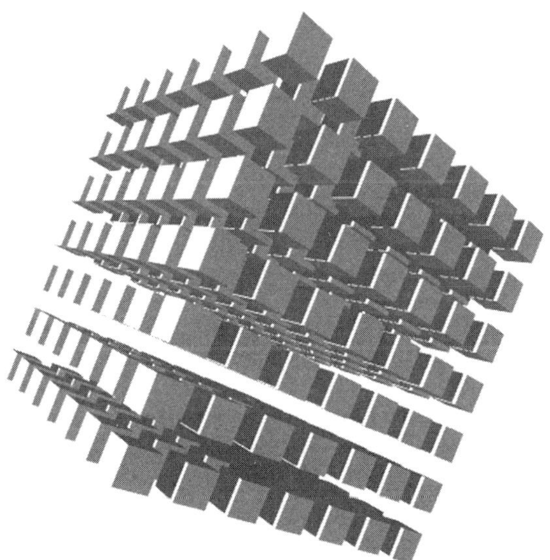

FIGURE 2.25 The cubic array rendered and ready to fly through.

Circular Arrays

Using the Multi-Replicate command, you can arrange objects in a circle. Doing this manually can be a time-consuming task, while using the Multi-Replicate option makes it easy. Here's how to create a circle of standing stones:

1. Place a Stone primitive on your workspace. Stand it up vertically, and elongate its height until it has the appearance of a standing stone (like those found at Stonehenge). Its size should be 85, 20, 42, or close to these dimensions.
2. Select Object Space. Go to the Multi-Replicate dialog while the stone is selected. We will need a total of 12 stones, so the number in the dialog should read 11 replications. Input the following data: Offsets of 0, 50, 50: Rotations of 0, 30, 0. Click on the check mark.
3. After the stones are replicated, select all of them. Go to the Rotation tool in the Edit toolbar, and rotate until they are all facing toward the center of the circle. With the group selected, apply a preset material. Render and save (see Figure 2.26).

FIGURE 2.26 The Top view of the stones, and the finished standing stones example after rendering.

Ribbon Path Arrays

A Ribbon path is a selected path transformed into an object. Ribbon paths are commonly used for Bryce animation purposes. Here, we will look at Ribbon paths for another purpose altogether, as a way to create special array objects. This subject is not covered in the Bryce documentation.

The idea for creating arrays with the help of Ribbon paths is straightforward and simple to understand, as long as you understand the basics about Ribbon paths first. You can apply this method to any Ribbon path in your scene, but for a basic understanding, we will import sample Ribbon paths from the Bryce Library. Go to the Create toolbar, and bring up the Objects menu. Select the Path Library (all the paths here are Ribbon paths), and load in the *Oval Racetrack* Path. Clicking on the check mark loads the Oval Racetrack Ribbon path to your scene (see Figure 2.27).

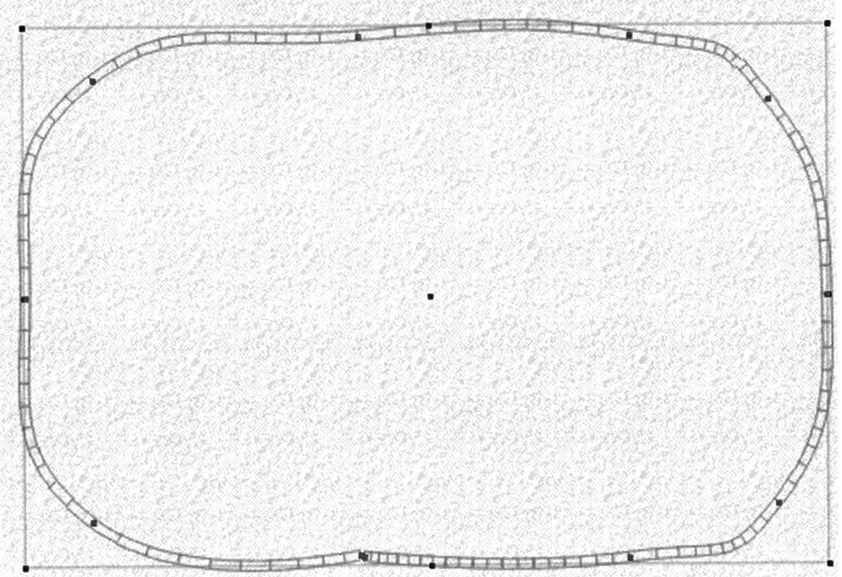

FIGURE 2.27 The top view of the Oval Racetrack Ribbon path.

If you want to explore this technique with your own paths, just make sure you translate them to Ribbon paths first, by selecting them and choosing Create Path from the Object menu.

THE WILD RIBBON BRIDGE

1. With the Racetrack Ribbon path loaded, we'll create a Bridge object. Using primitive objects, create a 3D form similar to the one shown in Figure 2.28.
2. Link the grouped Bridge section to the Ribbon path. The easiest way to link objects is to select the Link icon in the object's Attributes list (the third icon from the top), and click-drag to the object you want to link to. The grouped bridge component will snap to the Ribbon path after linking. With the Bridge section still selected, use the Replicate (not Multi-Replicate) command seven times. This will clone the Bridge section seven times on top of the original section.

FIGURE 2.28 This is the start of our Bridge object, a 3D form made from two cylinders and two Cube primitives.

You can also use the Duplicate command to do this. The difference between the two is that Replicate will create the clones with their original orientation, and Duplicate will create the clones in whatever orientation the object has been rotated to.

3. All of the sections are linked to the path, so they can be moved anywhere on the path. From the Top view, move the sections so they touch one another in a line, and rotate as necessary (Y rotation in Object Space). You should have a composite object that looks like the one in Figure 2.38. Do not delete the Ribbon path unless you unlink every section, or you will delete the sections along with it. Group the sections and the path. Pick an interesting camera angle, render, and save to disk (see Figures 2.29 and 2.30).

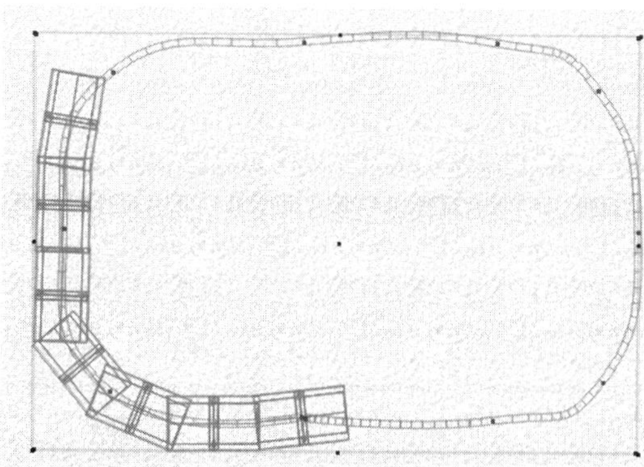

FIGURE 2.29 This is a Top view of the replicated sections placed in position on the Ribbon path.

FIGURE 2.30 A completed Bridge rendering.

OBJECT SUBSTITUTION MODELING

Here's another modeling tool that is unique to Bryce. We might even call this modeling technique a "post modeling" alternative, since it works on model constructs already composited in your scene. Follow this exercise:

1. Place an imported model from your choice of CD-ROM model collections in your scene. It should be a model that has multiple grouped parts; for example, a human figure. Select the model if it is not already selected.
2. Go to the Convert Selection To menu in the Edit toolbar (activated by clicking and holding on the double arrow icon at the top right of the toolbar). With the grouped figure selected, go to the Cylinder icon. Each part of the imported figure is replaced with a cylinder (see Figure 2.31).

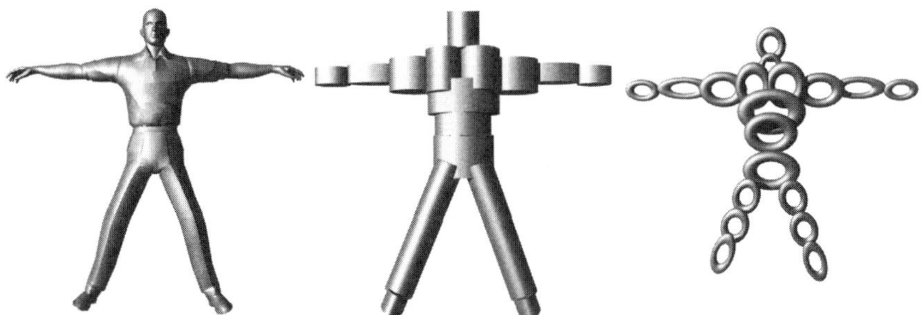

FIGURE 2.31 The original imported figure is on the left, and the cylinder Object Substitution figure is in the middle. At the right is an Object Substitution accomplished with Tori (multiple Torus objects).

PRIMITIVE MAN

Our Primitive Man is neither Neanderthal nor Cro-Magnon, but refers to an anthropological model built entirely of Bryce primitives. This is one way to create simple characters for populating a Bryce world, without importing more complex character models. Do the following:

1. Open Bryce. Delete any Ground Plane that might be in the Bryce document by selecting it and pressing Delete.
2. Select the Camera. Click on the "A" symbol to bring up the Camera Controls window (see Figure 2.32).
3. Use the Camera settings shown in Figure 2.33.

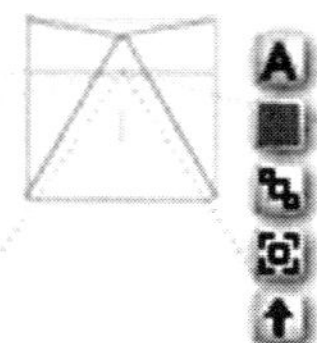

FIGURE 2.32 Click on the "A" symbol after selecting the Camera.

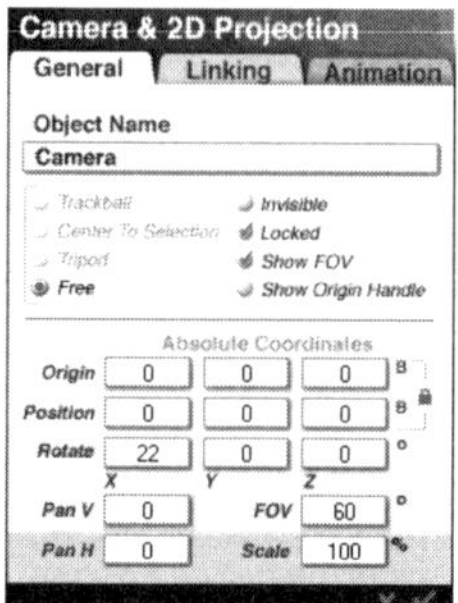

FIGURE 2.33 Use these values for the Camera settings.

4. Go to the Front view. Click on the Sphere primitive in the Create toolbar. This places a Sphere on the screen.
5. Use the same process to create a Torus primitive. Center the Torus over the Sphere. Click on the Link symbol with the Torus selected, and link the Torus to the Sphere. Do a test render (see Figure 2.34).
6. Create a Cylinder. Center it below the Sphere, and Resize and Rotate it (90 degrees on the Y-axis). Link it to the Sphere (refer to Figure 2.35).
7. You can move everything by selecting the Sphere, which is now the linked "parent" of the other two objects. Move these objects out of the way by moving the Sphere. Now it's time to create an arm.
8. Create the object shown in Figure 2.36. This object is made from a Cube (hand), two Ellipsoids (lower and upper arm), and a Cylinder (shoulder).

FIGURE 2.34 This is how your character should appear at this point.

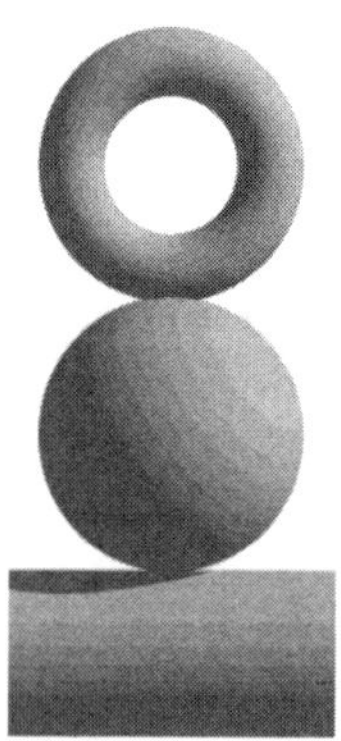

FIGURE 2.35 The Cylinder will act as the pelvic area of the character.

FIGURE 2.36 Create this object, composed of primitives, for the character's arm.

9. Link the Cube (hand) to the bottom Ellipsoid (lower arm), and the bottom Ellipsoid (lower arm) to the top Ellipsoid (upper arm). Link the top Ellipsoid (upper arm) to the Cylinder (shoulder). The Cylinder (shoulder) is now the Parent object in a Linked chain.

When you resize or rotate the Parent object, scaling and rotation is passed down the Linked chain to the Child objects.

10. Resize the Cylinder (shoulder) so that the Linked chain looks proportional to the rest of the character. Rotate as shown. Link the shoulder to the Sphere. Your character should now resemble Figure 2.37.
11. Duplicate the Linked chain of the arm by selecting the shoulder and going to Edit > Duplicate. In the Edit toolbar, click on the downward-pointing arrow next to the Resize tool, and select *Flip X* from the list. This creates the flipped duplicate for the other arm. Move the other arm into place. It is already Linked to the Sphere, since it duplicates the Linkage of the source arm (see Figure 2.38).

FIGURE 2.37 The arm is Resized, Rotated, and Linked to the Sphere (chest/abdomen).

FIGURE 2.38 Now our Primitive Man has two arms.

12. Click on one of the shoulder Cylinders, and Duplicate. We want to remove the Linking, so while the duplicated shoulder Cylinder is selected, click on the "A" symbol. This brings up the Cylinder's Object Attributes window. Under the Linking tab, select *None* from the *Object Parent Name* list. This removes the Link. Click on the check mark to complete this operation (see Figure 2.39).
13. We are going to use the Linked arm chain duplicate we just created for creating the legs as well. Move the new Leg object into place on one side of the character's body, and Rotate as shown. Duplicate and

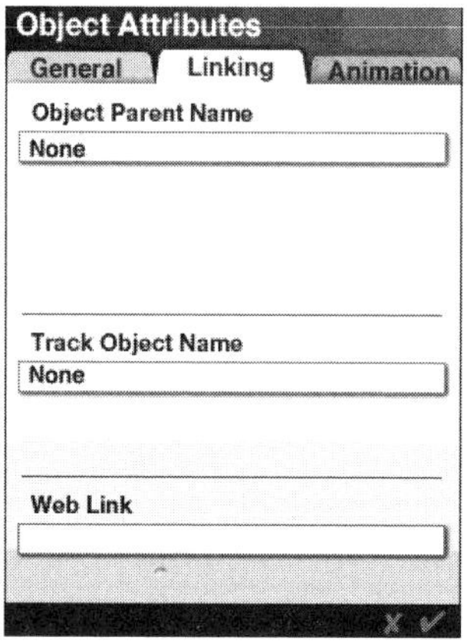

Object Attributes
General Linking Animation
Object Parent Name
None
Track Object Name
None
Web Link

FIGURE 2.39 Remove the Link in the Object Attributes window under the Linking tab.

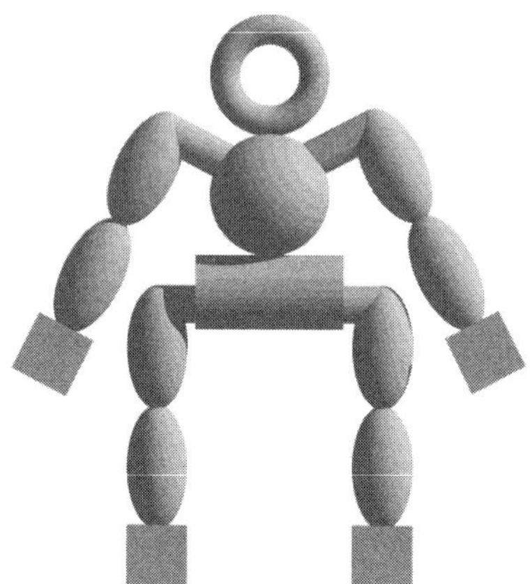

FIGURE 2.40 The completed Primitive Man model.

Flip to create the other leg. Both leg Cylinders are then Linked to the pelvis Cylinder of the character. When completed, your character will resemble Figure 2.40.

14. Since all of the body parts are Linked, rotating any Parent component also rotates all of the Child objects in the hierarchy below it. Let's rotate the Left Forearm, which should bring the Hand along. Click on the Left Forearm (which is really the arm on the right side of your screen, considering that the character is facing front). Rotate it (see Figure 2.41).
15. The forearm rotates and the hand accompanies it, but something is radically wrong: the forearm detaches from the upper arm. We have forgotten one important item: the object's Origin Point placement.

FIGURE 2.41 The Forearm is rotated, but it looks strange.

The Origin Point is the fulcrum of any objects, the point that determines the center of rotation and scaling.

16. Bring up the forearm's Object Attributes window. Under the General tab, click the Show Origin Handle option. Close the window by clicking on the check mark (see Figure 2.42).
17. You will see a bright green dot on the selected object. This is the Origin Handle (also called Origin Point and Pivot Point interchangeably). Rotate the object back into position. Use a Selection marquee, and surround the entire character. Go to Objects > Show Object as Box. All of the character's parts are now displayed as boxes. Select each part, one by one, and Show Origin Handle. Now you see boxes, with each showing its Origin Handle (see Figure 2.43).

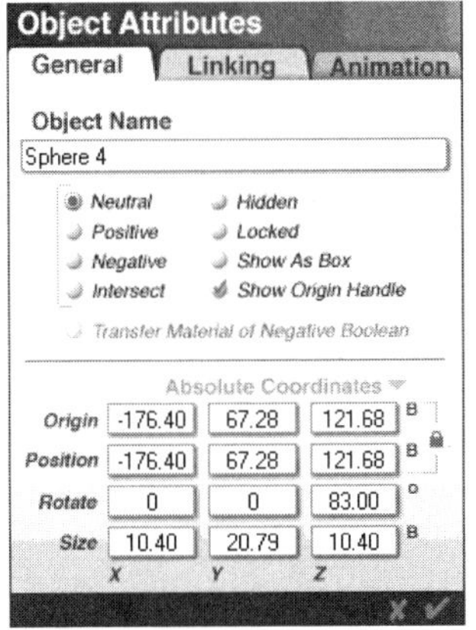

FIGURE 2.42 Select Show Origin Handle.

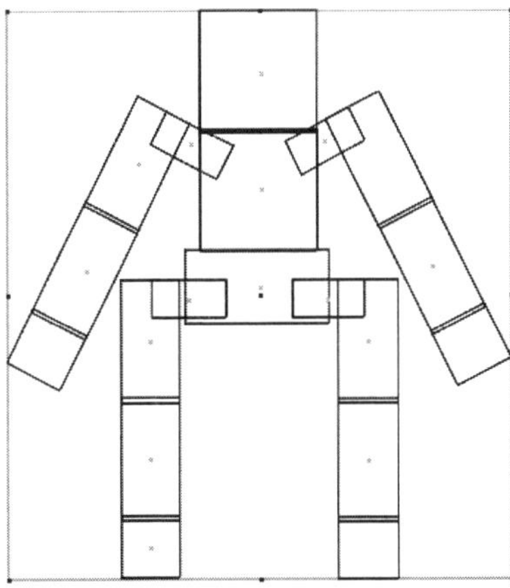

FIGURE 2.43 All of the character parts are displayed as boxes, with each part's Origin Handle visible.

18. You will want to move each component's Origin Handle (click and drag) to the place from which that component will rotate; for example, the forearms should rotate from the elbow. First, however, you have to correct something. Moving Origin Handles in a Linked Hierarchy moves the Child objects. Therefore, you have to unlink everything, move the Origin Handles, and then relink. Sorry about that, but this teaches you that certain processes in developing a Linked object must happen in a specific order. Mistakes are the best way to learn creative processes so you won't forget the lesson again (see Figure 2.44).
19. Now, Rotate selected parts to pose the character. Everything should work perfectly!

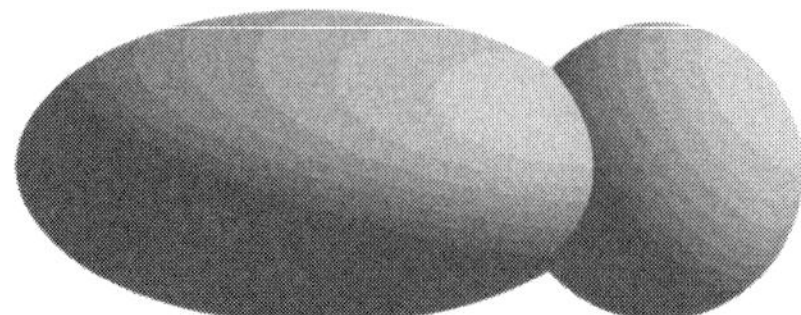

FIGURE 2.44 The parts are unlinked, the Origin Handles are moved into place, and everything is relinked.

This is called an *Articulated Model.* Use a metallic gold preset material on all of the Primitive Man's components, with Object Mapping.

Prim Tower

One of the best uses for object primitives is to use them to create towers and buildings. This can range from castles to skyscrapers, and include unique buildings of your own fantasy design. Here's what we mean:

In this exercise, the assignment of preset Materials is up to you.

1. Place a Stretched Cylinder on the screen. Go to the Top view, and Move the Origin Handle away from the object about six widths of the object. Select Edit > Multi-Replicate. Select a Quantity of 4, and a Y Rotation of 72 degrees (see Figure 2.45).
2. From the Top view, you will see that you have created a perfectly symmetrical pentagonal array of columns (see Figure 2.46).
3. Place a Cylinder at the center of the column array. Resize it so that it is about two-thirds as wide and deep as the columnar array, and

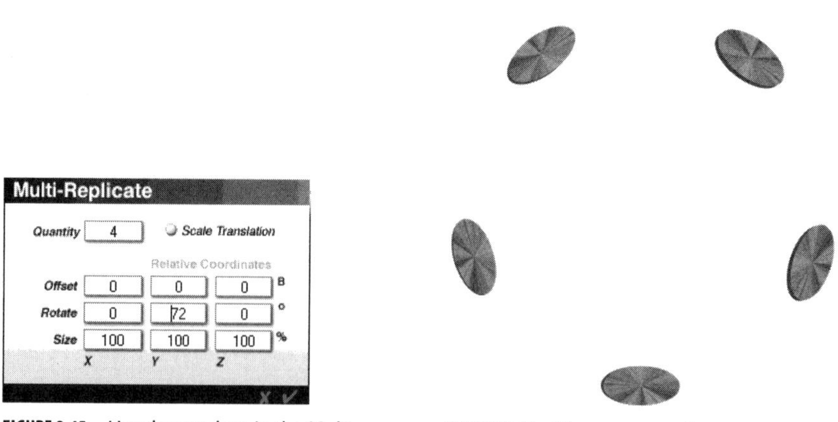

FIGURE 2.45 Use these values in the Multi-Replicate window.

FIGURE 2.46 The pentagonal array as seen from the Top view.

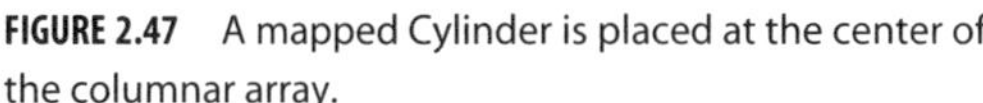

FIGURE 2.47 A mapped Cylinder is placed at the center of the columnar array.

FIGURE 2.48 A Cylindrical base is added.

equally as high. Use any Material you like on it—we used Wild & Fun/Office Building 2 with Object Mapping (see Figure 2.47).

4. Add a flattened Cylindrical base, a bit wider than the columnar array (see Figure 2.48).
5. Cap the model with a Duplicate of the flattened Cylinder. Group everything, and name it "Part_01."
6. Multi-Replicate the object. Set Quantity to 4, and Size to 90% on the X- and Z-axis. Move the replicates so that you create a stack of objects. Cap everything with a Pyramid primitive, group everything, and name it "Building" (see Figure 2.49).

FIGURE 2.49 The tower.

Once you have one fancy building, you can duplicate it to create other configurations, such as this walled fortress (see Figure 2.50).

FIGURE 2.50 Multiple towers.

MOVING ON

In this chapter, we demonstrated a number of ways that you can create and modify models in Bryce using primitives. In the next chapter, we'll look at a special type of Bryce models, and the ways you can customize them: Trees.

CHAPTER

3 Trees

One of the most requested attributes that Bryce users have pleaded for over the years has been the capability to create foliage on the spot. Great news! Bryce 5 adds this feature in a major way with the new Tree modeler. To access the Tree modeler, click on its icon in the Create toolbar (see Figure 3.1).

FIGURE 3.1 Click on this icon to place a default Tree in your scene.

When you click on the Tree icon, a default Tree object is placed in your scene (see Figure 3.2).

FIGURE 3.2 The default Tree object is placed in your scene.

Clicking on the Edit icon in the Edit toolbar brings up the Tree Lab panel (see Figure 3.3).

Using the downward-pointing arrow beneath the preview accesses the preview options lost. Selecting Rendered Preview from that list instead of the default Wireframe allows you to get a better idea of what's happening as you edit the parameters.

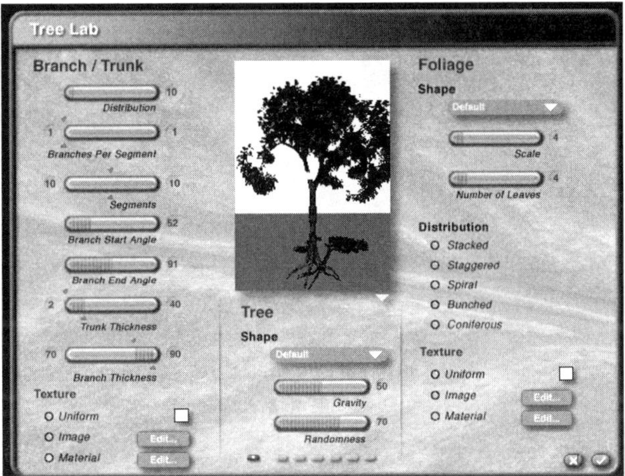

FIGURE 3.3 The Tree Lab appears.

PARAMETERS

The controls for customizing your tree are separated into the following groups: Branch/Trunk Values, Branch/Trunk Texture, Tree Shape, Foliage Shape, Foliage Distribution, and Foliage Texture.

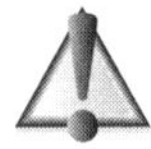

Trees models can be severely RAM intensive. If you push all of the values to the max, you are just about guaranteed to choke Bryce, with unpredictable results.

Branch/Trunk Values

Using the accompanying sliders to control the value settings for scaling the Branch and Trunk components represented under this heading, you can create a myriad of different Tree objects, even when the Tree and Leaf types remain the same. In addition, because a Tree is just another object in Bryce, you can also scale the Tree with standard scaling operations on any or all axes. See Figure 3.4 as an example.

Branch/Trunk Texture

Branch/Trunk Texture can be a color, a Material Preset, or an image taken from your own image files.

FIGURE 3.4 On the left, the default Tree object was given 8 Branches per Segment, with 10 Segments. The Branch Start Angle is 180 degrees, and Trunk Thickness is set to 70. The Tree on the right references the same model, but with the following parameter changes: Branches per Segment =1, Branch Start Angle = 90 degrees, Distribution = 40, and Trunk Thickness = 3. Compare the two models.

When accessing the Material Lab for a Tree, do it from the Tree Lab controls (the Edit buttons). Selecting the Materials Lab in the standard manner, from the Document Window, is to be avoided, since this will not map Material Presets or image data correctly to the tree.

Tree Shape

When you access the Tree Shape presets list, you are presented with over 60 tree varieties. When you need to place specific tree types in your scene for scientific accuracy, this is the place to go. To remain accurate, you'll want to select the same Foliage Type as well (see Figure 3.5).

GRAVITY

The Gravity setting ranges from 0 to 100, and is set at 50 by default. Gravity controls the direction of the branches, either toward or away from the ground (see Figure 3.6).

FIGURE 3.5 Left: Sycamore. Center: Mangrove. Right: Douglas Fir.

FIGURE 3.6 This Ginkgo tree displays a Gravity value of 0 on the left, and 100 on the right.

RANDOMNESS

Using slider ranges from 0 to 100 creates random forms from the same parameters. Use this operation when you want a group of the same trees, but want to avoid having them appear identical.

MEMORY DOTS

Use one of the six Memory Dots to recall your favorite Tree parameters.

Foliage Shape

The same 60+ Foliage Types are listed here as the Tree Types. Usually, you'll want to match them up, but you don't have to. Be creative, and see what the tree looks like when you select one Tree Type and a different Foliage Type (see Figure 3.7).

You can *Scale* the foliage in a range of 1 to 20, and set the *Number of Leaves* in a range from 0 to 20.

FIGURE 3.7 Here's an Apple tree with bamboo foliage.

FIGURE 3.8 Left to Right: a Sumac tree with distribution set to Stacked, Staggered, Spiral, Bunched, and Coniferous.

Foliage Distribution

The foliage can be distributed on the tree in one of five ways: Stacked, Staggered, Spiral, Bunched, and Coniferous (see Figure 3.8).

Foliage Texture

Foliage Texture is handled the same way as Trunk/Branch Texture is. Edit the desired texture from the Tree Lab, using the Edit buttons to access either the Materials Lab or your image files.

THE ENCHANTED FOREST

I don't know how you feel about creating 3D scenes that can't be distinguished from "reality" (whatever that is), but I like to push things beyond what the everyday provides, even if it's only observable in some corner of the image or animation. The great thing about computer graphics as it is evolving before our eyes is that the new tools allow us to blend our experience of the real with our experience of the dream, exactly how Andre Breton defines surrealism in his *Manifestoes of Surrealism* (J. J. Pawvert, France 1962). What does it take to evoke enchantment anyway? It certainly demands some perception of the surreal, a witness that or a suspicion that some of the laws of physics might be in question, even if for a brief fleeting glimpse. Some would argue that fantasy, especially surrealist fantasy, is not a way of escaping reality at all. Others see surrealist fantasy as a way of deepening reality and our experience of the world beyond what science alone would have us commit to.

The only way to break through one's own perceptual boundaries and preconceived notions is to come face to face, or more literally eye to eye, with something uncomfortable and out of the ordinary. In film, both horror and science fiction themes do that quite well, especially with the assistance of the new computer graphics tools. For the computer graphics enthusiast working in a setting less glamorous than Hollywood, the new prosumer tools (like Bryce) offer almost as much high-end output as the tools used to create major films. In fact, many off-the-shelf computer graphics applications are being used today to create big budget effects, so the line between what you can potentially create and what Hollywood generates, as far as computer graphics goes, continues to blur. As far as readily available software is concerned, we could point to a dozen or more applications that continue to push the creative edge for all users. Bryce stands out as one of these tools.

Creative work, all creative work, unfolds between two opposite poles. At one end is your pre-flight map, your plan. Whether you mentally visualize what you want to do and some or all of the elements, or commit your ideas to paper or an electronic sketch, there is some hint of the structure involved. Sometimes, the structure you visualize is very detailed and tight, and at other times, it might be just a general concept. Either way, you will have some indication, based on your experience, of the tools you are going to use to get there. At the other end of the spectrum, however, is your capacity to turn on a dime, to allow your creation to lead you into new areas of exploration, instead of just forcing your work to *stick with the plan*. Between these two poles, the magic of the creative moment takes place. You must be prepared and astute, while at the same time remain flexible enough to surrender all preparation to the moment as the work evolves.

I planned this project fairly vaguely. I knew I wanted a circle of trees, some reflective water, and a ground of some sort to place these elements on. I also knew that I wanted to use Bryce 5 as the creative vehicle. Other than that, the specifics of what enfolded took over and led the way as the project progressed.

Jumping In

Any of the following steps can be adjusted and varied, as your muse demands. Do the following in the order presented unless and until that occurs:

1. Open Bryce 5. Go to the Top view, and orient the Camera as shown in Figure 3.9. This gives you a more intuitive sense of direction.
2. Delete the Ground Plane. Lock the Camera in position, and turn the Atmosphere off. Use a white background for now.
3. We might as well get to the star actor first. Go to Camera view. Go to the Create toolbar and click on the Tree icon. This places a default tree in your scene (see Figure 3.10).
4. At this early point, we're going to create a star tree actor, surrounded by a supporting cast of tree players. This first tree will be the star actor. Make sure the default tree is selected, and bring up the Tree Lab by clicking on the Edit icon in the Edit toolbar. The Tree Lab appears (see Figure 3.11).

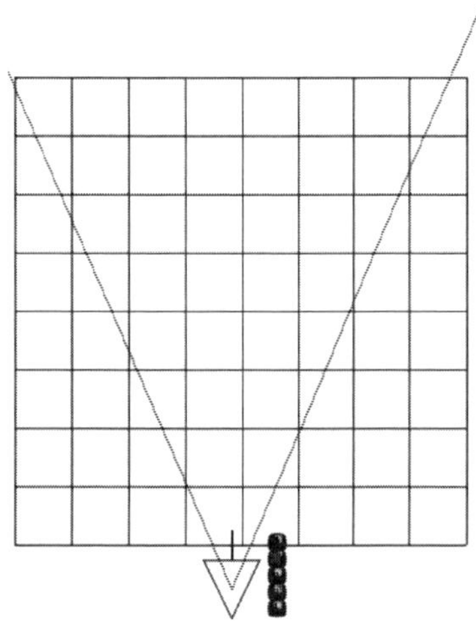

FIGURE 3.9 Orient the Camera so that East (sunrise) is at the top of the screen as seen in the Top view.

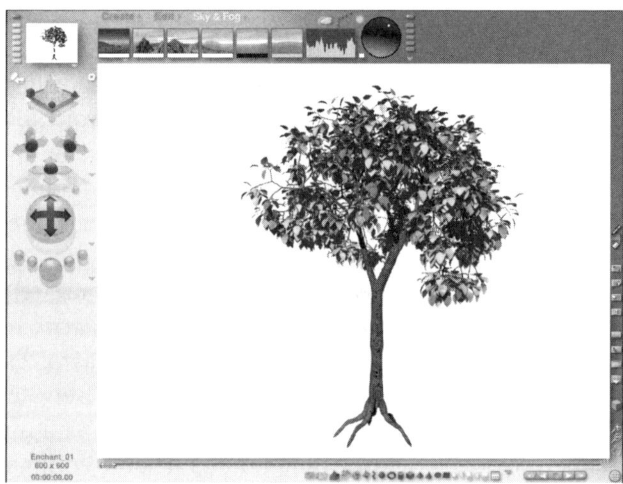

FIGURE 3.10 A default tree is placed in the scene.

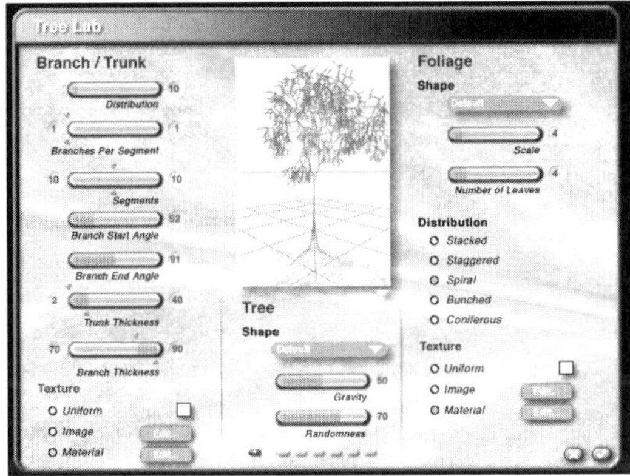

FIGURE 3.11 The Tree Lab appears.

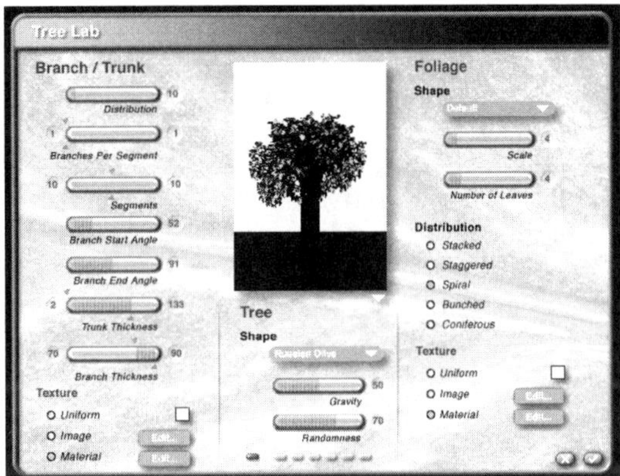

FIGURE 3.12 Use a Russian Olive as the initial tree shape.

5. Select a Russian Olive as your initial tree shape. Set the Trunk Thickness to 133, and do a rendered preview to get an idea what the tree looks like (see Figure 3.12).
6. Make the Branch Start Angle 80, and the Branch End Angle 32. You can experiment with your own parameters here, but these angles were suitable for this design.
7. Set the texture to Material, and click on the Edit button to bring up the Materials Lab.
8. In the Materials Lab, select the Glasses>Another Marble 2 material (yes, let's explore the use of a glass material for the tree). Always set the tree's materials in the Tree Lab, as opposed to selecting the object on screen and doing it from there.
9. Go to the Deep Texture Editor for this material, and use the parameters shown in Figure 3.13.
10. Set the parameters in the Materials Lab as shown in Figure 3.14. Note that the mapping is different for the two component textures.
11. Accept the material, which returns you to the Tree Lab.
12. Use a White Oak Foliage Shape, with a size of 12 and Bunched Distribution.
13. Set texture to Material and Edit. In the Materials Lab, select the Plasma Fire material from the Complex FX folder. Use Object Space mapping. This will make the tree look like no other in existence.
14. Accept all the alterations, and do a test render to see what you have created (see Figure 3.15).

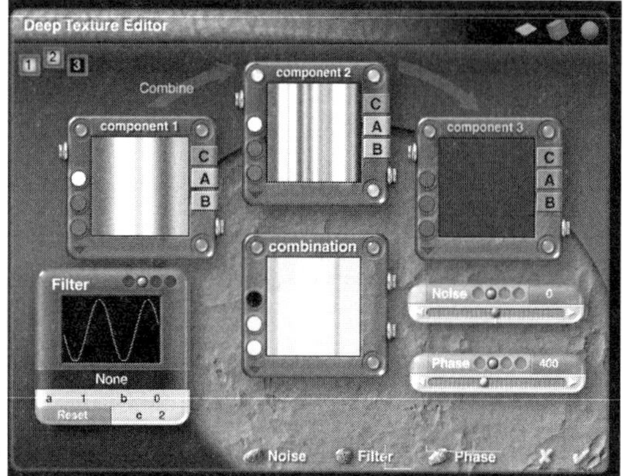

FIGURE 3.13 Use these parameters.

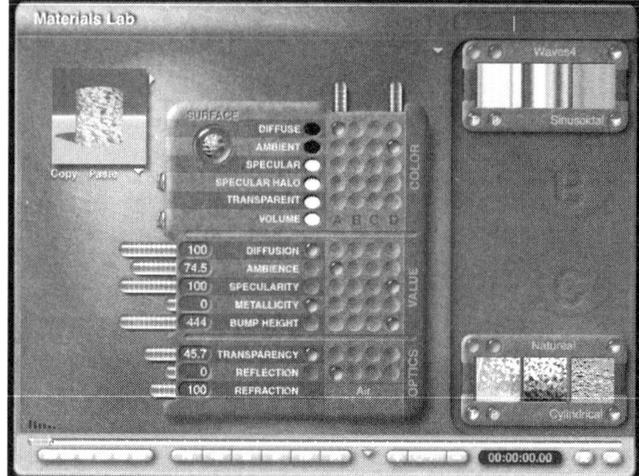

FIGURE 3.14 Set the Material parameters as displayed here.

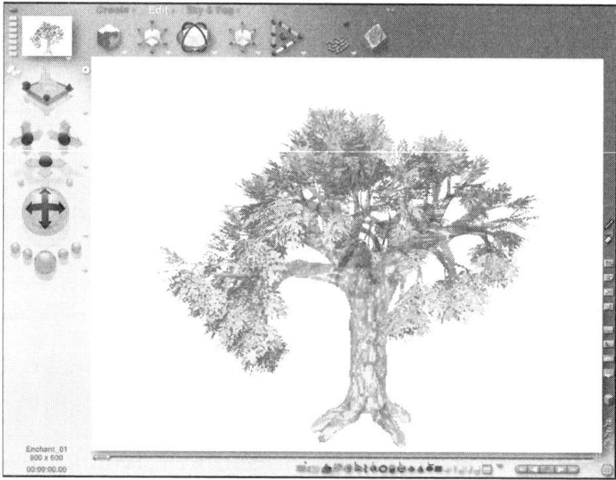

FIGURE 3.15 The rendered tree has a special personality.

15. Now for the main supporting actors. All you need to do is design one tree, and duplicate and scale for the others. In all, we'll want about eight surrounding trees, forming a circle around our star. You can experiment with the tree form and foliage until you get something you like. When it's finished, Duplicate and randomly Scale, placing the surrounding arrangement in a circle around our main actor. Here, we used a Red Oak with Hornbeam Foliage, both with standard materials (see Figure 3.16).
16. OK. So far, this looks like a manicured group of trees, but hardly a forest. We need an indication that there are many more trees in the scene. You could place another 30 or so trees in the background, but

FIGURE 3.16 The ring of trees surrounds the special member.

Bryce would probably choke on that many polygons. Instead, we'll use the new Metaball objects in Bryce for background trees. Go to the Top view, and place six large and flattened Metaballs in a circle around the inner ring of trees as shown in Figure 3.17. Use a Foliage 1 material from the Miscellaneous Materials library to map them (see Figures 3.17 and 3.18).

As sometimes happens in the middle of a project, the tree texture we had so painstakingly created for the central tree just didn't look right. Therefore, we altered it to the Dali-esque Marble material from the Rocks&Stones folder.

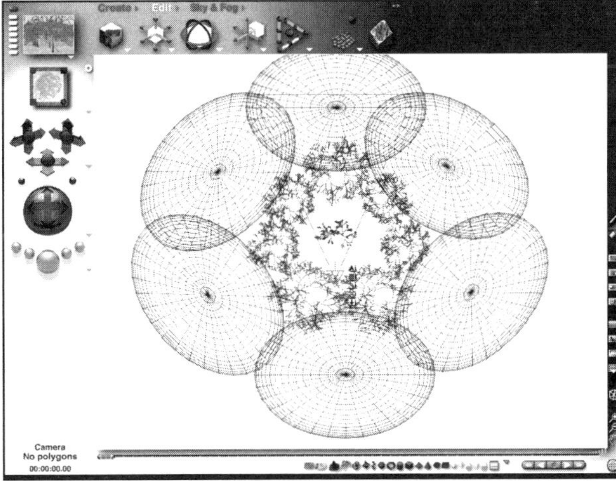

FIGURE 3.17 Use Metaballs for the background foliage.

FIGURE 3.18 The rendered result, displaying the background foliage.

17. Add a Ground Plane, and map it with the Storybook Grass material from the Miscellaneous Materials library.
18. Add a flattened Cylinder at the base of the central tree, and map it with a reflective water material.
19. Create a rock, duplicate as needed, and place a ring of rocks around the reflective pool. MarbleBronze Fusion works as a nice material for the rocks. Add any sky you prefer. Place a Radial light over the center tree, and use the Light Lab to configure a Gradient for it, as shown in Figure 3.19.

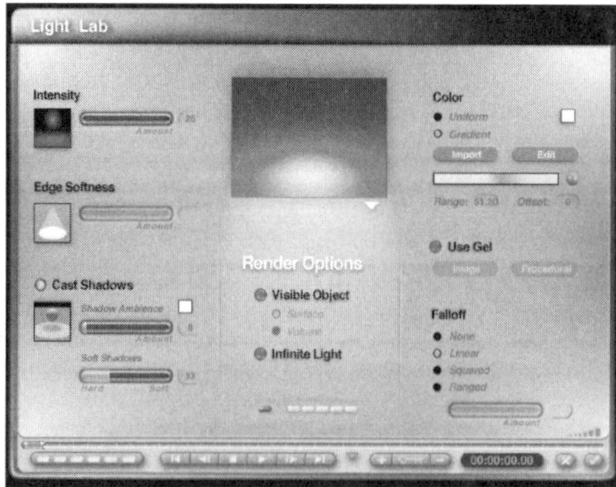

FIGURE 3.19 Use these parameters to configure a colorful Gradient for the light.

FIGURE 3.20 Looking down on the clearing from a slight angle.

FIGURE 3.21 When viewing the forest from a distance, it's a good idea to hide the outer foliage—the form is clearer this way.

20. Do some test renderings, and change whatever calls for your attention. This project can be taken much further with a little dream time and effort on your part (see Figures 3.20 through 3.23).

FIGURE 3.22 Here's a view with a voyeur's camera, allowing you to secretly peek through the ring of trees at the central tree of mystery.

FIGURE 3.23 Looking up at the top of the central tree.

THE USER LEAF

The last item in the Foliage Shape list is *User Leaf*. Here's where you can really create unique leaf shapes. The shape of the leaf, and its texture, are taken from content you create for the Picture Editor, as accessed under

Image>Edit under Textures in the Tree Lab. The image you place should have an Alpha channel (which determines the actual shape of the leaf), while the image determines the look. Do the following:

1. Create a leaf shape and texture of your own design in an image editing application such as Corel PhotoPaint or Photoshop. Save it to disk (see Figure 3.24).

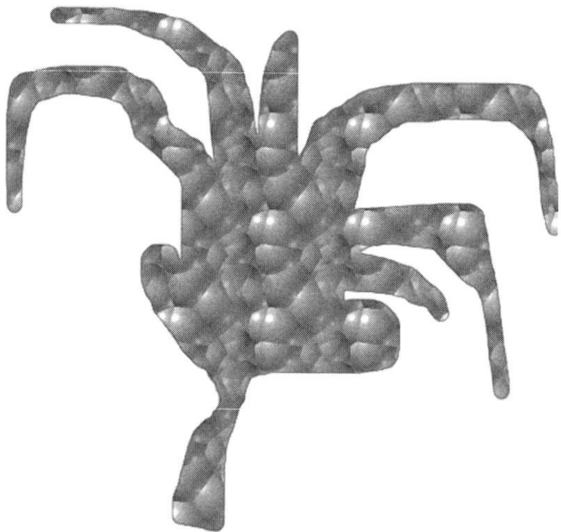

FIGURE 3.24 Here's one example of a leaf design.

2. Open Bryce and create a tree. Under Foliage Texture, click on Image>Edit. This brings up the Picture Editor (see Figure 3.25).
3. Load your leaf image and its Alpha channel into an empty slot in the Picture Editor (see Figure 3.26).

FIGURE 3.25 The Picture Editor appears.

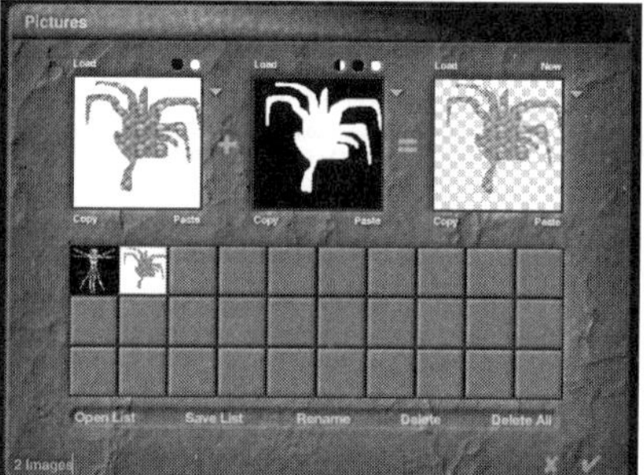

FIGURE 3.26 Load your image in the Picture Editor slot.

4. Click on Materials, and then on Edit. Your leaf image should now be present as a texture in the Materials Lab image preview. Set the buttons as shown in Figure 3.27.

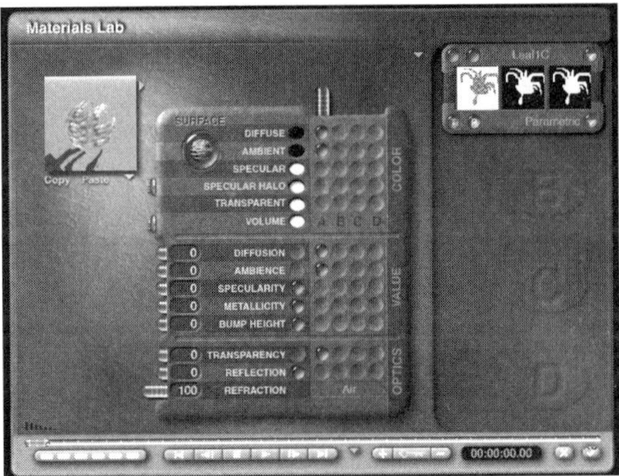

FIGURE 3.27 Use these parameters.

That's it. Your image now determines the shape and texture of the foliage. Configure the rest of the tree settings and values, and render your personalized tree (see Figure 3.28).

FIGURE 3.28 A tree with personalized foliage.

Use this technique for creating alien foliage on a Bryce planet.

If you own a digital camera or a scanner, you can take pictures of real leaves to use as your tree foliage.

MOVING ON

In this chapter, we explored the creation and modification of Tree objects. Next, we look at Metaballs.

CHAPTER

4 Metaball Models

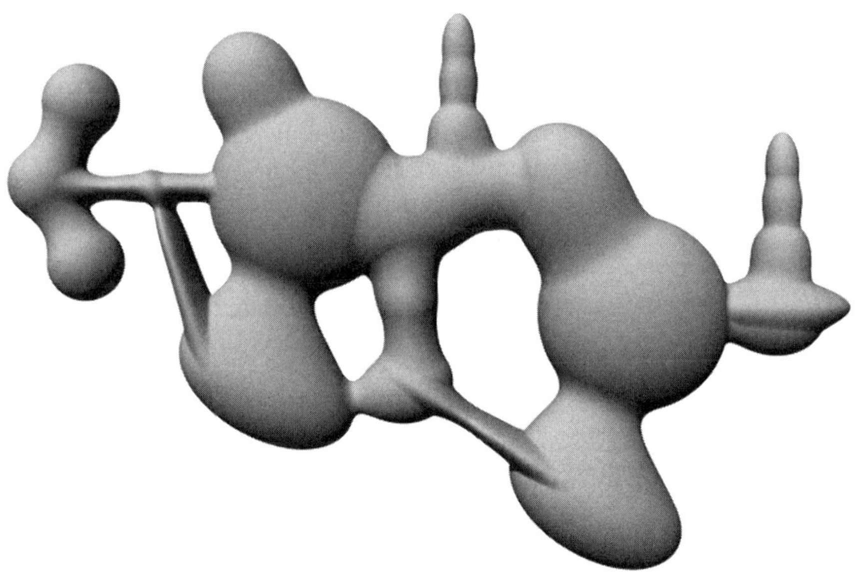

Creating a model with Metaballs is different from any other modeling process. That's because Metaballs have a personality all their own, a personality that takes some getting used to. When we say "personality," you might think we're stretching a point, since the term is usually reserved for living things. Yet, Metaballs do indeed seem to be alive in some sense. Metaballs literally reach out with a force that either attracts or repels other Metaballs within their area of influence.

RULES FOR METABALLS

Keep the following items in mind when you work with Metaballs:

- Metaballs are used to create more organic objects, and to emulate gelatinous surfaces.
- Materials assigned to Metaballs blend across the area of contact with other Metaballs.
- Negative Metaballs carve out spherical spaces in nearby Positive Metaballs. The size of the indentation is relative to the proximity of the Negative Metaball and its size.
- Metaballs can be grouped to form separate modeled elements.
- Grouped Metaballs no longer interact with other Metaballs in their vicinity.
- The further away one Metaball is moved from another, while remaining in the area of influence, the thinner the bridge that connects them.
- The larger a Metaball is, the more extensive its area of influence over other Metaballs.
- Duplicating a Metaball on top of itself increases its size and area of influence.
- To save time, keep your eye on the Nano Preview when working with Metaballs.

GENERAL OPERATIONS

To place a Metaball in the scene, click on the Metaball icon in the Create toolbar (see Figure 4.1).

FIGURE 4.1 The Metaball icon in the Create toolbar.

If Bryce Metaballs are new to you, do the following:

1. Click twice on the Metaball icon to place two concentric Metaballs in the scene.
2. From the Camera view, move one of the Metaball wireframes while keeping an eye on the Nano Preview. When you see the Metaballs interact in an interesting way, render to preview (see Figure 4.2).
3. Make the left-hand Metaball larger to explore their altered interaction (see Figure 4.3).

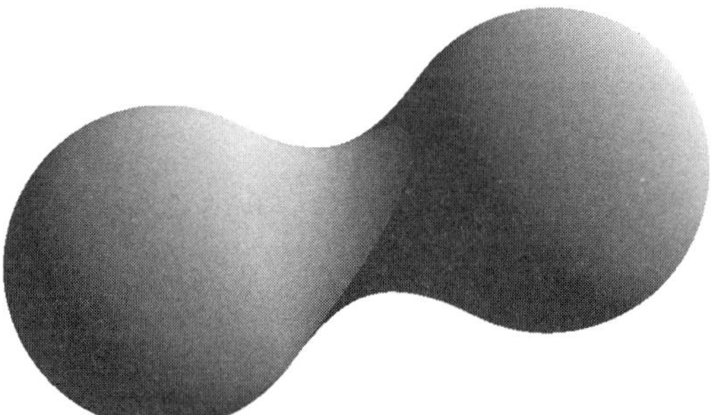

FIGURE 4.2 Two Metaballs interacting.

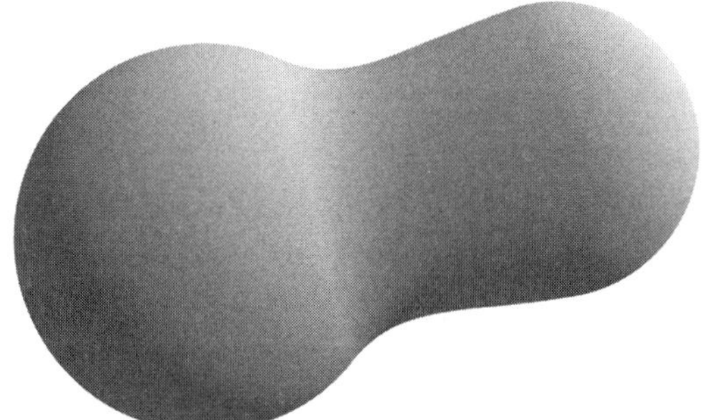

FIGURE 4.3 Notice that the "bridge" between the Metaballs is thicker now.

4. Scale the left-hand Metaball smaller, and move it closer to the larger Metaball so that a bridge forms (see Figure 4.4).
5. Squash the smaller Metaball. Notice that the bridge formed with the larger Metaball remains very smooth (see Figure 4.5).

FIGURE 4.4 Notice that smaller Metaballs have less "power" to form bridges.

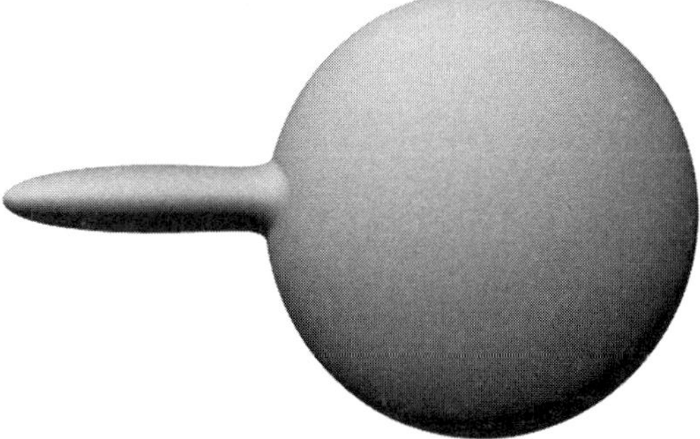

FIGURE 4.5 Metaballs can be scaled on any axis.

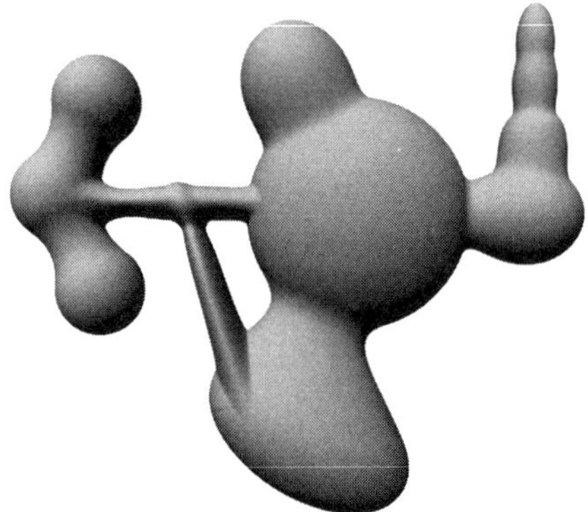

FIGURE 4.6 Create a unique Metaball object.

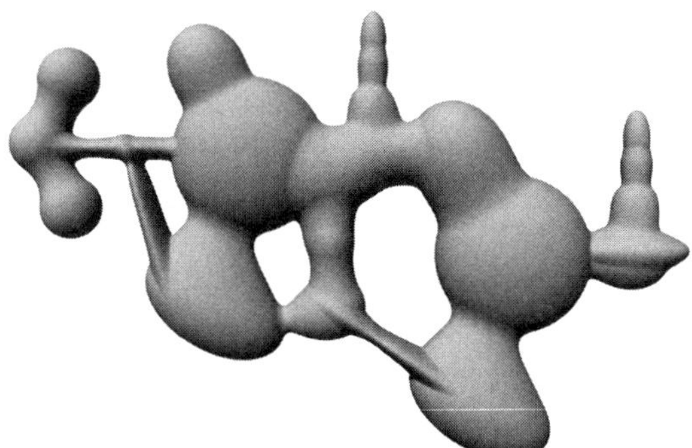

FIGURE 4.7 Save your object as a group.

6. Create your own unique Metaball object from any number of Metaballs you prefer. Use Scaling, Stretching, and Rotation on some of them until you get something interesting (see Figure 4.6).
7. Select all of the Metaballs, and Edit>Duplicate. Without deselecting any of the duplicated objects, move them so that they interact with the others. Adjust as necessary to create a more complex form. When finished, Group All and save to your Objects Library (see Figure 4.7).
8. Apply a material to your Metaball object, and create a scene that uses it (see Figure 4.8).

FIGURE 4.8 Place your Metaball object in a scene, and render.

METABALL SUBTRACTION

Metaballs come in two flavors: Positive and Negative, So far in this chapter, the tutorials have targeted Positive Metaballs only. You can also access Negative Metaballs. To do that, we'll need to expose what Bryce people call an *Easter Egg*.

What's a Bryce Easter Egg? *A Bryce Easter Egg is an undocumented feature. Ever since its inception, Bryce developers have hidden some of Bryce' features away, not alluding to them in any documentation. There are a dozen or more of these hidden features that can only be accessed if you know the right key combination, rather like going on an Easter egg hunt for hidden treasures. One place you can go to for downloading some data that exposes a number of Easter Eggs is the BSmooth site (www.bsmooth.de/bsolutions/).*

Although the BSmooth site lists a number of Easter Egg descriptors, you will not find any data there for creating Negative Metaballs in Bryce 5, so here's what to do:

To create Negative Metaballs in Bryce 5, click on the Metaball icon while holding down the Shift key.

That's it. Although simple enough, this is an undocumented feature. Now that you know how to do it, let's walk through a couple of exercises.

The Metaslice

Here's how to create a slice in a Metaball, using Positive and Negative Metaballs. Do the following:

1. Create a Positive Metaball in your scene, and go to the Front view. Zoom in so you can see the Metaball clearly.
2. Create a Negative Metaball, squashed to about 10% of its original dimensions on the X-axis. Enlarge by about 10%. Place it inside of the Positive Metaball so that both are centered. Allow the Negative Metaball to protrude slightly above and below the Positive Metaball in the Front view. Use the Top view for alignment (see Figure 4.9).
3. In the Front view, duplicate the Negative Metaball and rotate on its Z-axis, so you have an arrangement that looks like Figure 4.10.
4. Render, and you will see that the Positive Metaball has been sliced into four sections (see Figure 4.11).

Use a similar technique to slice any Metaball in your projects.

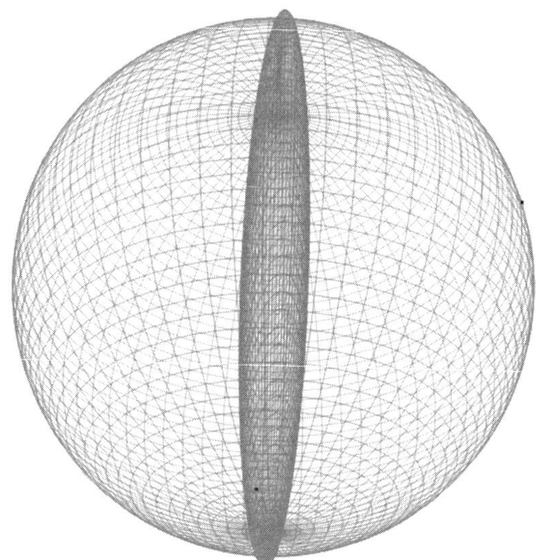

FIGURE 4.9 Place the stretched Negative Metaball inside the Positive one like this.

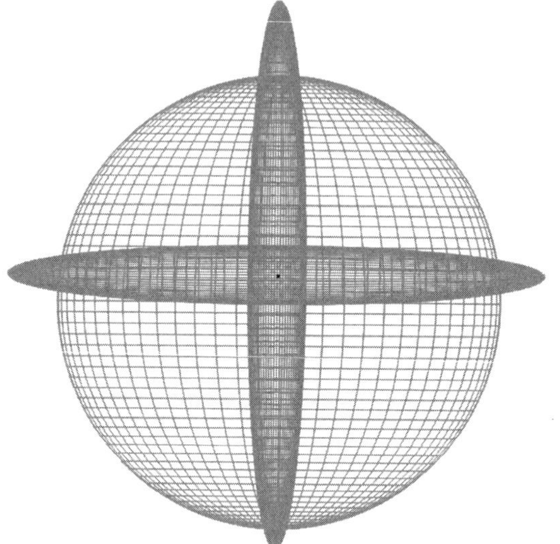

FIGURE 4.10 Create this arrangement.

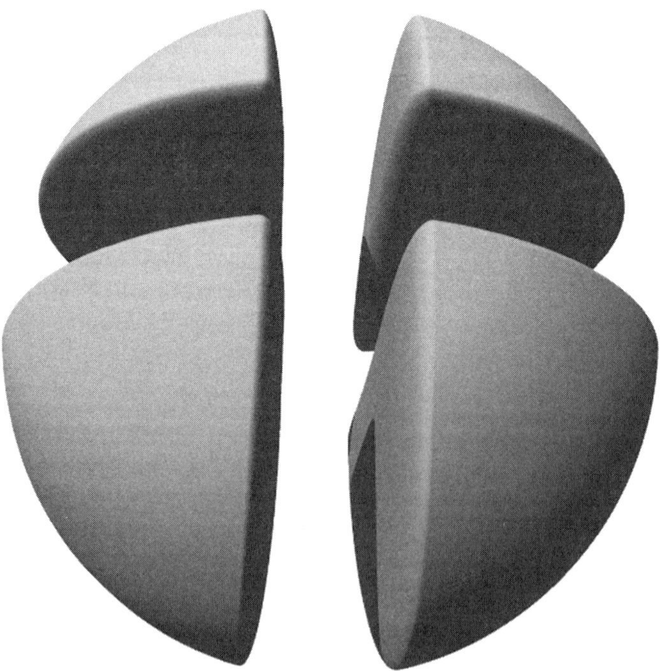

FIGURE 4.11 The original Metaball has been sliced twice.

The Metadrill

Use this technique to drill holes in Metaballs. Do the following:

1. Create a Positive Metaball, and zoom in on it in the Top view.
2. Create an arrangement of five Negative Metaballs that protrude from the top and bottom of the Negative Metaball, and are squashed on their X- and Z-axis (refer to Figure 4.12).
3. Render to preview (see Figure 4.13).

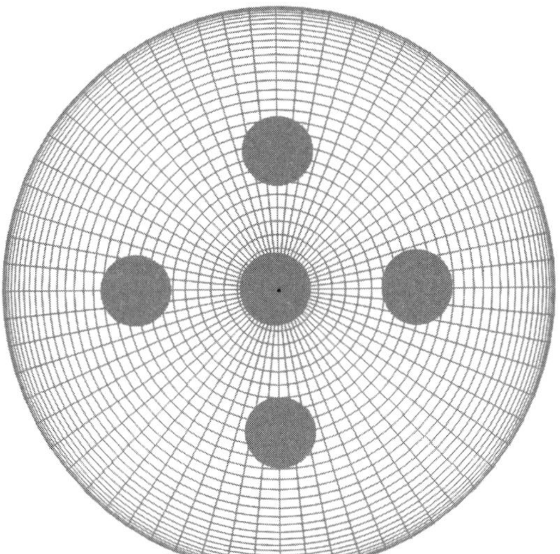

FIGURE 4.12 Create this composition of five Negative Metaballs piercing a Positive Metaball (Top view).

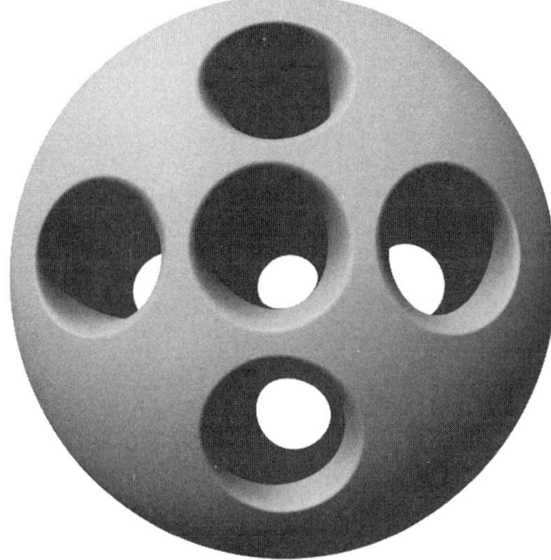

FIGURE 4.13 The Metaball displays holes that go all the way through.

To create holes that pierce just a portion of the surface of a Metaball, either shorten the Negative Metaball(s) on their Y-axis or move them upward (see Figures 4.14 and 4.15).

Use the Metaball indentation method to create a crater-pocked moon for a Bryce planetscape (see Figure 4.16).

COMBINING NEGATIVE AND POSITIVE METABALLS

You can use Metaball modeling to create some interesting characters for your Bryce worlds. Just make sure to observe the following two points:

- Create each specific body part separately. Use Negative and Positive Metaballs as needed.

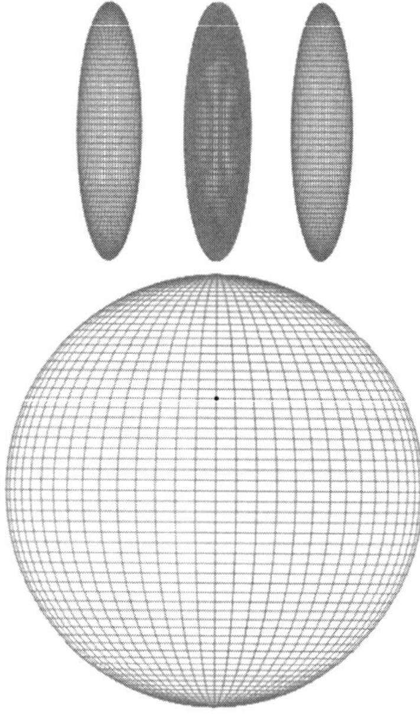

FIGURE 4.14 Moving the Negative Metaballs to this distance...

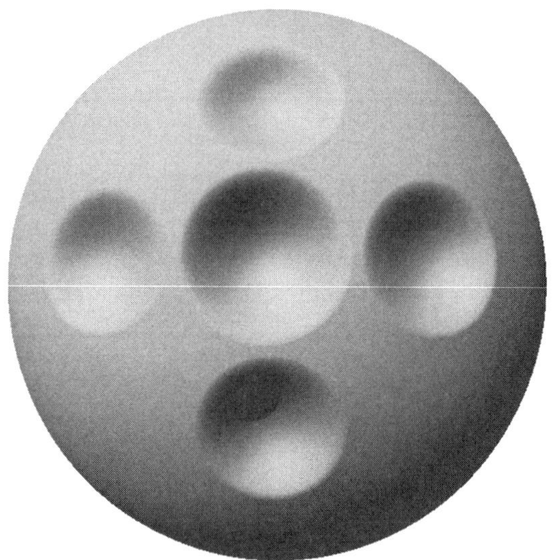

FIGURE 4.15 ...creates indentations instead of holes.

FIGURE 4.16 Create a crater-pocked moon.

- Group each finished body part so that it doesn't stretch out when brought into the proximity of another Metaball.

The Metabeast

You can customize the following tutorial to suit your own designer's eye. What's really important is that you understand the concepts involved.

THE HEAD

Do the following:

1. Create a multi-Positive Metaball construct, following the design shown in Figure 4.17.

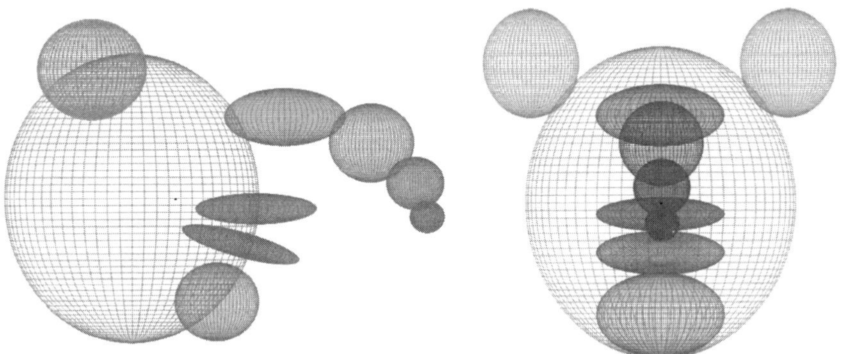

FIGURE 4.17 Create this construct (Front and Right views).

2. Create three Negative Metaballs; scale, and place as shown in Figure 4.18. The large Negative Metaball shapes the head, and the two smaller ones carve out eye sockets.
3. Add additional Metaballs to shape the head further if you prefer. Create two black spheres to use as eyes, and place (see Figure 4.19).
4. OK. One more operation. Create ears from flattened Metaballs, and place. Group All. Save the finished head group to your Objects Library (see Figure 4.20).

BODY AND NECK

1. Create a body for your character by using Positive and Negative Metaballs. Use your imagination, and keep an eye on the Nano

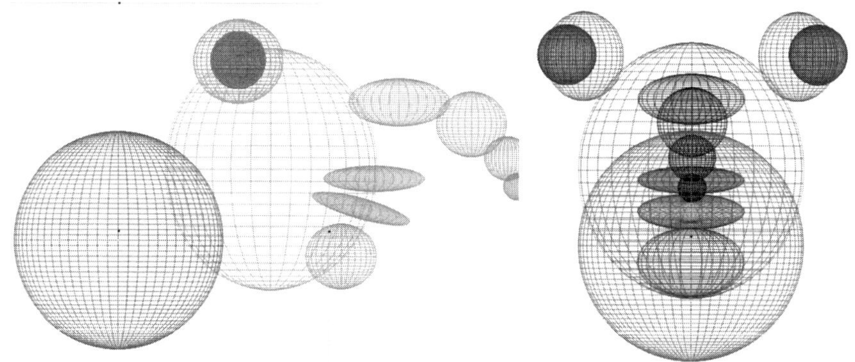

FIGURE 4.18 Create three Negative Metaballs as shown here (Front and Right views).

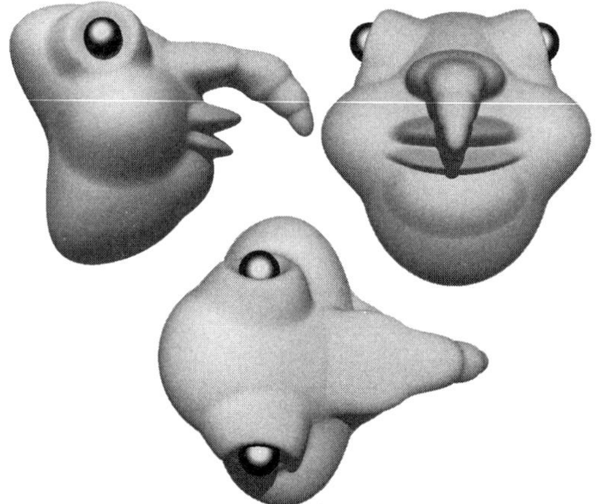

FIGURE 4.19 This is the almost-finished head, with a few more shaping Metaballs added.

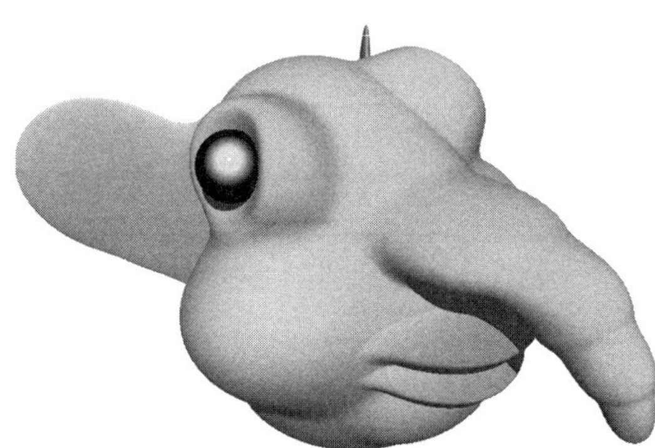

FIGURE 4.20 Now the head is complete.

Preview. Use a scaled and squashed Negative Metaball to create a separation of the buttocks.

2. Create the neck from Positive Metaballs. Use Linking to attach selected Metaballs to each other so the neck can bend. Group All as Body, and save to your Objects Library (see Figures 4.21 and 4.22).

Test the model so far by placing the head group on the neck of the body group. Perform any tweaking as necessary (see Figure 4.23).

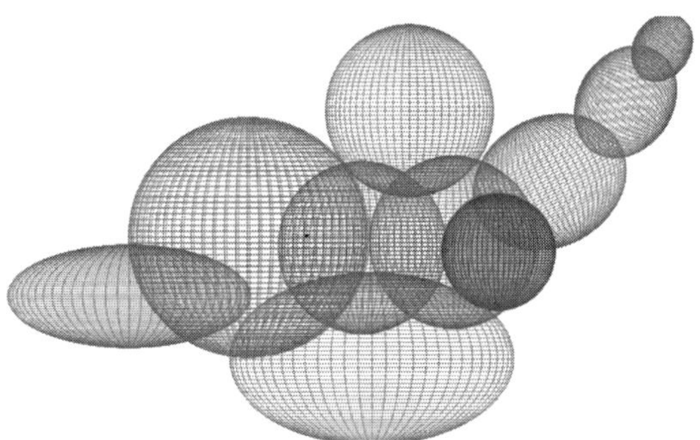

FIGURE 4.21 Here is the wireframe of the Metaballs.

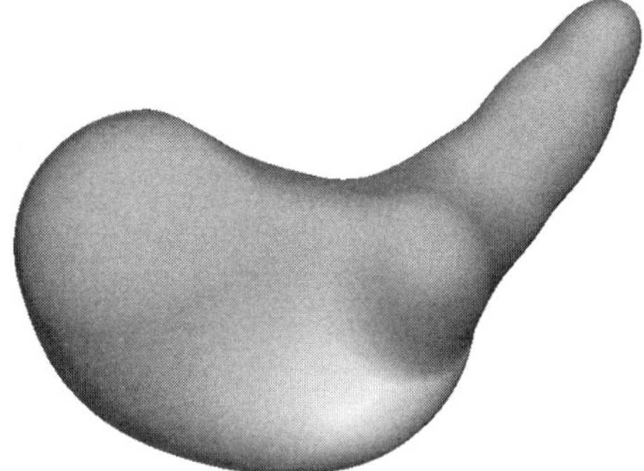

FIGURE 4.22 This is the result of the construct.

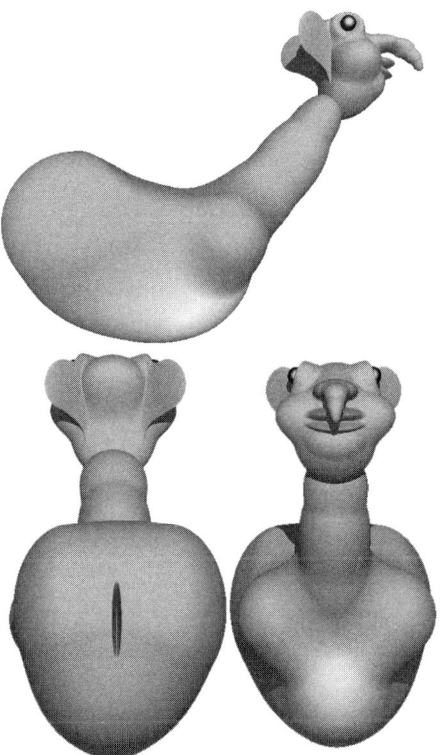

FIGURE 4.23 Test the model's looks so far.

LEG PARTS

We are going to create one leg part, and Duplicate/Scale it to create all eight needed leg parts. Do the following:

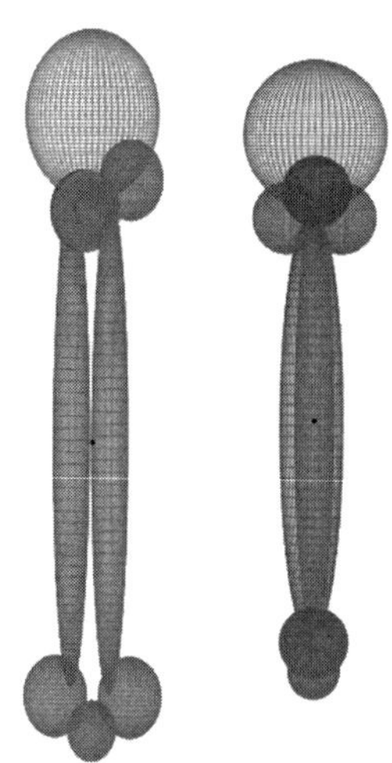

FIGURE 4.24 Front and Side views of the design.

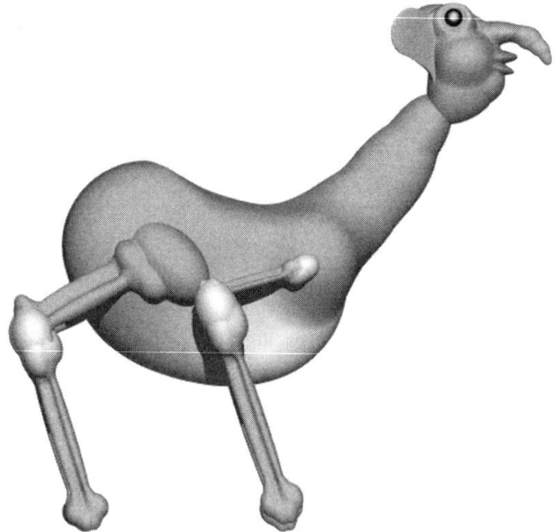

FIGURE 4.25 Duplicate the leg parts, and scale as needed for the four legs.

1. Create a Positive Metaball. Scale it down about 80%, and then stretch it along its Y (vertical) axis. This creates a cylinder-like form.
2. Using scaled spheres and the cylindrical forms, create the Metaball leg element. Notice that the elongated Metaballs, when placed in proximity, create tendon-like forms as they blend. Group (refer to Figure 4.24).
3. Duplicate and Scale as needed, and place to create four legs. Don't worry about the seams that are showing right now. Do a test render (see Figure 4.25).

FOOT

We'll create the foot separately. Do the following:

1. Create a foot from Positive Metaballs (refer to Figure 4.26).
2. Duplicate and place to create the four feet (see Figure 4.27).

TAIL

Creating the tail is the last step. Do the following:

1. Create a tail from Positive Metaballs. Group, and save to your Objects Library.
2. Scale as needed, and place on the Metabeast (see Figure 4.28).

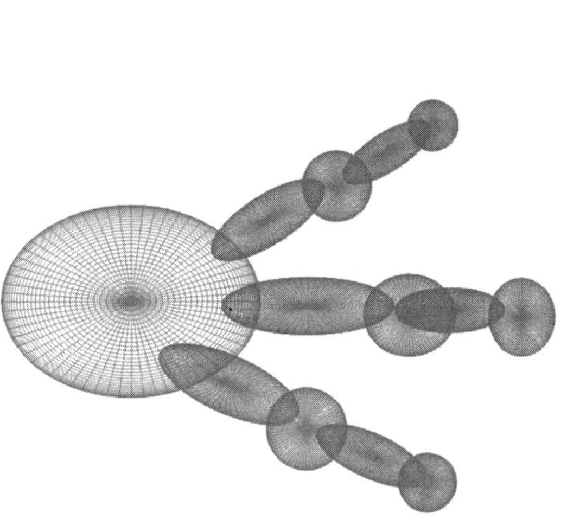

FIGURE 4.26 Create a foot. Use this design, or your own ideas.

FIGURE 4.27 Create the four feet, and place.

FIGURE 4.28 Create and place the tail.

A RULE FOR RENDERING COMPLEX METABALL CONSTRUCTS

Use the groups to create poses for your object, but before rendering, remove all groups. This allows the Metaballs to blend, removing any unpleasant seams (see Figures 4.29 and 4.30).

FIGURE 4.29 On the left is the character with groups, while on the right the groups have been removed (except for the tail).

FIGURE 4.30 Your Metabeast is ready to graze!

COLOR ME BLENDED

Metaballs possess an attribute that aids your texturing capabilities for complex models tremendously. Metaballs not only blend their structures with other Metaballs in their vicinity, they also blend their textures. Whether the blended Metaballs have different colors or different complex textures and materials, smooth blending takes place. Here's a fun experiment:

1. Create a structure as shown in Figure 4.31. There are four Positive Metaballs on the outside, and one Negative Metaball in the center.

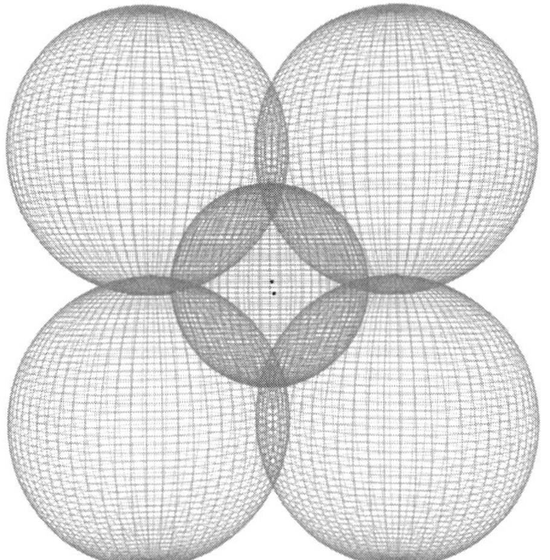

FIGURE 4.31 Create a Metaball structure like this.

FIGURE 4.32 This is the form you created.

2. Render to see what it looks like (see Figure 4.32).
3. Notice that the form is a default gray—not very pretty. Select the five Metaballs one at a time, and apply a different color or material. Now, render it again (see Figure 4.33).

Keep this in mind when you create complex organic or mechanical objects constructed from a number of Metaballs.

FIGURE 4.33 Wow! That's much better. Notice that the Negative Metaball lends its color or material to the total object as well.

MOVING ON

In this chapter, we explored the wonders of Metaball objects. In the next chapter, we'll take a peek at Boolean operators.

CHAPTER

5 Booleans

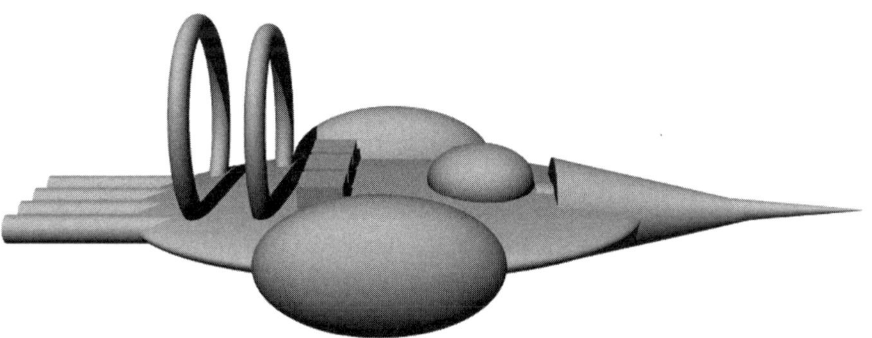

Imagine that you are very young, and that you have just started to learn about numbers. If you can, try to recapture that astounding realization that there are some "things" in the world that are not things at all. You can't hold a number in your hand or place it on a shelf, yet you can use numbers to shape real objects in the everyday world. Numbers have power, and learning about the power of numbers allows you to adjust and reconfigure the reality that surrounds you. By this time in your life, it is obvious that you can combine numbers to create other numbers, through addition, subtraction, and by other operations. The term *operations* is very important when it comes to understanding how Booleans can be manipulated. Operations, in computer graphics lingo, are situations that you set up in order to create a specific result. 1 + 1 = 2, for example, is an addition operation. 3 – 1 = 2 is obviously a subtraction operation. Now imagine that instead of being just abstract concepts, you could transform numbers into objects, while still maintaining the power that numbers possess to engage in number-specific operations. Imagine that this power of numbers could be transferred to any object you desired. The objects that you have transferred the power of numbers to would have a dual "personality." On the one hand, they would still be objects, defined by their shapes and volumes. On the other hand, they would also contain the power of numbers, the capability of being added to or subtracted from other objects with a similar power of numbers. In the computer graphics and animation world, these unique objects are called Boolean objects.

You can perform three basic operations with Boolean objects:

- You can add Boolean objects together to create an object whose form combines the forms of all of the objects in the Boolean operation designated as *Positive*. Positive Boolean objects can intersect, but the parts of their forms that intersect will be dismissed in the resulting combined object.
- You can subtract a *Negative* Boolean object from a *Positive* Boolean object. This operation takes note of where the objects intersect, carving a depression in the Positive Boolean object and reshaping its surface so that the new surface at that point matches the intersecting surface of the Negative Boolean object. The non-intersecting parts of the Negative Boolean object disappear from view.
- The third Boolean type is known as *Intersection*. You need at least two Boolean objects defined as Intersection types to create a resulting object. In Boolean Intersection, the resulting object is created from the parts of the intersecting forms that overlap, and the remainder of the objects disappears from view.

BOOLEANS IN BRYCE

There are two steps to remember when executing Boolean modeling operations in Bryce, as different from other applications:

1. Determining whether a selected object is positive, negative, or intersecting, by checking the appropriate designation in the object's Attributes window (see Figure 5.1).

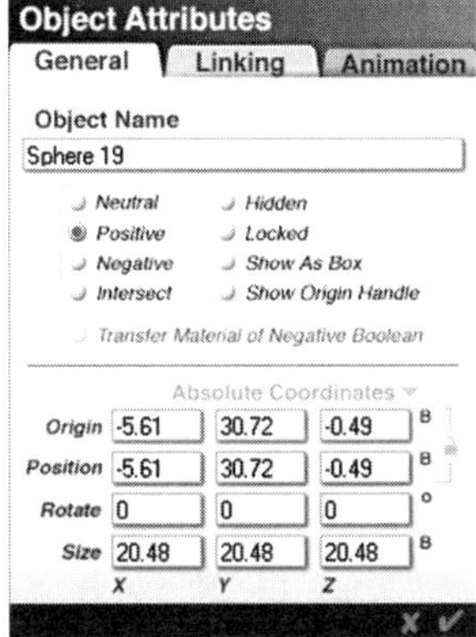

FIGURE 5.1 Check the appropriate designation in the object's Attributes window.

2. Grouping all of the Boolean objects into one Group.

Before you begin to create your own Boolean constructs, you might want to investigate some of the Boolean models included in the Bryce Object library (see Figure 5.2).

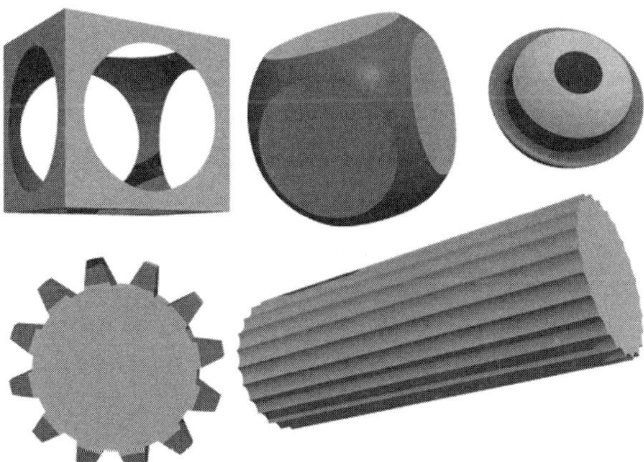

FIGURE 5.2 Sample Boolean objects included in the Boolean collection in the Object library. A careful study of the construction of these objects will help you when designing your own Boolean models.

At first, the fact that Boolean models are represented on-screen with all of the object components displayed instead of hidden might be confusing and seen as a liability in Bryce. Later, when you animate Boolean models, you'll appreciate this attribute.

BASIC BOOLEAN MODELING

Here are a few ideas for constructing some basic Boolean models.

Wine Glass

1. Create an elongated Sphere for the body of the glass, and map it with a Standard Glass material. Use a light-blue color in the Diffusion channel to tint it. Make the elongated sphere Positive in the Attributes dialog.
2. Create a Cube that intersects the elongated Sphere about halfway down. Make the Cube Negative, and group it with the elongated Sphere. Your object should resemble the one at the left in Figure 5.3.
3. Duplicate the object, and make the duplicate 10% smaller. Place the duplicate inside the original object, and apply a red glass material to it. This is the liquid, as illustrated in the middle of Figure 5.3.
4. Create the glass stem and the base. The stem is a Cylinder, and the base is a squashed Sphere. Use their Attributes dialogs to check Boolean Intersecting, and group both together. Place them in position, and group the entire glass. The result should be similar to the illustration on the right in Figure 5.3.

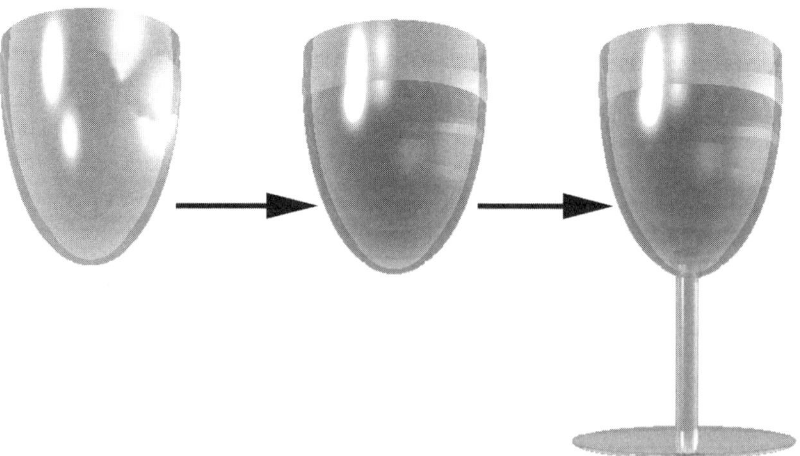

FIGURE 5.3 The Wine Glass object, from start to finish.

Be aware that glass exacts a severe rendering time penalty, because Bryce has to trace all of the lights that interact with the object's refraction and reflection. Glass objects can cause a scene to render 5 to 10 times slower, depending how large they are and if antialiasing is on or off. One solution is to render the scene without the glass objects, and then to *Plop Render* only the glass objects on top of the background.

A Boolean Chair

1. Start by placing a Cube in your workspace. Resize it to twice as high as it is wide and deep. Apply a wood material to it in Object Space. In its Attributes dialog, make it Positive. Refer to the left illustration in Figure 5.4.
2. Create three elongated rectangular blocks to be used to cut away spaces for the legs and top from the Right view. Give each block of the three a Negative Boolean attribute. Place the blocks so they cut away unwanted parts of the Positive block, and Group All. Render a preview. Refer to the middle of Figure 5.4.
3. Ungroup everything. Create two more blocks to cut away unwanted parts of the chair from the front to back, and make them Negative Booleans. Create cutaways for the back of the chair slats, and make each a Negative Boolean. For the last Negative Boolean, create a cube that cuts away the excess from the bottom of the chair. Place a shiny red cushion on the chair by adding another cube resized to fit. Now, Group All for the final render. Refer to the right-hand illustration in Figure 5.4.

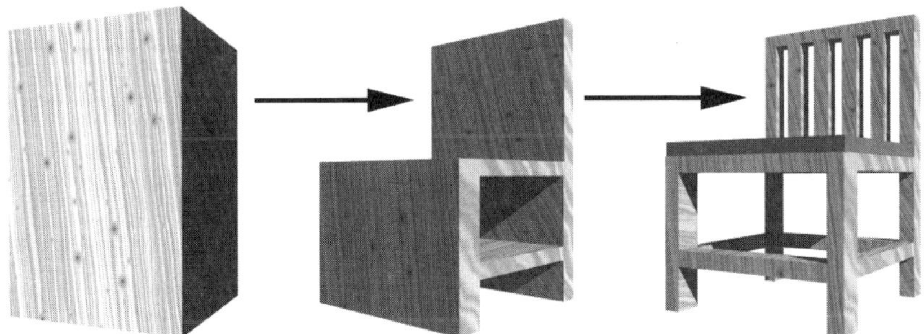

FIGURE 5.4 The Boolean chair.

Intergalactic Boolean Ship

Space ships go hand in hand with computer graphics, and using the Boolean techniques we have investigated, you can create mega-vehicles in Bryce. Try your hand at this model by using any number and variety of Bryce Primitive objects only, and then combining and grouping them as Positive and Negative Booleans. See what you can come up with (see Figures 5.5 through 5.7).

ADDING COMPLEXITY

Once you have modeled your ship, one of the best (and easiest) ways to make it even more complex is to Duplicate it and scale the duplicate(s) down. Then, place the duplicates on the original, and Group. You can

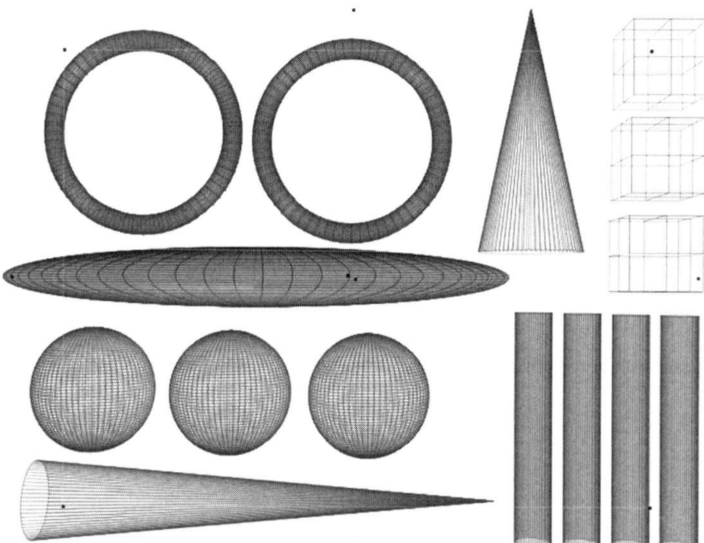

FIGURE 5.5 The components we used.

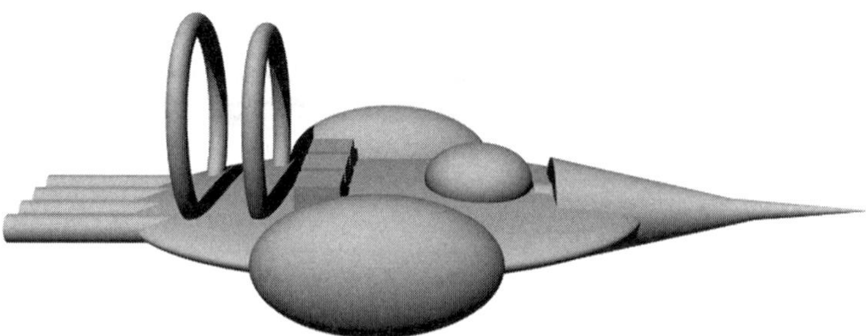

FIGURE 5.6 The pieces are put together and the Boolean types determined. Here's a test render before grouping.

FIGURE 5.7 When all the parts are Grouped, Boolean operations are enabled, and the sculpted form is revealed.

create some fantastic forms using this technique, even though the components are very basic (see Figure 5.8).

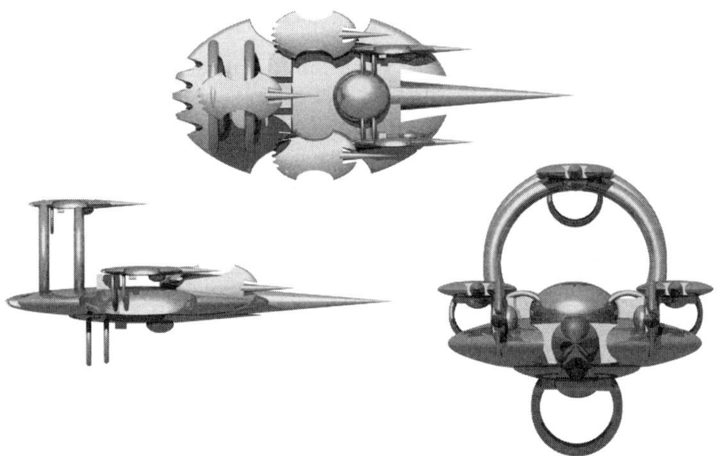

FIGURE 5.8 Adding scaled-down duplicates to a model is a simple path to complexity.

Repeating this process can help you create even more complex objects, like this space station (see Figure 5.9).

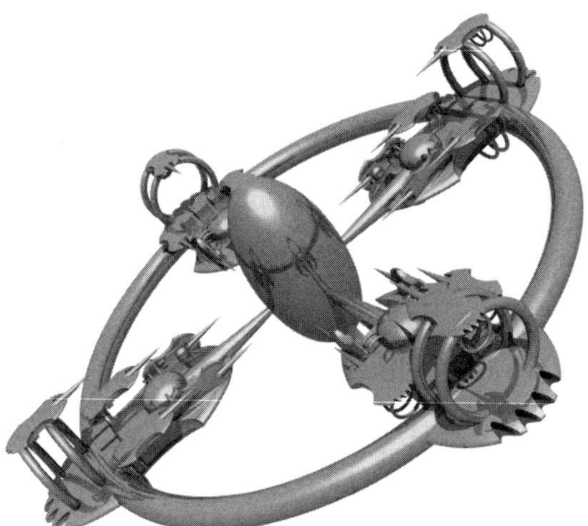

FIGURE 5.9 There is no end to the potential complexity of the resulting object, using this duplication-and-place technique.

You can refer to this technique as *Boolean Self Symmetry*. How many times can you repeat the process to create evermore complex objects? Until the polygon count gets too large for your system to handle.

A FEW MORE BOOLEAN EXERCISES

If you would like to polish your Boolean skills further, follow along with these added tutorials.

A Boolean Object-Presets Tower

There are a number of preset Boolean objects in the existing Boolean Library. This first exercise shows you one way to use them to create a more complex Boolean object: a tower. Do the following:

1. Open the Boolean Library by clicking on the right arrow next to the word *Create* in the toolbar. Select the first item in the list—*Boolean Objects*. This opens the Boolean Library (see Figure 5.10).
2. Look at the selections. Click on a selection to create a component to build part of a Boolean tower. Click on the check mark to accept your choice, and close the Library. Do this four more times until you have five components.
3. All of your components have been placed on top of each other in the workspace. To separate them and build the tower, select each in the

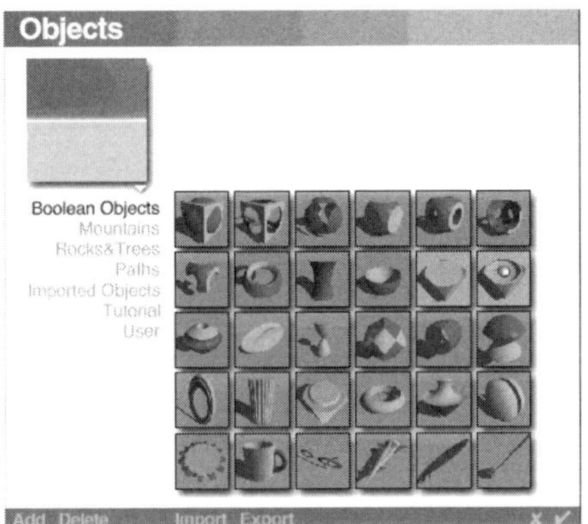

FIGURE 5.10 The Boolean Objects Library opens

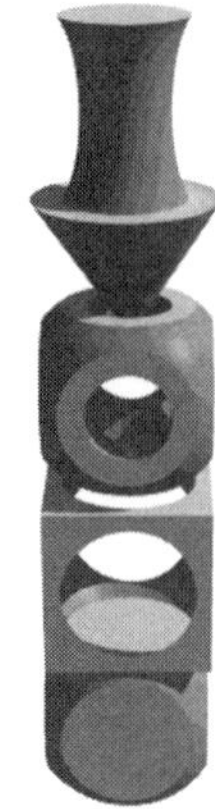

FIGURE 5.11 The Boolean tower. Yours might look different due to your selection of components.

stack and move it vertically until the tower contains the components stacked one on the other in the order you desire. The tower is complete. Render to preview. Do not delete the objects yet (see Figure 5.11).

Saving Boolean Objects to the Library

Saving your Boolean objects to the Boolean Objects Library means that they can be accessed in any future Bryce project. Do the following if you need the practice:

1. Place a Selection marquee around all of the objects in the tower. Group them (Objects > Group Objects).
2. Open the Boolean Objects Library with the group selected. Click Add. Name the new Boolean object *Tower_01*. It now appears as a selection in the thumbnail previews (see Figure 5.12).

A Mountain Tunnel

Boolean objects can drill holes in Terrain objects. Do the following to explore this possibility:

1. Go to the Create toolbar, and click on a Terrain Object icon. This places a Terrain in your workspace. Use the Front view and zoom in on the Terrain object so it fills the screen.
2. Go to the Create toolbar again, and place a Cylinder in the workspace. Enlarge it so that it can be used to cut a tunnel in the Terrain.

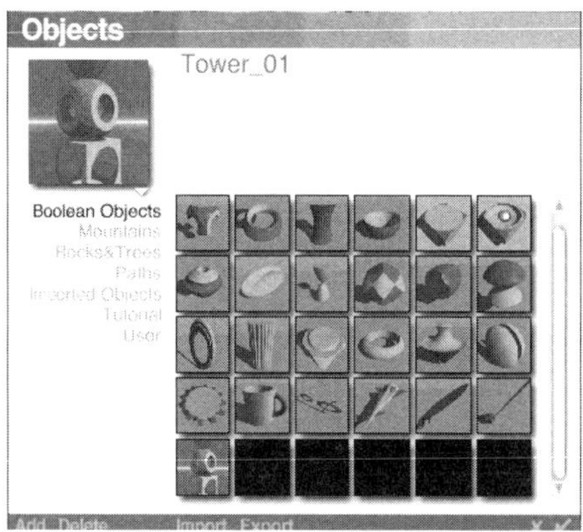

FIGURE 5.12 Save the Tower object to the Boolean Objects Library.

Map the Terrain with any Terrain Material in the Materials Editor (Parametric Mapping), and map the Cylinder with the Wild and Fun>Carnival Tent Material. Rotate the cylinder and Resize it so that it is embedded in the Terrain, and you can see it poke out the other side (see Figure 5.13).

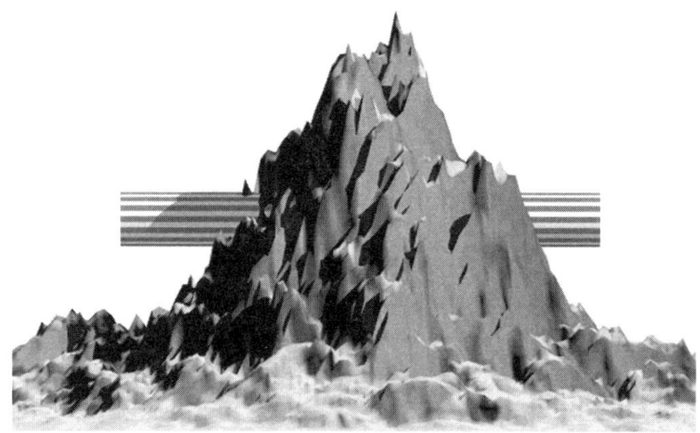

FIGURE 5.13 Embed the Cylinder in the Terrain object.

3. Select the Cylinder, and open its Attributes window. Click on *Negative* and *Transfer Material of Negative Boolean*. This means that the striped material will be mapped to whatever negative space is involved. Click on the check mark to apply the settings (see Figure 5.14).

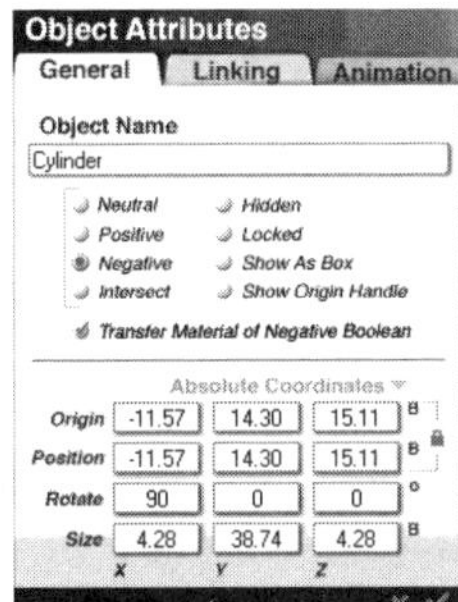

FIGURE 5.14 Configure the cylinder's attributes.

4. Select the Terrain object, and open its Attributes window. Click on Positive, and click on the check mark to apply the settings.
5. Use a Selection marquee to select both the Terrain object and the Cylinder, and Group. When you Group Boolean objects, they interact. You have just created a striped tunnel through the Terrain object. If you did not check the *Transfer Material of Negative Boolean* attribute for the cylinder (the Negative Boolean), the tunnel would have the same material as the rest of the Terrain object (see Figure 5.15).

FIGURE 5.15 The finished tunnel through the Terrain object, ready to admit any traveling objects.

Terrain Cuts Terrain

Using a Cylinder to cut a tunnel or a cave into a Terrain object is interesting, but not if you want the look of a natural object. When wind or water cuts a tunnel or cave, there are uneven pieces in the mix. When you want a more natural model, you can use a more natural object to create the Boolean cut. Do the following:

1. Go to the Create toolbar, and place two Terrain objects in the scene. Resize one so that it is cylinder-like for use as a cutter. Make it a Negative Boolean, and map it with a Terrain material of your choice. Check *Transfer Material of Negative*, and apply the settings.
2. Make the other Terrain object a Positive Boolean. Place the cutter in position to create a tunnel or cave, and group both Terrain objects. The cut now looks more jagged and natural (see Figure 5.16).

FIGURE 5.16 The cut looks more jagged and natural this time.

Boolean Piglets

Using Primitive objects and Boolean operations, you can create unique objects. Do the following to create what we call a *Boolean Piglet*:

1. Place these diverse Primitive objects in a scene, and go to the Front view (see Figure 5.17).
2. Decide which objects are to be Positive or Negative, and apply the necessary attributes. Move the objects together to form a construct that takes advantage of the Positive and Negative Boolean types, as shown in Figure 5.18.
3. Objects > Group Objects to create the Boolean structure (see Figure 5.19).

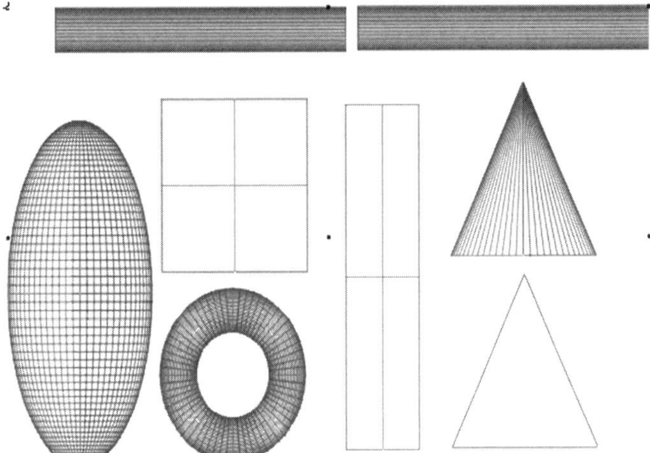

FIGURE 5.17 Place these diverse objects in a scene.

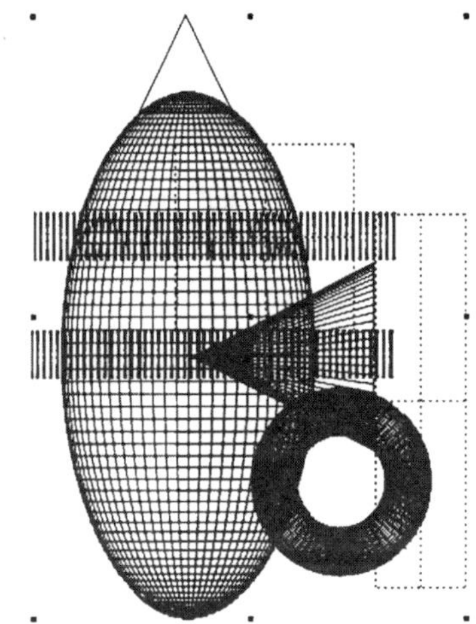

FIGURE 5.18 Apply Positive and Negative attributes, and move the objects so they overlap according to this example.

4. When your object is designed to your liking, duplicate it to create a family of objects. Place them in accordance with your designer's eye to create a surrealist painting (see Figure 5.20).

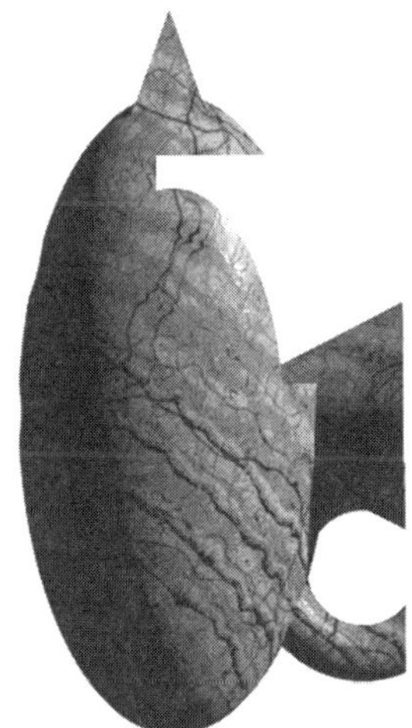

FIGURE 5.19 Group to create the Boolean structure.

FIGURE 5.20 Your painting might look different from this example. The form is definitely abstracted from that of a real-world pig, but the idea is there.

A Fancy Boolean Archway

Using Booleans to create archways is one of the simplest ways to create these complex design elements. Do the following:

1. Create a large Sphere. Flatten it on the Z-axis to reduce its depth. Map it with the Eroded Granite material from the Rocks&Stones Library of preset materials. Make the Sphere a Positive Boolean (see Figure 5.21).
2. Create a flattened Cube. Scale and move it so that it cuts into the Sphere as shown in Figure 5.22. Make it a Negative Boolean.

FIGURE 5.21 Start with a large Sphere.

FIGURE 5.22 Create a Negative Boolean flattened Cube.

3. Create a series of four Negative Boolean Cylinders. Arrange them in a pattern so they cut through the flattened Sphere as shown in Figure 5.23.
4. Map the Cylinders with the same material as the sphere. Group All, and render to preview. Your archway should resemble that shown in Figure 5.24.
5. Save the object to your Objects Library. Create a scene that uses the object, or several of them (see Figure 5.25).

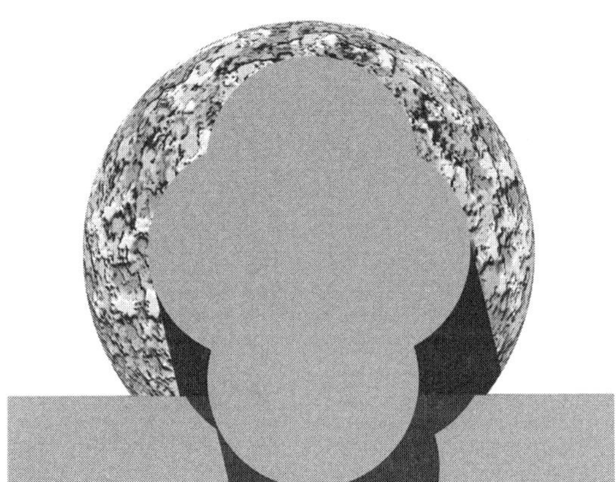

FIGURE 5.23 Create and arrange the Cylinders like this.

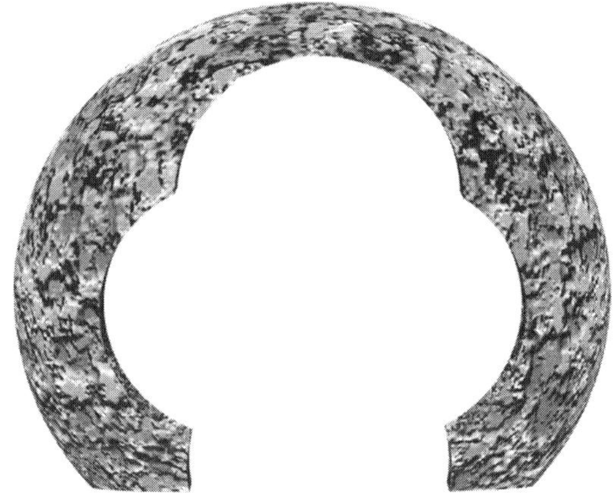

FIGURE 5.24 Your fancy archway is completed.

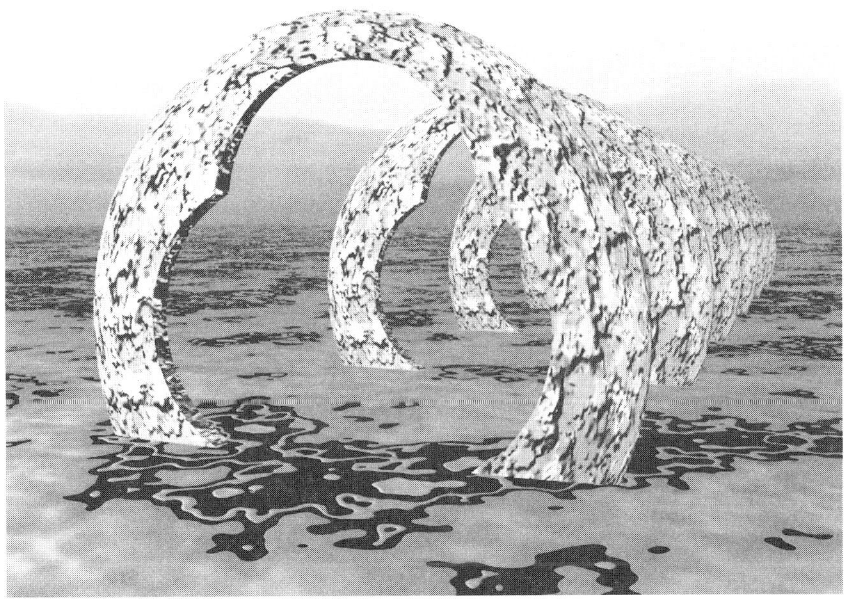

FIGURE 5.25 The archway can add just the right touch to your Bryce scene.

MOVING ON

In this chapter, we focused on using Booleans to create a range of objects. In the next chapter, we'll take a look at Terrains.

CHAPTER

6 Terrain Models

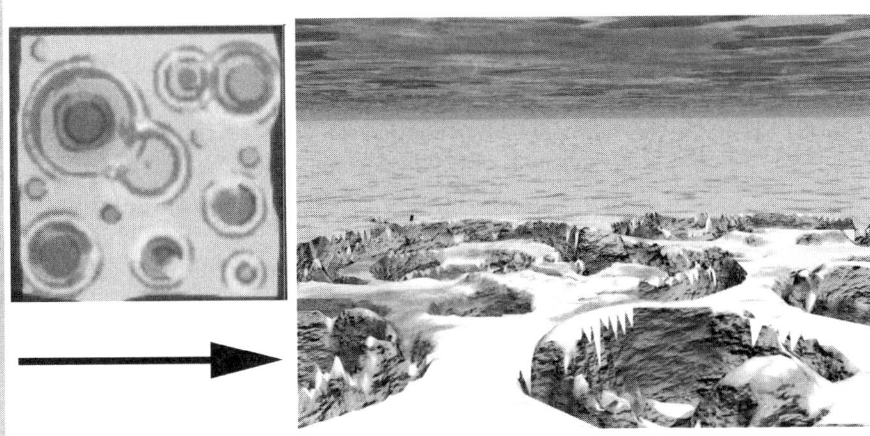

Bryce offers you different types of terrain for your worlds. The two main terrain types are flat infinite planes and 3D outcroppings. What is usually referred to as a *terrain model* in Bryce is the latter, although we will also attend to Bryce infinite planes in this chapter.

GETTING GROUNDED

When the word *"terrain"* is used in a Bryce world, it generally refers to a specific Bryce element. A Terrain object has depth, or what is known as extrusion on the Y World Space coordinate system. Common Terrain objects include hills and mountains on infinite Ground Planes, but the possibilities do not end there. True Terrain objects can be edited in the Bryce Terrain Editor. Four items represented by icons in the Create toolbar are associated with Terrain: Infinite Planes, Terrain, Stone, and the Symmetrical Lattice (see Figure 6.1). Of these four items, only two can be edited in the Terrain Editor: Terrain and the Symmetrical Lattice. You might also consider trees to be Terrain objects, but because we have already covered trees and the Tree Editor in Chapter 3, "Trees," there is no need to cover that topic again in this chapter.

FIGURE 6.1 The four items in the Create toolbar associated with Terrain: Infinite Planes, Terrain, Tree, Stone, and the Symmetrical Lattice.

Terrain and Symmetrical Lattice objects can be infinitely customized and modified in the Terrain Editor—but what about the Ground Plane and the Stone objects?

The Infinite Planes

Bryce has three infinite planar objects: Cloud, Water, and Ground. Each loads into the workspace at different heights. Each really attains its distinctive personality by the materials mapped to its surface. Since each of these three planes can accept any materials, and each can be moved to any height desired, there is no real difference between the three infinite planes except for their default height, which can be altered in all cases. You can easily map a cloud material to a Ground Plane, or a water material to a Cloud Plane. Although they have separate icons, any one will suffice for the others. The difference depends on their material settings, which distinguishes them from their counterparts. Keep this in mind when we talk about the Ground Plane, since what is said can apply equally to the other two planes. Each of the infinite planes can be stacked, rotated, and even "drilled" with Boolean objects.

Holding down your mouse button on an infinite plane allows you to select either a Surface or Volume plane. Volume planes can have their thickness scaled (like any other 3D object). Boolean cutting operations performed on infinite planes work best if the plane is Volumetric, because you'll be able to see that the cut has thickness.

STACKED GROUND PLANES

The reason for stacking Ground Planes is primarily to create more complex textures. To do this effectively, the top Ground Plane(s) must be either moderately transparent overall, or must have materials that are wholly transparent in spots (see Figure 6.2).

FIGURE 6.2 Here is an illustration of two stacked Ground Planes. The bottom plane is mapped with a stone material, while the top one is mapped with partially transparent horizontal bars with totally transparent areas in between. Notice how the object reacts when placed on the bottom plane, and the shadow cast on it by the bars on the top plane.

Stacked Ground Plane Project Ideas

Here are some suggestions for projects that would benefit from stacked Ground Plane techniques (see Figure 6.3):

- Apply a ground fog to the top plane, and a normal surface to the bottom plane. You might even use several planes on top to simulate layered fog. The top plane(s) either could have a splotchy material with see-through sections, or be textured as an overall transparent with muted color.
- Create a multicolored checkered surface by stacking two Ground Planes fairly close together. Map the bottom one with a left-to-right striped material in green. Map the top plane with a front-to-back striped material in red, with 100% transparency between the stripes, and 50% transparency for the color.
- Create a swampy effect by using two or more Ground Planes stacked moderately close together. Map the top plane with the *Disco Kelp* material found in the Complex Materials Library.

Be aware that the use of transparent stacked planes comes at a cost. Raytraced transparency in Bryce consumes many times the amount of rendering time as compared to opaque materials.

FIGURE 6.3 There are three stacked planes here. The top one is mapped with a water material, the middle one with the Disco Kelp material, and the bottom one with a rocky material. Notice that objects stuck in this mystical swamp show through the top layers, and that the "kelp" creates shadows on the bottom layer.

ROTATED GROUND PLANES

Depending on where you place your camera and how you apply materials to planes, you can create some powerful optical illusions. Using multiple rotated infinite planes compounds their infinite nature and creates some startling optical illusions when you animate the camera moving through them. The trick is to look at them from the correct position to see what is going on (see Figure 6.4).

FIGURE 6.4 These two Ground Planes were placed at a 20-degree angle to each other as seen from the camera. The right plane was mapped with a Steel cage material, so you can see through it to the left-hand plane. Strange things happen when you double infinity. Flying at an even distance above the right-hand pane would cause the left plane to recede further below you.

The Infinite Corridor

Infinity can be infuriating, because there's no way out, no end. Inexorably, infinity goes on forever, as this exercise disquietingly demonstrates. Do the following:

1. Load two Ground Planes into your scene. Rotate them so that they are each standing vertically (90 degrees on the Z-axis in World Space), and facing each other with a space in between. Make the camera look down this infinite corridor.
2. Now, Rotate each plane on its Y-axis three degrees, so that the camera is placed at the narrow end of the corridor, and the corridor gradually opens wider at the end. Place the sun in front of the camera so that the corridor is illuminated from the front.

If you travel the camera down this corridor, you will never reach the sky at the end. What will happen, however, is that the sides will seem to recede slowly as the corridor widens and the planes diverge. The effect is like that of a dark curtain gradually opening to the sky. The corridor will always be there, though, as a look to either the left or right will prove (see Figure 6.5).

FIGURE 6.5 Looking down the infinite corridor at the sky beyond.

DRILLED GROUND PLANES

Another undocumented feature in Bryce is that infinite planes can be treated like any other object when it comes to Boolean operations. This means that you can take any object (primitive or imported) and use it to drill holes in the infinite plane. If the plane is a Volume type with a Surface type stacked below it, light will shine in the hole to reveal the material of the plane below. Drilling numerous holes in the top plane will multiply the effect. If you "traveled" in the space between the planes, it would be pitch dark until a hole let sky and light through. If you placed an object (like a futuristic habitat) on the lower plane and let it rise above the upper plane through a hole, you would enhance the suspicion of the viewer that there was an entire world beneath the one he was looking at. You could then journey down into that murky world, as a virtual spelunker.

A Breath of Air

Here's an exercise that will allow you to explore one of the drilled plane effects:

1. Create two Ground Planes in your world. Make sure there is space between them, and make each parallel to each other and to the Bryce horizon line, as seen in the Front view.
2. Apply materials (your choice) to each plane. Place the camera between them. Your preview should show a completely black scene.
3. Use a Cylinder standing on its end to cut a hole in the top plane. Place another Cylinder object on the bottom plane, poking up through the hole. Place the Camera so it is in the space between the planes, looking up at the Cylinder #2 and viewing the sky. If you like, you can also place a light in some part of the space between the planes, mysteriously illuminating some of the dark space in the distance.

Make sure that Haze is set to 0, or you'll get a dim horizontal line across the screen (see Figures 6.6 and 6.7).

FIGURE 6.6 A hole in the upper world reveals a spire and the mysterious terrain below.

FIGURE 6.7 The same scene as viewed from below.

Stones

When you need to place a cliff or other sharp escarpment in your Bryce world, it's worth considering the use of a Stone rather than a Terrain object. Why? Because Stones can be resized as large as a Terrain object without the squarish base that a Terrain has. The only detriment in using Stones for this purpose is that they can't be edited in the Terrain Editor, which might be fine if the object looks the way you want it to at the start. If you don't like the shape of the Stone that is placed in your scene, simply delete it and click the Stone icon again. Do this until the Stone object meets your expectations. There is one more alternative, which is to use the Objects Library in the Create toolbar. The Objects library has a special folder called "Rocks," which contains preset stones. Make sure you save

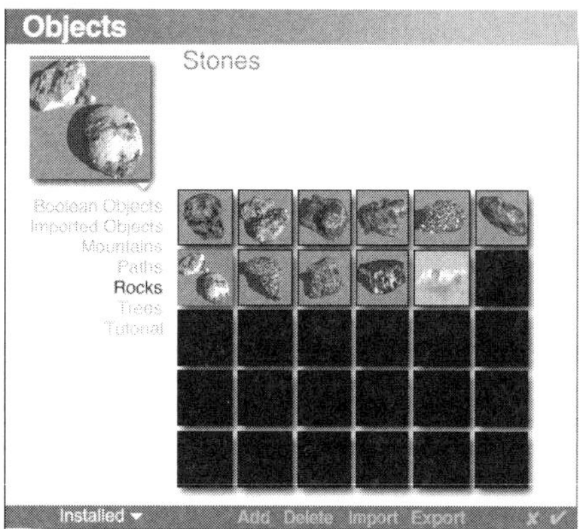

FIGURE 6.8 The Rocks section of the Create/Objects Library has a number of Stone objects from which to choose. You can save your own favorites here as well.

FIGURE 6.9 Stone objects make great seaside cliffs.

your own favorite Stone objects to this library when you find one that pleases your designer's eye (see Figure 6.8).

When you need a bunch of different Stone shapes, but want them all to exhibit the same material texture, just Copy the Material (Edit menu) and paste it to the other Stones. Stones used as larger Terrain elements should be moved so they intersect one another (see Figure 6.9).

Terrain and Symmetrical Lattice Objects

Having touched on Ground Planes and Stones, it's time to move on to the two object types that can be edited: Terrain and Symmetrical Lattice objects.

TERRAIN OBJECTS

The *Mountains* folder in the Objects library is the first place to go to explore preset Terrain designs. It's also important to notice that the Terrain objects stored here give some indication that Bryce Mountains can be more than mountains, but include a variety of object concepts that lie somewhere between a geological outcropping and an abstract object. Letters, for example, can be translated into rocky objects that look like mountains from the side, while retaining their alphanumeric appearance from the Top view. There is no reason why you can't do this with your own company or personal logo (see Figures 6.10 and 6.11).

Remember the exercises we did that included the rotation of infinite planes? The same thing can be done with Terrain objects. You can literally turn mountains on their side in Bryce, creating surrealistic rock

FIGURE 6.10 The Mountains presets.

FIGURE 6.11 This Bryce Terrain object is included in the Mountain folder in the Objects library. It appears as a mountain from the side, and is logo-like as seen from the top.

walls, and even using the Terrain object as a wall of a medieval house. Although Terrains are normally used to create awesome mountain ranges, you do not have to be constrained to this use alone (see Figure 6.12).

When you want to cover your backdrop with mountains and hills, it might not be necessary to use more than one Terrain object. Since Terrain objects can be resized on any axis and rotated, one replicated Terrain object can serve as multiple objects when used with different sizes and rotations (see Figure 6.13).

FIGURE 6.12 This exquisite tiled grating, through which the desert and sky can be appreciated, was created by Multi-Replicating a preset from the Mountains presets folder in the Objects library.

FIGURE 6.13 This scene was created with just one replicated Terrain object, which was resized and rotated to produce the different geological looks. Even the grassy hills in the foreground were constructed from the same Terrain object. Different materials were used to map some of the clones.

By turning a Terrain object upside down, you have a perfect meteor crater, or even a receptacle for a crater lake (see Figure 6.14).

FIGURE 6.14 When a Terrain object is flipped vertically, it becomes a hole in the ground. Placing an object inside a hole enhances the depth effect.

SYMMETRICAL LATTICE OBJECTS

Symmetrical Lattice objects are objects mirrored vertically. For this reason, they can be used to create objects with balanced top/bottom or left/right symmetry. This is especially useful when you need to create mechanical objects, or fantasy terrain such as floating mountains (see Figures 6.15 and 6.16).

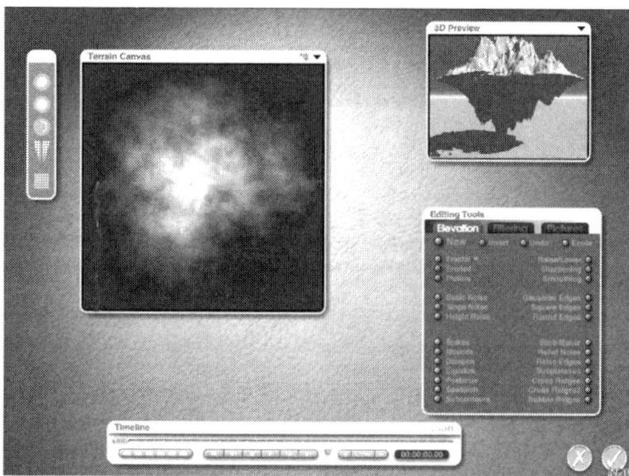

FIGURE 6.15 A default Symmetrical Lattice object as it appears in the Editor.

FIGURE 6.16 A Conic map was applied to this Symmetrical Lattice to produce the effect seen here, which was then texture mapped with a Psychoactive Christmas Ball material.

You can also use a Symmetrical Lattice object to fake a reflection, since the mirrored bottom half is always the same as the top half. If you take a journey "below" the liquid surface, you will still see the reflected lattice, an interesting optical illusion if you travel from below to above the surface in an animation. The surface doesn't have to be a common transparent surface, but can also be a surface with "holes" in it, with no reflective capabilities at all.

EDITING TERRAINS

Mastering any technique can be a rather elusive pursuit, especially if the tools in question offer near infinite variations. For example, you could never hope to exhaust your options when editing terrains. What you can hope to accomplish is to gain a comfortable degree of familiarity with the terrain editing tools and techniques, although you are always free to combine them in exciting and novel ways. The Editor is activated by selecting its icon in the Edit toolbar. The Editor addresses the following items: Terrain, Symmetrical Lattice, Torus, Stone, or Mesh. Editing a Torus allows you to adjust the size of its inner diameter. Editing a Stone is the same as editing a Mesh object, in that you can select to either smooth the polys or have them faceted. Editing a Terrain or Symmetrical Lattice brings up Bryce's major editing interface (see Figure 6.17).

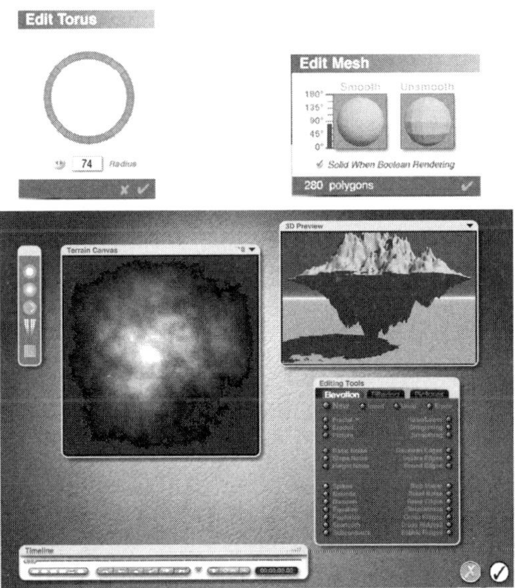

FIGURE 6.17 The three editing windows: Torus Editor, Mesh/Stone Editor, and the full Terrain/Symmetrical Lattice Editor.

We will look at some Terrain object editing examples, so you can achieve definitive geometry using various tools and techniques in the Terrain Editor. The first step is always to use the Terrain icon, so that a Terrain object is placed on the screen. This object is only a proxy object, so that the Terrain Editor can be accessed. It is seldom that you will want to use the default Terrain object without editing it. If you want to explore these methods on a Symmetrical Lattice instead of a Terrain object, just make sure you click on the Symmetrical Lattice icon to place its proxy on screen first (see Figure 6.18).

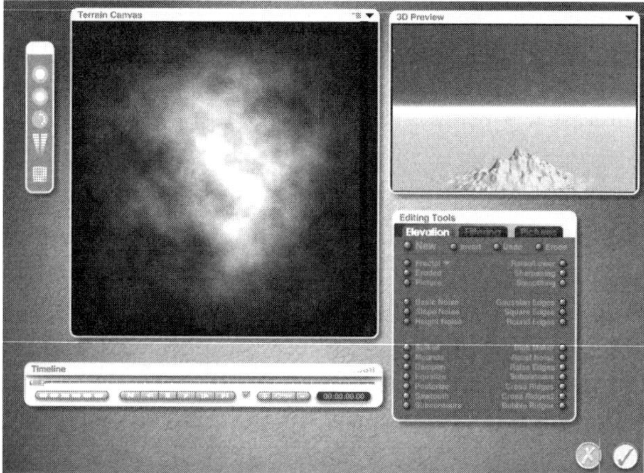

FIGURE 6.18 In order to understand and work through these examples, you must be working familiar with all of the tools and options in the General, Filtering, and Pictures tabs of the Terrain Editor, as well as the options in the rest of the Terrain Editor dialog.

CREATING AND CUSTOMIZING OBJECTS IN THE TERRAIN EDITOR

Look at the pictures that accompany these examples. The instructions that follow tell you how the object was produced with specific tools and options in the Terrain Editor. If you work through these exercises, you will be well on your way to mastering the Terrain Editor.

The Cross-Sloped Cabin Roof

With a Terrain object selected in your workspace, open the Terrain Editor and click New in the Terrain Editor General tab, so you can start with a blank 3D canvas. Then, do the following:

1. Click on Cross-Ridges 2. A cross-ridged roof shape will be created. This object has no sides if ported to your workspace at this point, so we have to create some (see Figure 6.19).

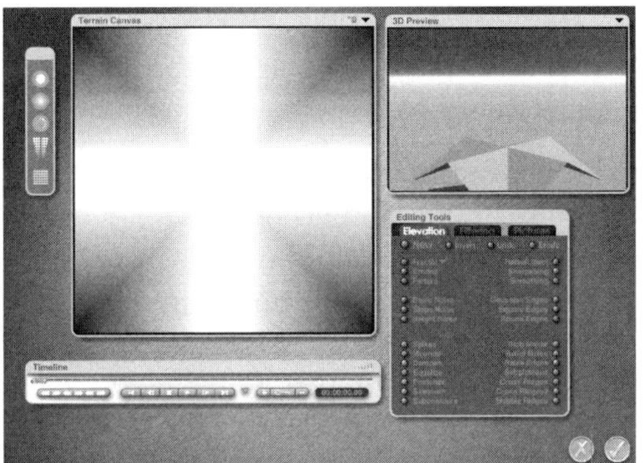

FIGURE 6.19 The Cross-Ridge 2 operator creates a nice Roof object.

FIGURE 6.20 Here is the roof placed on a basic house, created from cubic blocks.

2. Click on Erode, and then on Undo. This sets up the Effects brush. With Paint Effect selected, draw your brush down the perimeter of the Cross-Ridged shape. You have added rough vertical faces to the object. They are somewhat random and cracked, but this will be just right for the roof we want. Place the roof on your workspace. For smooth vertical faces, click and drag on the Square Edges operator (see Figure 6.20).

Variations Ad Infinitum

Starting with the basic Cross-Ridge operator in the Terrain Editor, you can create an almost infinite array of roof variations. This is done by exploring various other effects operators after you apply the Cross-Ridge or Cross-Ridge 2 effect (see Figure 6.21).

FIGURE 6.21 Here are just a few examples of roof variations that can be created in the Terrain Editor in seconds, using the Cross-Ridge as a base.

Petrified Forest

With a Terrain object selected in your workspace, open the Terrain Editor and click New in the Terrain Editor General tab.

1. Create a group of Mounds by clicking and sliding the mouse (LMB on Windows systems) to the right over the Mounds operator.
2. Create a series of SubPlateaus by sliding the mouse (LMB on Windows systems) to the right over the SubPlateaus operator.
3. Write the Forests Terrain object to the scene.
4. Add some height (Y World axis) when you return to the workscreen. Use any suitable material to add a convincing color.

This is a useful object because adding groups of trees any other way is rendering prohibitive. Used in the distance with a 50% to 60% haze (light green), and a 70–70 Fog setting (light green), this technique provides a realistic forest. These trees can be especially effective when reflected in water across a lake. Submerge the base beneath the Ground Plane or underlying terrain (see Figure 6.22).

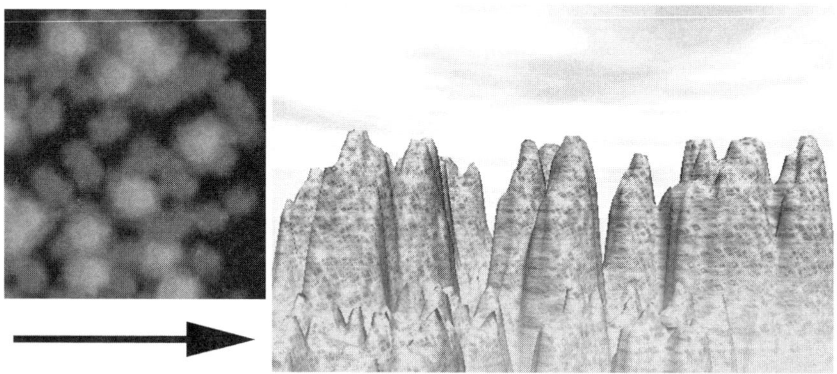

FIGURE 6.22 Using the Mounds and SubPlateaus operators in the Terrain Editor creates a convincing forest.

Volcano

With a Terrain object selected in your workspace, open the Terrain Editor and click New in the Terrain Editor General tab.

1. Create a basic Volcano cone shape by clicking on the Blob Maker operator.
2. Select a mid-level gray with the Elevation brush, and click 10 times in the middle of the cone. This flattens it out.

3. Select a black Elevation brush, sized smaller than the flattening brush in step 2, and click 10 times in the middle of the flattened cone. This bores a hole for the calendra.
4. Click on Erode, and then on Undo. Use a Paint Effect brush to go around the perimeter of the volcano, adding selective cracks and fissures. Paint from the inside outward in shaky, uneven strokes. When satisfied with the preview model, write the object to your workspace.

You can resize the volcano or duplicate it as needed in your scene. Later in the book, when we look at Illusion from Impulse Software, we'll demonstrate how to create a realistic flame for the volcano (see Figure 6.23).

FIGURE 6.23 The volcano lives on earthly and alien terrain.

Standing Stones

With a Terrain object selected in your workspace, open the Terrain Editor and click New in the Terrain Editor's Elevation tab.

1. Use an Elevation brush to paint in seven standing stones as seen from the top. Use a maximum white ranging to a medium white, so they all have separate heights.
2. Use the Eroded Effects brush to give the stones a little character, and then click and drag right on the Smoothing function twice. Write the object to your workspace.

This group of stones looks very nice reflected in water, so our example shows a reflective pool around the stones. A Torus is used as a border for the water (see Figure 6.24).

FIGURE 6.24 The standing stones look more mysterious when reflected in a pool of water.

House Interior

With a Terrain object selected in your workspace, open the Terrain Editor and click New in the Terrain Editor General tab.

1. Create the Top view of rooms in a house, like a floor plan. Use the smallest and whitest brush possible. Draw the walls as straight as you can.

One way to get straight lines in the Terrain Editor is to slide your mouse along the edge of a ruler when drawing. The simplest way is to hold the Shift key down while dragging.

2. Use the Smoothing operation twice, by clicking and dragging the mouse to the right over the Smoothing function. Accept the object, and write it to your workscreen.
3. Use a series of resized Cubes to cut windows and doorways in the walls (see Figure 6.25).

River Canyon

With a Terrain object selected in your workspace, open the Terrain Editor and click New in the Terrain Editor General tab. Then, do the following to create a Terrain object that emulates a river canyon:

1. Click on these three operators in the following order: Cross Ridges 2, Cross Ridges, and Eroded. This will produce a blocky structure.
2. Use a medium-sized solid-black Elevation brush, and trace a meander from the upper left to the lower right of the object. This is the start of your riverbed.

FIGURE 6.25 You can add lights and position the camera for a walkthrough of the rooms. Add furniture as needed, or live in it very frugally until you can afford to furnish it.

3. With the same brush, and select a medium-gray color. Trace next to the meander on either side. This cuts away some of the sheerness of the cliffs next to the riverbed.
4. Click on Erode, and then on Undo. Use the Effects brush to add some erosion to the sides of the cliffs that face the riverbed. Write the object to your scene.
5. Use a material on the Terrain object (Planes and Terrains/Grassy Peaks works well). Add a Water Plane to the scene, and map a material to it (the "Nice Water" material will do nicely). Nestle your camera over the river for a nice view, and render (see Figure 6.26).

FIGURE 6.26 Rollin'... Rollin'... Rollin' down the river.

Castle Fortress

With a Terrain object selected in your workspace, open the Terrain Editor and click New. Get ready for a medieval thrill.

1. Use a medium-sized Elevation brush set to 100% white to paint in the four towers at the corners of your Terrain Editor workspace. The best way to do this is to click the same number of times for each tower, assuring that they will be of equal height.
2. Select a color two shades darker than the towers for the walls. Draw a line between the towers to create the walls. Try to make them as straight as possible, but don't be concerned if they wiggle a little. The Terrain Editor will interpolate them and make them straighter.
3. Write the castle to your workspace, and add Boolean cutaways as needed. If it is to be used as a distant edifice, you don't have to do much more detail work. Use a rock material to texture the object (explore the Barnacles material), and set it on a mound in your world, adding a 50% Haze (see Figure 6.27).

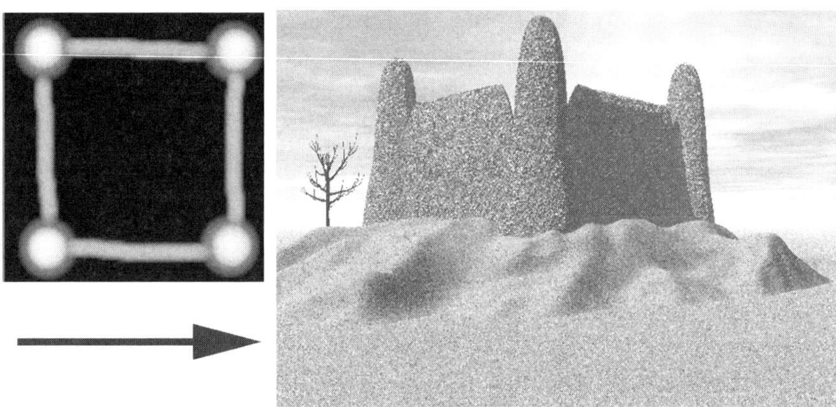

FIGURE 6.27 The old castle sits on a misty hill, remembering its past days of glory.

Machine Panel

With a Terrain object selected in your workspace, open the Terrain Editor and click New in the Terrain Editor Elevation tab.

1. For this exercise, we are going to use one of the preset Terrain maps in the Bryce folder. Click on Picture in the General tab, and then find the Terrain Maps folder. Select the City2 map.
2. Click on Posterize, and drag the mouse to the right as far as it will go. Click on the Raise/Lower function, and drag the mouse to the right

so that the object has its height lowered by about two-thirds. Write the object to your workspace.

For a neat effect, stack these panels, or variations of them, and set them in place as a backdrop for a high-tech room. You can even create the background for a bridge of a spaceship in the same manner (see Figure 6.28).

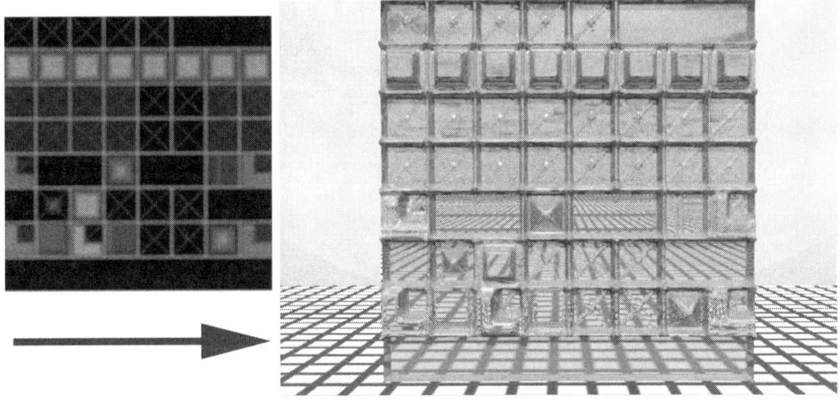

FIGURE 6.28 This object creation technique gives you instant techno props.

Craters

With a Terrain object selected in your workspace, open the Terrain Editor and click New in the Terrain Editor General tab. Then, do the following:

1. Create a solid block by clicking and dragging right as far as you can over the Raise Edges operator. This produces a solid block (colored white).
2. Lower the height of the block to about one-third of its size by selecting the Raise/Lower operator, and clicking and dragging to the right while watching the 3D preview.
3. With a 70% white Elevation brush of medium size, pick the place for your first crater. Click over the area as you watch the circular area raising itself in the 3D preview. This will be the wall of the crater.
4. Now, select a 70% black Elevation brush a bit smaller than the raised area. Click and watch the hole being formed. Make the hole about twice as deep as the walls of the crater are high.
5. Repeat this process to develop several craters in the block.
6. Click on the SubContours operator, and then on Undo. Select the Effects brush, resize it to Minimum, and paint some erosions onto each of the crater's walls. Watch the 3D preview as you are working.

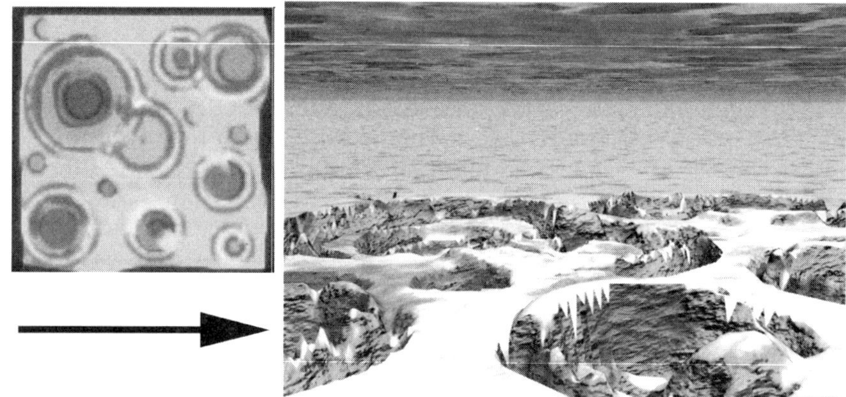

FIGURE 6.29 Cratered environments can be produced quickly and interactively in the Terrain Editor.

Repeat this process with SubPlateaus. When finished, write the object back to the workspace (see Figure 6.29).

Avoid using complex material if you want to see the craters more clearly, or they might be hidden by the material. On the other hand, materials that work by altitude work well on craters, since they paint the upper parts differently and allow the crater to stand out.

CityMap Picture Blend

With a Terrain object selected in your workspace, open the Terrain Editor and click New in the Terrain Editor Elevation tab.

1. Load the Cones preset from the Terrain Maps folder into the first channel of the Pictures tab.
2. Load the City1Mask.tif preset into the second channel.
3. With options set to Blend, click and drag on the Blend arrow until the final picture area shows about a 50% blend between the two Terrain Maps. Use the Bladerunner material to map the terrain object (see Figure 6.30).

GENERAL TERRAIN EDITOR TIPS

- To quickly black out an area of your Altitude map, select Darkest Color and No Smoothing on the brush. Click the mouse once over the area needing deletion. This is also how holes are cut in objects, after selecting a very dark shading.

FIGURE 6.30 Blending the cones with the CityMap 2 gives the cityscape a much more bizarre look, like something out of this world.

- To create jagged "stairstepping" object elements, paint down your brush with Smoothing off. Select the "lowest" step first, with the darkest shade. Then, move progressively brighter, painting down the next highest step. Doing this inside of the Terrain Editor creates circular or partially circular steps, since Bryce has no rectangular brushes for this operation.
- Use the edge of the Altitude Map window as a straightedge when you need to paint a line along the perimeter of the object. This is especially useful when applying effects with the paintbrush.
- For altering the ho-hum symmetry of an object, load a different graphic into the Alpha channel in the Picture tab. Use the Blend slider to mix the original graphic and the Alpha graphic on screen. This is very useful when creating cities whose buildings look too similar from just the Altitude map. The Blend can also be used as a keyframe, so that it can change over time, creating unusual and experimental effects.
- Work with a Grid Size that gives you the level of detail you require. The higher the Grid Size, the smaller the brush you can paint with, and the finer the resulting detail.

Hiding or Deleting an Object's Square Base

If your Terrain objects appear with a square base and you do not want to see the base in the rendering, you can do one of the following:

- Terrain objects always have a square base, while Symmetrical Lattice objects can have theirs painted out (when they have one).

- If the object is sitting on an opaque plane (like the Ground Plane), just move it down so that the base is hidden by the overlying plane.
- If the object is in transparent water, move the base of the object below an opaque plane that lies below the water plane.
- If the object is to float in the air (floating or inside of a cloud) or in space, then use a Symmetrical Lattice initially in the design phase instead of a Terrain object.
- If the Symmetrical lattice object displays a base, you can use the Edge tools in the General tab to paint it out, or alternatively, you can apply selective Erosion on the edge with the effects Paintbrush.

An alternative method to all of these options is to group a Negative Boolean Cube at the positive object's base, cutting off the visibility of the base for the viewer, or to painstakingly use negative Boolean Spheres to cut away the superfluous parts of the base on the sides of the terrain.

CREATING ALTITUDE MAPS

You can create Altitude maps in the Terrain Editor with the paint tools provided, or you can create them in a separate paint application, and import them into the Terrain Editor afterward. It is best to use the internal painting tools for editing and touchup in most cases, and to create new Altitude maps outside of Bryce. External bitmap painting applications give you far more painting options, and they usually have large filter plug-in libraries to alter the image further.

Internal Altitude Map Painting

Using the Painting brush to edit a Terrain Elevation map is where the Terrain painting process in Bryce really shines. By clicking on any of the terrain creation operations (like Mounds or Erode), and then clicking UNDO, the effect selected before the UNDO was activated becomes the operation your brush will use in the editing process. This allows you to carefully paint the effect over selected parts of the Altitude map, as opposed to targeting the entire altitude map for the effect. Let's look at some examples. Here are some tips for using the Terrain Editor's painting tools and options These tips assume that you have spent time exploring the Terrain Editor's painting options, so that the terms are familiar to you.

- Add Erosion and Fractalization selectively with the Effects brush. This allows you much more control over your models.
- Create a negative (inverse) of your image in a paint application, and store it with the positive image. In the Pictures tab, load the inverse image into the second channel. Use the Blend slider to mix the two.

The result will be an object slowly reversing its geometry. At midpoint, this obliterates the object, while at either end of the spectrum, it allows either the positive or negative object to exist.

- Use the Paint Effects brush with Relief Noise to add a touch of volume to elements of the image. This process puffs out the selected elements each time you use it, so you will be able to control the shaping of the object by small amounts each time.
- With the Hard/Soft selector turned all the way to Soft, the Elevation brush acts more to smooth a selected altitude than to carve holes, even with the grayscale indicator turned all the way to black. When you want to carve a hole in the top of an object, turn the selector to Hard.
- For more subtle applications of an Effects brush, try using short clicks instead of clicking and dragging the mouse.

External Altitude Map Painting

Bryce can translate 24-bit, 256-color, or black-and-white bitmap art into Altitude maps. Since the final operation uses a 256-color palette or smaller, it's better to work in index color modes of 256 colors or less in your paint application to produce the Altitude map art, although a 24-bit RGB image is useful for color mapping the terrain. There are any number of external applications to use for this purpose, including some personal favorites:

Corel Painter. Painter is a most innovative bitmap painting application. It has loads of diverse brushes for painting any effect you can imagine, and many you can't. Painter also has f/x brushes whose image content creates innovative Altitude maps in Bryce. Chief among its tools is the Image Hose, allowing you to spray randomized graphics. Many of the Image Hose libraries contain brushes that translate well when used as Altitude map data in Bryce. Painter can use most Photoshop plug-ins, and it is a multiplatform application (see Figure 6.31).

Adobe Photoshop. Although Photoshop has limited painting options compared to Painter, it is king of the hill when it comes to filters. Photoshop has its own extensive list of internal f/x filters, in addition to its invitation to developers for external plug-in filters. The Photoshop Lens Flare filter creates smoothly sculpted conic spires in Bryce's Terrain Editor (see Figure 6.32).

You can apply Photoshop filter effects without leaving the Terrain Editor. Just go to the Filtering tab and select the downward-pointing arrow at the bottom right. Click on "Select Plugins Folder" to locate your filters, and they will be displayed in the list. From there, simply choose one to bring up its settings window, and apply the effect!

FIGURE 6.31 A Painter 5 graphic, produced with the Hexagonal Tile effect, translated to an Altitude map in Bryce. The hexagons range in brightness, so they are perfect for creating skyscrapers that range in height—a classic urban skyline.

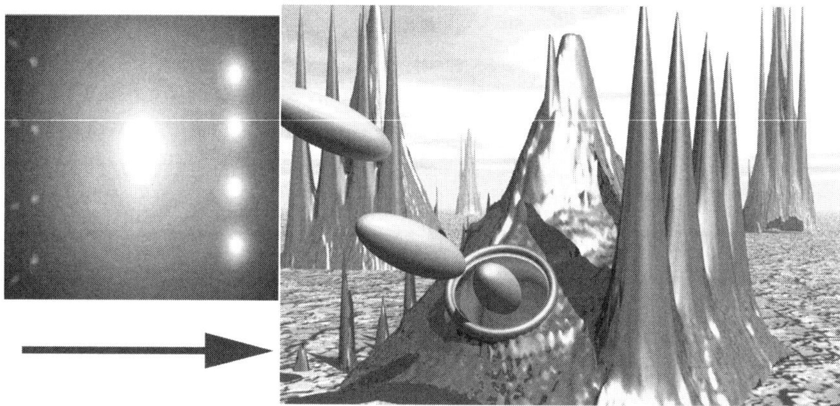

FIGURE 6.32 A Photoshop graphic, produced with Photoshop's exclusive internal Lens Flare filter, translated to an Altitude map in Bryce. The 3D object it created is on the right. ... "Where ships of dreams amaze the eyes and golden spires touch the skies."

Corel PhotoPaint. Corel's PhotoPaint will access most Photoshop plug-in filters, and also includes many of its own unique effects. Many of its filter selections are versions of separate applications that come with PhotoPaint, yet have to be purchased as extras for other painting software. PhotoPaint is a multiplatform application (see Figure 6.33).

For creating mountain objects in the Terrain Editor externally, use any method in your painting application that creates "cloud" graphics. 2D Clouds translate into superlative Altitude maps that then generate very

FIGURE 6.33 A PhotoPaint graphic, produced with a Ripple Fill, translated to an Altitude map in Bryce. The Terrain is grooved all the way around, providing a troth for an object to roll. Smoothed out, this would even suffice for a marble raceway. The circular path could also lead to a temple on top. Flattened out, this could also be a terraced rice paddy, with the right texture.

realistic Terrain objects. This is because clouds, like mountain objects, are based on fractals.

Generating Altitude Map Data from Photos

A digital photograph is produced by any photographic method that results in data that can be read into the computer. That data can then be imported into Bryce as an Altitude map for Terrain object creation. There are a number of devices that can be used to generate digital photographs, including:

Digital still-camera input. Until a few years ago, consumer-priced digital still cameras were capable of producing only low-resolution output. Recently, this has changed dramatically, with the introduction of dozens of cameras capable of capturing very fine detail, and priced to fit most computer arts budgets. You will need either the proper inputs on your computer (composite or S-VHS) to access the images in the camera, or a camera that writes images to a floppy or FlashPix disk (see Figure 6.34).

Scanned photographs. Most computer graphics art and animation studios, and many home computer workspaces, have a scanner. A scanner can generate very detailed images from original or printed photographs (see Figure 6.35).

Video grabs. If you have access to a video camera, and if your computer has an add-on card that has a video input (usually Composite and/or

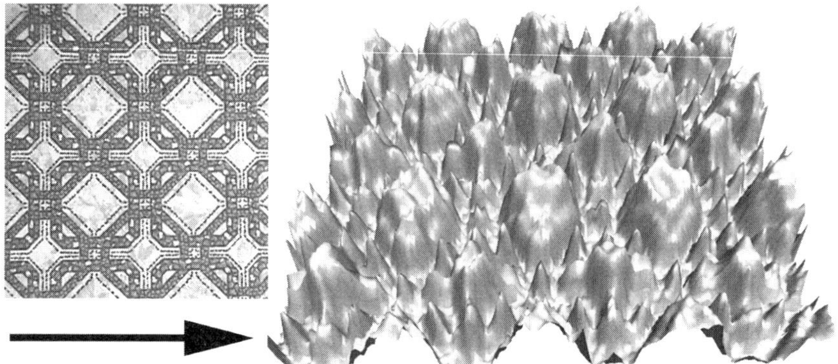

FIGURE 6.34 An original digital still-camera image of some floor tiles, translated to an Altitude map in Bryce. The tiled floor translates into what appears to be a 3D egg carton.

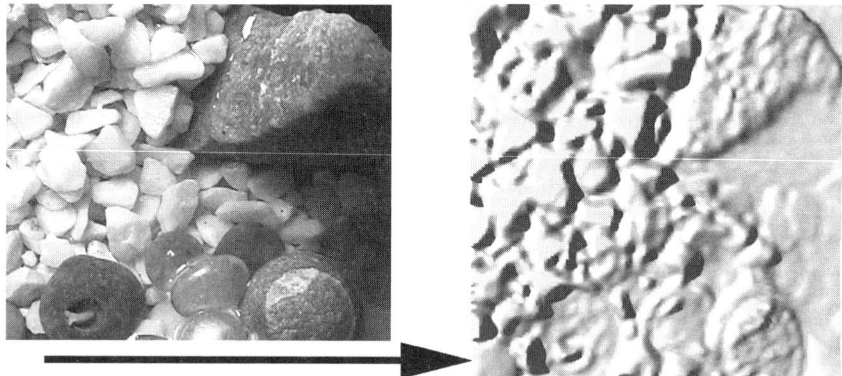

FIGURE 6.35 An original scanned photograph of some pebbles, translated to an Altitude map in Bryce.

S-VHS), you can grab still-frames from a video. You can also grab frames from a videotape (see Figure 6.36).

Photocopy. This is an option that many artists neglect, but one that can serve you well. The newer office copiers produce photographic or near-photographic output, in color or grayscale. Sometimes, however, the older office copiers that produce "poor" output create just the right look for interesting Altitude maps, after the copy has been scanned into the computer. You can even move the original artwork on a copier while it is doing its job, creating interesting grayscale smears that look intriguing when turned into altitude maps in Bryce (see Figure 6.37).

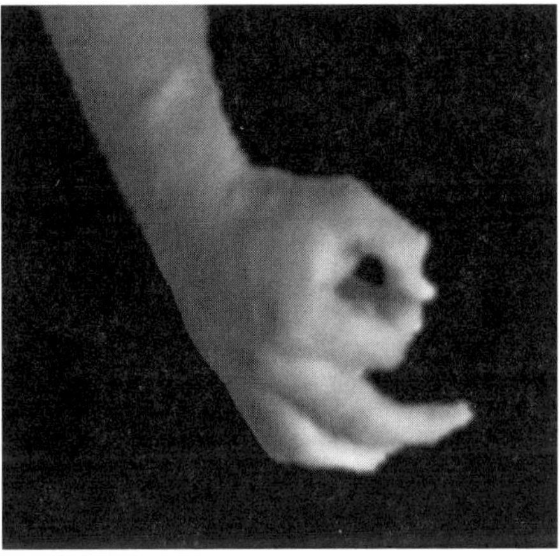

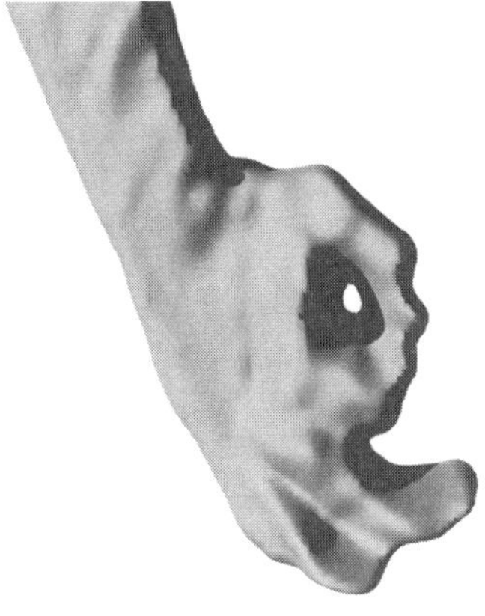

FIGURE 6.36 A frame from one of the author's videotapes, translated to an altitude map in Bryce. The base was cut away by a Negative Boolean Cube. Blur was applied in the paint application, and smoothing in Bryce.

FIGURE 6.37 A photocopy of an original image, translated to an Altitude map in Bryce. Black was used to outline the image in the paint application, and again in Bryce's Terrain Editor.

Preparing Photos for Bryce Use

There are several things you can do beforehand in your paint application to make photos more suitable for translation into 3D objects in Bryce's Terrain Editor:

- **Use a Blur filter several times on the image.** This tones down the areas that are prone to be translated as 3D spikes.

- **Enhance the contrast of the image.** This will make altitude data more obvious to Bryce, and make the 3D object smoother at the start.
- **Change 24-bit color into grayscale.** This allows you more options in the paint application, so that you can visualize what the translation might look like.
- **Delete unwanted data.** This can be very important. If you need to translate facial information to 3D, for example, there is no need for the background. For translation in the Terrain Editor, make the unwanted data pure black. For translation in the Materials Lab make the deleted parts of the photo white. If you need both translations, create two images, one with a white backdrop and one with black. This allows you to precisely map colored image data on a 3D object later on.

It is often necessary to use a black Elevation brush on the image after you apply Smoothing in the Terrain Editor, since Smoothing can cause the background black level to turn gray. This might be necessary even though you used black to outline the image in the paint application.

Copyrights. *Don't neglect the copyright laws when it comes to gathering photographic art for your Bryce Altitude maps. The photography in most magazines and books, unless otherwise noted, is copyrighted; so are the images in most videos. Select either copyright-free imagery, or contact the publishers of commercial publications to obtain permission to use their images. Publishing copyrighted photos on the Internet is especially troublesome when it comes to using copyrighted material without permission, since so many people might see your work. Be safe, and get permission or use only copyright-free material.*

Plug-In Filters

Plug-in filters enhance the capabilities of the application they are folded into. There are hundreds of plug-in filters available for paint applications, each one offering new and exciting image enhancement and modification capabilities. One of our favorites is the Terrazzo plug-in from Xaos Tools. With this plug-in, you can take any selected area of an image and use it as a basis for the creation of a kaleidoscopic tiled graphic. Using this plug-in as a device for creating a Bryce Altitude map, the resulting objects offer new 3D possibilities (see Figure 6.38).

Scanning Real-World Objects

You can scan more than 2D images on your scanner. You can also place a variety of 3D objects on the scanning platen (being careful not to scratch

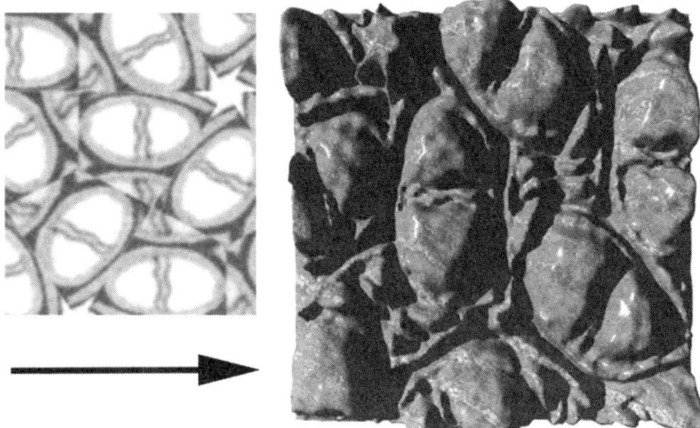

FIGURE 6.38 An image created with Xaos Tools Terrazzo filter, translated to an Altitude map in Bryce. This object is reminiscent of rusting beetle carcasses.

the glass). Exploring and experimenting, you can wind up with a graphic that translates into an interesting Altitude map for applying to a Bryce Terrain object (see Figure 6.39).

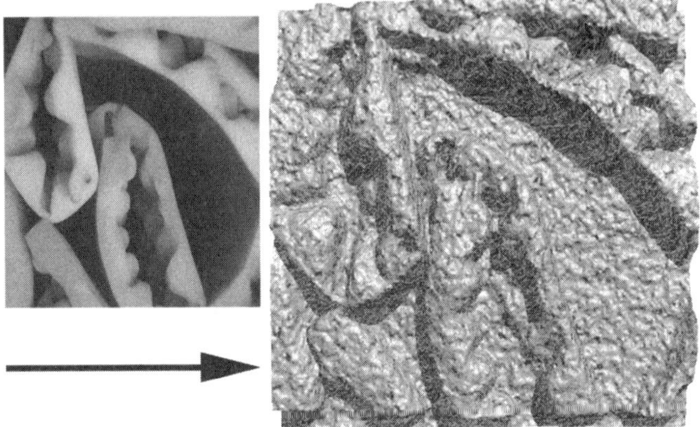

FIGURE 6.39 This object was created by scanning pieces of foam rubber on end, and translating the image into an Altitude map in the Terrain Editor.

Two-Color Bitmaps as Altitude Maps

This is the best way to generate sharp symmetry, good for producing mechanical and architectural objects in Bryce's Terrain Editor. Remember, however, that you are working in the Terrain Editor, basically changing organic objects such as mountains into human-constructed artifacts when you need sharper objects, and that some anomalies will probably be present. There are ways to minimize them by using the smoothing operation after the bitmap has been read in, but there will usually be a few jagged anomalies left. If this bothers you, then you should not be creating objects in the Terrain Editor. Instead, you should be creating them in a more suitable external 3D application, exporting them in a format that Bryce can read, and using them from there. Terrain objects will have some organic and unsymmetrical terrain attributes most of the time, no matter what the Altitude map looks like.

No matter what painting application you use to create the two-color (black and white) original art, or even if is processed from a color or grayscale photo, it can be altered by a number of filters as well. Black-and-white art creates a Bryce Terrain map that has only two altitudes, low and high. Black-and-white art can, however, be transformed into grayscale Altitude maps in Bryce by using various modifications on it (such as smoothing, eroding, and combining it with other images assigned to an Alpha channel). Once translated to grayscale, an image has the potential to include 256 different altitude variations (see Figure 6.40).

FIGURE 6.40 This object began as a vector drawing in Macromedia Freehand, was ported to Photoshop and saved as a two-color TIFF, and was then translated to an Altitude map in Bryce. A Negative Boolean Cube was used to cut away the base. This is a good technique for creating fancy wrought iron fences.

Redundancy Altitude Maps

This information is not mentioned in the Bryce documentation, and it can help you create startling objects quickly in Bryce.

Here's another awesome technique for creating a variety of Altitude maps for Bryce, a method that uses Bryce itself as the initial image engine! To repeat, an Altitude map is comprised of a series of 256 grays, with each gray standing for a separate altitude as seen from the Top view. The darkest gray (or 100% black) generates the lowest altitude. The lightest gray (100% white) generates the highest altitude. The rest of the gray spectrum produces intermediate altitudes, depending on their range from black to white. The magic of it is, Bryce can produce Altitude maps from your 3D scenes. Here's how:

1. Using a variety of Bryce Primitive objects, create a customized scene. Stack some of the objects on top of one another, resize some larger and some smaller.
2. Delete the Ground Plane, and set the sky to the Pure White backdrop option. This is just for viewing, since this process never renders the sky anyway.
3. Go to the Camera view. Now, here's the necessary alteration: position the objects as if you were looking down on them from the Top view. The rendering will only work as a camera rendering, but in order to create a suitable Altitude map, we have to configure the objects in the Camera view as if they were seen from the Top view.

It doesn't matter how many or where your light(s) are, since the image produced will pay no attention to lights.

4. Turn Normal Antialiasing on. Go to the Documents presets, and select the Distance Render option. Distance Rendering is normally used to produce image masks for Photoshop or compatible applications. Render and save the image.

Notice that the farther the objects are from the camera, the lighter they are. Brightness will translate into "higher" altitudes in the Terrain Editor.

5. Delete all of the objects from the scene. Create a Terrain object or a Symmetrical Lattice in your workspace. With the object selected, go to the Terrain Editor. Click New to remove the object, and click on Picture to load in a graphic.
6. Find the Distance render you just saved, and load it in as an Altitude map. Click on Invert to reverse the altitudes. Use whatever other alteration methods you like to alter the object, or leave it as is. Click on the check mark to write it to the 3D workspace.

The more you explore this technique of object creation, the more adept you will become at foretelling the outcome. Remember that when you generate the object, the Terrain object can then become the subject of another Distance Render, which can then be translated in the Terrain

Editor as another Altitude map. Multi-Replicating the object, and repeating the Distance Rendering over and over again, can lead to a further exploration of this process. The resulting object is textured by the one material. Since every part of it is in one glued together grouping, rendering time and storage space are saved, as compared with the original collection of objects. It's not a complete solution, but it is a way to generate objects that can't be sculpted any other way. This technique can be used to create complex-looking skyscraper facades whose polygon counts are low (see Figures 6.41 and 6.42).

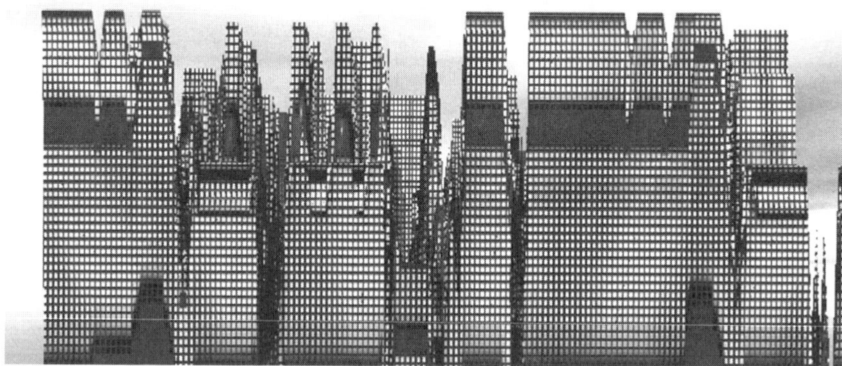

FIGURE 6.41 A modern skyline created with the Reduction method in the Terrain Editor.

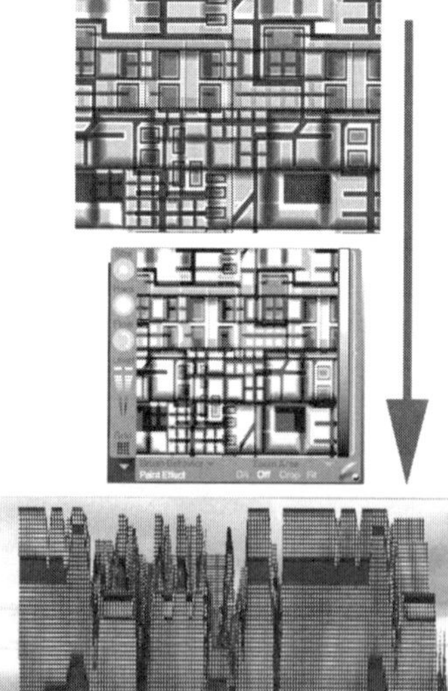

FIGURE 6.42 This figure illustrates the consecutive steps in this unique process, from creating a Camera view of a collection of objects, to the final resulting 3D object. There are infinite variations to explore.

Here's a variation on the previous method. There's more than one way to skin a carrot, and more than one way to perform this object creation option. Instead of using Distance Rendering, use normal Perspective Rendering. Set the objects up so they are seen from the Top view, and select the Pure Black Sky option (delete the Ground Plane). When the rendering is imported as an Altitude map, you won't have to invert it. Make sure that Shadows are turned off on all objects, or the shadows will become object data.

You can also render Altitude maps in Bryce from the Render options. These renderings show the actual height of objects, with white being high and black being low. Although Distance Renders will only work from the Camera view, Altitude Renders work in any view. To get grayscale maps from the Top view, you have to move the object up or down in the World Y-axis.

1. Create a row of seven Spheres. Group them, and Duplicate twice. Rotate the groups so that they each use the first Sphere as in a stack, as seen from the Top view. Move each group to a different height (Y-axis), using the Front and/or Right views as a guide.
2. Delete the Ground Plane, and set the sky to the Pure Black backdrop option. This render process does render the backdrop color.
3. Go to the Top view. Use the Altitude option in the Render selections with Normal Antialiasing on, and render the view. Export the image to disk.

It doesn't matter how or where your light(s) are, since the image produced will pay no attention to lights, only to the comparative altitude of the objects. Notice that the closer the objects are to your eye from any view, the lighter they are. Brightness will translate into "higher" altitudes in the Terrain Editor.

4. Delete all of the objects from the scene. Create a Terrain object or a Symmetrical Lattice in your workspace. With the object selected, go to the Terrain Editor. Click New to remove the object, and click Picture to load in a graphic.
5. Find the Altitude render you just saved, and load it in as a Terrain Editor Altitude map. No need to invert the map this time, since with a black background, altitudes are in the expected places. Use whatever other alteration methods you like to alter the object, or leave it as is. Sincc spheres are translated into poles by this method, you could use an Erode brush effect to give them scraggly surfaces, and use them as a tree group. Click on the check mark to write the object to the Bryce workspace (see Figure 6.43).

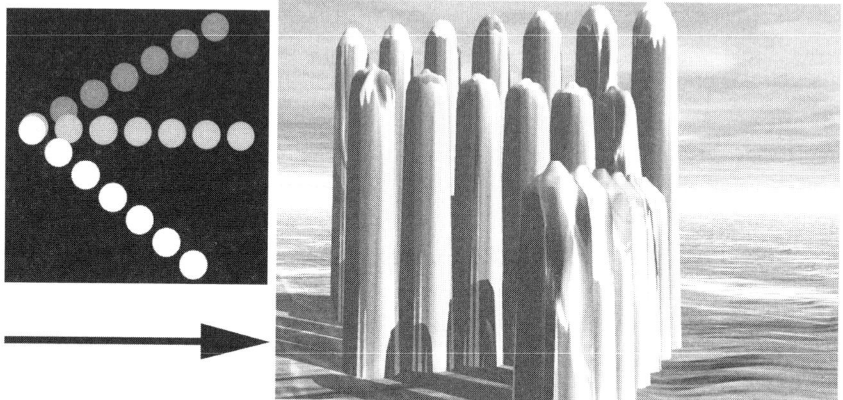

FIGURE 6.43 From a stack of spheres to a finished group of poles, using the Altitude rendering method as a precursor to Terrain mapping creates useful objects.

Every Material Is an Object!

If you can turn bitmaps into objects in the Terrain Editor, then it doesn't matter what application generates the original bitmaps. Bryce can generate bitmaps, so Bryce itself can transform them into objects. Bryce can wrap objects in Materials, and some of these materials make perfect Altitude maps. Here's how to translate a selected material into an Altitude map.

1. Create a Flat Plane as seen from the Camera view. Zoom in on it so that it fills the entire screen.
2. Go to the Materials Presets, and select the Miscellaneous/Urban Dwelling material for the plane.
3. With Normal Antialiasing on, render the Camera view. Save the image.
4. Place a Terrain object on the screen, and go to the Terrain Editor. Click New to begin a new object, and import the bitmap of the material wrapped plane you just saved.
5. Tweak as necessary, and write the new Terrain object to your Bryce world.

After importing a material as a Terrain map, try using the Elevation and Effects tools on it to give it more complexity and character (see Figure 6.44).

The Filtering Tab

Any of the models we have developed and investigated in this chapter can be customized and explored further by using the graph options in the

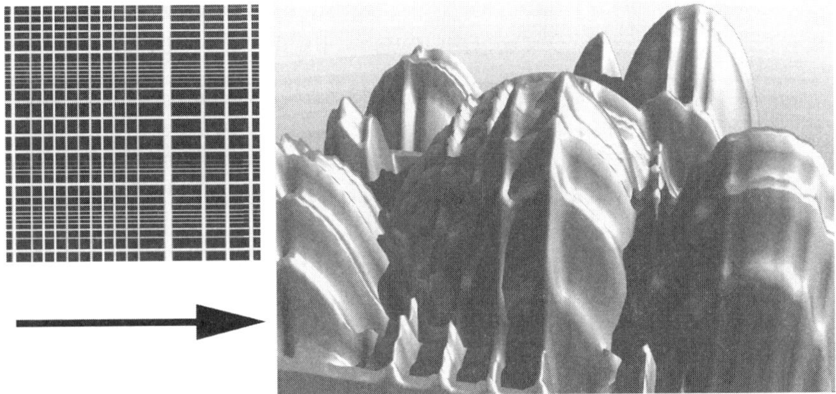

FIGURE 6.44 Every material you use or customize in Bryce can be transformed into a Terrain object. This cityscape began as a Bryce material, and by importing the graphic into the Terrain Editor, and painting in the domed elevations, it was transformed into a 3D object.

Filter tab in the Editing Tools window of the Terrain Editor (see Figure 6.45). Filters are preset modification operations, represented by graphs, that apply global reshaping processes to the Terrain model. The shape of the Filter curve compares to a silhouette of a cross-section of the intended effect. If there is no Terrain model present, the filter process will create a stand-in model. The Elevation and Effects brushes are fully functional when you are in the Filters environment. Here's one method to use when you want to test filtering options on your models.

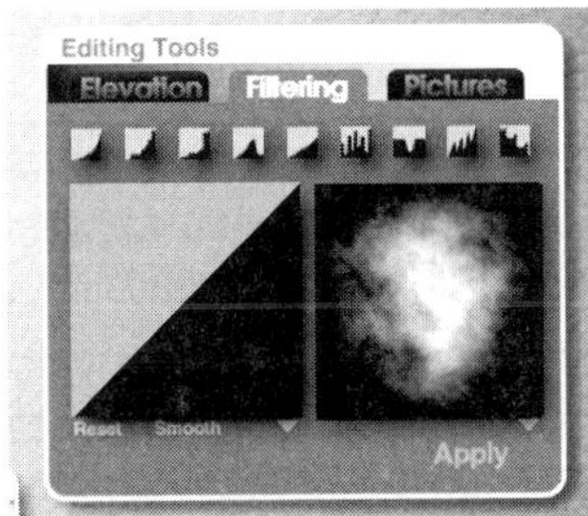

FIGURE 6.45 The Filtering tab in the Editing Tools window of the Terrain Editor.

1. After bringing in a Terrain object, or creating one in the General tab from either painting tools or an imported picture, switch to the Filter tab.
2. Notice that your topography appears in two places: in a preview screen of the Filter tab, and in its customary position at the right of the

tab. You can continue painting on the topography in the customary view. The topography preview displays whatever filter has been selected, and how it will affect your model if/when it is applied.

If you click and hold on the Filter preview, the 3D preview model will change to what it will look like when the filter is applied, and snap back when you release the mouse button (Left Mouse Button for Windows users). It is important to do this regularly, since it gives you a comprehensive look at the potential changes.

3. Click on one of the Filter presets, or draw your own in the left-hand Filter window. Notice that the right-hand preview of the topography changes to match the filter operation. Click Smoothing as many times as needed to smooth out the Filter curve a step at a time.
4. Click the Reset button at any time to return the Filter preview to the same topography as your original model, as shown in the topography on the main Edit screen to the right.
5. Using the downward-pointing arrow beneath the Filter window, access the Filter parameter options list to explore applying Vertical, Horizontal, Vertical Add, or Horizontal Add modifiers of the Filter shape to your model. Although these operations instantly alter your model in real time, you can always click on the Undo function in the General tab to start over again.

Remember that the Undo function only covers one operation, and that altering your model more than once in succession will mean that only the last operation can be undone. Unless you are just exploring, or know exactly where you are headed, alter your model one step at a time.

6. Apply as many filters, or customize each in the drawing window, as you like, paying attention to the preview topography as you go. When you reach a satisfactory point in your filtering process, apply the filtering alterations to the model. See Figure 6.46 for examples of how one model was altered in the Terrain Editor by just Filtering transformations. You must be willing to spend time exploring the Filtering process to get the hang of it.

If you have the RAM that allows you to run more than one application at a time, you can decrease the amount of time it takes to port a graphic to the Terrain Editor as a Topographical map. Just copy the selected graphic to the Clipboard in the painting application, and paste it in the picture slot in Bryce. This allows you to preview the intended object much faster than saving it to disk and reading it again. It also fosters a more robust exploration of image-to-object translation.

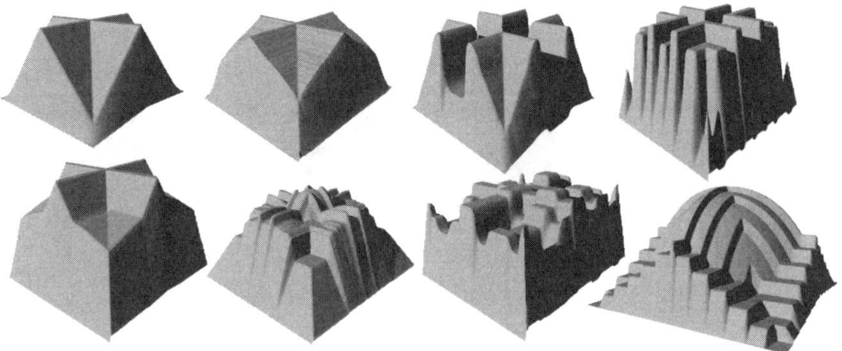

FIGURE 6.46 The original model, our by-now familiar Cross Ridges 2 preset, is shown at the upper left, while the rest of the models are variations created by using different types of Filtering options in the Terrain Editor.

A FRACTAL F/X ENCYCLOPEDIA

In the Terrain Editor's Editing window, under the Elevation tab, is the Fractals effect. If you click and slide your LMB over the button next to this effect, a Bryce Classic Fractal is applied to your Elevation map, creating spiky artifacts on your Terrain model. Many Bryce users, however, miss seeing the small downward-pointing arrow next to the Fractals effect, a place where even more magic resides. Clicking on this arrow opens the Fractals options list, which holds 27 different fractal types that can be applied. By default, the Bryce Classic fractal is selected, but you can choose any of the others to affect your Terrain map. In Figures 6.48 through 6.52, all of the 27 fractal types are shown as applied to a default terrain. Use these examples as a visual encyclopedia when you need a reference that shows you what each of the 27 options does. Of course, you can always apply more than one fractal, and you can paint the fractal effects on with your Effects brush.

Painting Fractal Effects

When you want to paint the Fractal Effects on your Elevation map, as opposed to applying the effect globally, do the following:

1. Go to the Terrain canvas window in the Terrain Editor. Click the Menu icon at the top right, next to the arrow. The options will appear (see Figure 6.47).
2. Under Paint Behavior, open the list and select Paint Effect.
3. Hold down the Spacebar, and select one of the Fractal options from the list.

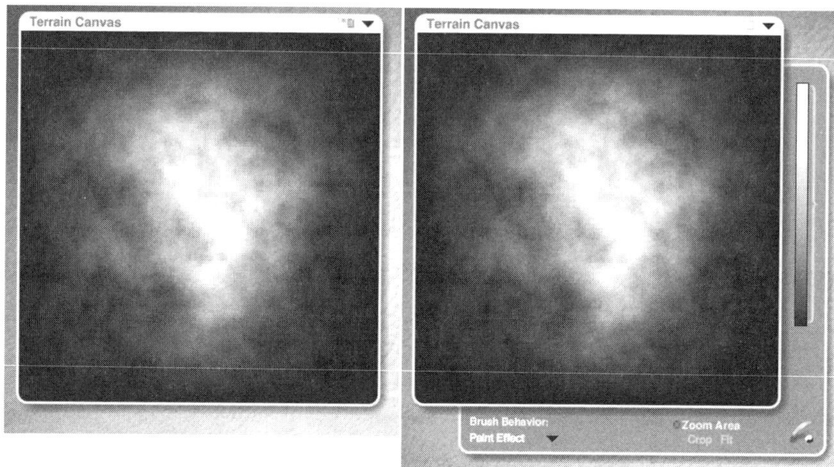

FIGURE 6.47 On the left, the options are hidden. On the right, after clicking on the Menu icon, the options appear.

4. Scale your brush size as needed, and paint the selected Fractal Effect on the canvas.

See Figures 6.48 through 6.52 for a visual encyclopedia of all 27 Fractal Effects. Use these images to get an idea of what each Fractal Effect does to a terrain.

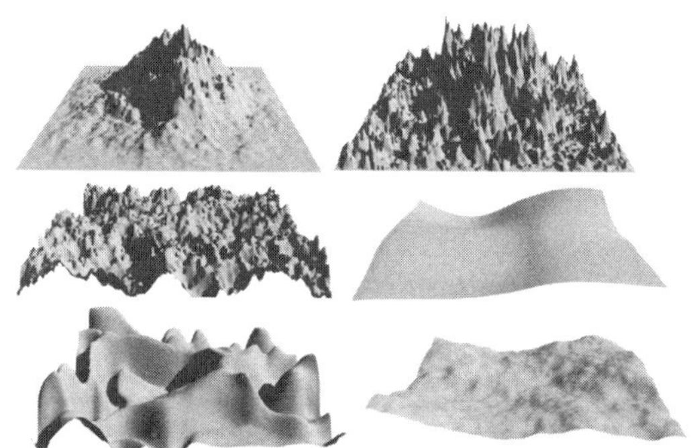

FIGURE 6.48 Upper left to lower right: The default terrain with no Fractal Effects applied, Bryce Classic Fractal, Ridged MultiFractal, Perlin Hills, Rounded Dunes, and Classic Fractal (different from Bryce Classic fractal).

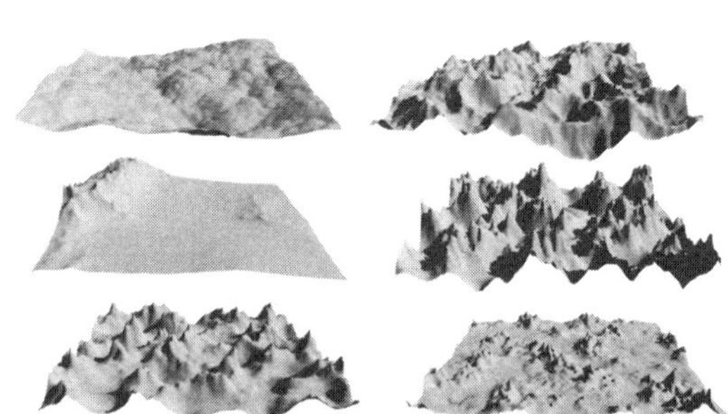

FIGURE 6.49 Upper left to lower right: Round Hills, Slick Rock, Ridges, Rolling Hills, Alpine Valleys, and Chaotic.

FIGURE 6.50 Upper left to lower right: Pocked, Crystalline, Lava, Metamorphism, Metamorphosed, and Fractured.

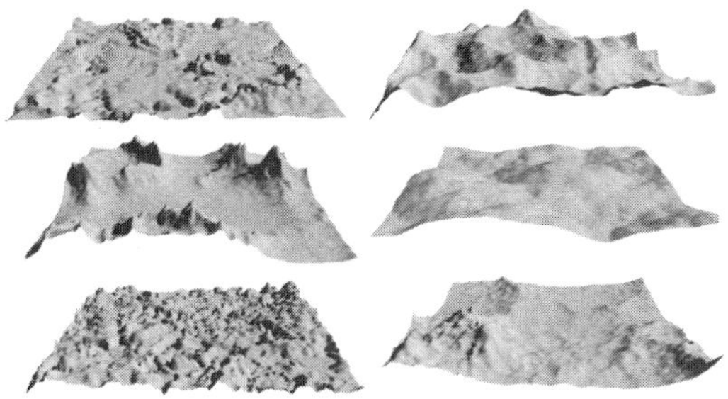

FIGURE 6.51 Upper left to lower right: Weathered Dykes, Warped Slickrock, Warped Ridges, Zorch, Warped Zorch, and Mordor.

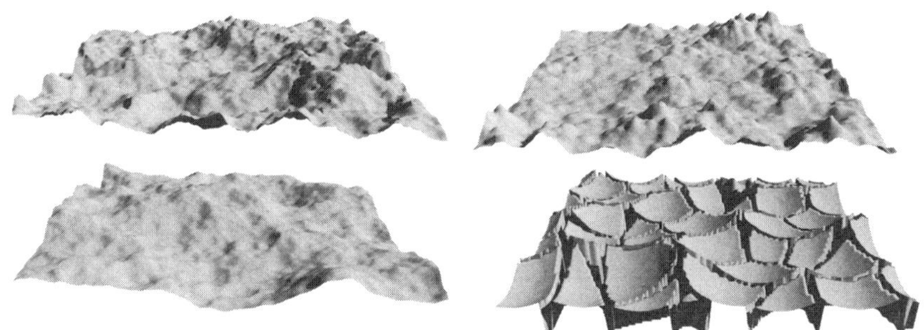

FIGURE 6.52 Upper left to lower right: Shattered Hills, Cauliflower Hills, Planet X, and Mud Cracks.

Note that Figures 6.48 through 6.52 show the 27 Fractal Effects applied globally to a default Terrain model. Also remember that you can click on the Fractal command as many times as you like in the Terrain Editor, and that each click will create a different variation of the same Fractal Effect. Stop when the preview displays one you like.

Tiling Fractal Terrains

At the bottom of the Fractal options are four additional commands that allow you to set up a tiled parameter: North, South, East, and West. Selecting one of these options creates a terrain that when duplicated and moved can be used to create a much larger surface area. This is very useful when you need a larger surface area that has the same appearance as the fractal you set up originally (see Figure 6.53).

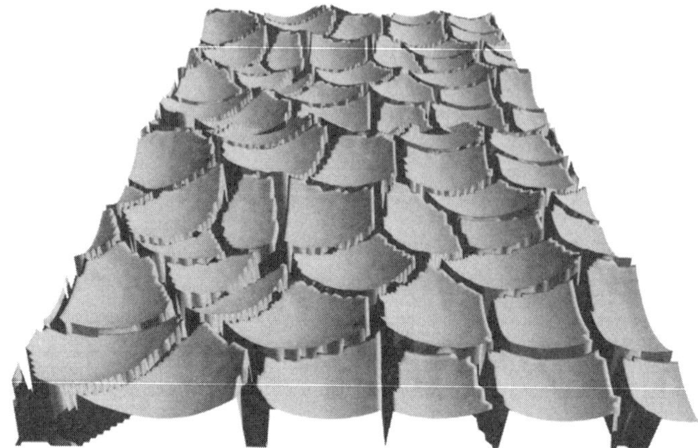

FIGURE 6.53 In this example, the Mud Flats fractal is tiled to the North, enlarging the terrain look.

MOVING ON

In this chapter, we focused on creating and modifying Terrain models. In our next chapter, we explore a related topic: Terrain objects.

CHAPTER

7 Terrain Objects

Now that you have read and worked through the last chapter, and understand how to use the Terrain Editor, it's time to put your knowledge to use to create a more complex model. We're going to create a 3D model of a customized truck, using Terrain modeling techniques and a few other processes you were introduced to previously.

We are using the term *Terrain object* to distinguish what we are doing from creating a *Terrain model*. A Terrain model maintains its terrain-like form (hill, mountain, valley, etc.), while a Terrain object can be used to create any form at all. The similarity between the two is that they are both open to being customized in the terrain editing process. If you have not yet worked through the last chapter, and have no experience with Bryce terrain editing, it is imperative that you return to the last chapter and work through it.

THE SYMMETRICAL LATTICE

The Symmetrical Lattice is a variant, as we have seen, of a Terrain model. We will use the Symmetrical Lattice exclusively in this chapter for our Terrain object needs. This is because the Symmetrical Lattice appears in the Terrain Editor with no Flat Plane to worry about. Click on the Symmetrical Lattice icon in the Create toolbar to place a Symmetrical Lattice in the scene, and open the Terrain Editor to see what we're talking about (see Figure 7.1).

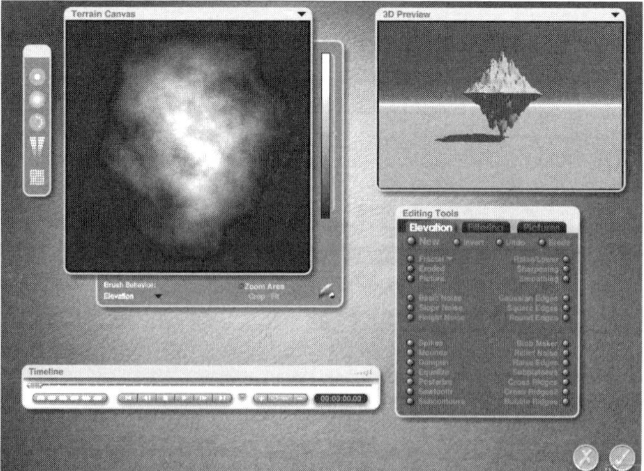

FIGURE 7.1 A Symmetrical Lattice as it appears in the Terrain Editor.

As you can see when you look at the Terrain Canvas window, the Top view of the Symmetrical Lattice shows a dark red area around the object. This red area indicates that there is no data present. If this were a Terrain model, you would see a black area around the model, which would indicate that there is data present, a Flat Plane.

Move the Elevation Brush Color (the red dot in the left-hand slider) all the way to the bottom. This allows you to paint in the dark red color that removes anything you paint over. Use an Elevation brush to paint out about 50% of the edges of the Symmetrical Lattice. Look at the 3D Preview to appreciate what you have accomplished (see Figure 7.2).

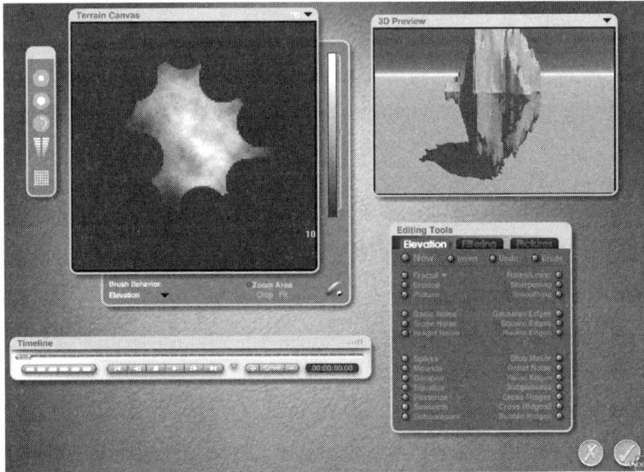

FIGURE 7.2 Paint out the edge data of the Symmetrical Lattice with an Elevation brush set to the dark red color.

Click New in the Editing Tools window. The Symmetrical Lattice disappears, and the Terrain Canvas is completely dark red. You are still in Symmetrical Lattice mode, however, so anything you paint in the Terrain Canvas window will have the same vertical symmetry as a Symmetrical Lattice. Move the color slider to the top position to select a maximum white color, indicating the highest elevation, and paint down a large circle in the Terrain Canvas. You have created a cylindrical object (see Figure 7.3).

Actually, as you can see, the object is a bit more barrel-like, with somewhat rounded edges at the top and bottom. It also has a few jagged anomalies at the center. These are artifacts of the terrain editing process. Sometimes, through smoothing and other devices, you can reduce these artifacts, but most times, you'll just have to live with them. Remember that

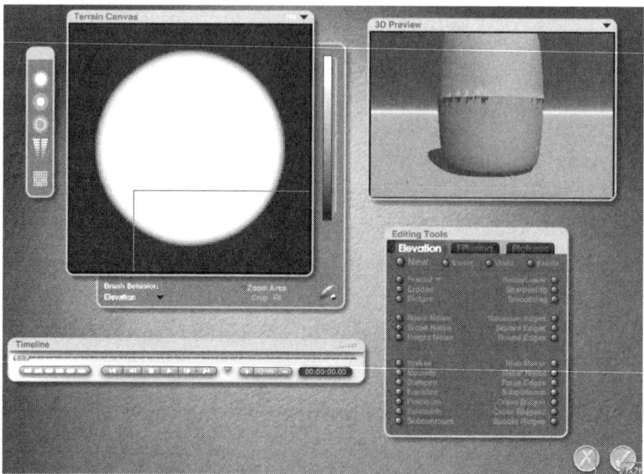

FIGURE 7.3 Create a cylindrical object.

the terrain editing process in Bryce, whether applied to terrains or symmetrical lattices, was not really designed to create other objects. The fact that you can use it for that purpose creatively stretches the capabilities of Bryce.

With your cylindrical object still in place, drill a hole in it. This is accomplished by selecting a smaller brush size, and using the lowest color setting (the dark red color) (see Figure 7.4).

Using variations of these preparatory steps will allow you to create some pretty complex objects for your Bryce worlds. Let's proceed with our truck. Do the following:

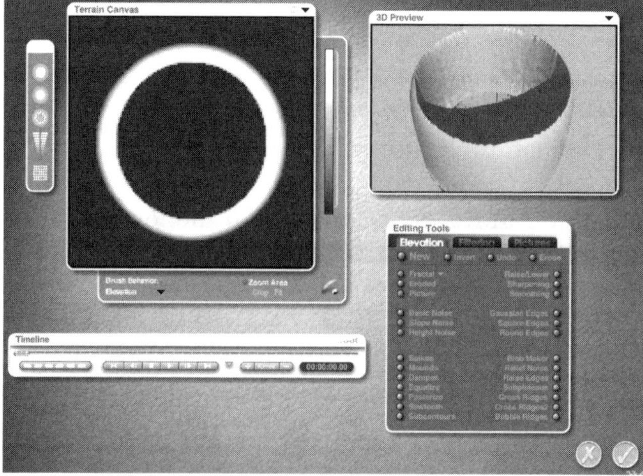

FIGURE 7.4 Drill a hole in the cylindrical object.

1. Place a Symmetrical Lattice in your scene, and open the Terrain Editor.
2. Click New. This erases the object. Use a maximum height (white) Elevation brush to paint a large white area on the Canvas.
3. Using the minimum (dark red) Elevation brush, reshape the area so that it resembles Figure 7.5.

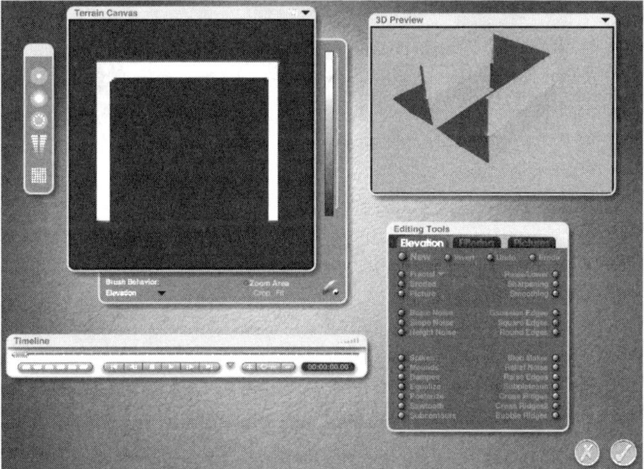

FIGURE 7.5 Create this shape.

Remember to hold the Shift key down to create straight edges.

4. Close the Editor. The resulting object should resemble Figure 7.6.
5. Create a Cubic object. Color it black, and make it Negative. Use a red material on the Symmetrical Lattice object, and make it Positive.

FIGURE 7.6 Your object should resemble this illustration.

FIGURE 7.7 Cut some window holes in the cab.

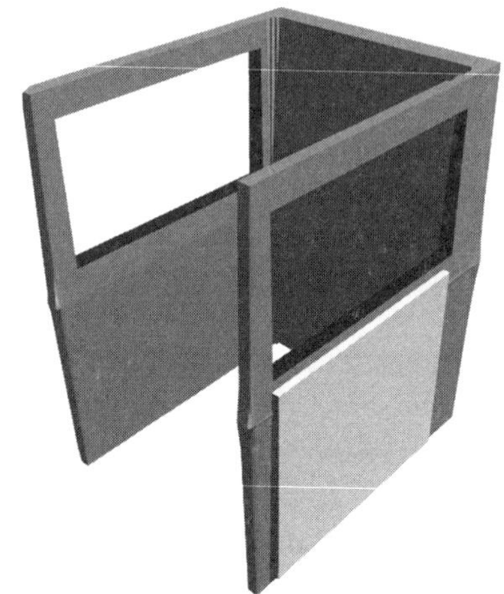

FIGURE 7.8 Create and place door panels.

Place the Negative Cubic object so that it cuts window holes in the truck cab, as shown in Figure 7.7.

6. Use flattened Cubes for the door panels. Make them yellow, and place in position (see Figure 7.8).
7. We'll group things again a bit later, so don't worry about that now. Create side windows from much-flattened Cubes, and place in position. Use a bluish glass material on them (see Figure 7.9).
8. For the front window, we'll use an edited Symmetrical Lattice. Place a Symmetrical Lattice in the scene, and open the Editor. Select New, and use Elevation brushes (maximum and minimum) to create the form shown in Figure 7.10.

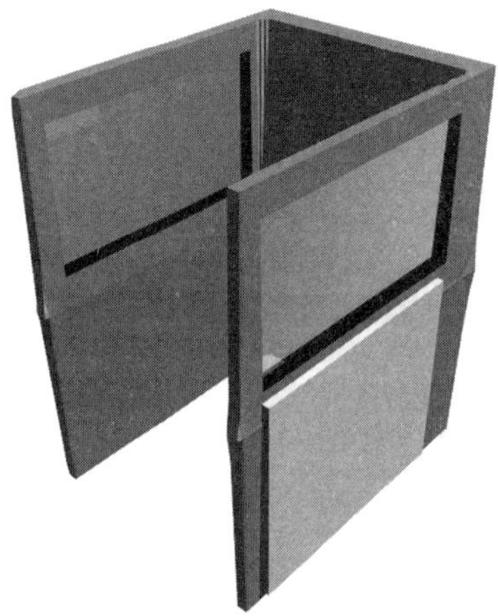

FIGURE 7.9 Add some glass windows.

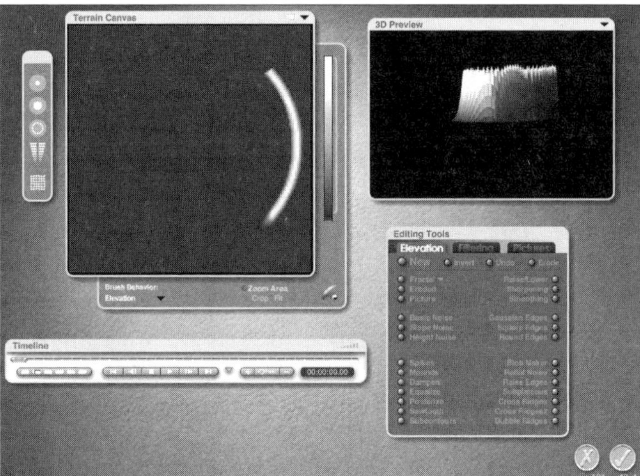

FIGURE 7.10 Create this form.

9. Place the object in your scene, and map with a blue-green glass material. Scale it so that it can be used as the front windshield, and tilt the top backward slightly. Don't worry about the ragged edges at the top and bottom, because they will be hidden later on (see Figure 7.11).
10. Create the cab roof by using two Cubic primitives, one Positive and one Negative, as a Boolean group. The final roof should slope toward the front of the cab (see Figure 7.12).
11. Place a Symmetrical Lattice in the scene and Edit. Select New. Create the form shown in Figure 7.13.

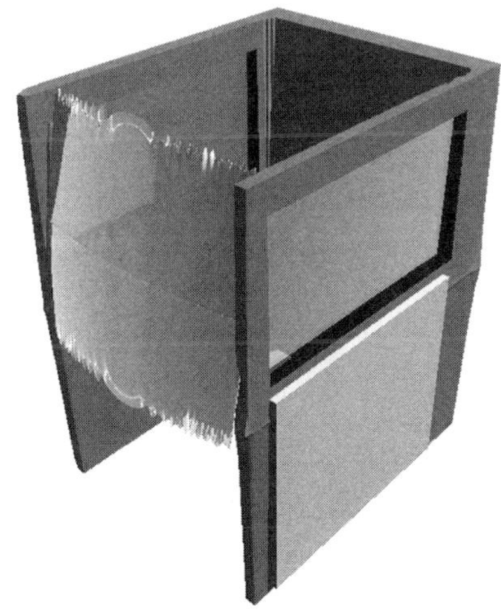

FIGURE 7.11 Create the front windshield.

FIGURE 7.12 Create and place the cab roof.

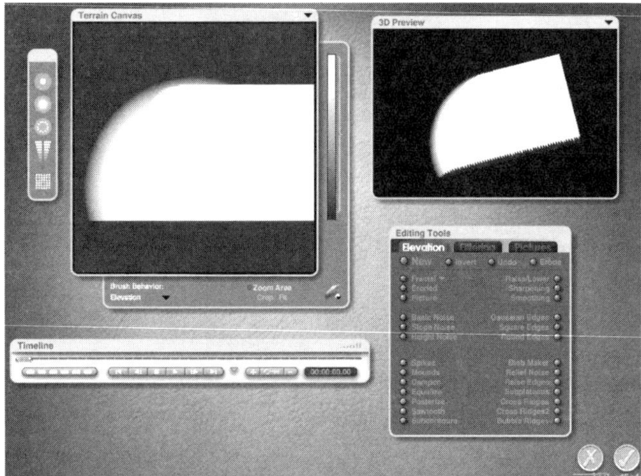

FIGURE 7.13 Create this form for the hood.

FIGURE 7.14 A perfect hood!

12. Notice how perfect this process is for the hood. When scaled, rotated, and placed, the normal seam that separates one half of the symmetrical lattice from its opposite half is perfect for the hood (see Figure 7.14).
13. Now for the connecting part of the cab that attaches to the rear bed. Create the form shown in Figure 7.15 by using the now familiar Symmetrical Lattice method.
14. Scale and place the connecting frame at the back of the cab, as shown in Figure 7.16. Give it a flat black color.

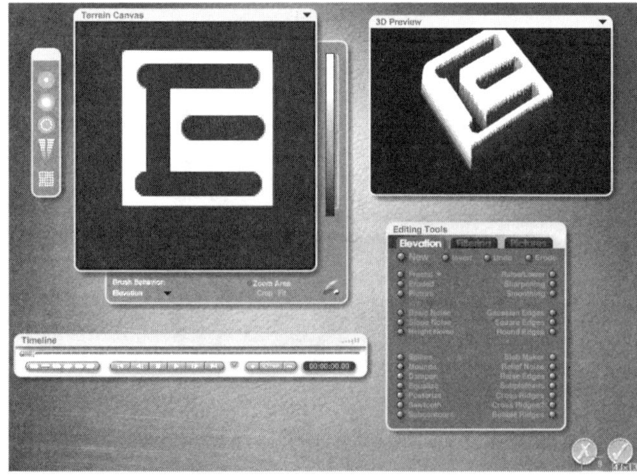

FIGURE 7.15 Create this form.

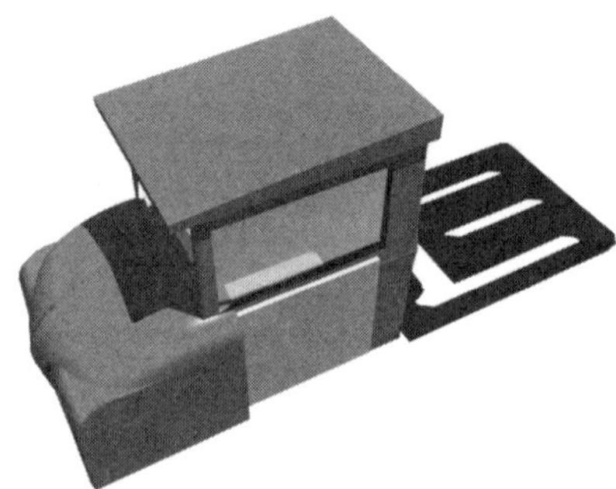

FIGURE 7.16 Place the frame as shown.

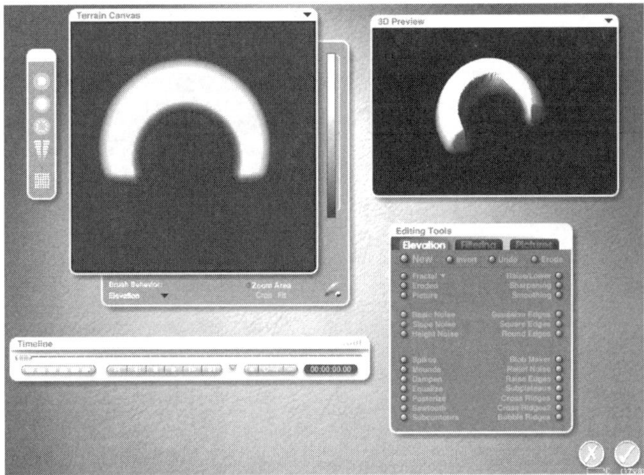

FIGURE 7.17 Create a basic fender.

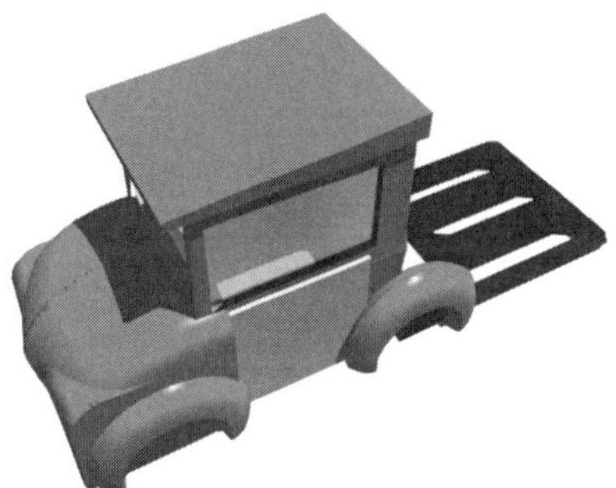

FIGURE 7.18 The fenders are placed in position, two on each side.

15. Create a basic fender by using the Symmetrical Lattice method (refer to Figure 7.17).
16. Duplicate, Scale as needed, and place four fenders (refer to Figure 7.18).
17. Place a box at the back of the can that rests on the frame (see Figure 7.19).
18. Create half of the front grill using the Symmetrical Lattice method. You can explore your own design options, or use the form shown in Figure 7.20.

FIGURE 7.19 A box is added.

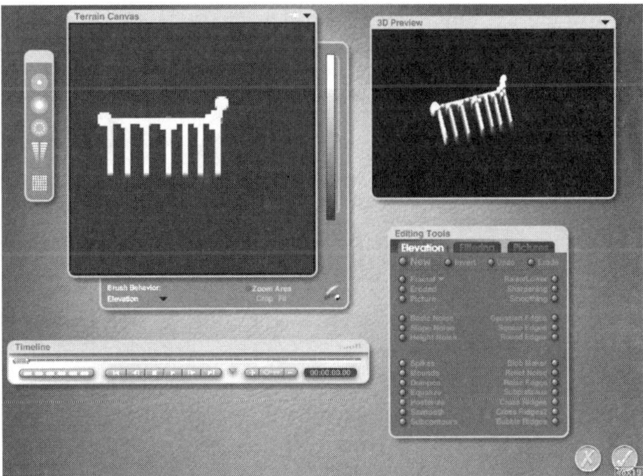

FIGURE 7.20 Design half of the front grill.

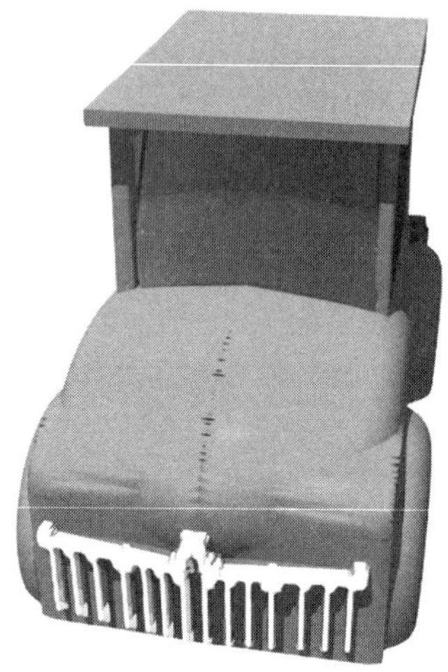

FIGURE 7.21 The grill is added.

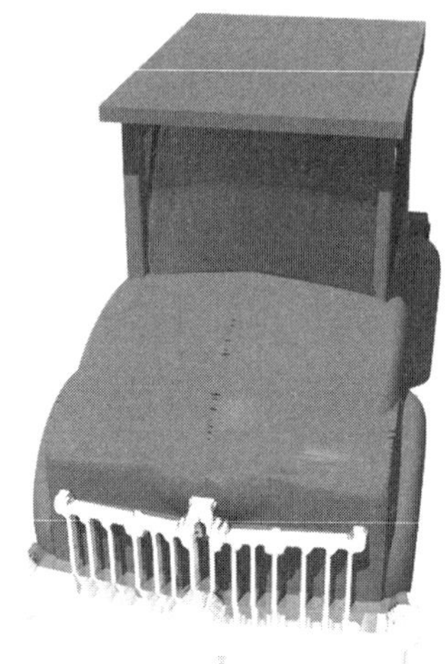

FIGURE 7.22 Create and place a front bumper.

19. Scale, Rotate, and place one half of the grill. Duplicate and Mirror (flip on the X-axis) to create the other half. Apply a chrome material (see Figure 7.21).
20. Using the same basic technique you just used to create the grill, create half of the bumper. Use your own design (see Figure 7.22).
21. Using the symmetrical lattice method, use your own imagination to create a profile of the hood ornament. Don't worry too much about detail, since it will be fairly small (see Figures 7.23 and 7.24).

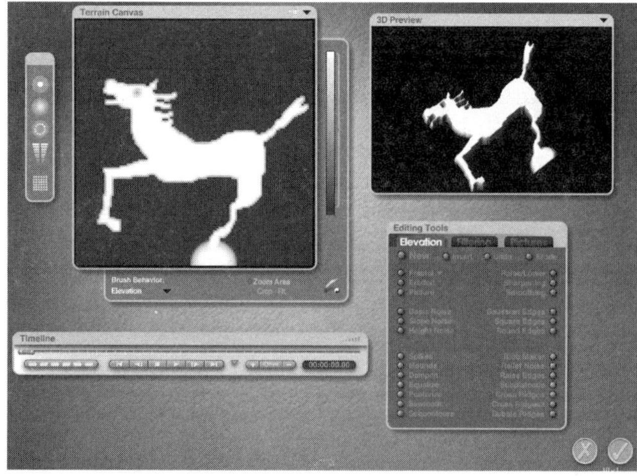

FIGURE 7.23 Here's one idea.

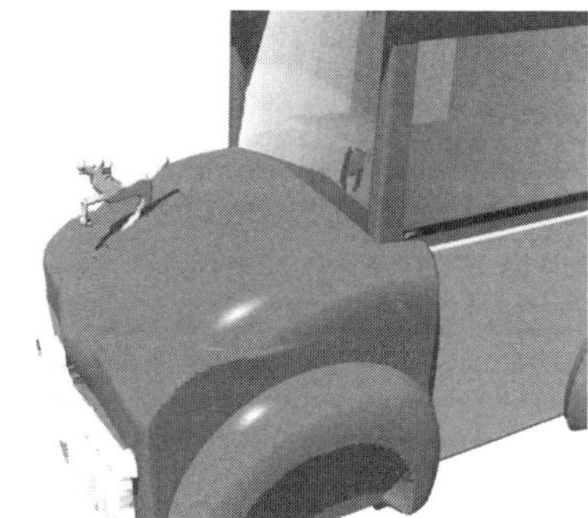

FIGURE 7.24 Scale, position, and place the hood ornament.

Then again… If you want a more realistic hood ornament, you can create a silhouette (or import a clip art one) and use it as the Elevation map. You could also import a horse model from CuriousLabs' Poser, but that would be a lot of polygons added to the scene. It all depends on how close you intend the camera to be to the hood ornament, how much RAM your system has, and the extent of your hard drive space.

22. Let's place a couple of horns on the hood. To do this, create the horns from elongated Cones, and use additional Cones as Boolean cutters to create a hollowed-out cavity (see Figure 7.25).
23. Using the same concept that you used to create the horns, create and place a cylindrical smokestack for the exhaust (see Figure 7.26).

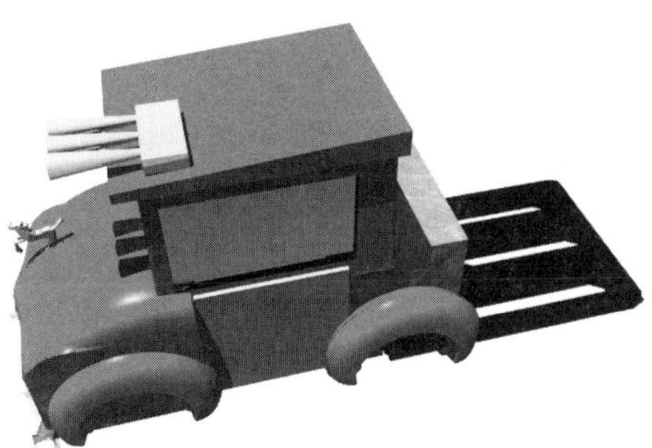

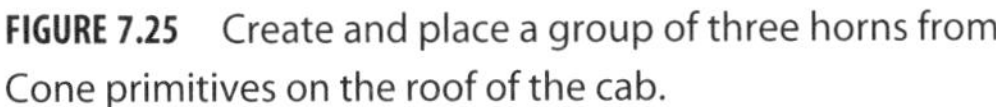

FIGURE 7.25 Create and place a group of three horns from Cone primitives on the roof of the cab.

FIGURE 7.26 Create the exhaust pipe.

24. Create a light from three Cones. Make one Cone Positive, and a slightly smaller one Negative to cut a cavity in the Positive Cone. Make both chrome. Make a third Cone about the same size as the Negative Cone, and color it with whatever color you want the light to be. Group all three cones. Duplicate as needed, and place (see Figure 7.27).
25. Three more steps, and the cab will be complete. Create door handles from scaled Cubic primitives, and place.
26. Create some side mirrors from two scaled Cylinders for the struts, and a flattened Cylinder for the mirror. Group, and place on each side (see Figure 7.28).

FIGURE 7.27 Create and place some lights.

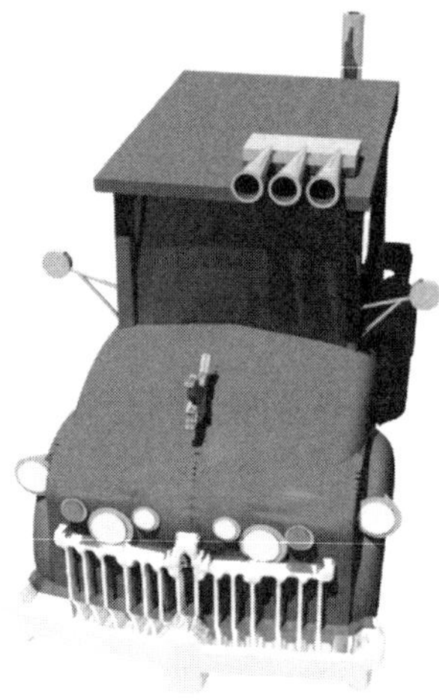

FIGURE 7.28 Create and place side mirrors.

27. Use the Symmetrical Lattice method to create the form shown in Figure 7.29.
28. The form you just created should be Rotated, Scaled, Duplicated, and positioned as the two running boards between the truck's fenders (see Figure 7.30).
29. Select all of the elements you have created so far, and Group them. Name the Group *Truck Cab*. Save it to your Objects Library folder.

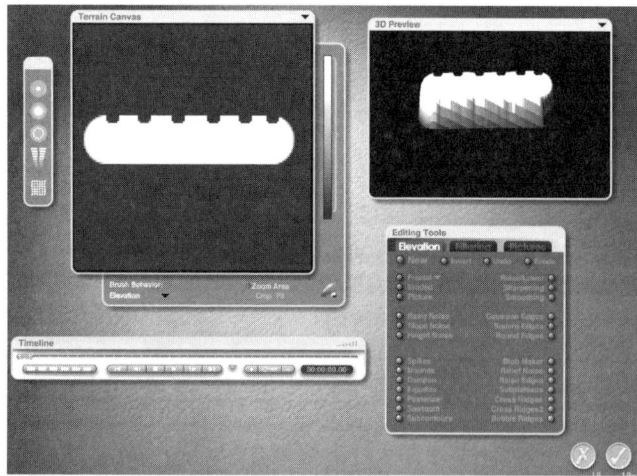

FIGURE 7.29 Create this form using the Symmetrical Lattice method.

FIGURE 7.30 The running boards are placed in position.

Tires

As you can see, the truck can doesn't have any tires yet. Let's create a tire. Do the following:

1. With a symmetrical lattice in your workspace, open the Editor and click on New. Create a large circle with the maximum white brush, and a smaller medium-gray circle inside of it.
2. Notch the edges of the larger circle with a dark red to cut away all content (refer to Figure 7.31).

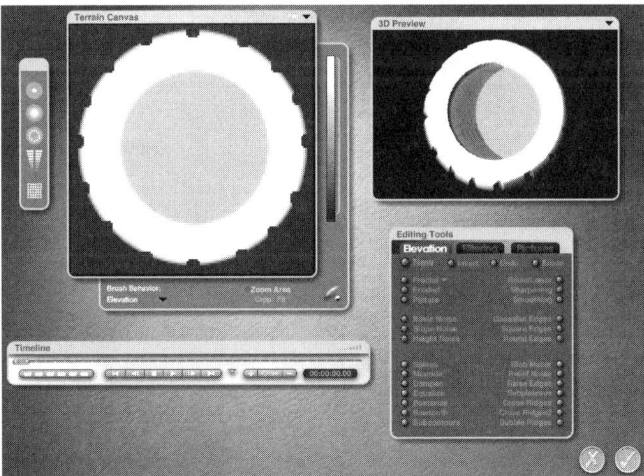

FIGURE 7.31 Create this form.

3. Place the object in your scene, and color it black.
4. Place another symmetrical lattice in the scene, and open the Editor and select New. This time, we'll create the internal part of the tire. Create a form that resembles that shown in Figure 7.32 with various-sized Elevation brushes.
5. Scale and Rotate as needed. Place the internal part of the tire inside the outer tire, and Group. Name it Tire1 (see Figure 7.33).
6. Duplicate to create all four tires for the truck cab. Link each tire to the cab (see Figure 7.34).

If your project demands it, you can always create a seat, steering wheel, and other additional components inside of the cab.

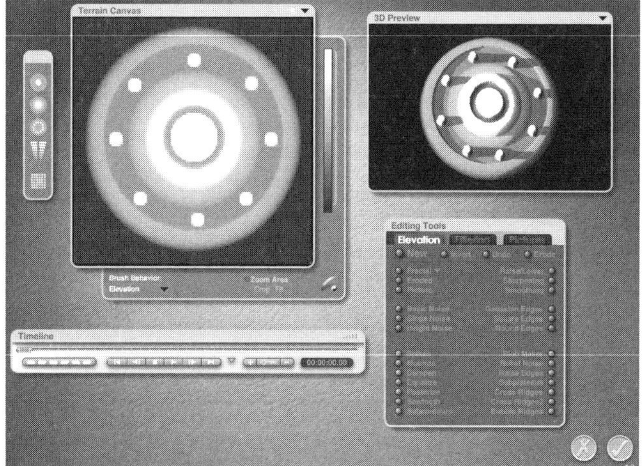

FIGURE 7.32 Create this form.

FIGURE 7.33 A finished tire.

FIGURE 7.34 The tires are positioned and linked to the truck cab.

The Trailer

Compared to the cab, the trailer is a simple matter. You already have the wheels. The trailer form can be cylindrical for a fuel or milk truck, or box-like for the standard hauling rig. It can also be a flatbed, with some additional item loaded on it. Once you have saved the truck cab to your Objects Library, you can use it for a multitude of purposes and projects. Create any trailer type you like, and link some wheels to it. Figure 7.35 shows one possible example.

FIGURE 7.35 Here's one trailer example for the truck.

A Logo

Here's one way to create a scalable logo for your truck. This method works best when the logo area is flat. Do the following:

1. Create the contents of your logo in a 2D paint or drawing application (like Photoshop, Painter, FreeHand, Illustrator, or another suitable application). Also create an Alpha channel for the image content so its background will drop out. Save the image as a TIF file (see Figure 7.36).

FIGURE 7.36 On the left is the image content, and on the right the Alpha channel content. Your image content will, of course, look different.

FIGURE 7.37 Locate and place your logo image in an empty Picture Editor slot.

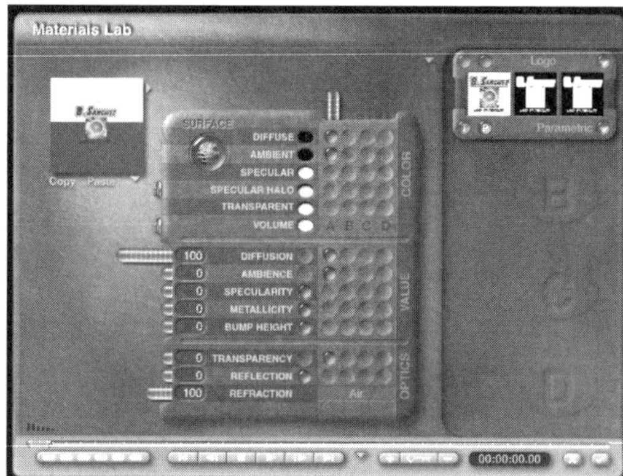

FIGURE 7.38 Use this configuration setting.

2. In Bryce, create a 2D Picture Object. When the Picture Editor pops up, place your logo in an empty slot (see Figure 7.37).
3. Configure the Materials Lab exactly as shown in Figure 7.38.
4. Your logo maps perfectly to the 2D Picture Object in Bryce, and the background drops out (see Figure 7.39).
5. Save the mapped 2D Picture Object to your Objects Library. Open your truck project.
6. Import the 2D Picture Object you saved earlier. Scale and Duplicate as needed. Place the logo on the truck where you want it to appear, and Group it with the truck trailer and/or cab (see Figure 7.40).

FIGURE 7.39 The logo appears in Bryce.

FIGURE 7.40 The truck with the logos attached.

License Plate

Using a similar process you engaged in to create the logo for the truck, you can also create a license plate or plates. Do the following:

1. Create the image for the license plate in a 2D-image application (see Figure 7.41).
2. Using Object Front mapping, place the image on a flattened Cube with similar dimensions to the image. Duplicate and Rotate for both plates, and place and Link to the cab and trailer (see Figure 7.42).

ON THE CD

This truck model weighs in at about 3MB, and has over a million polygons. It can be found in the Projects folder on the CD-ROM that accompanies this book.

FIGURE 7.41 Create your license plate's image content.

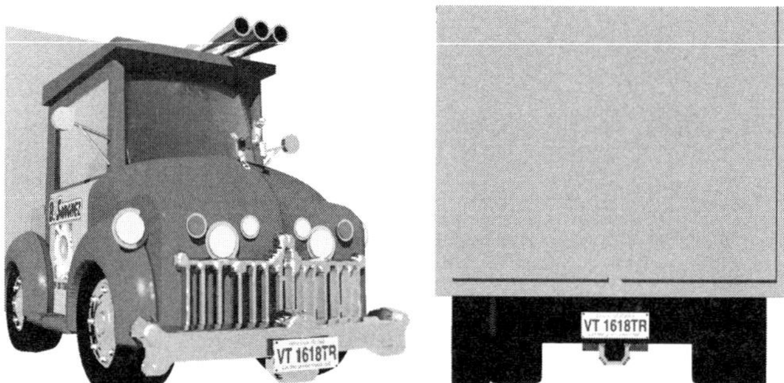

FIGURE 7.42 The plates are positioned and Linked.

MOVING ON

In this chapter, we demonstrated how to use the Symmetrical Lattice as a base component for creating non-terrain forms. In the next chapter, we'll take a closer look at 2D Picture Objects.

CHAPTER

8 2D Picture Objects

A 2D Picture Object is an image mapped to a plane, usually with a transparent background. Using 2D Picture Objects, you can add hundreds of elements to a Bryce world without the memory overhead that would be necessary if all of those elements were 3D models. There is a problem, however. The liability is that 2D Picture Objects have no real depth, or Z dimension. If a 2D Picture Object is mapped to a Flat Plane (which is usually the case), placing the camera at an angle other than perpendicular to the plane will result in the image seemingly warping. If the output is to be an image, this can be compensated for by rotating the plane so it remains perpendicular to the camera. The real problems arise in an animated view of the scene; any movement of the camera might reveal that the 2D Picture Object is not really a 3D model, but merely a flat planar image map. As long as the camera doesn't rotate to reveal the "edge" of the mapped 2D Picture Plane, an animation can be carefully constructed without any anomalies.

The 2D Picture Object icon is located in the Create toolbar, and is shaped like a Hermetic Man with multiple limbs (see Figure 8.1).

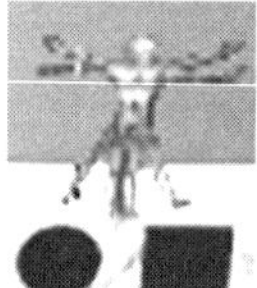

FIGURE 8.1 The icon for the 2D Picture Object.

Clicking this icon will place a vertical 2D Picture Object plane in the scene, and automatically open the Texture Source Editor so you can find the image you want to reference.

WHAT YOU NEED TO KNOW

In order to do the tutorials in this chapter, you need to know the following,:

- How to place a 2D Picture Object in a scene
- How to place content in the Texture Source Editor
- How to create Alpha Channel images or Layers in a paint application
- How to use Alpha Channel data in Bryce
- General mapping procedures for Bryce Materials
- Working with Photoshop plug-ins

- How to create a Stone with the Stone icon
- How to use Poser if you own it

Mastering the Materials Lab Controls

In this tutorial, you will refresh your knowledge concerning the image controls in the Materials Lab, as they apply to placing a texture on a 2D Picture Object. Do the following:

1. Click the 2D Picture Object icon in the Create toolbar to place a 2D Picture Object in the scene. The Materials Lab opens automatically, waiting for you to locate the image content (see Figure 8.2).

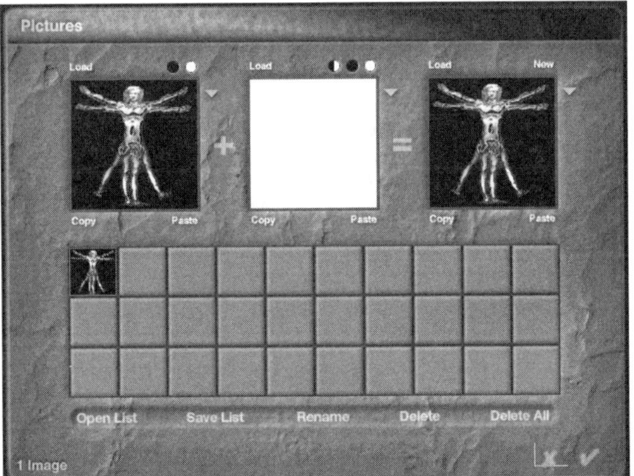

FIGURE 8.2 The Materials Lab opens, displaying the default image.

2. Take note of the three large image areas. The first is for the image content and color, and the second represents Alpha Channel data. Alpha Channel data determines the transparency of the final image. The image and the Alpha Channel data, when combined, create the final image. The final image is displayed in the third image area to the right of the other two. By default, the second image area is solid white. White in the Alpha area means that any content represented by white is opaque. Since the Alpha Channel area is solid white, the result is no transparency. This being the case, the content in the first image area is the same as the final image at the right. It's like saying 1 + 0 = 1.

3. Go to the controls at the top of the Alpha Channel image area, and click on the black circle. This tells Bryce to give the entire image a solid black Alpha channel, which says that in the final image at the right, no image data will be apparent. Notice that this is exactly the case. This is like saying that 1 – 1 = 0.
4. The Alpha Channel image area can reference images as well as solid blocks of color. Click Copy below the first image area, and then click Paste below the Alpha Channel image area. A version of the Hermetic Man image is pasted in the Alpha Channel image area. Look at the final image area to the right. The final image shows the blacks dropped out, so that only the lighter areas remain (see Figure 8.3).

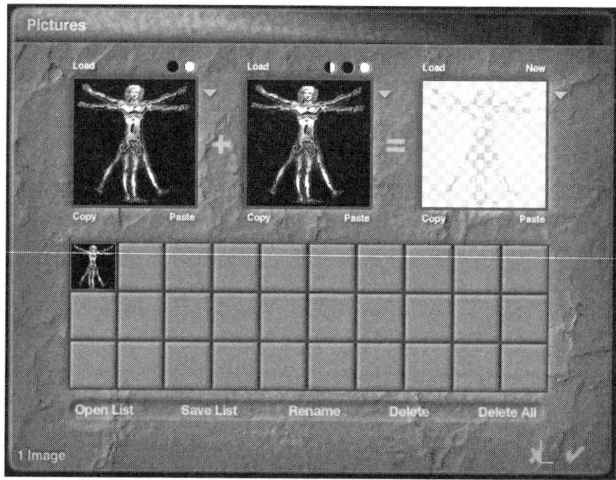

FIGURE 8.3 The blacks have dropped out.

5. What has really happened is that the image in the Alpha Channel area is a grayscale image. Solid blacks in the image are now transparent, and solid whites are opaque. Every other shade of gray has some degree of transparency. Click on the half-black/half-white circle above the Alpha channel, and the whole scheme is reversed in the final image (see Figure 8.4).

There are two reasons why the reversal control is included in the Alpha Channel area. One is that it's a neat way to create transparency effects for your scene. The other is that different graphics and animation software defines 100% transparency as either black or white, so this allows you to adjust your imported image data. accordingly.

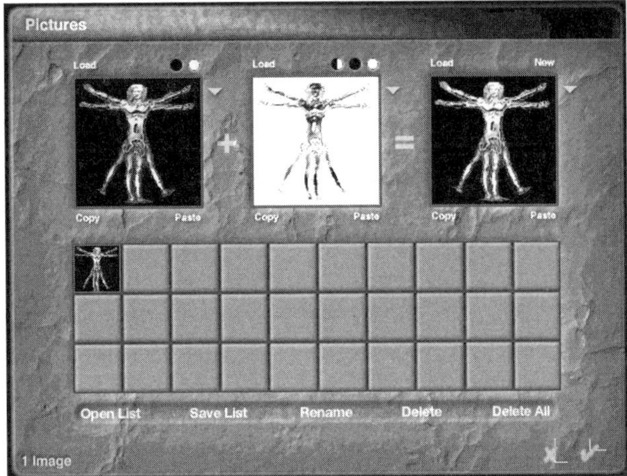

FIGURE 8.4 The transparency/opacity is reversed in the final image.

6. Note that you also have black and white circle controls over the first image area. Using these controls results in the final image being based entirely on the content in the Alpha Channel area, and in a grayscale image. Use this method to create very fast Alpha Channel information. As you know from your work in previous chapters, the Terrain Editor translates grayscale data to 3D object height data, so the Materials Lab can be used in a roundabout way to create 3D object data. Explore this possibility when you have some spare time.
7. Click on any one of the small squares at the bottom of the Texture Source Editor. A File window opens up, allowing you to locate the image content that will be placed in the first image area. You can have a lot of image content ready to use for Material channels by filling these slots, and then applying the images as you like in the Materials Lab.

Creating 2D Picture Content

Creating your own image content for use on a 2D Picture Object is required when you are developing original scenes. Do the following:

1. Open Corel Painter, Photoshop, or any other 2D painting application. We prefer Painter for this exercise because of its unique *Image Hose* tool. If you are using Painter, create an Image Hose composition of flowers on a white or black background. If you are using Photoshop or another application, create a freehand painting of your choice on a black or white background. In either case, do not use the background color for foreground content (see Figure 8.5).

FIGURE 8.5 Here, the Image Hose in Painter is used to create a picture of Green Fronds on a white background.

2. Next, you want to select the background color wherever it appears, and then select Inverse (which selects the image and not the background). Paint the image solid black. If the background is black, paint the image solid white. You'll wind up with a silhouette of the image content.
3. The silhouette is your Alpha Channel content, so save the image with an "A" at the end. For example, if your original image was saved as "Leaves," name this image "LeavesA." That will tell you what the content is when you look for it later.
4. In Bryce, place a 2D Picture Object in the scene. When the Materials Lab opens, click on a new slot. Place the color image in the first preview area, and load the Alpha image into the Alpha Channel area. Click the reverse control if you need to, and the content without the background will appear in the final image area (see Figure 8.6).
5. Accept the texture. Duplicate the 2D Picture Object a few times in the scene, and move the duplicates at random distances from each other front to back. Keep the camera level with the objects. You have created a large amount of image data for the scene without taking up anything near the amount of memory that a similar 3D object would require. This is the best way to create details in the distance, like

FIGURE 8.6 The final image will be the data without the background.

forests or crowds or flocks, thereby saving the placement of your 3D objects for the foreground (see Figure 8.7).

Image/Alpha content mapped to a plane will cast shadows and reflections just as a 3D object does, although camera placement must be taken into consideration.

FIGURE 8.7 Although only you will know that the content is just an image mapped to a plane, the viewer will see this as a collection of 3D objects.

Alpha to 3D Object

The rest of the tutorials in this chapter will use the Fronds.tif, FrondsA.tif, Moss1.tif, and Moss1A.tif images in the Images folder on the companion CD-ROM.

Bryce figures that you are going to map Alpha/image data to planes because you want to use the resulting object as non-warped background content. However, what if you know that the content will warp, and in fact are planning on it? Then, of course, your creative options suddenly expand. Let's explore this a bit. Do the following:

The advantage of mapping objects as opposed to planes is that they exist in 3D. That means that no matter where the camera is placed, the object will still be appreciated, although you might have to adjust the initial texture placement to make sure everything looks okay from selected vantage points. Please note that strictly speaking, whether the targeted object is a 2D Picture Plane or a true 3D object, the result is still a Picture-based object.

1. Place a Sphere in the scene. Open the Sphere's Materials Lab.
2. Go to the Texture Resource Editor in the Sphere's Materials Lab.
3. Place buttons in the Texture A column for Diffuse, Diffusion, and Transparency, as shown in Figure 8.8.

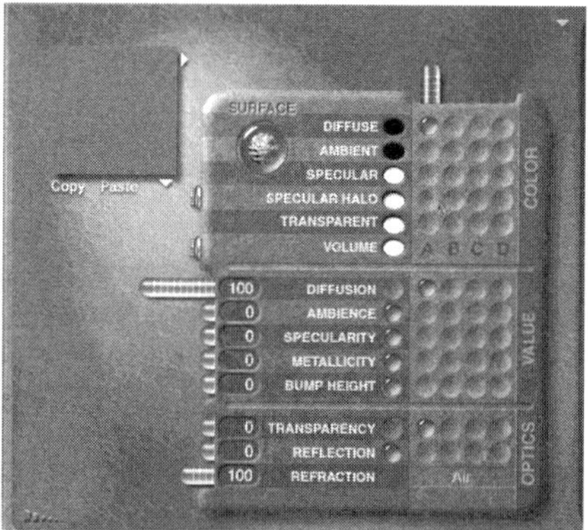

FIGURE 8.8 Place the buttons as shown here.

4. Go to the Texture Source Editor. Load the Fronds.tif image in the first image area, and the FrondsA.tif image in the Alpha Channel area. Make sure the finished image displays the Fronds without a background. This is what your Texture should look like in the Texture Resource Editor.

5. Set Spherical Mapping in the Materials Lab, and accept the texture. Render the sphere (see Figure 8.9).

FIGURE 8.9 The sphere, mapped with the Fronds image and Alpha data.

6. Rotate the sphere on its vertical axis, and render again. You will notice that the texture wraps all the way around. Try the following in the sphere's Materials Lab to alter the look of the sphere's texture:
   - Alter the texture's Scale, Rotation, and Offset values with the Edit Texture controls.
   - Alter the Mapping Type to Cylindrical, Object, Parametric, Random, or any of the other Mapping Types, and preview the results. Select the one that looks best for your needs.

You will notice that the texture appears a bit blurry. This is because the original image was created at 300 × 300 pixels. To get a sharper texture, create images at larger resolutions—1024 × 1024 and 2048 × 2048 pixels will create sharper images for the textures, and sharper-edged Alphas as well.

Creating Moss and Mold

Here is a very interesting way to enhance your Bryce objects. By using this Alpha technique, you can create all types of moss and mold textures on any selected object. Do the following:

1. Click the Stone icon in the Create toolbar to place a Stone in the scene.
2. Use a Pitted Concrete Material (from the Rocks & Stones Materials Library) with Object Mapping to texture the stone (see Figure 8.10).

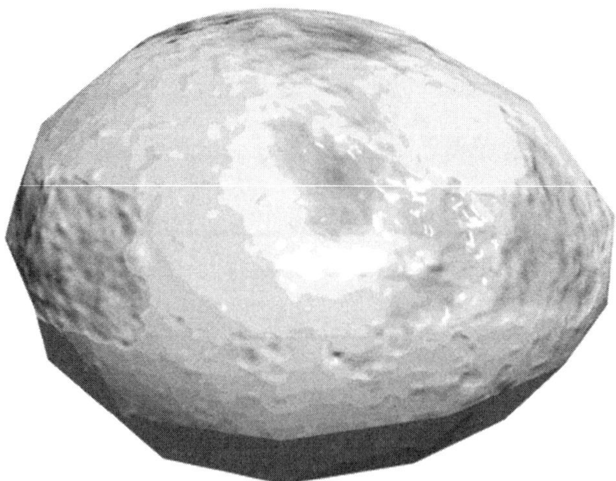

FIGURE 8.10 The stone is mapped with the Pitted Concrete Material.

ON THE CD

3. Use your favorite bitmap paint application to create an image sized 1024 × 1024 pixels to create your idea of some moss. Save the image, and then create and save its Alpha as described previously. As an alternative, you will find Moss1.tif and Moss1A.tif in the Images folder on the companion CD-ROM.
4. Back in Bryce, Duplicate the stone, and enlarge the duplicate so it extends just a bit around the source Stone object. Open the Texture Resource Editor for the duplicated and enlarged stone, and load the Moss1.tif and Moss1A.tif images (or load the ones you created) (see Figure 8.11).
5. Use a Parametric mapping to smear the texture at the bottom of the stone. Place the stone on a reflective water surface, and then Render and Save (see Figure 8.12).

Multi-Alpha Terrain

One complaint that users have about Bryce is that there is no way to map foliage to a Terrain. This is not true, since there is a way to do it using Alpha imagery, just as if you were creating a 2D Picture Object. Do the following:

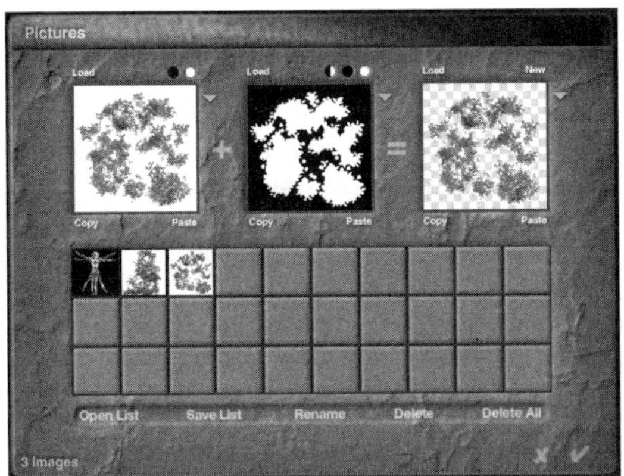

FIGURE 8.11 The Moss and its Alpha image are loaded into the Texture Source Editor.

FIGURE 8.12 The dripping moss texture is overlaid on the original stone texture.

1. Place a Terrain in the scene, and use a New Mexico Cliffs material on it. We are using this material because it is devoid of foliage (see Figure 8.13).
2. Duplicate the Terrain, and enlarge the duplicated version about 5%, just enough to make it extend beyond the source Terrain's boundaries.

FIGURE 8.13 The Terrain is devoid of foliage.

3. Load the Trees1.tif texture and the Trees1A.tif images in the Texture Resource Editor to create the image content needed for the foliage. Map it to the duplicated Terrain. Use a Parametric mapping with XYZ Scaling set to 15. The result will be a Terrain that from a distance will seem to be covered with patches of foliage (see Figure 8.14).

FIGURE 8.14 The bare Terrain now supports a thriving green matte.

Slime, Oh Wondrous Slime

Through your personal explorations, you by now realize that Bryce offers you two texture modes: Surfaces and Volumes. Although, as we have shown so far, you can create some interesting texture concepts by using Alpha/image textures in standard Surface mode, there are a few effects that are far more effective when applied in Volume mode. One of these is a super slime material, which can also emulate mold and rust as well as other material effects. Although we will cover Materials more in the next part of the book, it is natural to jump ahead a bit here because this exercise is so connected to your previous work with 2D Object Planes. Do the following:

1. Place a Stone in the scene, and map it with the Archeological Find Material from the Rocks & Stones Library. Use Object Space mapping.

2. Create a Duplicate of the Stone. Open the Duplicate's Materials Editor, and switch to Volume mode. Use Random Mapping, and an XYZ Scale of 3%. Use the Trees1.tif and Trees1A.tif images in the Texture Source Editor. Set the parameters as shown in Figure 8.15.
3. Render to preview. You can alter the values in the Materials Editor, but the ones noted are good defaults (see Figure 8.16).

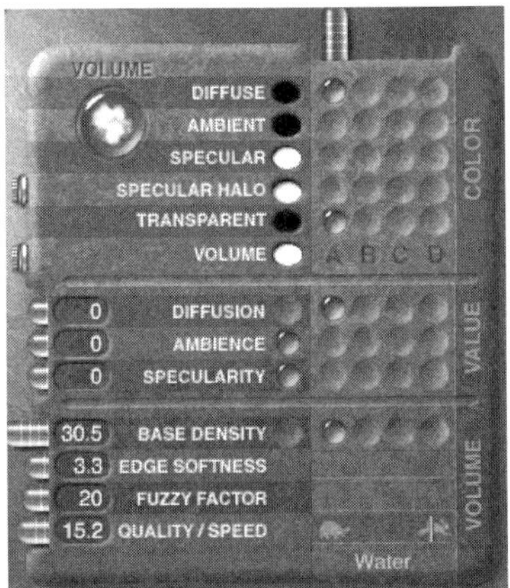

FIGURE 8.15 Set the controls as shown here.

FIGURE 8.16 The result will look like a combination of alien slime and melted pistachio ice cream.

The Random mapping type creates whorls such as those produced by viscous elements in motion. These are also called caustics in some applications.

Panoramic Backgrounds

Developing Panoramic backgrounds is also possible with Alpha image mapping techniques. A Panoramic background is used to give viewers the sense that they are surrounded by scenic content as the camera pans from a stationary position. Of course, you can do this by using a circle of 3D objects, but that can get rather memory intensive if the objects are complex, and the storage for a scene that uses so much 3D data can get huge very quickly. Here's a way to test your 2D Alpha/Image mapping skills further. Do the following:

1. Create a Cylinder in your scene. From the Top view, enlarge the Cylinder and place the Camera at its center. Refer to Figure 8.17 for the relative sizes.

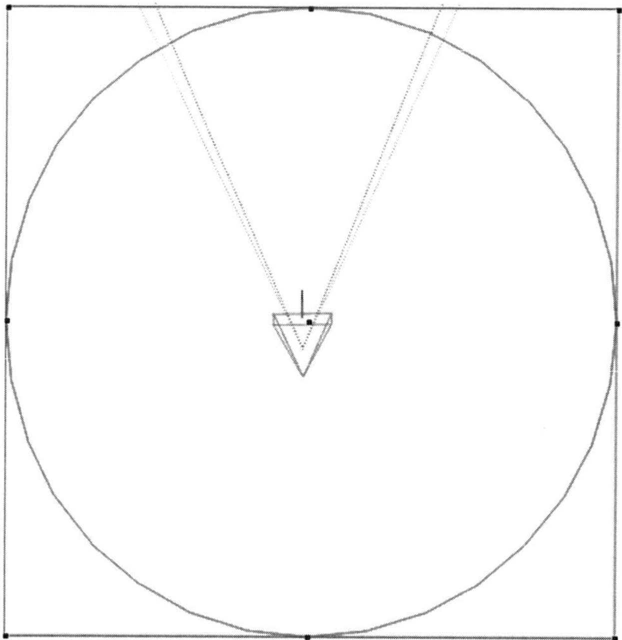

FIGURE 8.17 Place and enlarge a Cylinder, and place the Camera at its center.

2. Use any Alpha/Image texture you prefer on the Cylinder. Use Cylindrical mapping, and try different Scale percentages, since no two images will respond the same way. Render, and you will see that the mapping is blurred. This is because the Cylinder is so big, and it is exactly what we want.

A blurred background simulates what is known as Level Of Detail (LOD). Neither the eye nor the camera sees distance objects with the same detail as foreground objects.

3. Place another image closer to the Camera, and map it with a detailed material. This emphasizes the effect. No matter which way you rotate the Camera, a view of the Cylinder mapping will be there (see Figure 8.18).

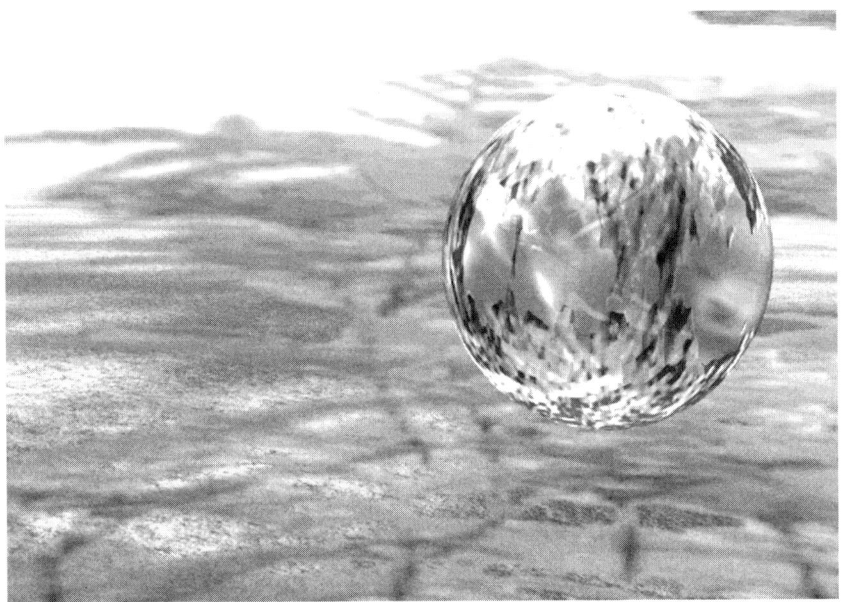

FIGURE 8.18 The mapped Cylinder emphasizes the LOD effect.

MOVING ON

In this chapter, we explored the creation of objects and texture effects using 2D Picture Object methods. The next part of the book is devoted to the use and exploration of Bryce materials.

CHAPTER

9 Material Presets

THE SOUL OF THE MATTER

Objects without color and texture live in a bleak, soulless void. They can be animated in complex and intriguing ways, go through complex maneuvers that give them breath and life, but there will still be something uncomfortably missing. There will be nothing but their shapes to distinguish them from other actors in the scene. That will not be enough, and your audience will scarcely be able to distinguish objects from backdrops, and the observers will not want to remain in attendance for too long. What an object seems to be *made of* tells us more about its potential character, its motivation, than its form alone can convey. A space ship that's all shiny and glistens in the light of a star has a very different emotional impact than one that is rusty and looks dented in spots, and each of these attributes has an effect on the story we are telling. A green tinted dinosaur is much less awesome and terrifying than one whose scales can be seen subtly shifting as it stalks its prey. In an animation, liberties might be taken to make textures simpler because movement hides texture detail. However, when the same object comes to rest, perhaps for long periods of time, the eye begins to notice textural detail. At that time, we look for definitive information so that disbelief, essential to the storyteller's art, can be willingly suspended.

Adding Textures in Bryce

There are two ways to add textures to objects in Bryce. One is to opt for *procedural materials,* and the other is to address object with *bitmap graphics.* Each has its purpose, as well as its weaknesses and strengths.

BRYCE PROCEDURAL MATERIALS

Using procedural materials in Bryce is fostered by the fact that there is such a rich source of materials presets from which to select. Each of these presets can be customized in infinite ways in the Materials Lab. A procedural material is a mathematical formula that contains basic image information. The magic of Bryce is that you are given intuitive control over this data without having to be a mathematician. Procedural materials are, in most cases, dependent on fractal algorithms (or formulas). This means that no matter how "close" you get to a procedural fractal material, there is always more detail to appreciate. Whereas procedural material in other applications tend to have a "computer" look, the procedurals in Bryce have been created to emulate organic textures and other environmental f/x as much as possible. Your work in Bryce will depend on how much comfort and understanding you have concerning the application and customization of procedural materials 90% of the time, with the other 10% devoted to your awareness of how to use and modify bitmaps as textures.

BITMAP TEXTURES

As you have already seen by working through the tutorials in previous chapters, Bryce is no slouch when it comes to incorporating bitmap images in materials.

When and Where to Use Bitmap Textures

The biggest liability for using bitmap textures as compared to procedurals is that when you zoom in on a bitmap, you are sure to see the pixels enlarge as you draw closer, to the point that it becomes irritatingly obvious that the object's texture is a bitmap and not a "real material." This can be somewhat addressed by blurring the original image, but too much blurring also adds its own degree of non-believability. Bitmap textures are best used when you are not going to zoom in on an object, or when the pictorial information is not vital for close-up inspection. Human portraiture, for example, must be handled through bitmapped graphics. There are no procedurals (yet) that allow you control over the design of a unique face, although who knows what the future holds? Bitmaps are also vital when you want to apply a specific facade to an object, especially useful in the texture mapping of buildings as seen from a city street. In one operation, a bitmap can be applied to an object that would require the kind of variables that a procedural just cannot handle, except perhaps in stacking and manipulating procedurals in layers. However, even when layered, the look of objects in the real world need recognizable and randomized textural appearances. Although Bryce procedurals can accommodate your needs in most cases, specific bitmapped graphics might be required for that extra hint of reality.

THE BEST OF BOTH WORLDS

You can combine both procedural and bitmap materials in a *texture sandwich* in Bryce. In most cases, you will opt for one method of texturing over another, but there are situations that demand the layered sandwich approach as well.

Look at the World Around You

The first step in judging, valuing, and evaluating textures is to look at the world surrounding you right now. Look at your computer. If the case were made of wood instead of metal, would that affect you or your work habits in any way? If your important other entered the room, seemingly made of water and clouds, would your surmise about who they are be altered? If the trees outside of your window took on the appearance of precious metals, would you be able to categorize the natural world the same way you do now? Computer artists and animators are always playing with the material looks of reality, sometimes to emulate those looks more closely than a photograph, and other times to shockingly alter our perception and comprehension of the world we take for granted and think we know.

Procedural Materials Organization

There are a number of ways we could organize procedural materials. What we have chosen to do is to go from the surface to the depths. The surface is like a high-level computer language, which allows you easy access to usage without much knowledge of programming. You can compare it to a visual programming language, accessible to all comers. This surface language is represented by Materials Presets in Bryce, which also includes the beginning discussions and examples concerning Volumetric Presets. The next level down offers you more customizing control over events, perhaps comparable to a computer language such as Basic. Here is where you can get behind the screen to control more of what is going on. In Bryce, this is represented by the *Materials Lab*. Included in the Materials Lab are both the Alpha Channel and Refraction indexing, among other channel-related elements. At the depths are controls for the controls, akin to a computer language such as C++, where you maneuver around with some knowledge that everything you do has mega-consequences for the higher levels. This requires more experience and exploration than higher-level manipulations do. In Bryce, this is represented by the *Deep Texture Editor*.

Procedural Materials topics are arranged in chapters as follows:

- *Materials Presets* (including Volumetrics) in this chapter (Chapter 9)
- *Materials Lab* in Chapter 10
- *Deep Texture Editor* in Chapter 11

BITMAP TEXTURES

Applying bitmap textures is done in the Materials Lab. In order to distinguish procedural mapping topics from bitmap topics, we have separated the bitmap focus out from other procedurally targeted work in the Materials Lab (Chapter 10), and instead will present it on its own. This is very important, because it allows us to center on information and examples vital to understanding how to work with bitmap textures in Bryce. This includes wrapping bitmaps on objects in different ways.

We begin by looking at the Bryce Materials Presets.

MATERIALS PRESETS

The simplest and quickest way to add a material to your selected object(s) is to access the Materials Presets Libraries, click on any material represented, and check the Apply mark. To access the Materials Presets Libraries, click on the downward-pointing arrow next to the word *Edit* in the Edit toolbar.

About the Materials Presets Libraries

There are 14 libraries listed in the Material Presets list.

CLOUDS AND FOGS

Clouds are moderate to highly expensive to render, dependent mostly upon their transparency and size. Antialiasing is also a large factor in rendering time, since a cloud can have so many edges to smooth. Cloud and Fog materials should be differentiated from the Cloud Plane. The Cloud Plane is addressed by its own presets, and in general, renders very quickly. Cloud and Fog materials are targeted to specified objects, many times a sphere or cube. You might consider the following as common targets for Cloud and Fog materials:

- Ground fog in the morning or evening over the Ground Plane. Use a Fog material that has elevation-dependent transparency, so that it gets thicker and more impenetrable as it gets lower to the ground.

Sometimes this effect can be enhanced by using a higher Haze setting as well, so you get both vertical and horizontal fog effects. Using a high Fog setting can interfere with and negate an assigned Fog material effect.

- Clouds around a mountain summit. These can be colorized normally, taking their tint from the sun color, or colorized red for vaporous clouds around the top of a volcano.
- *Flyover* clouds. These are mapped to Cloud Planes lower than the Sky Plane, so that you can see through them to the ground below. It also allows you to rise above the clouds, where your Sky Plane might show a sunny sky.

If you need to map Cloud materials to a Flyover Plane, it's better to use a sandwich of three or four planes, separated from each other by an intervening clear space. Map each of the planes with a high transparency, on the order of 70% or more. This allows you to animate each plane, so the total effect looks randomized, with clear spaces suddenly appearing and disappearing as the camera aims at the ground below.

- *Progressive disclosure* is a term used to indicate that a targeted object in a scene is slowly brought into focus. Parting or slowly disappearing clouds mapped to an intervening plane can serve nicely in this capacity (see Figure 9.1).

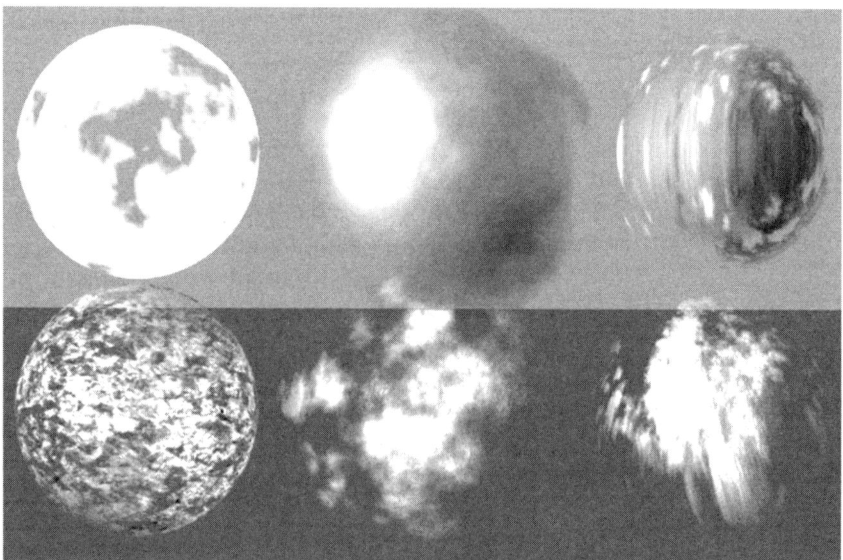

FIGURE 9.1 Clouds and Fogs materials are shown wrapped on spheres. From upper left to lower right: Wispy Afternoon, Smokestack, Marbled Clouds, Planet Atmosphere, Bright and Bumpy, and Turbo Clouds.

COMPLEX EFFECTS

This library of materials can be used to develop strange and evocative Bryce worlds. The materials with high levels of transparency and turbulence can be rather expensive to render, but they are so interesting to fold into a scene that you won't mind the extra rendering time. Besides, this gives you a chance to go get a sandwich. Some uses worth considering for these materials include (see Figure 9.2):

- Green Lit is a favorite material for creating fake lights, from vehicle headlights to stars. Used in this manner, no lighting or shadows are produced, which is just perfect for illuminating faraway object.
- Lit Rays is the perfect material for emulating laser beams and other light effects.
- Alien Disco Ball has the perfect shimmer for making a robot look all the more menacing and invincible.
- Copper Bump is the material to explore for shields, antique dinnerware, and sculpted Dali-esque forms sitting on an infinite Ground Plane.
- The Retina Projector material can be used when a human eye has to be superseded by something the Terminator would be comfortable with.
- Bleeding Moon Glass is very expensive to render because of its high transparency settings, but it allows you to create alien textures that look very eerie, especially when sitting in layers in front of the camera.
- The two Fire materials can be used to light campfires or forests, or even for that spurt of flame from a volcano. Just wrap them to a vertically elongated sphere.

GLASSES

The most important thing to remember about glass is that it bends (refracts) light. Because of this factor and transparency values, it can be very time consuming to render. Your computer has to figure out what the objects behind the glass will look like when warped by the light rays being bounced around, and that takes time. If the glass is also reflective, then more calculations have to take place. It is not unusual for a Glass object to add an hour to every rendered frame in a sequence, turning a five-hour rendering into days of computer tie-up. This being said, however, when you need glass, you need glass (see Figure 9.3).

Glass objects should always have other objects behind them, since to believe an object is glass is enhanced by how objects behind the Glass object are warped by light rays and refraction.

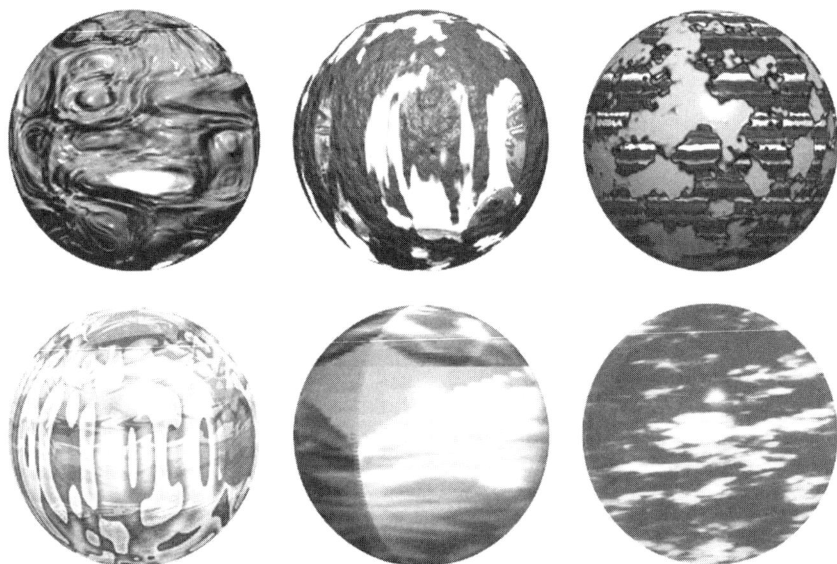

FIGURE 9.2 Among the materials found in the Complex Effects library are (top left to bottom right) Oily Bronze, Water Puddles, Chocolate Coated Bricks, Disco Kelp, Shiny World in a Glass, and Lost Marble.

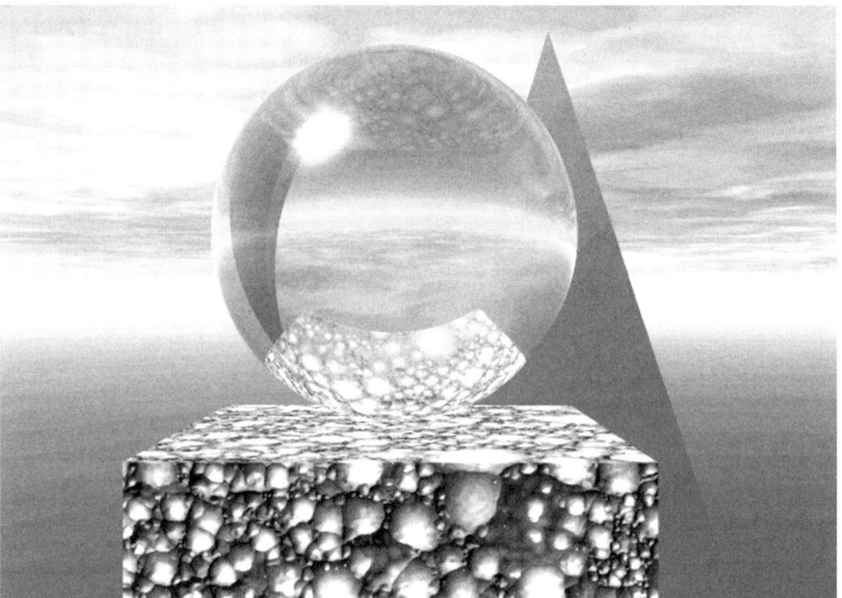

FIGURE 9.3 As light rays are traced after having been reflected and refracted by the glass sphere, the scene on the globe is warped and reconfigured. This sphere is mapped with the Standard Glass material.

Glass Tips

Here are a few tips on how you can add some magic elements to your Glass objects, and even make your Glass objects render faster.

- When glass gets too thick, it will be impossible to see through even at 100% transparency. This is especially true of solid glass spheres. One thing you can do to thin out the sphere is to use a Boolean trick.

  1. Make a Sphere, and map it with a glass that has a 100% transparency (you can use the one of the three Bubble Glass preset materials). Make a Duplicate of the Sphere.
  2. Resize the Duplicate so it is 5% smaller than the original, without moving it, and make it a Negative Boolean object. The cloned Sphere now rests inside the original.
  3. Make the original Sphere a Positive Boolean object, and Group it with the Duplicate inside. This creates a sphere with a hollow inside, and the glass material will react very differently to transparency levels. You can achieve a similar effect by simply mapping a single Sphere with Bubble Glass, but this alternative gives the globe a little more thickness to refract the light. If you made both Spheres Positive, then cut a Boolean hole in them with a Negative Boolean object, the hole would show the walls where the Sphere has thickness (see Figure 9.4).

- To save some rendering time, render your scene first without the Glass object. Create the Glass object and place it when the first render is done. Now, Plop Render the Glass object. Even with antialiasing on, this method saves time.
- Place objects that are vertically or horizontally straight lined (e.g., chairs, poles, or window frames) behind Glass objects. You will be able to see and appreciate the warping effects of the glass more clearly.
- Use a Spotlight or Globe light to one side of a Glass object to enhance the color shadows being cast.

LEAVES

These are material presets designed specifically to map the leaves on a Tree object from the Tree Lab. That does not mean you can use these materials for anything else. In fact, you are always encouraged to explore and see what happens when you break the rules!

FIGURE 9.4 Compare this picture with Figure 9.3. Here, the Sphere is mapped with the Bubble Glass 3 material. In this variation, transparency dominates over reflection. Look closely, and you can see the thickness of the walls of the glass.

METALS

Every metal you can think of is either represented here as a preset or is made possible by altering the preset by tweaking any attribute in the Materials Lab. Use the pitted and eroded metallics when you want a spaceship, robot, or household item to have more character. Use more than one metal in a scene so that the viewer is drawn into reflections of reflections (see Figure 9.5).

Transparent metals in this folder seem to render a bit quicker than transparent glass, and in some cases can be a valuable substitute that saves you rendering time.

MISCELLANEOUS

Personally, we dislike the name of this material presets library folder. How about *Stupendous,* or even *Awe Inspiring*? There are no superfluous or throw-away materials living here, but a collection of extremely useful and novel items. Some of the best Ground Plane materials are included here, especially when it comes to Bump mapping. Some uses include (see Figure 9.6):

FIGURE 9.5 The spheres, stacked from bottom left to bottom right, use Christmas Ball 9 and 17, Brushed Silver, Polished Gold, Brushed Bronze, Transparent Aluminum, and Eroded Gold materials. All have highly reflective surfaces, a characteristic of metal.

- Moon Lava and Moon Lava II can both be used both as a Ground Plane map and also to make a Sphere look like a far-off moon.
- Cracked Clay Pot transforms ordinary stones into artifacts from an archeological dig.
- Acid Build Up is a wonderful material for mapping the sides of an active volcano, or the ground below it.
- City Lights I and II are the materials to select when the world is dark, and your tour bus is flying above populated terrain.
- Foliage I and II should be used as materials for trees and other flora that is created by Boolean operations. Be careful, however, since this material can add many hours of rendering time to an unsuspecting project.
- Pearl Beads and Alien Cherries add authenticity to Stone objects and collections of rusty metal, respectively.

PLAINS AND TERRAINS

This library features a series of materials perfect for giving your mountains and Ground Planes that lived-on look. From the spring mud to the winter snow, a large number of environments are represented here. All

FIGURE 9.6 Moon Lava, Cracked Clay Pot, Acid Buildup, Death Star in Progress, Mud-Bark Fusion, Pearl Beads.

of the Planes and Terrains presets can be infinitely customized in the Materials Lab (Chapter 10) and Deep Texture Editor (Chapter 11). It's advisable to investigate all of the materials included here, so your explorations won't be hampered by attraction to any specific material over another at first. You will probably find yourself, however, gravitating to ones whose overall feel you especially like. Some materials seem to work better on Planes or Terrains, while some look good on both (see Figure 9.7).

When you are placing mountainous terrain in your world, consider using another lower Terrain object as the base. Nothing looks less natural than a mountain sitting on a Flat Plane. Better to place it on a low-lying series of foot hills. When you do this, the lower terrain should have the same material as a Ground Plane so they blend;. At times, mountains, lower terrain, and the Infinite Plane can all have the same material.

ROCKS AND STONES

This library contains materials meant to be applied to Rock and Stone objects, but you will be limiting your creativity if you don't stretch their purpose to include at least planes, terrains, and anything else that might benefit by these materials (especially stone Poser statues). Some are more

FIGURE 9.7 Cones make excellent models for previewing materials that are to be targeted to terrain objects. The materials on these six cones are Grassy Peaks, Iceberg, New Mexico Cliffs, Antique Pots, Etched Rock, and Grand Canyon

"expensive" (time consuming) to render than others, but most of these selections have the very convoluted and intriguing looks that you just can't resist.

Using Stone Materials

Here are some tips and hints for using Stone materials on objects (see Figure 9.8):

- Place random stones in a scene to give it a more realistic look. Make the stones different sizes, and give them different orientations, planting some deep in the ground. Use one material for most or all of them, so as not to make your scene too busy.
- Use complex materials on stones closer to the camera, and simple materials (or even just color) on stones further in the distance, You will have a more realistic scene that will render in less time.
- Use a simple material on a stone, Multi-Replicate it, and use the stones to build an edifice. Examples would be a small cabin, an altar, a stone bridge, or an archway.
- Use Boolean operations on stones to build Stone objects. Examples would be a bowl, ornament, or alien structure. Use a material that fits the item you are creating.

FIGURE 9.8 A feast for the Bryce rock collector, from the left: Riverbed, Barnacles, Granite Eroded, Stone Wall, Cave Wall, and Alien Sandstone.

- A Rock object has so many facets, that having just one in your scene that is duplicated, and then rotated and resized, usually suffices for a multitude of items. Before you duplicate or Multi-Replicate a rock, assign a suitable material to it.

SIMPLE AND FAST

Don't be fooled by the title of this library. Besides assigning basic colors to objects, several of our favorite materials live here. We are referring specifically to Pale Blue Metal, Yellow Gold, Mirror, and the six Woods presets. Pale Blue Metal is a great all-around material to apply to buildings in the distance, and Yellow Gold renders with absolute believable clarity. Mirror is not only great when it comes to completely reflective surfaces, but is also super when it comes to mapping virtual water. From high up, the mirror surface makes water look very convincing, without all the time it takes to render most of the water presets. The woods serve all of your needs for wood looks, from finished cabinetwork to rough plywood. All of these materials can be customized in the Materials Lab, as we shall see later (Chapter 10). Render time for any of these materials is very fast (see Figure 9.9).

FIGURE 9.9 Six Spheres, showing the six wood materials from the Simple and Fast materials presets (from the top left): Warped, Light, Bleached, Plank, Walnut, and Polished Walnut.

TRUNKS

This library of materials presets, added in Bryce 5, was created especially for trunks of trees generated in the Tree Lab. That doesn't mean you can't use them for anything else, however, so exploration is strongly advocated (see Figure 9.10).

FIGURE 9.10 Six spheres, showing six selected Trunk materials (from the top left): Tulip Tree, Birch, White Pine, Coconut Palm, Italian Cypress, and Scotts Pine.

TUTORIAL AND EXTERNAL FOLDERS

These folders are mainly for your use when saving (adding) your own customized materials. You can delete the few materials in the Tutorials folder, leaving room for more materials of your own design. If you design a material that falls within one of the categories already covered by another folder in the library (rocks, glass, metal, etc.), think about saving it to that existing folder instead of another folder. It'll be easier to locate and use later.

WATERS AND LIQUIDS

Waters and Liquids are generally more expensive to render than most other materials, except for clouds. This is because Waters and Liquids generally include degrees of turbulence and transparency. Since ray-traced light waves have to penetrate transparent surfaces, and the computer has to figure out the math involved in any turbulence, more time has to be taken for the rendering. You will notice this most when rendering large patches of water, or infinite and volumetric water planes. Water effects, however, are some of the most thrilling attributes of Bryce, so you will no doubt be patiently waiting as they render (see Figure 9.11).

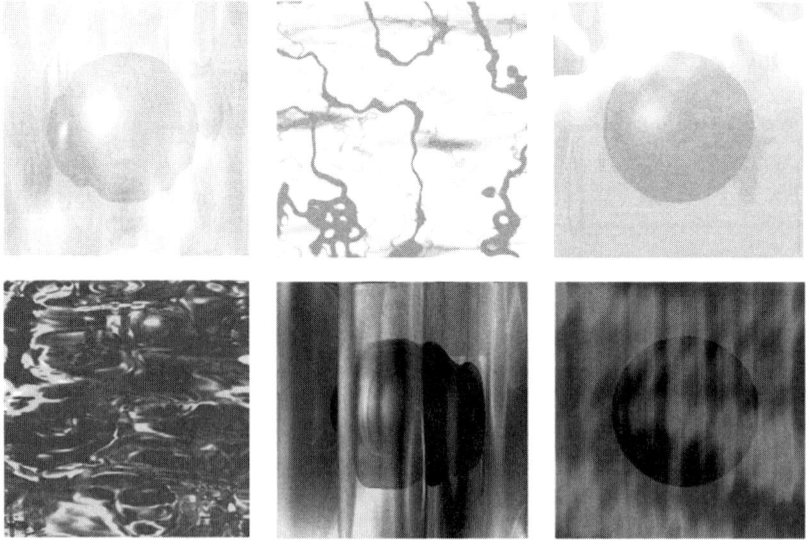

FIGURE 9.11 Here, a series of Water and Liquid materials are mapped to a cube. The materials used (from the upper left) are: Rosewater, Foamy Seawater, Pollution Waterfall, Santraginus V, Caribbean Resort, and That Thing from Abyss. A gold sphere has been placed just below the surface on each, to give you some idea of each liquid's transparency.

Unless you already have one, it is highly advisable that you purchase an accelerator card for your PC or Mac if you are planning to be spending a lot of time doing Bryce rendering. A medium-level accelerator card runs somewhere in the neighborhood of $100, and it can save you hundreds of hours in rendering time a month. For Bryce professional use, including animations for film (which require larger file sizes and antialiasing), you should consider the best accelerator card you can afford. Although Bryce offers effects and options found in no other graphics or animation application on the market, it does not offer super speedy raytracing. A fast machine and an added accelerator card will make your Bryce work all the more pleasurable, and will certainly handle your water material rendering with ease. It's also best to install as much RAM as you can afford.

WILD AND FUN

Some of Bryce's most experimental materials are included in this presets library folder. When you are seeking to attract the viewer with strange alien environments or excursions into the dream world, drop by this library of materials. The names of the materials, incorporating descriptive words like "Dali," "Tyrel" (from the movie *BladeRunner*), "Alien," and "Psychoactive" give you a strong hint that using these materials will tell the audience they are not in Kansas anymore. Some possibilities for the uses these materials might be put to include (see Figure 9.12):

- Use the Dali Bee material on a human head model, or even a whole Poser figure. The result will be similar to some of Salvador Dali's

FIGURE 9.12 Dali Bee Stripes, Tyrel Building, Alien Tree Bark, What Are You Looking At?, Peeling Paint, and Psychoactive Christmas Ball.

famous works. This material also produces surrealistic effects when targeted to Fruit objects such as apples, oranges, and bananas.

- The Guilded Cage material makes very modernistic skyscrapers that can reflect the city in which they are placed.
- The Tyrel Building material, a salute to the film *BladeRunner*, creates interesting effects on buildings, spaceships, and can even be used to map a Ground Plane for an infinite city flyover.
- One of the most awesome and effective materials to wrap on a robot is Alien Tree Bark, with Robot Fungus adding a touch of deterioration.
- The What Are You Looking At? eyeball is perfect for adding eyes to any suitable object, anthropomorphic or machine.
- Peeling Paint makes an excellent Ground Plane material.
- Easter Egg Dye 2 and Rustic Vein are perfect when you need to create that used and worn look on a spaceship.

VOLUME

Although Volume materials is just another preset folder in the Materials library, it deserves very special attention. Volumetric materials, and the concept of volumetrics in general, is a new way of thinking about models and materials across the board. What is a Volumetric object? A Volumetric object is any object that is constructed of mass throughout. Most imported models are not volumetrics, since they display a hollow inside when they are ungrouped or cut away. Some are volumetric, because they look solid when you turn their elements in space. Bit volumetrics in Bryce have to do with Infinite Planes, and specifically with the Water and Cloud planes. These planes are normally wrapped with 2D textures. You can fly through them, but your journey to the other side is instantaneous. In the real world, flying through clouds or swimming through water is a volumetric experience. Depending how thick the clouds are, or how deep the water is, it will take you a certain amount of time to break through or touch bottom. Until you do pass through, you are presented with a constant vision of the material that the element is made of. This is the exciting new magic of working with volumetric Infinite Planes, and also with the materials that address them.

In addition to flying through volumetrics is the appreciation and realism of what an object looks like when it is partially immersed in a volumetric material. It slowly disappears, just as you would expect. Water Plane volumetrics are especially beautiful this way, treating the poles of a pier or a partially submerged boat as real objects would be treated by the liquid's refraction, the capability of the liquid to bend light.

Volumetric materials deform the objects they address by a process known as *Deformation mapping*. Bump mapping makes it look like an object has bumps and dents, while Deformation mapping actually produces bumps and dents. This allows lights to play very differently, and more realistically, on objects mapped with volumetric materials. Bump mapping is just another surface mapping type, while volumetrics soak the object to the core with the material being applied (see Figure 9.13).

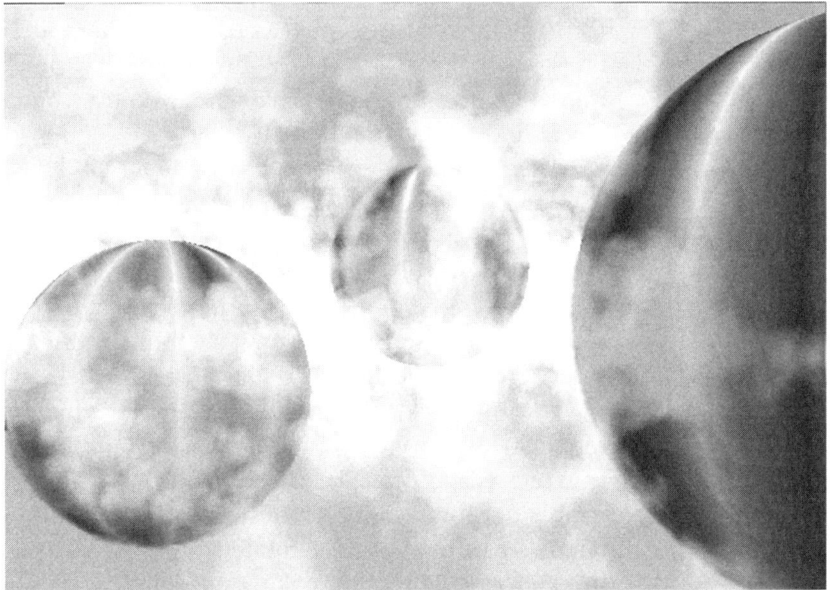

FIGURE 9.13 These three Spheres were set at different distances from the camera inside of an infinite volumetric Cloud Plane. Notice how different layers of the material reveal and hide the objects.

It is extremely expensive to render volumetrics, because the computer has to calculate the volume mapping for the transparent layering that's taking place. Antialiasing is especially expensive, because volumetric materials have a lot of edges to smooth out. Unless your project demands very high-end output (animation for TV or the movies), do not use antialiasing when working on a volumetric sequence, or use just the minimum. What we said previously about the need to use a fast machine and an accelerator card bears repeating here. Without the right hardware configuration, using volumetrics for graphics or animations projects is prohibitive.

USING VOLUMETRIC MATERIALS

One of the first uses for a volumetric material is an infinite Volumetric Plane. If you click and hold the mouse on any of the three Infinite Plane icons (Water, Cloud, or Ground), you can select either a Volumetric or a 2D Surface Plane. The default is the 2D Surface Infinite Plane.

The magic of volumetric substances is that you can move through them with the camera. Many times, attempting to move through a non-volumetric object with the camera will cause Bryce to crash, especially during an animation. Since Volumetric Planes are infinite, you could move around in a Volumetric Infinite Plane forever. Volumetric substances other than the Infinite Planes are not infinite, so you can fly through them and see what's on the other side. Dimensional travel, dream sequences, and moving from one environment to another; all of this and much more is possible when you use volumetric materials on an object or Infinite Volumetric Plane.

The Volume materials in the Materials Library represent a number of materials specifically designed to work with volumetric objects, but that's not the end of it. Any of the water or cloud/fog materials can also address any Volumetric object, including Volumetric Infinite Planes. You are free then to set up an underwater scene. Just make sure that the material has some transparency. Better yet, it should have an active Alpha channel so that there are patches in the substance where no material exists.

Like any object that accepts a volumetric material, a Volumetric Infinite Plane has apparent internal mass. On an Infinite Plane, this volume is expressed (and can be altered) in the Y-axis, or height direction. Remember, as discussed previously, that any Infinite Plane can also be rotated, so Infinite Planes rotated on their X-axis 90 degrees become infinite walls, and then make it possible to have something else waiting on the other side. The effects that can be imagined and designed with Infinite Planes and volumetric materials have no end. Here are some ideas:

- Fly a craft through volumetric clouds, with the camera following close behind. What you will see are the clouds breaking over the craft as it enters thicker and thinner patches of volumetric material.
- Use the Blood Corpuscles volumetric material preset, with the camera buried deep in the object. It's like being on the other end of a cosmic microscope.
- Create a Volumetric Infinite Plane (choose any of the three Infinite Planes), and map it with a volumetric fire material. It is left to your imagination what this environment emulates, but you probably don't want to go there.
- Create a world with two Volumetric Infinite Planes, one above the other with a space between. Make the top plane a volumetric cloud material, and map the bottom Volumetric Plane with a water material (use a high transparency of 60% or more). Create an animation

that allows the camera to dive from a starting position on top of the Cloud Plane through the Cloud Plane and down under the water. Bury a treasure object at the bottom of the Volumetric Water Plane as a final target.

- Create a Volumetric Infinite Water Plane. Make it 80% transparent with a simple aqua color material. At different levels inside the volume, place a series of objects. Place rocks at the bottom of the water volume, and a very low but bumpy Terrain map with a sandy material. Look at the scene from above with the camera, and render either graphics or an animation. If you decide on doing an animation, move a visible light through the water so its path includes different depths. You can muddy the water by using the Polluted Waterfall material.
- Create a cube, and map the Dented Planet volumetric material to it. Move the camera so that one face of the cube fills the screen. Render an animation that allows the camera to slowly move closer to the cube. The dented planet material is a deep fractal, so that no matter how close you get (as log as you don't actually touch the object), the more detail you will see.

Use Volumetric materials prudently and rarely. Most of the elements in a Bryce scene can be mapped quite effectively through normal material mapping. When volumetrics are called for, try to limit their use to objects that absolutely require them.

BOOLEANS AND VOLUMETRICS

You can use Boolean objects to cut Volumetric objects, including the volumetric materials used to map them. The "transfer materials from the negative object" option should be turned off in the Negative object's Attributes list (see Figure 9.14).

Adding/Deleting and Importing/Exporting Materials

When you are performing these operations, here are some things to keep in mind:

- Instead of deleting a material preset, consider exporting it out to a separate folder for later use. Export similar presets to the same folder for later import. Then, you can safely delete the item in any Material Presets Library.
- When you add (save) your own material creations, see if they fit under one of the other preset categories. If you developed a nice Rock material, for example, add it to the existing Rocks and Stones Library. It will be a lot easier to find and use later.

FIGURE 9.14 The volumetric material Dented Planet was mapped to this Sphere. A Negative Boolean Cylinder, with the Transfer Materials option off, was then grouped with the Positive Sphere forming a hole. The volumetric material is a fractal, so that more detail is always available the closer you get.

- If you are saving an object with a customized material wrapped on it, there might be no need to save the material separately. Remember that objects are saved with materials attached, so importing the model imports the material too. You could save a group of objects with similar materials, perhaps a group of wine glasses with materials customized for each. Loading that object to the scene would then allow you to copy its material, and paste it on other needed objects. It might be easier to classify materials according to the object class to which they belong, especially if that object class is not represented in the Materials Presets Library (e.g., lizard skins, fabrics, or other material classifications). Lizard skins could be added to a lizard model, fabrics to a rug model, and so forth. This would give you the instant ability to load in the representative object as well as the material.
- If you have developed a series of interesting materials, think about sharing them with other Bryce users. This can be done by uploading them to a specific Bryce Web site (search the Web for a suitable site), or by contacting Corel directly.

MOVING ON

In this chapter, we began our exploration of materials use in Bryce by detailing the uses of the collection of Materials Preset Libraries. In the next chapter, we move on to the Materials Lab.

CHAPTER

10 The Materials Lab

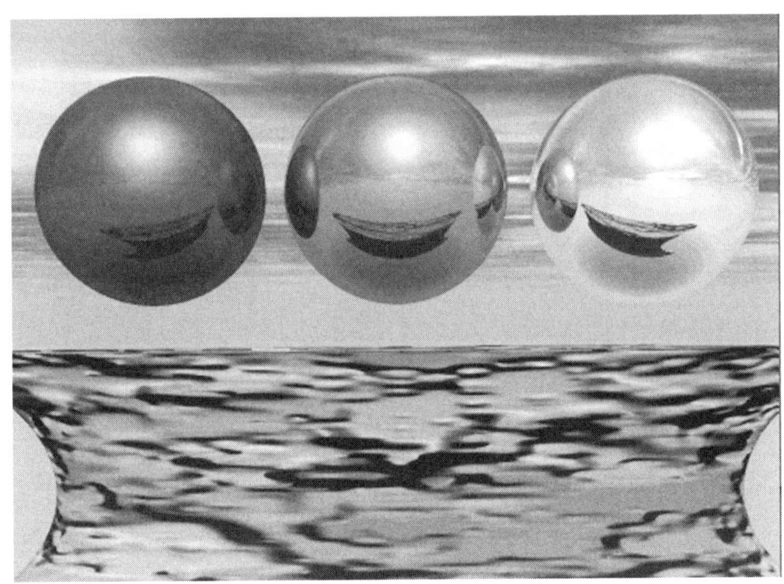

When the presets in the Materials Library no longer seem adequate or exciting, it's time to learn how to create and customize your own materials. This is accomplished in the Materials Lab and also by using the tools in the Deep Texture Editor (Chapter 11). The Materials Lab can be accessed in four ways: by selecting Edit Material in the Objects menu, by using the hot-key combination Control-M (Mac and Windows), by clicking on the Material icon in the Edit toolbar, or by clicking on the "M" in the selected object's Attributes List. All of these methods bring up the Materials Lab (see Figure 10.1).

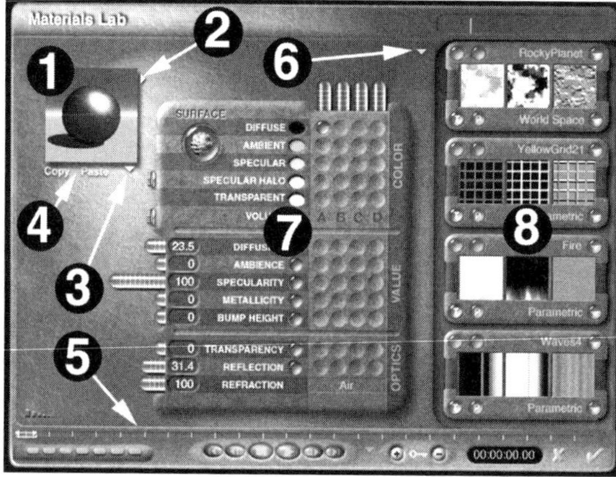

FIGURE 10.1 The tools and components of the Materials Lab.

Materials Lab Components

Refer to the Figure 10.1 numbered keys:

1. The Materials Nano Preview window presents a picture of the material as it looks when placed on an object. Be aware that these renders can take time, especially if you have chosen complex materials or volumetrics. It's important to remember that placing your mouse cursor in this window and holding down the Left Mouse Button (Windows) will allow you to interactively turn the object to view the material from different vantage points.
2. This is the switch for bringing up the Materials Presets, which are very handy when you are designing your own materials. The presets act as category selections, so if you are designing a Wood material, you might want to base it on an already existing Wood preset. After designing your own material, you would activate the presets in order to Add and/or Export it through this dialog.

3. Activating this switch allows you to select a basic 3D form on which the Materials Nano Preview will display your material. If you are working on a selected imported object in your world (DXF, OBJ, 3DMF, 3DS, LWO, etc.), the view in the Nano Preview will default to a Sphere to display the material. If you are working on a Terrain object, you can show the actual Terrain object mapped with your material by selecting Current Selection from this list. Use the Up Close option when you want to Add (Save) a new material, since the preview will show it more clearly.
4. The Copy/Paste functions become extremely important to remember when you are animating a material because they allow you to paste the same material to the beginning and end frames in an animation (or anywhere else the material is supposed to return to its original look). Other than that, these switches work the same way as the Copy/Paste Materials commands in the Edit menu.
5. This is the Animation toolbar.
6. This switch gives you access to items that affect the Material Shading Modes and options. The following sections provide details to consider when using the items in this list.

MATERIAL SHADING MODES

You can select from among Normal, Blend Transparency, Fuzzy, and Light.

- Use the Normal mode to write the material to the object so it renders in a standard manner, with the expected hard edges and material details. No modifications are made to the material.
- Use the Blend Transparency mode when you want the black areas of an image's Alpha Channel to drop out, in accordance with the channel that is selected (A, B, C, or D). The Transparency Slider is normally set to a value of 0, so that the non-white elements of the material show as opaque. Use this setting to show an object as if it were constructed from a skeleton.
- In Fuzzy mode, the apparent density of the object is read. More dense areas remain opaque, while less dense areas are rendered as more transparent. A Sphere facing the camera, for example, is interpreted as having less density at the edges, so these become fuzzed out. A perfect way to use this mode is to emulate LOD (Level of Detail). Objects farther from the camera in a 3D scene should not be as sharp as objects closer to the camera. Use fuzziness to add vagueness to objects in the distance, and your depth perception of the scene will be

enhanced. The only caution is not to fly closer to the fuzzy objects, because they will remain fuzzy and cause perceptual confusion for the viewer.

- Use the Light mode when you want to transform an object into a pseudo-light. The color of the light is a combination of the Diffuse and Volume color settings, and the amount of transparency is set by the Transparency Optics slider. When given a material texture, the resulting object looks rather ghostly, and can be used to evoke feelings of mystery in a Bryce world.

Objects assigned the Light mode need not be devoid of material textures. If they derive their color and/or value from a Diffuse row, then they will show that material in accordance with the Diffuse slider setting. See the example at the right in Figure 10.2.

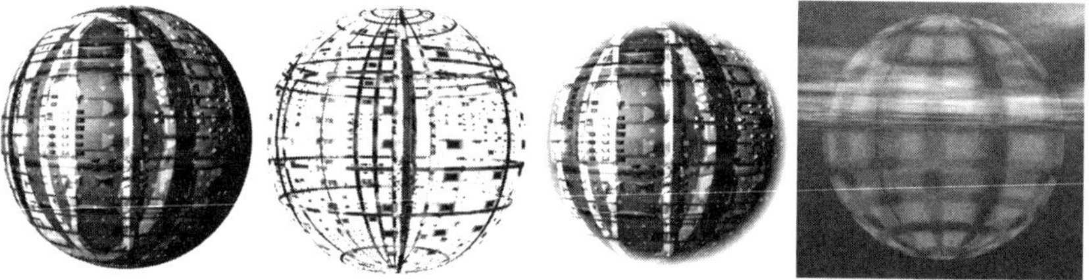

FIGURE 10.2 From left to right, the same material wrapped to a figure in Normal, Blend Transparency, Fuzzy, and Light modes. The Light mode example has a material assigned in the Diffuse row.

ADDITIONAL MATERIALS OPTIONS

In addition to the Shading mode selections contained in this list, other attributes of the selected object can be controlled from here. Each performs an important function in how your object looks and behaves on screen.

Additive

Normally set to Off, click it On when you want to add all of the material settings to the area behind the object as opposed to the object's surface. Psychedelic illusions and solarization effects are many times the result, although each instance has to be explored on its own.

Cast/Receive Shadows

This setting gives you ultimate control over how an object behaves in the light in your scene. Normally, you will want to leave these settings defaulted to On. In creating storyboards, however, or flatter illustrations for print output, they can be switched Off. This produces a scene that shows no obliteration of material on the objects targeted for no shadowing. There are also ways to create special effects, shadows cast from objects that are invisible.

Distance Blur

It is advisable to always check this item when you are writing materials to an Infinite Plane. Blurring the distance enhances depth perception, making foreground elements appear sharper.

Volume Blend Altitude/Distance

These options have a direct relationship with the color the Volume attribute is set to. Volume Blend Altitude will gradually blend the selected Volume color from 100% to 0% along the vertical distance (altitude) of the object. Volume Blend Distance will blend the Volume and Diffuse colors from background (farthest distance from the camera) to the foreground (closest distance to the camera). This is another way of emphasizing depth and enhancing the LOD (Level of Detail), since objects farther from the camera will be darkened out as compared with foreground objects. This is definitely an option to apply when your foreground actors are begging to be distinguished in a busy scene from more distant elements. Think about using it whenever your scene shows a deep panorama. As the camera moves farther into the scene, closer objects lighten and become more defined, so it's also an excellent animation device.

The Color, Value, and Optics Controls

There are three distinct parts to this palette: Color, Value, and Optics. Color deals with how colors are applied to the selected object, and where they are accessed from. The Value section of the palette deals with how Value (light) is interpreted, and where this information comes from. The third section of the palette deals with assigning discreet optical properties to the object that affect its density and ability to alter light (see Figure 10.3).

The two buttons at the left of the palette, Randomize (top) and Reset (bottom), are useful for creating initial materials that can then be customized. In order to get a better understanding of how the Materials Lab works, it is advisable to click the Randomize button a few times, and watch how the screen and the Nano Preview of the material changes.

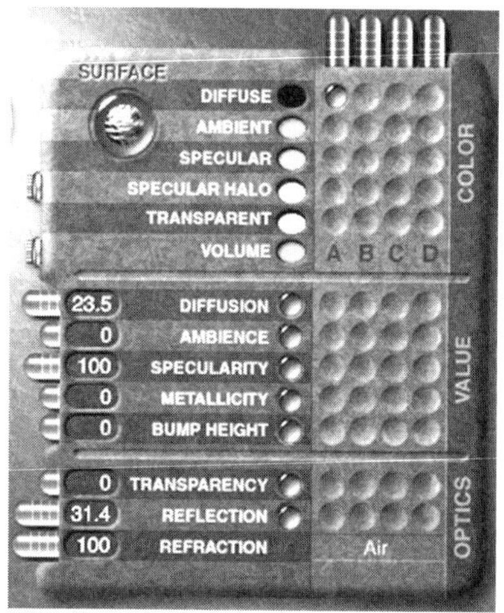

FIGURE 10.3 The Color, Value, and Optics palette.

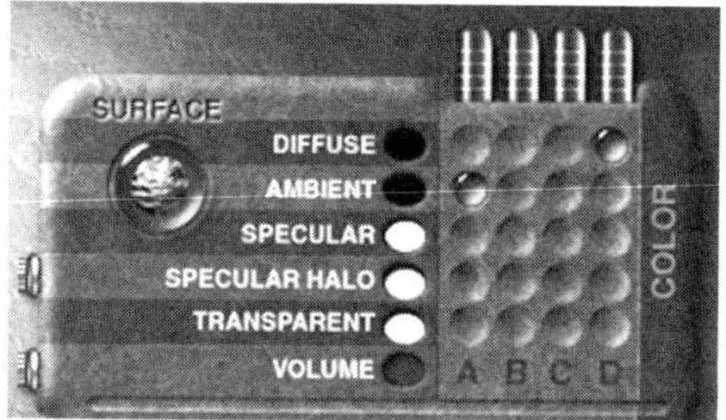

FIGURE 10.4 The Color Controls section of the Color/Value/Optics palette.

COLOR CONTROLS

The Color settings occupy the top third of the Color/Value/Optics palette. Like the Value and Optics settings, they can take their data from either a palette color or from one or more of the four texture channels (see Figure 10.4).

See the AB and ABC Channel Mixing information later in this chapter.

There are six associated color sources that you can manipulate in order to apply color to your selected object: Diffuse, Ambient, Specular, Specular Halo, Transparent, and Volume. Using the sliders at the left and top of each color option, you can control the amount and extent, as well as the resource (where the color is being taken from), of each of these components. The left-hand sliders determine "how much," while the sliders at the top determine "*from where*" and "*to what extent.*" This will become clearer as you read on and explore by doing.

Diffuse Color

Diffuse color is the color of the light that emanates from the material from all directions. Assigning a basic blue color as the material. for example, would show a bright blue when the Diffuse color slider is moved to 100, and black if the Diffuse color slider is set to 0. If, a texture is set to be the place the Diffuse color is being taken from instead of a palette color, then the overall color of the texture will be brightest when the Diffuse color slider is set to 100%, and very dark when the Diffuse color slider is set to zero. For different material effects, both palette and texture based, adjusting the Diffuse color slider is usually the first thing you do. To test out its effect, assign the Pale Cyan material to an object. You'll notice that the Diffuse color slider is set to 100%. Render the object to see what it looks like. Now, go back and set Diffuse color to 50% and render the object again. Not only is the object darker, but its 3D definition is weaker. Diffuse color can take its hue from a palette color, or from the Alpha channel of one or a combination of up to three of the four materials channels.

You can set the Diffuse color of an object to 0 in order to turn it into a silhouette against a light backdrop. Set Ambient color to 0 as well.

Ambient Color

Ambient color is the trickiest to apply, because it can easily throw the color in a scene off balance. In other applications, this is called a "Glow" color. It sets the color of an object to be displayed no matter what, in light or in darkness. If used consciously, it can create effects such as streetlights and lit windows. If used haphazardly, it can destroy the capability of an object to receive the right shadowing, and throw off the balance of a scene, giving the object a washed-out overexposed appearance. The best advice? Use Ambient color with care, and alter it subtly.

A nice effect is to set Ambient color high enough, which varies with each material, so that when the object is in the dark, part of it lights up. This can happen when Ambient color is taken from a texture separate from the Diffuse texture, and not from a palette color. In the light, both textures will contribute to the object, while in the dark, only the Ambient texture will be visible. This allows you to see window lights in a cabin as the sunlight disappears.

Specular Color

Objects that are shiny have specularity, or a hot spot that appears when a light shines on them. Specular color is the color of the hot spot. The amount of a set color applied to the hot spot is determined by the slider next to Specular color. Try using a complementary color as a specular color; that is, for a red object use green Specular (or vice versa), for a yellow object use violet Specular (and vice versa), and for a blue object use yellow Specular (or vice versa). This is a painter's trick to make objects seem more light sensitive. The same trick works well with the color of shadows.

Specular Halo Color

The Specular halo is the blurred edge around the Specular hot spot. Try to use complementary colors here too. Remember that the Specular halo indicates the finish of the material. A hard, shiny, metal material has a small hot spot with not a lot of halo. A buffed metal, or a plastic, has a larger halo. Some substances have more halo and little or no hot spot, such as buffed wood. Other materials, such as fabrics, have neither.

Transparent Color

What happens to an object with a color assigned to its Transparency color attribute depends on either Normal or Blend Transparency selected in the Materials Options list. If Normal is selected, a color assigned to the Transparency control, and 100% Transparency evoked with the slider, the object will "hold" that color as a glow.

The Normal setting is very useful when you need to show a treasure chest full of jewels. Assign a Transparency color to the selected object(s), and move the slider to 100%. Diffuse and other color settings should be set to 0.

If Blend Transparency is selected, at 100% Transparency the object will vanish. If the Blend Transparency color assigned to Transparency is drawn from a texture, then the material will be transparent where the texture's Alpha channel is black at 0% transparency. As the Transparency amount increases, the portion of the material identified in the Alpha channel as white will also start to become invisible. At 100%, the material (and the object it is assigned to) will disappear (see Figure 10.5).

Volume Color

Volume color is the color with which an object is filled. It acts in concert with the Transparency color. For example, if the Volume color is yellow and the Transparency color is blue, the object (in Normal mode) will look green at 100% transparency. That's because light shines through both the Transparency color and the Volume color. Altering just one of these colors over time creates interesting internal light effects on the object.

Although you can assign a Volume color to a material, the object that the material is targeted to will not display that Volume color when you cut it with a Boolean object.

FIGURE 10.5 This example shows how an object disappears as its Transparency Color setting is increased from 0 to 30% to 60%. The color in this case is being drawn from a Texture channel pattern. Diffusion Color is set to the same texture pattern at 100%.

VALUE CONTROLS

The Value settings occupy the middle third of the Color/Value/Optics palette. Like the Color and Optics settings, they can take their data from either a palette color or from one or more of the four texture channels. The five Value settings include Diffusion, Ambiance, Specularity, Metalicity, and Bump Height (see Figure 10.6). Value controls deal with "how much" of that element will be applied to the material, also known as its *intensity*.

See the AB and ABC Channel Mixing information later in this chapter.

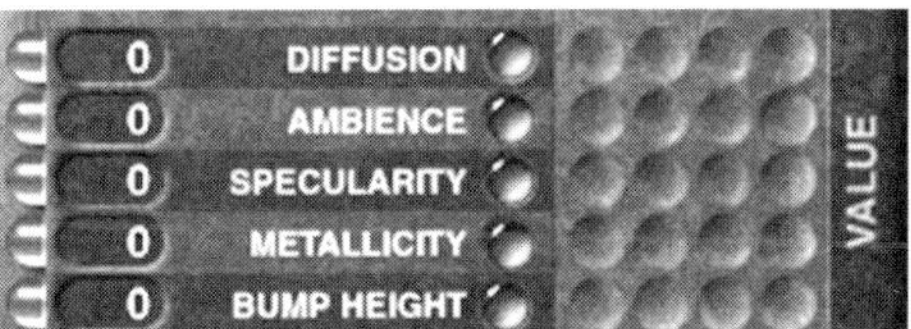

FIGURE 10.6 The Value Controls section of the Color/Value/Optics palette.

Diffusion Value

How much of the Diffusion component should be applied to your material? If the Diffuse element is based on either a Color palette assignment or a texture in one or more of the ABCD Texture channels, the Diffusion Value slider will determine how strong its presence will be in the material. In most cases, Diffusion value is set to 100%, but you can always explore what other amounts produce by looking at the Materials Nano Preview window.

Ambience Value

How much of the Ambience component should be applied to your material? If the Ambience element is based on either a Color palette assignment or a texture in one or more of the ABCD Texture channels, the Ambience Value slider will determine how strong its presence will be in the material. In most cases, you should be wary of setting the Ambience value too high, or you will wash out the texture. An exception might be a material that suddenly suffers a blast effect from a cosmic or nuclear device.

Specularity Value

How much of the Specularity component should be applied to your material? If the Specularity element is based on either a Color palette assignment or a texture in one or more of the ABCD Texture channels, the Specularity Value slider will determine how strong its presence will be in the material. You should adjust the Specularity value based on the material you want the assigned object to be made of. Turn it up for metals and plastics, medium up for woods and metallic liquids, and off for softer materials such as fabrics.

Metalicity Value

This value is one you will probably use less than the others. It works in conjunction with the Specularity controls to filter light for metallic material. The best suggestion for its use is to explore various settings in concert with a range of Specular settings. If you left it alone, you would probably never notice the difference in your productions.

Bump Height Value

Computer artists and animators love Bump mapping. Bump mapping applies what looks like height values to parts of a material, although no real distortion of the underlying geometry of the object ever occurs. There are two types of computer artists, those who apply Bump mapping gingerly and with care, and those who apply it with abandon everywhere. Bump mapping looks best when applied with the object in mind. Mountains close up look great with a lot of Bump mapped materials, while mountains in the distance need no Bump maps. Stones and rocky cliffs usually benefit, while smooth surfaces couldn't care less. The Bump Mapping value slider is one that has both positive and negative settings, ranging from –999 to +999. Negative values reverse the look of the Bump map, so what looks raised with a Positive setting will look depressed with a Negative one. Bizarre animation effects can be generated by reversing the two over time (see Figure 10.7).

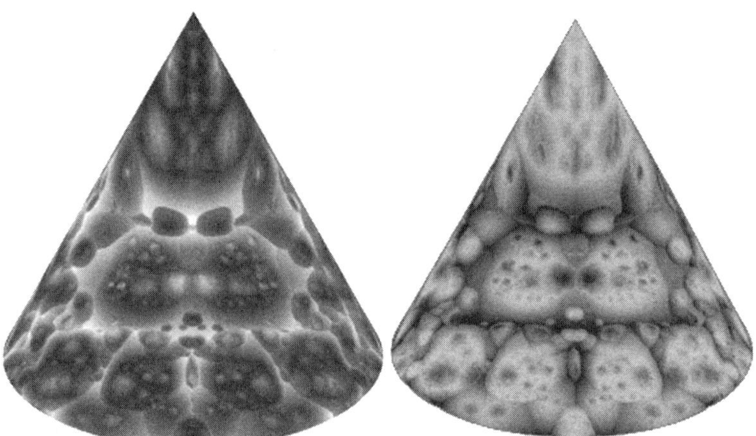

FIGURE 10.7 Here are two Bump mapped cones. The one on the left has a +100 Bump map, while the one on the right displays a –100 value. The same material was used on both. Can you see the difference? The Alien Rock texture with symmetric tiling was used.

OPTICS

Optics occupies the bottom third of the Color/Value/Optics palette. Like the Color and Value settings, Optic elements can take their data from either a Color palette or from one or more of the four Texture channels. The Optics controls address Transparency, Reflection, and Refraction (see Figure 10.8).

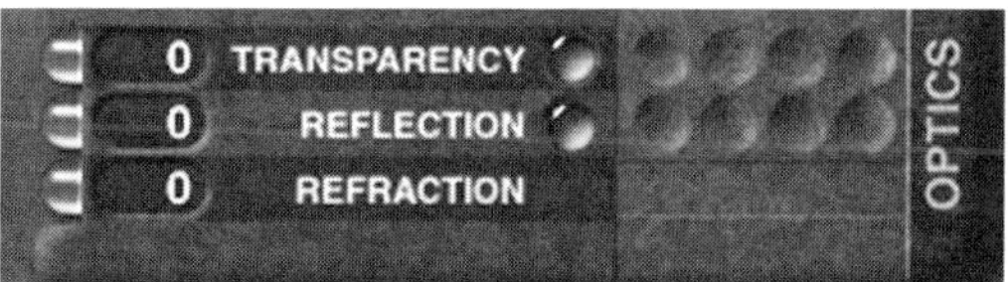

FIGURE 10.8 The Optics Controls section of the Color/Value/Optics palette, with controls for Transparency, Reflection, and Refraction.

See the AB and ABC Channel Mixing information later in this chapter.

TRANSPARENCY

We have already referenced the ways in which the Transparency gets its referenced data, from either the Color palette or Texture channels. This slider in the Optics channel controls how much transparency is to be used, ranging from 0 to 100%. Depending on where the transparent data is coming from, and what you want your object to look like, you will have to alter the settings until you achieve what you want. Refer to the *Color* and *Value* sections covered previously.

REFLECTION

A completely Reflective object is a mirror, while an object with no reflection bears no witness to the world around it. Most metals are at least partially reflective, and metals such as chrome are almost mirrors. Polished wood can be very reflective, ranging up to a maximum of 75%. Still water can also be reflective as a mirror, which is why in some cases you can use a mirror as a water substitute for water in a scene. This slider controls the amount of reflectivity an object possesses (see Figure 10.9).

FIGURE 10.9 These three spheres illustrate a 25% Reflectivity, a 55% Reflectivity, and a 100% Reflectivity. The object was placed in the foreground to give the spheres something to reflect.

REFRACTION INDEXING

A Refraction Index indicates the mass of a material as compared to that of a vacuum. The Refraction Index of a vacuum is 1.0000, so all other materials have a higher Refraction Index than 1.0. The more massive a substance is, or dense, the higher its Refraction Index number. Clear, clean air has a Refraction Index number close to 1.0, but the more hazing and particulate the air gets, its Refraction Index number rises. Clean water, on Earth, has a Refraction Index of 1.33 at 20 degrees Celsius. At different temperatures, however, and with various pollutants added, the Refraction Index of water increases. The Bryce Refraction Index numbers range on a scale from 0 to 300, and compare with standard Refraction Index numbers by moving the decimal point two places to the right. For example, a standard Refraction Index of 1.00 is represented by a Bryce number of 100. All research texts that deal with optics, and many that deal with physics, list Refraction Indexes for hundreds and even thousands of materials. Working in Bryce, only the purist will explore the use of Refraction Indexing when designing a material. In the service of these individuals to whom Refraction Indexing is both important and useful, we have prepared a partial Refraction Index table (Table 10.1) that lists the more common materials.

TABLE 10.1 Using the Refraction Index Control in Bryce

MATERIAL COMPONENT	STANDARD MEASUREMENT	BRYCE EQUIVALENT
Air	1.00029	100+
Acetone	1.36	136
Alcohol	.329	33
Calspar	1.486 to 1.66	149 to 166
Crown Glass	1.52	152
Crystal	2.00	200
Diamond	2.417	242
Emerald	1.57	157
Ethyl Alcohol	1.36	136
Fluorite	1.434	144
Quartz	1.46	146
Glass	1.5 to 1.9	150 to 190
Ice	1.309	131
Lapis Lazuli	1.61	161
Liquid Carbon Dioxide	1.20	120
Polystyrene	1.55	155
Quartz	1.553 to 1.65	155 to 165
Ruby	1.77	177
Sapphire	1.77	177
Salt	1.55 to 1.65	155 to 165
Topaz	1.61	161
Vacuum	1.000000	100
Water (Clear, 20 C)	1.333	133

The refraction controls in Bryce go from 0 to 300—100 is air, and 150 is water. This effectively moves the decimal point over two positions from the standard calculations, so the Bryce column lists the materials in Bryce equivalents that you can use in the Materials Lab.

AB and ABC Channel Mixing

Bryce offers you two magical ways to combine more than one channel to create composite mixed materials. Each is unique to Bryce. Because the four channels are referred to as ABCD, these techniques are named according to the channels they address: AB and ABC. In general, AB mixing allows a blend of the A and B channels so that the information in each is composited on the selected object in an altitude sensitive manner. The data in the A channel is written to the bottom half of the object, while the B channel data is written to the top half. ABC mixes are a little different. The data is written so that there is a mix of the data from A and B, mixed through the Alpha channel data of C. Let's look at some examples so you can see these mixing effects in action.

The top sphere on the left in Figure 10.10 shows a Diffuse Color map in channel A, while the bottom figure displays Diffuse color in channel B. The composite material contains the A channel data at the bottom, and the B channel data at the top, both blended seamlessly in the middle.

Figure 10.11 shows an ABC mix of Diffuse Color channel patterns. The Alpha channel of C allows a mix of the A and B channel data. The

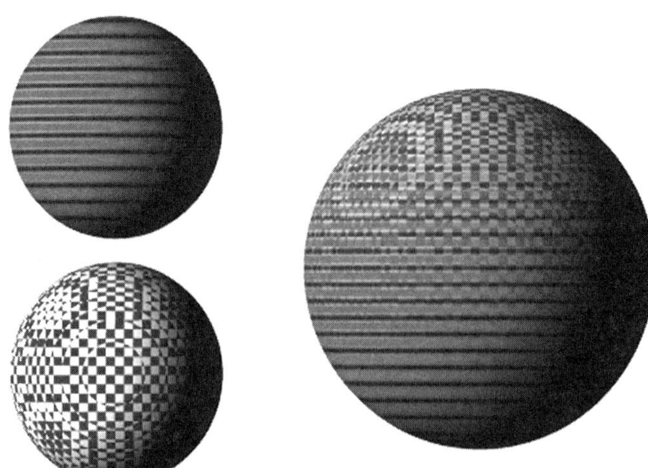

FIGURE 10.10 This is an AB material with data taken from the A and B Diffuse color channels.

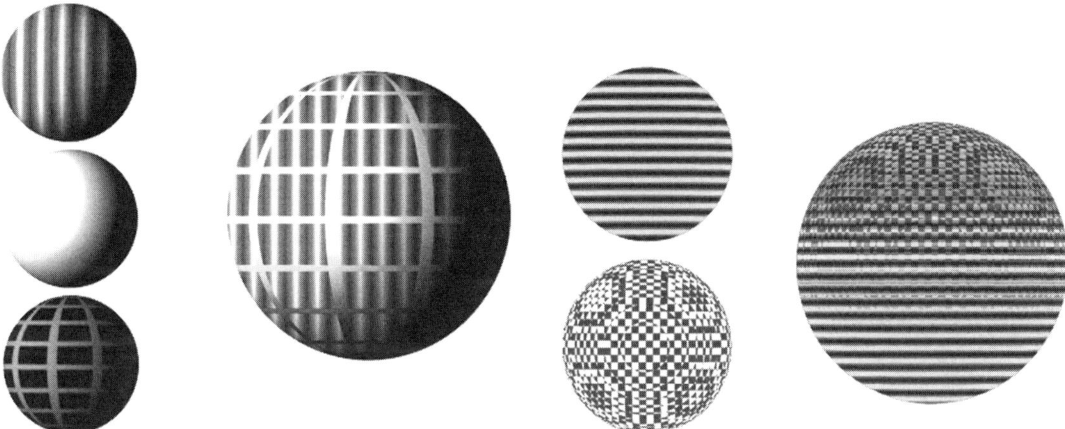

FIGURE 10.11 An example of an ABC material mix.

FIGURE 10.12 This is an AB mix of data from the Ambience channels. Each Ambience channel was set to 100%.

light areas of the Alpha channel show the B color data, and the dark Alpha areas show the A data.

In Figure 10.12, Ambience channel data was used in an AB mix. Although similar to Figure 10.10, the characteristics of Ambient light would create a very different object in the scene than Diffuse color channel data. This object would literally glow in the dark, whereas the Diffuse AB mix object would vanish if no light were shown in the scene.

Now let's see what happens when we develop an AB mix material from the Transparency channel data. Look at Figures 10.13 and 10.14 for the results.

FIGURE 10.13 AB channel Transparency data was used to create this AB mix material.

FIGURE 10.14 This figure uses the ABC channel mix method with Transparency, Diffuse, and Ambient color. The result is a wicker ball whose construction lies beyond known physics.

The Four CAB (Color, Alpha, Bump) Channels

The four CAB channels are used to customize and create the component textures that are ingredients for a material (see Figures 10.15 and 10.16).

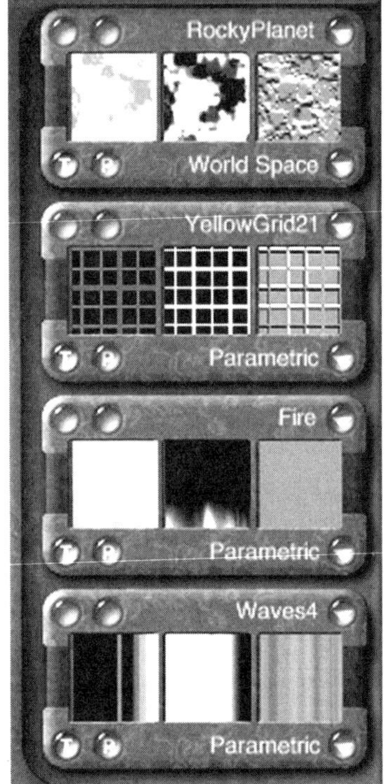

FIGURE 10.15 The ABCD Color-Alpha-Bump channels, where textures are created and customized as ingredients in a material.

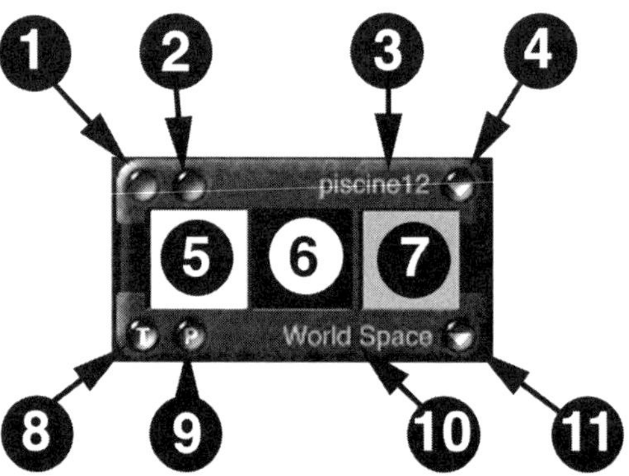

FIGURE 10.16 Each CAB (Color-Alpha-Bump) channel contains the same modification tools.

TRANSFORMATION OPTIONS

Clicking on this button brings up the Transformation Options dialog. You should always bring up this dialog if you want to resize, rotate, or reposition a texture component of the material, since it is activated the same way as the transformation items in the Edit toolbar, and is intuitive to use. Keeping an eye on the Nano Preview of the material, you can get a very good idea of how your manipulations are affecting the material. Each of the ABCD channels offers this tool, and the tool affects only the texture or picture in that channel (see Figure 10.17).

The range of the Size Transformation Options can be extended, by manually inputting numbers, up to plus or minus 1,000,000.

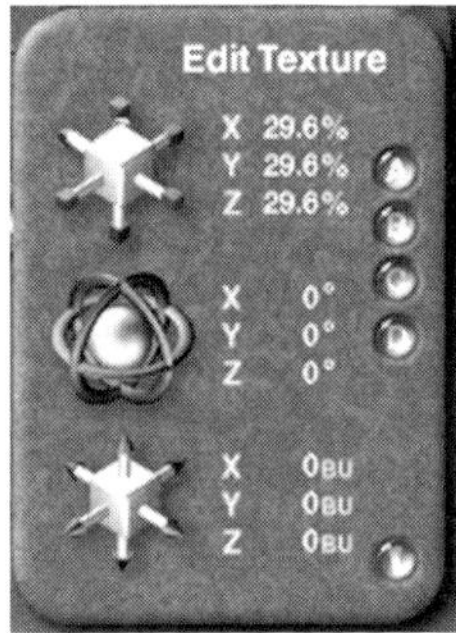

FIGURE 10.17 Bring up the Transformation Options whenever you need to resize, rotate, or reposition the textures in a channel for the material you are designing or customizing.

EDIT BUTTON

Clicking on this button brings up the Deep Texture Editor for customizing procedural textures, or the Picture Editor if you are working on a bitmap texture.

TEXTURE NAME

The name listed here is taken from the texture you are customizing, as imported from the Texture List at the right.

TEXTURE LISTS

Clicking on this button allows you to access and import a procedural texture from the Texture Lists. There are five Texture Lists you can access, each with dozens of items not found or displayed in the Materials Presets Library. The Lists include Basic, Bump, Clouds, Rocks, Sand, Psychedelic, and User.

In designing your own procedural textures, make this your first stop. Select a texture from one of the lists that sounds interesting, and use it as a starting point for your own creations.

COLOR ATTRIBUTE THUMBNAIL

A thumbnail view of the Color attribute of your texture is displayed here. This is the information that is accessed when you manipulate the Color controls for that channel.

ALPHA ATTRIBUTE THUMBNAIL

A thumbnail view of the Alpha attribute of your texture is displayed here. This is the information that is accessed when you manipulate the Value controls for that channel.

BUMP ATTRIBUTE THUMBNAIL

A thumbnail view of the Bump attribute of your texture is displayed here. This is the information that is accessed when you manipulate the Bump Height controls for that channel.

PROCEDURAL TEXTURE TOGGLE

The four component textures can be either Procedurally or Bitmap based. This button selects the Procedural option. This means that editing of the texture is done in the Deep Texture Editor.

BITMAP PICTURE TOGGLE

The four component textures can be either Procedurally or Bitmap based. This button selects the Bitmap option. This means that editing of the texture is done in the Picture Editor.

Clicking on the Bitmap Picture toggle and then on the Procedural Texture button randomizes the texture for that channel.

MAPPING TYPE NAME

This text displays the current Mapping Type.

MAPPING TYPE LIST

This button brings up the Mapping Type List. There are Mapping Types, ways that your texture can be placed on the selected object in your scene. They include Object Space, World Space, Parametric, Parametric Scaled, World Top, Spherical, Cylindrical, Reflection Map, Random, Object Top, and Object Front. In addition, you can elect to use the Symmetric Tiling option with any of these choices, and Scale Pict Size can be chosen for scaling the picture to match the size of your object. Some hints about Mapping Types follow (see Figure 10.18):

- **Object Space**: This is the most common choice for mapping a material on an object, which scales the texture to the object proportionately. This is the most common Texture mapping for objects that will move in a scene, since the texture realistically moves as a glued part of the object.

- **World Space**: Do not use World Space mapping if the object is in motion. World Space Texture maps remain stationary, so when mapped to moving objects, the texture makes it look as if it is being projected from a stationary position, and sliding across the object.

Moving an object with a World Space mapping texture placed on it can create some interesting effects. It can substitute for a light projected image, since in a sense, the texture is being projected from the world light. Explore this possibility, and save an animation that uses it as a sample. Note that World Space mapped objects also look strange when the object is rotated on any 3D axis.

- **Parametric**: This mapping can be substituted for object mapping, but is especially vital when it comes to mapping imported WaveFront (OBJ) and 3DS objects. It allows you to remap the object with the texture map saved out from their original applications, and results in perfect texture maps. DXF objects cannot use Parametric maps.
- **Parametric Scaled**: Scaled Parametric maps address every part of an object with a separate map. This can be very useful for mapping reptiles with textures that look a little different for each body part, but confusing on primitives. See the Scaled Parametric cube in Figure 10.18.
- **World Top**: This is worth exploring when mapping Infinite Planes. It comes out a bit differently than a standard World Space map. If the selected object has a vertical dimension, World Top is not a good choice, since it will streak the sides of an object.
- **Spherical**: Although useful on Spherical objects, the polar region of the texture shows a crunched-together mapping, which is not very pretty.
- **Cylindrical**: Cylindrical mapping is best used to emulate labels on cans or bottles.
- **Reflection Map**: Reflection maps are projected on your objects as if from a spherical projector surrounding the scene. Use them on Spherical or Terrain objects. Reflection maps do not work well on cubes.
- **Random**: This is the mapping type to select when you want to create splotchy surfaces, perfect for terrains, rocks, and alien world objects. Resize the texture to accommodate the object being mapped. This is also the mapping to use when you want to create marbleized materials, camouflage, or cow hide.

- **Object Top**: The map is applied to the top of the object, and streaks the sides. This is great for woods, since it produces both grain ends and streaks.
- **Object Front**: The map is applied to the front of the object, and streaks the other sides and top/bottom. This works best on objects that remain with their front facing the camera. This is great for woods, since it produces both grain ends and streaks.

New Mapping Type Options in Bryce 5!

There are a number of new Mapping Type options added to Bryce 5 (see Figure 10.19). They include the following:

Sinusoidal: This option applies a sine wave-based look to the material. It's a nice alternative to the Random mapping.

Object Side: This one is the final option to Object Top and Object Front, completing the trio.

Object Cubic: This option has been noticeably missing prior to Bryce 5, giving you the capability to apply a Cubic object mapping type. Apply this one to Cubic objects and object volumes.

World Front/World Side/World Cubic: Three new World mapping types. Use on objects that will remain stable and glued in place in the scene. See Figures 10.18 to 10.20.

Never apply World mapping types to objects you intend to place in motion, unless the effect you want is to have the material sliding across the object as the animation commences.

FIGURE 10.18 Some of the various mapping types create alternate looks with the same texture. From top.left: Object Space, World Space, Parametric, Parametric Scaled, World Top, Spherical, Cylindrical, Reflection Map, Random, Object Top, and Object Front.

FIGURE 10.19 New Mapping Types featured in Bryce 5 from the same material (Eroded Granite) on a sphere: Sinusoidal, Object Side, Object Cubic, World Front, World Side, and World Cubic.

FIGURE 10.20 Symmetric Tiling can produce interesting variations of a texture, like knots in wood or geometric floor tiles.

Clicking on the Picture button and then on the Texture button randomizes the texture for that channel.

Volumetric Materials

Volumetric materials soak the selected object with the selected texture inside and out, in effect, making the texture a full 3D participant in the construction of the object. You can only appreciate the internal existence of the material if the object has degrees of transparency assigned to it, however, or if a Boolean cutter slices part of the object away (see Figure 10.21).

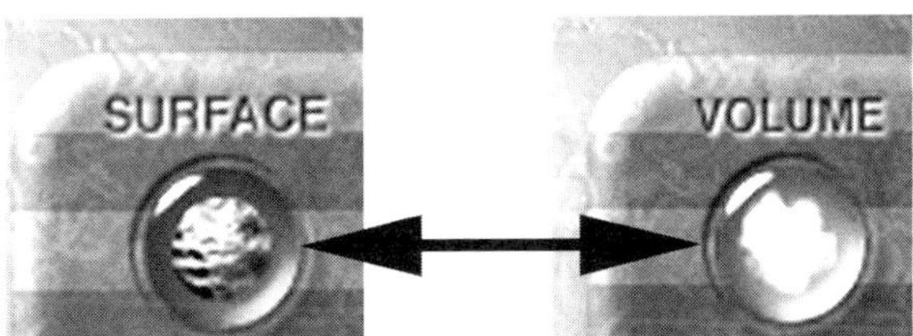

FIGURE 10.21 The Surface/Volume toggle on the Color/Value/Optics palette switches between surface and volumetric material modes.

VOLUMETRIC SHADING MODES

Three shading modes make an appearance in the Shading Modes list when you select the Volumetric material type: Flat Shading, Full

Shading, and Light Sensitive. Base Density controls the transparency of the object. Set to 100%, the object displays no internal material. Set to 0%, the object displays maximum material.

FLAT SHADING

Flat Shaded Volumetric materials are displayed as flat mapped 2D surfaces inside of the object.

FULL SHADING

Full Shaded Volumetric materials are displayed as 3D volumes. Circular dots become spheres. This allows you to fly through them, just as you would through any other objects in a 3D scene. The only thing to keep in mind if you want to do this is the stiff rendering cost of volumetrics in general.

LIGHT SENSITIVE

Light Sensitive Volumetric materials only appear when you shine a light on them. They take on the color of the light, and respond best when the light is at full intensity (although more subtle effects can be generated when the light is at lower settings). This allows you to have objects in your scene that are invisible to the eye, and to make them appear as a light is turned in their direction (see Figure 10.22).

Using a Volumetric material on a Boolean cutter is the same as turning Transfer Materials off on the cutter, except that the part of the Volume material in back of the cutter is completely hidden from view (see Figure 10.23).

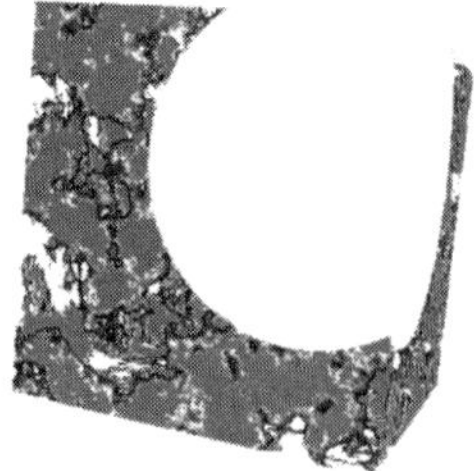

FIGURE 10.22 On the left is a Cube with a Volumetric material cut by a Boolean Negative Sphere with a surface material. At the right is the same situation, except that the Cube is also using a Volumetric material.

FIGURE 10.23 A Cube, shaded with a Volumetric material: Flat Shaded, Full Shaded, and Light Sensitive (with a spotlight shining in the Volume's direction).

Using Volumetric materials with Full Shading can suffice in many instances as an animatable particle system. All you have to do is make sure that the Texture channel is checked for Base Density, and that you have a suitable Volumetric material that gives you transparency. The best material to select for this purpose is the Ball Bearings material in the Volume folder of the Materials Library.

CREATING A NOVEL PARTICLE SYSTEM EFFECT

1. Create a Sphere, and use the Volume material Ball Bearings to map it. Tint the texture bright red. Make sure Full Shading is activated in the Shading List of the Materials Lab.
2. Make a Volcano in the Terrain Editor - and place the Volumetric sphere in the volcano opening.
3. Create an animation in which the Sphere both Rotates and Resizes (on the World Y-axis).

You can also use Light Sensitive Volumetrics for this exercise, so that the particles display only when a light is shined on them, although Full Shaded volumetric materials also take on the color of a light. This further enhances the animation effects (see Figure 10.24).

FIGURE 10.24 Lava spewing from a volcano is a perfect demonstration of how to use a Full Shaded Volumetric material to emulate a particle system effect.

VOLUME CONTROLS

When you switch to Volume instead of Surface material, the Optics section of the Materials Lab interface changes to Volume. The listings also change, because Volumetric materials must be addressed in different ways than Surface materials. The new command listings include Base Density, Edge Softness, Fuzzy Factor, and Quality/Speed.

Base Density

This is the most important Volumetric control whose use must be mastered. Using this slider, you can set the Base Density of a volumetric material from 0% to 100%. If all you are addressing is a color from the palette, then Base Density settings will have next to no effect on your material. The Base Density controls are meant to address materials with textures. Here is the best way to understand Base Density, and the design of Volumetric materials in general:

1. Create a Sphere in your workspace, and with it selected, open the Materials Lab. Choose the Volume mode.
2. Click in the Diffuse row on the first channel. Click in the Base Density row in the first channel. Leave all other commands set to the Palette button, with no other channels selected.
3. In the first channel (A), find or create a texture that has solid black in its Alpha component.

Base Density works best when the Alpha channel of the texture being incorporated has solid black in it. This is the section of the image that will drop out of the final material, leaving holes in the object on which the material is placed.

4. Set Base Density to 100 with the slider. This will be drawn as your texture with holes where the Alpha component is black. Move the Base Density slider to 50%. Surprise! Instead of creating a transparency, less of the texture is seen in the material. Move the Base Density slider to 0%. No texture material is seen in the preview (see Figure 10.25).

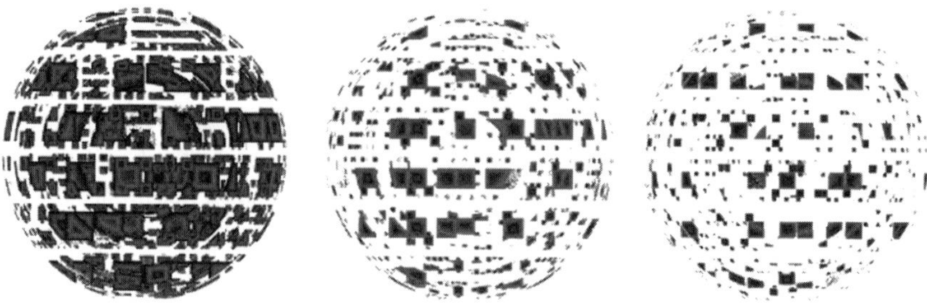

FIGURE 10.25 Following the preceding example, the Base Density settings are shown to control the density of particles in a Volumetric material, not its transparency. The left object is at 100% Base Density, and moves to 10% Base Density at the right.

PLATE 1. This truck was modeled entirely of Bryce elements, before being placed in a Bryce scene.

PLATE 2. Using Bryce Metaballs, you can create a myriad of creature forms.

PLATE 3. It's easy to supply your own leaf designs for a tree created in the Tree Lab as shown here.

PLATE 4. At the top are 2D Picture objects, modeled in 3D in ZBrush, and ported to Bryce for placement. At the bottom, you can see how effective it is to place a spotlight in a volcano.

PLATE 5. Extremely complex scenes are built one component at a time.

PLATE 6. The top image displays the KPT FraxFlame effects as applied to both a spherical sky and to other elements of a scene. At the bottom, a photographic image is applied as a bump map to a wall.

PLATE 7. Using components modeled externally and imported greatly increases your creative options.

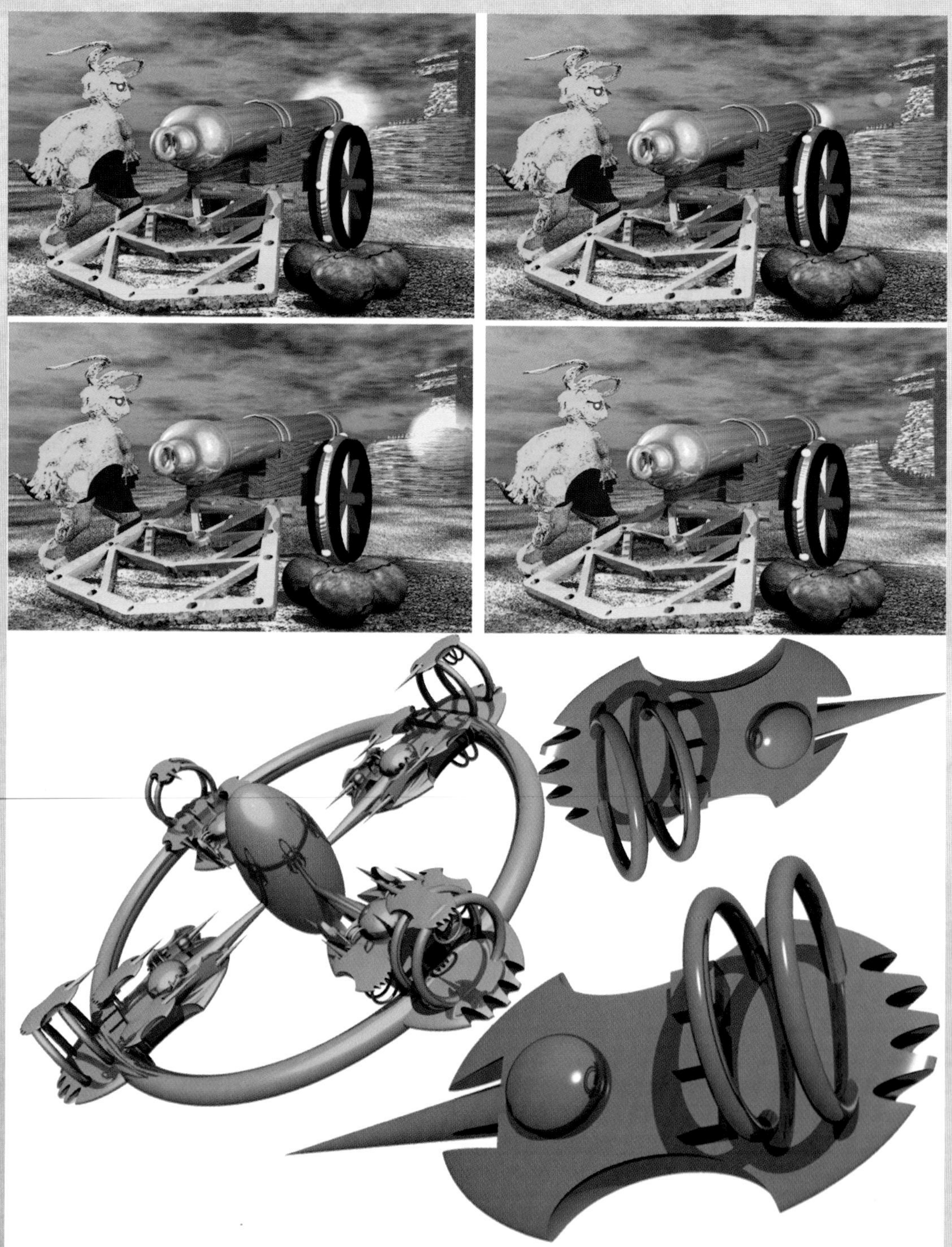

PLATE 8. Scenes from a cannon animation are shown at the top. Below are some complex models created with Metaballs and standard primitive components.

Using Base Density operations such as the one just described, you can create the famous "Beam me up, Scotty" effect from Star Trek. The reverse, of course, would be "Beam me down." Everything depends on having a good amount of black in the texture's Alpha channel: around 35% to 50%.

Edge Softness

This slider adds softness to the edge of the elements that make up your material. The effect is subtle, gradually blending the material into the background. As shown in Figure 10.26, the effect is almost impossible to discern.

FIGURE 10.26 This figure illustrates Edge Softness (top) and Fuzzy Factor (bottom) applied to a Volumetric material: Edge Softness: 20, 50, and 100; Fuzzy: 100, 200, 300.

Fuzzy Factor

This slider adds fuzziness globally to your material, rather like a fog that blurs everything out at maximum settings.

Quality/Speed

The Quality versus Speed setting is your only chance to influence the speed of Volumetric materials rendering. It is advisable to move the slider all the way down, and to opt for maximum speed over quality. The only situation that might influence you to select a more qualitative render would be an assignment to produce graphics or animations for a major print, broadcast, or movie project. Even then, you might find higher quality settings extremely prohibitive.

Multiple Materials on One Object Using the Boolean Way

Except for AB and ABC mapping in Bryce, you are not supposed to be able to apply more than one material to any single ungrouped object, but there is one rather convoluted way around this restriction. It calls for a little knowledge of Boolean operations, which I'm sure you already possess at this point. Here's how it works:

1. Place a Sphere in your Bryce world. We are using a Sphere as a quick example, although you can use this technique on any object, primitive or imported. Work in the Front view.
2. Duplicate the Sphere in place. Name the original "Sphere 1," and the copy "Sphere 2."
3. Use a Boolean Cube to cut off the bottom half of Sphere 1, and another to cut off the top half of Sphere 2.
4. In the Materials Lab, apply a different material to each hemisphere. Go back to your world, and make sure the halves line up. Link Sphere 2 to Sphere 1. Render and Save to disk (see Figure 10.27).

FIGURE 10.27 Using the Boolean technique described, the Sphere appears to be mapped with two totally different materials at the same time.

Multiple Materials on One Object Using Transparent Layers

An alternate way to create an object with multiple materials:

1. Duplicate the original in place, making sure that it doesn't move. Name the original "1" and the duplicate "2".
2. Resize the Duplicate so it is 5% larger.
3. Map a material to #2 that is 60% transparent. As yet another variation, map #2 so that it has holes in it (Alpha channel transparency). Whichever way you select, the object is to see through #2 to #1. Link the outer object to the inner one.
4. Render and Save to disk.

This technique is exactly the one you would use to wrap clouds around a planet.

If both objects are transparent or Alpha transparent, there's no reason you can't place these layers over the multi-material object shown in Figure 10.28. This process can be enhanced by repeating the steps as many times as desired.

FIGURE 10.28 The cage around this inner globe was constructed by using Alpha transparency on the cage material, with the Transparent Layers technique described in the preceding text. The objects were created in about 30 seconds.

Adding Bitmap Labels to Objects

This is a project that most computer artists and animators take on at some point, whether from their own interest or as an assignment. Every 3D application handles it somewhat differently. In Bryce, with the knowledge you have gained by working in the Materials Lab, this challenge can be met quickly. Here's how:

1. Develop a graphic of your label-to-be in a paint application, and make an Alpha map of it as outlined previously. Save it to disk in a format that Bryce can import.
2. Import a suitable object to wrap the label on, a bottle or glass. Use whatever material you want on it, and give the material a 55% transparency.
3. Create a Cylinder that fits around the middle of the object, which will act as your label object. Make the Cylinder about 5% larger than the object in circumference as seen from the Top view (that is, enlarge the label object's X and Z scale).
4. With the Label object selected, open the Materials Lab. Activate the first channel by placing the buttons in the Diffuse and Ambient Color slots, Diffusion and Ambience Value slots, and in the Transparency Optics slot. Open the Picture Editor.
5. Load the label art into the first window, and the Alpha map of the label into the second window. The Result window should show the label in full color.
6. Use Object Front mapping to wrap the label to the object. White areas of the label will drop out. Render the object, and save it to disk (see Figure 10.29).

FIGURE 10.29 By following the preceding tutorial, you should be able to wrap your own labels on a suitable Bryce object.

USING THE WRONG MATERIALS FOR THE RIGHT REASONS

An artist needs to know all of the rules and idiosyncrasies of the medium she or he is working in. As a computer artist and animator, you need to know how to use your computer as a creative medium. There is another reason for learning the rules when it comes to working within the constraints presented by your chosen medium: you have to know the rules so that you can consciously break them when you need to.

This is especially true when it comes to customizing and applying procedural materials, the materials found within the Materials Lab, and in the associated libraries. If you use only the materials you are "supposed to," those most logical for the task, then how will your work differ from everyone else's? It won't, and your work will have no discernible signature of originality. This is actually the central criticism leveled at computer art, because it is seen as the programmer's signature, not the artist's. Bryce is no exception, especially since it's so easy to accomplish basic tasks that look great. Click on a sky parameter, and the sky is painted in. Place Primitive objects in the scene, and they magically appear. Without a little bending and stretching of the rules, it won't matter who is responsible for the resulting artwork—you, another person, or the machine.

Every time you spend part of your creative juices on customizing the components of a scene, you start to develop work that bears the mark of your own mind and hand. That is why Bryce is such a massive creative tool. You are given every opportunity to stray from the expected path, and to mark the resulting work with your personal visual signature. The objects that you create, the way you compose them in space and time, and the global parameters of your scenes—all of these play a part in your personal artistic watermark. One area that especially stands out in Bryce as having the potential for customization and surrealistic exploration is that of tweaking and twisting the parameters of procedural materials in the Materials Lab and in the Deep Texture Editor (Chapter 11).

Creating Customized Materials

At the start of your Bryce experience, you will probably be in a hurry to see your rendered worlds. Some of the more subtle aspects and options might be passed over in a rush to render. As you become more familiar with how fast you can do the basics, the subtleties might start to attract you, and you will spend more time tweaking the finer features. Materials can be composed through the use of multiple channels, and even customized further by using a channel's Deep Texture Editing (Chapter 11) and Picture Editor processes. Perhaps you have already attempted some materials creation on your own, and you might even have a personal library that contains hundreds of your own material creations. Let's reinforce and deepen your general knowledge concerning materials before we push the topic to a more creative edge.

SURFACE MATERIALS CREATION TIPS

When creating Surface materials of your own, here are some points to note:

- Think of "Ambient" as "Glow." Ambient color will act as a glow color, especially when the object is placed against a dark backdrop and when lights are dimmed or off. Any part of the object that is in a shadow, even a self shadow, will show the Ambient color, while the part of the object that remains in the light will show the Diffuse color. If the Ambience Value is taken from an assigned channel texture, then that texture will glow wherever the object is in the dark or shadow. If you are using a pattern from a channel texture, keep the Ambience Value related to the value, and the Ambient Color related to the Color palette. This gives you a patterned texture that will be visible in both light and dark environments.
- As a general rule, keep a texture size set from 0 to 10 if you want to see the details of the texture. Larger sizes are good for effects, but look very speckled when targeted to small objects (especially without antialiasing on).
- Multicolor patterns (e.g., RGB Fabric) can behave better in the light and dark by attaching both the Diffuse and Ambient colors to the channel texture, while leaving the Value set to the Color palette.
- Keep the Ambience Value to 50% or less when applying a deep Bump map (50% and higher), or the Ambience will wash out the Bump map shadowing (see Figure 10.30).

Any smooth metallic texture looks like worn metal when you assign a Bump map from an appropriate texture channel (see Figure 10.31).

If you add a Bump map to an object in an animation, with 0% bump value at the start and 100% at the end, the object will look like it is being blistered by heat. A great use for this would be a ring of rocks too close to a departing rocket.

- Set the Ambient color to a darker hue (dark blue or even black) to preserve the underlying texture pattern, even when the Ambience value is set at 100%.

FIGURE 10.30 On the left, the Ambience is set to 30%, while on the right it is set to 100%. In both cases, the Bump map is set to 100%. Keep the Ambience setting low to emphasize the Bump map.

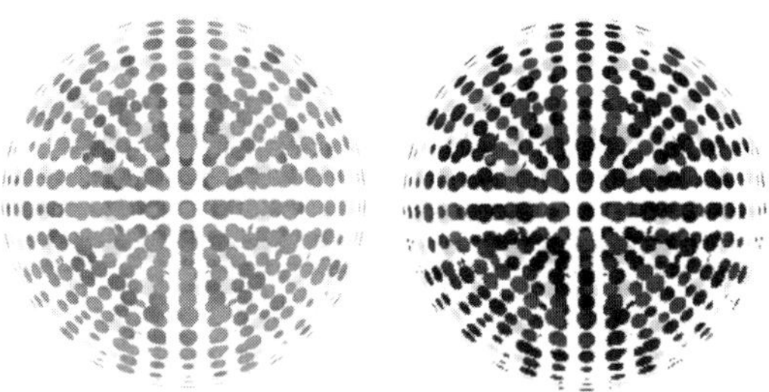

FIGURE 10.31 On the left is the default gold metallic material, while on the right it has been modified by adding a Texture channel Bump Height map (the texture used is Black and White from the Basic folder in the Materials Lab).

- With Transparency set to 100% and all other sliders set to 0%, the color of the transparent object will be a blend of its Transparent Color and the Volume Color. Moving the Diffusion value slider up at this point adds the Diffuse Color to the blended mix. Setting the Transparent Color to black effectively makes an object opaque, no matter what the other colors are set to.
- There might be a time when you want to turn on an object in the dark as if it were a light. This can be done with or without textures in the Ambient Color channel, since the Ambient Color will represent the light as a color or a texture. All you have to do is to set the Ambience Value to 100%, and use the Transparency Optics slider as the "light switch." The higher the transparency setting, the dimmer the object light; therefore, at a transparency of 100%, the light will be invisible. Material Options should be set to blend Transparency.

VOLUMETRIC MATERIALS CREATION TIPS

Be very careful about applying Volumetric materials to large objects, as this will send rendering time through the roof. As a caution, make objects mapped with Volumetric materials no more than about 15% of your total screen size whenever possible. Here are some points to take note of when creating Volumetric materials:

- Multilayered Volumetric materials can be used as layers with holes in them by controlling the material's Base Density. These are best used un-animated, since the rendering times are very high. Make sure that shadowing is On to increase the depth perception of the layers.
- Do not push the Quality/Speed slider all the way to the left, or you will be in danger of hanging up your system, because the preview render will take too much time.

- Setting the Fuzzy factor to 0 produces the most brilliant texture colors.
- By simply switching from Surface to Volume in the Materials Lab, all of your procedural surface materials can become volumetric.
- Use Flat Shaded Volumetrics for layered objects with holes in them, and Full Shaded Volumetrics if you are going to move the camera through them (see Figure 10.32).

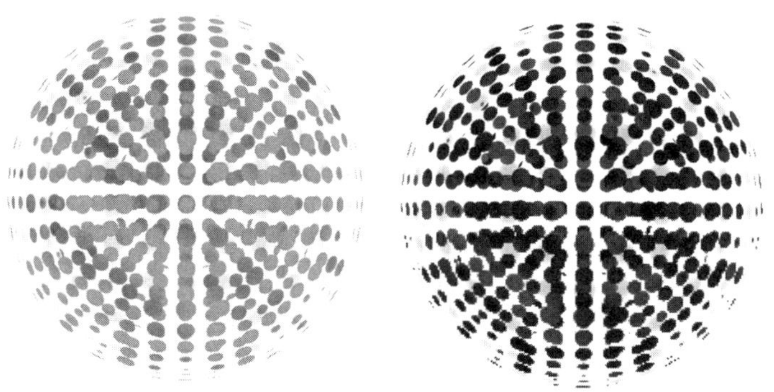

FIGURE 10.32 The same Volumetric material appears flat shaded on the left, and full shaded on the right. Full Shading creates 3D material pieces, but rendering times are much longer.

BITMAP MATERIALS CREATION TIPS

The first step in creating interesting materials that use bitmap pictures is to create or customize interesting bitmap pictures in your paint application. In general, they should be defaulted to 72 dpi (dots per inch) for use in Bryce, with a size of 640 × 480 or 420 × 240. Use the larger size when the camera is going to zoom in on the material, and use the smaller size when the material will remain a backdrop element. You can use any dpi ratio, but 72 dpi will suffice in most cases. Here are some points to take note of when creating bitmap-based materials on your own:

- Bitmap images will tile when you use any mapping but the Random option if they are resized to address the object more than once. The higher or lower you alter their size in the Materials Lab, the smaller the tiles will be.
- Using Random Mapping with a bitmap creates color patterns from the bitmap that can substitute for similar procedural texture looks. This works best if the image is constrained to no more than one hue, since more color results in a random dot pattern (unless you are looking for a random dot pattern, of course).

ALPHA STANDALONES

An Alpha image is a mask, and it does not have to have an accompanying cloned color image to be a valuable tool in the creation of a material. It can also serve to mask out an underlying procedural texture, or a totally different bitmap image. In this way, you can create bitmapped areas on an object (such as labels and other effects), mapped over another bitmap or a procedural textured material (see Figures 10.33 and 10.34).

FIGURE 10.33 The color image was loaded on the left, and the rectangular Alpha image in the center. The result is an image that displays parts of the color image inserted in rectangular areas, as shown in Figure 10.34.

FIGURE 10.34 The Alpha masked image shown in Figure 10.33 inserted in a Bryce 3D scene, wrapped on a sphere with a color sphere inside.

PLACING THE BITMAP IN A CHANNEL

Normally, the Bitmap picture is placed in the Diffuse Color channel, so that all of the color and image data in the image predominates. You can exercise other options, however. Figure 10.35 shows the bitmap image attached to different channels on the Materials Editor.

FIGURE 10.35 The same bitmap image as addressed to the following channel attributes: Diffuse (Transparency = 100%), Ambient, Transparent, Bump, Reflection, and Diffuse Random.

TILED BITMAPPED LOGOS

Tiling bitmapped logos are a rage on the Web, used most often for a page backdrop. Using the bitmap techniques already described, you can create infinite logo backdrops in Bryce (see Figure 10.36).

BITMAP/PROCEDURAL COMBINATION MATERIALS TIPS

The bitmap/procedural material effect uses a bitmap picture in one or more Color, Value, or Optics channels (Surface) in the Materials Lab. Here are some points to take note of when creating bitmap/procedural materials on your own,

- The most common way to fold in the bitmap is in the Diffuse Color channel, since this allows you to get all of the color from the image. Another suggested alternative is to apply the bitmap as a Bump map, especially if it is composed of an image that can be recognized in silhouette. This creates an embossed effect, and is especially attractive when tiled.

FIGURE 10.36 A plane tiled with bitmapped logos casts shadows on another plane below, mapped with a procedural texture material.

- The cloned object method allows you to paste the bitmap to a clone of the original object that is a few percentage points larger than the original object. This makes the Bump-mapped image look like a solid cutout above the object (see Figure 10.37).
- The multiple channel method allows you to mix procedural and bitmapped textures in one material, so the effect is a blend rather than a segmented layering. Use the following parameters to create one example of this type of composite material: Channel A and B are

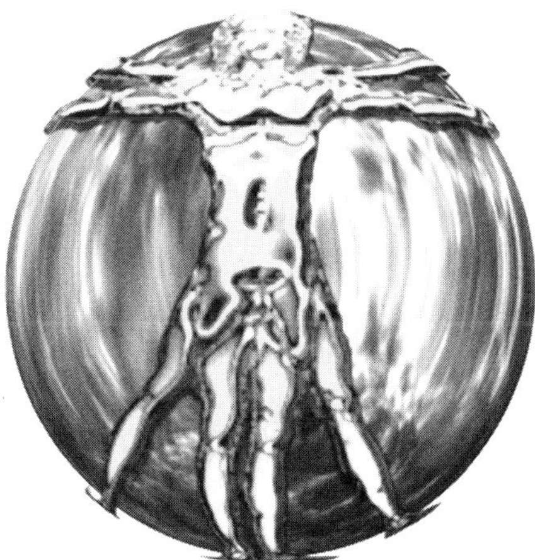

FIGURE 10.37 This bitmapped object is mapped to a clone of the original object, sized a few percentage points larger. Notice its 3D appearance, especially at the edges.

activated for Diffuse Color and Diffusion Value. Channel B is also activated for Ambient Color and Ambience Value. Channel A holds the bitmap image (the default LEO picture), which uses Object Front mapping. Channel B holds the galaxy texture from the Basics Library. Diffusion and Ambience sliders are set at 100% (see Figure 10.38).

FIGURE 10.38 An example of multiple channel mapping.

EXOTIC LAMINATES

True laminated materials present a different problem. A laminate is a combination of two materials, both of which must be present on the object. You cannot create two different materials in Bryce using just the Materials Lab, so another way has to be found to accomplish this effect. The elegant solution incorporates the use of the Advanced Motion Lab. Here's how:

1. Select one material, or create one, for frame 1 of an animation (animation length is your choice), and map it to an object. Select or create a second material for the last frame.
2. Open the Advanced Motion Lab with the object selected. Find the object in the list, and click on Material. For all of the parameters listed under Material, draw a straight horizontal line midway in the Motion Curve area. This effectively blends the two materials into one for the entire animation.

Use this technique to create the following exotic laminates: Double Wood, Wood-Stone, Double Stone, Cloud-Stone, Water-Cloud, Water-

Stone, Rock-Psychedelic, Mirror-Wood, Cloud-Metal, and more (see Figure 10.39).

FIGURE 10.39 From upper left to bottom right, these exotic laminates blend Rock and Wood, Red Fractal and Vortex, Carnival Tent and Clown Collar, and Gilded Cage and Disco Kelp.

MULTIPLES OF ONE

We called this "Multiples of One" because you need only one material mapped to a selected object to achieve this effect. It allows you to maximize the variability of one assigned material, by using it up to four times in different ways in each of the four (ABCD) channels in the Materials Lab. Do the following:

1. Place a Sphere in your scene, and select it. Open the Materials Lab.
2. Activate the A, B, and C channels for Diffuse and Ambient Color, and Diffusion and Ambience value (click on channel C for these attributes with Shift/Control held down). Activate the D channel for Bump height.

3. Use only one texture of your choice in all four channels. Vary the size, rotation, and mapping type in each channel. You now have a four-layered material that is based on different elements of the same texture (see Figure 10.40).

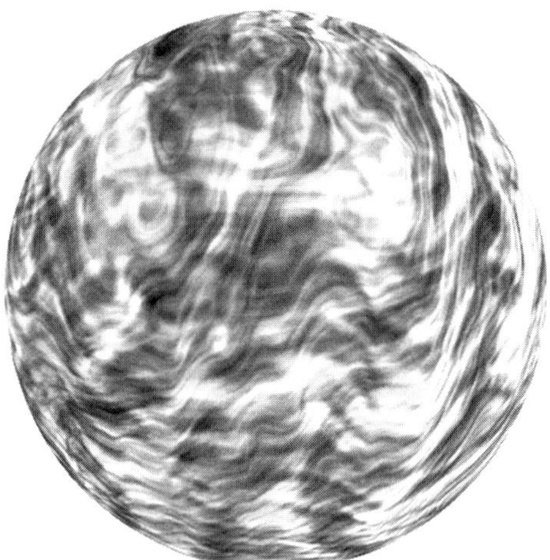

FIGURE 10.40 Startling material maps can result when you use the same material configured in different ways in each of the four ABCD channels in the Materials Lab, like this quadruple mapping of the Abalone texture from the Psychedelic folder. Each channel can also be independently animated, producing complex layered movements.

EMPLOYING THE CREATIVE MISTAKE

Why would you want to use the "wrong" materials on an object in the first place? There are two reasons. The first is that the "wrong" material might have a better "right" look than the "right" material. Let's look at a simple case in point. Bryce features both a Terrain/Plane Materials Library and a Rocks/Stones Materials Library. Placing material on a mountain, however, especially in the foreground, might work better if you use a Rocks/Stones material than one meant specifically for terrain. The Rocks/Stones material might display a more "realistic" and discernible texture at some distances than the "right" material from the Terrain Materials Library options.

The second reason to explore assigning the "wrong" material is more personal. It might be that a certain material expresses your compositional and aesthetic needs more than a standard material does. You might want to assign a cloud material to a solid in order to make the composition appear more ethereal or alien, or the opposite, assigning a metallic or rock material to a cloud plane. Both are valid reasons for using the "wrong" materials.

USING THE WRONG MATERIALS FOR MORE REALITY

"Reality" is a nebulous affair at best. Reality can be a shadowy monster that lurks in your bedroom, until the light reveals a bundle of clothes draped over a chair. Reality is broken all of the time by what we perceive at the moment. If you have been taught that red is evil, then the most striking red sunset will have overtones of evil intent for you. Some aspects of perception are ingrained in us because of what we have been taught, so reality can depend on mental and emotional attitudes as well. "Reality" also depends on experience. You might discover that the swastika has a deep history as a symbol of transformation in Indian culture, but if your grandparents escaped the terror of the Nazis, the "real" nature of the swastika will be forever colored by the stories you were told, and the horrors that the swastika of experience evokes. Reality is not neutral ground, but is colored by suspicion, education, cultural bias, personal experience, and more.

How might all of this affect your work in Bryce when you are deciding what material to apply to an object? The answer might depend on whom you are doing your work for. If you are creating art or animation for a client, then you have to listen carefully to their critiques. If they say that your "brick doesn't look like real brick," you have to find out what their definition of "real" brick is, and reshape the composition accordingly. If the Bryce work you are involved in is to bring your own vision to pass, and the brick material you just rendered doesn't look or feel "real" enough for you, then your own exploration will continue until it does.

Knowing this means that some of the following suggested alterations for achieving greater reality, or optional reality, might not work for all of your perceptive needs. If these suggestions leave you feeling unsatisfied, then simply use this as a procedure for exploration, and seek further for examples that satisfy you.

SIMULATING MATERIALS REALISM

Materials Realism is a term invented by a sculptor friend of ours (Dave Huber) to indicate that the materials used in a sculpted piece are to be used as is, and not painted or hidden. We are using it in a slightly different context to indicate that what a material's name is does not always determine its uses in a Bryce 3D composition. There is an alchemist's way of perception that also is used as the basis for this exploration—"like begets like." Keeping in mind all of the perceptual inconsistencies already discussed, there is one cardinal rule when you want to use the "wrong" materials to simulate an enhanced realism in your Bryce work.

THE CARDINAL RULE: EYES BEFORE MIND

When you need to assign a material to an object in your Bryce world, do not read the names of the materials. Instead, look at their thumbnails and see which ones "look like" the real-world material you have in mind, and select them accordingly.

A General Cloud Formula

If you load a Cloud material from the Materials Library, you will see that only its Bump Height and Transparency are allocated to a Texture channel. The rest of the texture draws its look from Color palette assignments, with both Diffusion and Ambience sliders set around 30%. This emphasizes the wispy nature of a cloud or smoke. The type is always set to Fuzzy. If you follow these standard settings, you can apply more than the standard Cloud textures to the Bump and Transparency channels.

You can, for example, apply a Rock texture, as long as you make sure it has Alpha and Bump attributes. Color doesn't matter, because clouds normally draw their color references from diffuse and ambient palette settings. If your alternate texture doesn't have Bump and Alpha attributes, just add them in the material's Deep Texture Editor (Chapter 11) (see Figure 10.41).

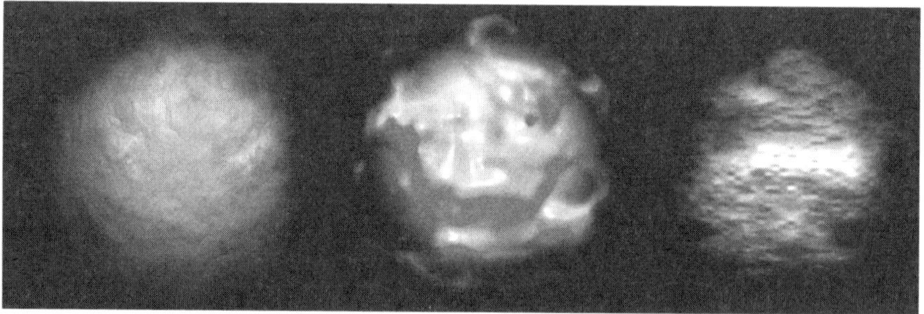

FIGURE 10.41 At the left is the Cloud texture LowSmog5; in the middle is the Rock texture StuccoBump. On the right is a texture from the Bump folder, Polychrome Bump. All make interesting clouds.

Standalone "realistic" clouds in the Bryce 3D sky are normally addressed to spheres, distorted spheres, or grouped spheres. Standalone clouds also work great in an animation when you set them in motion so they cast shadows across a landscape.

"Realistic" Planets

Just about any material wrapped to a sphere can emulate a planet, except perhaps a logo. There are some materials, however, that work better than others for this purpose, and many are not in the standard planetary categories (rocks and other terrains). What features does a material need to possess to be believable as a planetary texture, according to what we have been trained to expect of "reality?"

- It should fall into one of the three basic planetary classes: cratered, gas, or potentially "habitable" (by humanlike creatures). Habitable planets look more believable if they have cloudlike atmospheres and show some water areas.
- The features should not be too small, or the lack of detailed areas will detract from their believability.
- "Strange" anomalous features should be confined to smaller areas of the display (like the red spot on the planet Jupiter). If stranger features dominate, they can detract from the believability factor.
  For Gas Planets, make the sphere a Fuzzy type (see Figure 10.42).

FIGURE 10.42 Here is a selection of planetary objects (left top to right bottom), created with the following "wrong" materials: Red Fractal, Mushrooms, Barnacles (Sand), Cliffy Sand, Foamy Water, and Bleached Wood (re-colorized in the Deep Texture Editor).

- If you want a planet to show the lights of civilization when it rotates into darkness, use an Ambient texture with small gridded artifacts to map its dark side. The Ambience elements will not show when the planet is in the light.
- To create snowy poles on planets, embed spheres at the Northern and Southern Hemispheres, and use a snowy material map.

USING THE WRONG MATERIALS FOR A PERSONALIZED REALITY

Whose reality is it, anyway? If you purchased Bryce in order to simulate only what your camera sees on a summer afternoon on Earth, you are missing a major part of the creative fun and mesmerizing surrealistic explorations. Bryce is capable of more horizons than the one we see when we look out on our everyday world. Bryce is a creative tool for the surrealistic artist and animator. The goal of surrealism is to use seemingly identifiable elements to construct dreamlike visions, and Bryce (with a modicum of creative effort on your part) fits this role perfectly. Yes, you can use Bryce to generate lovely artwork that takes you for a ride on the Colorado River, with the Grand Canyon rising up majestically on each side. However, pushed just a bit further, you can also be riding on a lake of liquid mercury, past empty shards of lost civilizations. It is when you select a more personalized experience that your creation, customization, selection, and use of stranger, more variable materials can come into play.

Simulating Materials Surrealism

There are few rules that will guide you in the application of surrealistic materials; only the persistence of your own visions and dreams. Some Bryce users will move toward a radical materials approach, while others will prefer to subtly alter the materials in their scenes. Materials can be pushed towards more radical variations, and then adjusted until you feel satisfied.. Exactly what "right" is eludes any verbal description, because each Bryce world is so potentially unique (see Figure 10.43).

The three variations shown in Figure 10.43 are mapped as follows (from the top):

Top: Terrain = Office Building; Ground = Leopard; Figure = Mirror (Reflection turned down).

Center: Terrain = Green Bump Glass; Ground = GridRock; Figure = Water Puddles.

Bottom: Terrain = Dreams of Xanades Lake; Ground = Tyrell Building; Figure = Dali Bee Stripes.

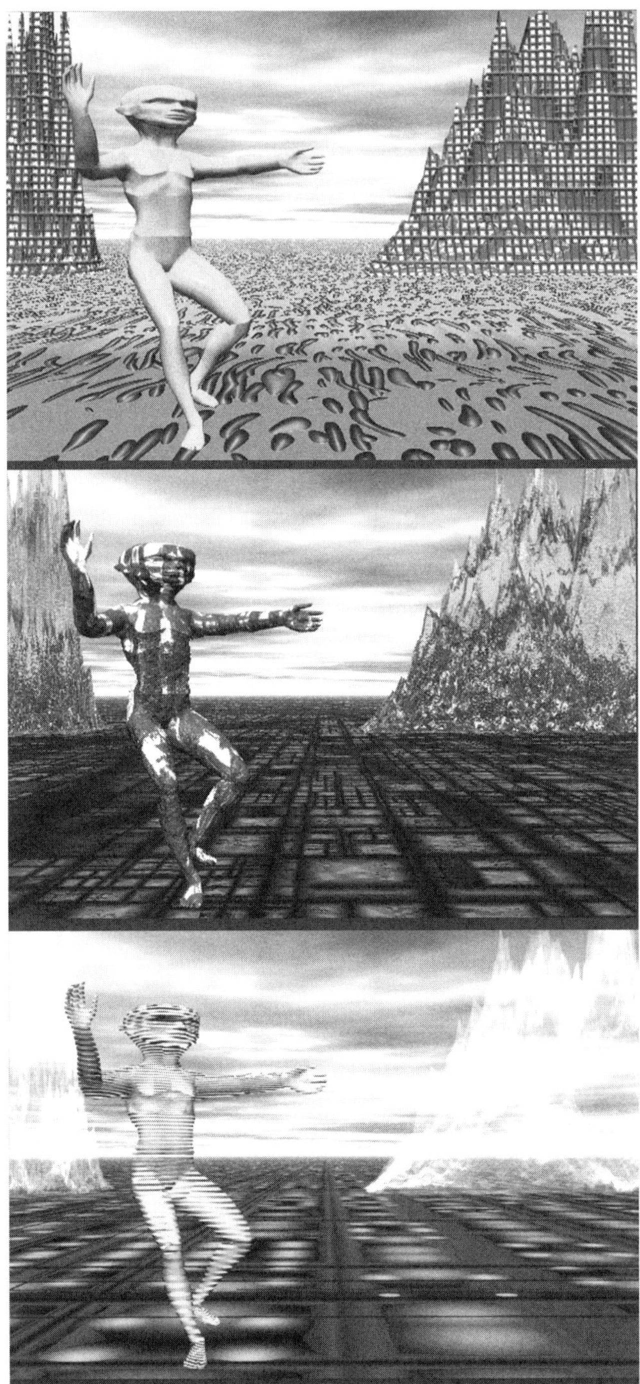

FIGURE 10.43 These scenes are based on the same composition, with only the materials differentiating the two. The materials give each variation a totally different look and feel.

MOVING ON

If you read and worked through this chapter carefully, you should by now have a much better understanding of how to navigate in the Materials Lab. In the next chapter, we'll take a look at the mysteries of the Deep Texture Editor.

CHAPTER

11 The Deep Texture Editor

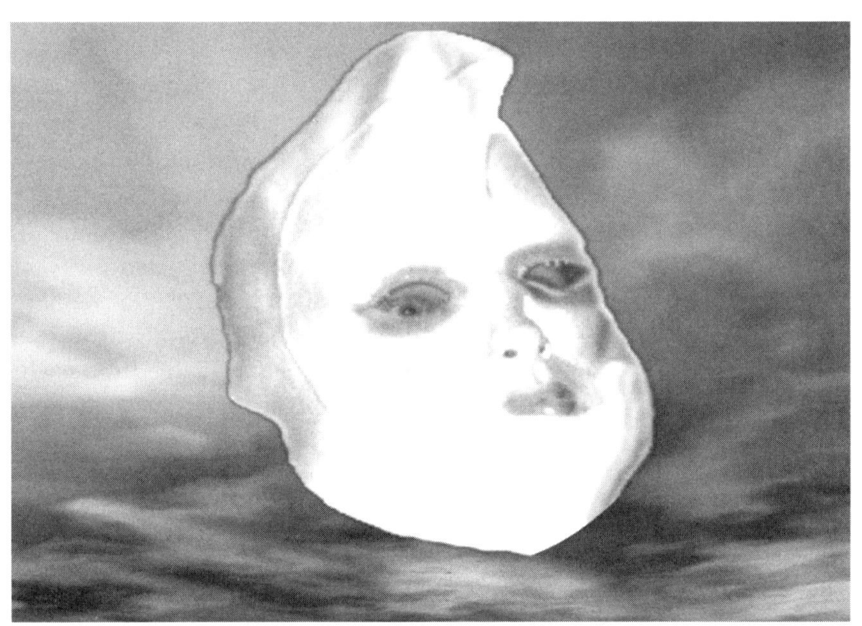

The magic of Bryce is that even the first-time user can create spectacular photorealistic scenes. Bryce also offers more complex alternatives, however, to the more experienced professional user. One path to these more customizable features is found in modifying and creating unique procedural and bitmap-based materials.

WHAT IS DEEP TEXTURE EDITING?

If modifying the ABCD channels in the Materials Lab is working at the molecular level, then using the Deep Texture Editor is working at the atomic and subatomic level. The most confusing thing about Deep Texture Editing at first is the similar nomenclature for the four channels. The use of "ABCD" to denote both attributes and components at every level of the Materials Lab throws everyone off balance at first. You just have to get used to how things work at every stage of the Materials Lab, and that means three things: practice, practice, and (oh yes), practice. This book can never substitute for learning by exploring and doing. That is especially true at this deeper level of materials creation.

The Deep Texture Editor is available from each of the four channels that comprise the Materials Lab component interface. These channels are called the A, B, C, and D channels. This is not to be confused with the three components that make up each channel: C (for Color), A (for Alpha), and B (for Bump map). The second button at the upper left of each component channel accesses that channel's Deep Texture Editor, as long as you are in Procedural Texture mode, and not Bitmap Picture mode (see Figure 11.1).

Once activated, the Deep Texture Editor's interface appears (see Figure 11.2).

The best teacher to guide you through the intricacies of the Deep Texture Editor is you. There is, however, a way we would like to suggest that you proceed. If you follow this method diligently, you will be able to proceed on your own direction after a few days of experimentation. The Deep Texture Editor is one of the most comprehensive procedural texture creation tools offered by any 3D application on the market. You can even use it to develop textures and materials for other 2D and 3D applications. Follow these steps to set up an easy-to-understand Deep Texture example:

1. With an object selected in your workspace, open the Materials Lab. Place an Activation Dot in the first row (the Diffuse channel) and first column. Go to that channel's Components interface on the right, and activate the Deep Texture Editor.

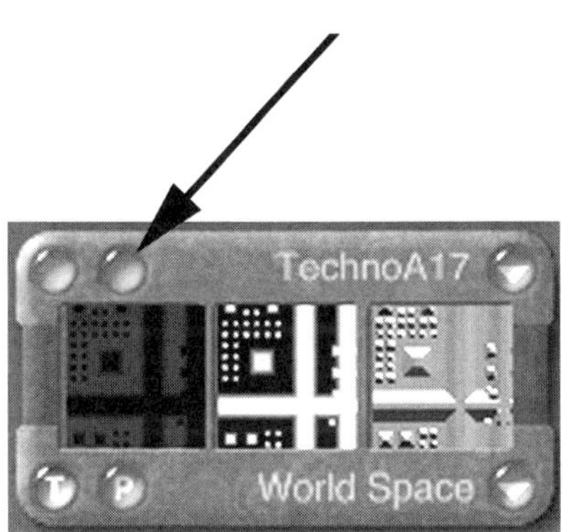

FIGURE 11.1 This is the button that activates your entrance into the Deep Texture Editor for each of the four component channels in the Materials Lab.

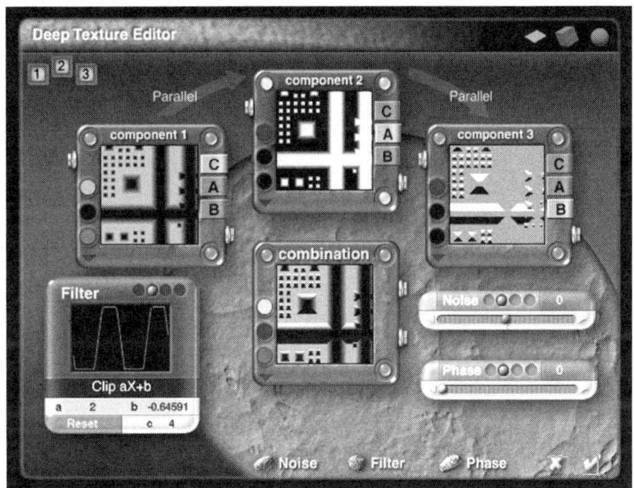

FIGURE 11.2 The Deep Texture Editor's interface and controls.

2. Make sure that all three Component lights at the upper left are on (they will be green). This activates the three component windows (marked Component 1, Component 2, and Component 3).
3. In Component 1, make sure only the C (for Color) is selected, and that A (for Alpha) and B (for Bump) are off.
4. In Component 2, make sure that only A is selected, and that C and B are off.
5. In Component 3, make sure that only B is selected, and that A and C are off.

You have just assigned Component 1 as your Color source, Component 2 as your Alpha source, and Component 3 as your Bump Map source. Shake your own hand for doing well.

6. Click the Randomize button on Component 1 to load a texture. Reset the CAB buttons so only C is selected. Repeat this until you like the pattern in Component 1.
7. Repeat this same process for Component 2, making sure that only A (the Alpha channel) is selected. Repeat this until you like the pattern in Component 2.
8. Repeat this same process for Component 3, making sure that only B (the Bump channel) is selected. Repeat this until you like the pattern in Component 3.

Now you have the three parts of a texture started in all three Component channels: Color in 1, Alpha in 2, and Bump in 3. Look at the Window marked "Combination." This shows you how the three Component channels are contributing to the total texture.

9. Go to the curved arrow that connects Component 1 and Component 2. A word there indicates how the data from 1 is being fed to 2. Click and hole on that word, and a list will pop up with a number of choices. Explore each choice, and watch the Combination window for a preview. Select whatever option looks good in the Combination window.
10. Repeat this same process over the curved arrow that indicates how Component 2 is passing data to Component 3. Stop when the Combination preview looks pleasing.
11. Explore the use of the Filter window on each Component and on the Combination preview, by selecting the appropriate button from the top of the Filter window. By clicking and dragging in the space in which you see a mathematical curve, you can alter the way in which data is filtered in the Component or Combination window you have selected. You can also hold your mouse (LMB for Windows users) over the name of the math function, and select another from the list. Explore in order to see what happens, and don't rush.
12. Add or subtract noise with the Noise slider to a selected Component or the Combination preview, until the resulting Combination graphic looks like something interesting.
13. Repeat this process of exploration using the Phase slider in the Phase operator. Stop when you have something worth using as a material.
14. Return to the Materials Lab, and use any of the controls to further tweak the texture you just designed for an original material. Finish by writing the material to the selected object. Render a preview. If the material is pleasing, add it to your Materials Library.

It is absolutely guaranteed that if you do this exercise 10 times, you will be so excited about using the Deep Texture Editor that your work in Bryce will become 100 times more interesting to you. Remember that Deep Texture Editing works on both Surface and Volume textures.

Referring to Figure 11.3, from top left to bottom right, these operations were performed one after the other. Although all of the textured materials are connected, you can see the subtle power of working in the Deep Texture Editor. The textures are detailed in the following notes, from upper left to lower right of Figure 11.3.

FIGURE 11.3 Here are some examples of a material whose texture has been customized in the Deep Texture Editor.

1. Original Basic Waves 5 Surface textured material.
2. Clip aX+b used as a formula in the Combination channel.
3. Procedural Blend added between Components 2 and 3.
4. Noise to –42 in Combination, and Phase to connect 1 to 2, and 2 to 3.
5. Snow Puddles formula added to Component 2, and Perturbed Noise to Component 3 with Altitude formula, Blend Max from 2 to 3, and Phase change of 770 on Component 3.
6. Blend random transition used between Components 1 and 2, and between 2 and 3. CAB channels switched on in all three Components.

If you use the Altitude transition between Components 2 and 3, with Color activated in each Component, the textured material you develop will be height sensitive. Color will change in relation to height. This is how the Terrain presets were built in the first place.

THE PICTURE EDITOR

Here are some additional details about using the Picture Editor as a texture tool. The Picture Editor is to bitmap images what the Deep Texture Editor is to procedural materials. Although you will probably spend most of your time in Bryce using procedural materials, there are times when a specific bitmap is called for. Actually, some of the procedural materials in

Bryce contain one or more channels that contain their own bitmaps. Each of the four material channels allows you to select either a procedural or a bitmap element at any time, for the creation of procedural/bitmap sandwiches in the final material.

Be wary of using any Bump Height mapping on imported graphics, especially photographs. Photos usually contain thousands of small defects that show up as particles when Bump mapped. The only way to minimize these artifacts is to apply Blurring several times in a paint application.

Bitmap pictures are configured in the Picture Editor, which is switched on from the Edit button in one of the ABCD channels (see Figures 11.4 and 11.5).

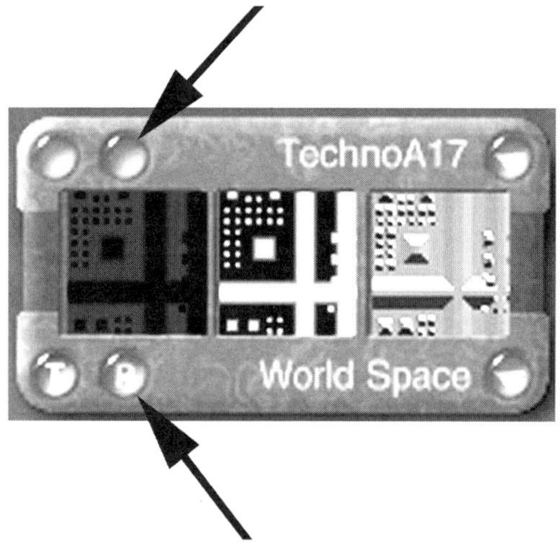

FIGURE 11.4 The Edit button activates the Picture Editor interface, as long as Picture (P) and not Texture (T) is also selected below it.

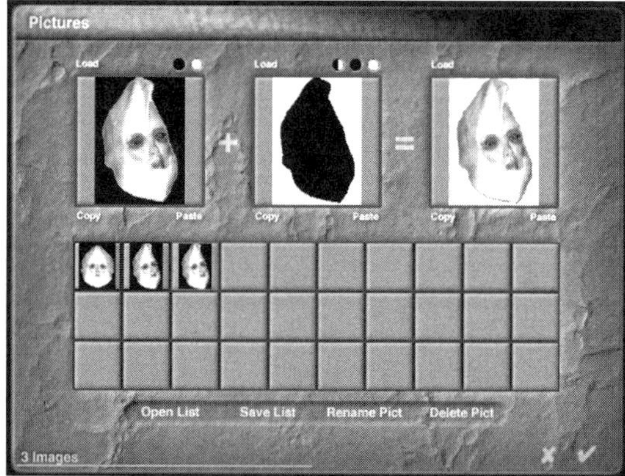

FIGURE 11.5 Once activated, the Picture Editor interface takes command of the screen.

Working in the Picture Editor

The Picture Editor interface is very straightforward, and not nearly as complicated as the Deep Texture Editor (see Figure 11.5, or look at the Picture Editor on your own screen). There are three main windows at the top: Original Picture, Alpha Channel, and Result. Below that are 30 visible picture thumbnail slots (scrolling gives you access to more). Each of these slots holds one bitmap picture. At the bottom are four commands. The first two allow you to export and import entire Picture lists, and the second two to Rename or Delete any Picture already on screen.

What you need to know about the Picture-Alpha-Result windows is something that initially will challenge your logical assumptions, but this is the way Bryce has been designed to work. When you want to add bitmapped pictures to the slots in the storage area below, you must click the Load button in the Result Window at the right, not the Picture Window at the left. This is very important. Loading a picture on the left in the Picture window will replace the current picture selected in the slot below. This is OK if that's what you want, but usually what is needed is to add a number of bitmaps in the slots all at one time. Here is the way to add new bitmap images in the Picture Editor:

1. Click the Load button above the Result window on the right.
2. After the image loads, click on Copy under the Result window.
3. Click on Paste under the left-hand Picture window.
4. If you want to add the same picture as an Alpha channel, click on Paste under the Alpha window. Note that adding another bitmap on the Alpha channel will act as a mask for the final result. Adding the same picture as an Alpha will drop out areas of the picture that are close to the dropout color. See the section that follows on creating an Alpha image in your paint application.

White areas of your Alpha image are normally dropped out. Click the half-moon (black/white) symbol above the Alpha window to reverse the information being dropped out. Look at the Result window to see a preview of how the Alpha is affecting the finished bitmap.

5. Finally, click on the check mark to return to the Materials Lab, where you can use any of the controls to adjust your Picture Texture further.

Creating an Alpha Mask in a Paint Application

You have to have an Alpha mask in the Picture Editor that duplicates the outline of the needed image, so it can be composited correctly against a Bryce scene, if you don't want the background frame of the image to show. If you want the framed content to show, however, you don't need Alpha channel data. Here's how to create Alpha data in any paint application:

1. Find the image you want, and load it into your bitmap painting application (Painter, PhotoPaint, Enhance, or Photoshop will do just fine). Paint out the area you do not want to appear with solid black.
2. Make a duplicate of the image. Make the area you *do* want solid black, and the rest of the background white. Save both images to disk.

3. Load the image with the black backdrop into the Picture Editor as the final result image. Load the Alpha mask into the Alpha window. You should now have three images that look like those in Figure 11.6.

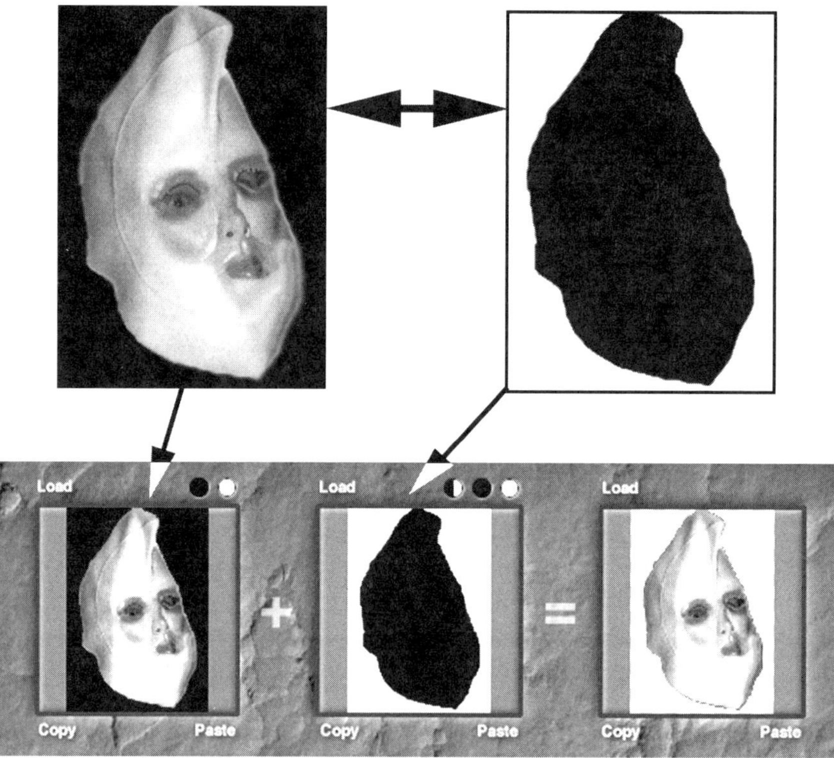

FIGURE 11.6 First, an Alpha mask created in your Paint application. Then, the original image is loaded into the first window, and the Alpha mask into the Alpha window. The result is a perfectly cropped image when mapped to a 2D Picture Plane in Bryce.

BITMAPS AS OBJECTS

When mapped on a Picture Plane, as we discussed in previous chapters, bitmaps can become objects in your scene. They are objects with no depth, so you can't orbit them. Doing so will ruin the illusion, as they will seem to get thinner and thinner and disappear, before emerging from nothing again. Kept as background elements, however, bitmapped planes make excellent elements in a Bryce world. The object you should be mapping to in your world should be the 2D Picture Object from the Create toolbar.

1. Place the 2D Picture Object where you want it, and make sure it is facing the camera head on. Open the Materials Lab, and the Picture Editor.

2. Repeat the steps listed in "Working in the Picture Editor" to import and adjust your bitmap. Return to the scene and do a preview render (see Figure 11.7).

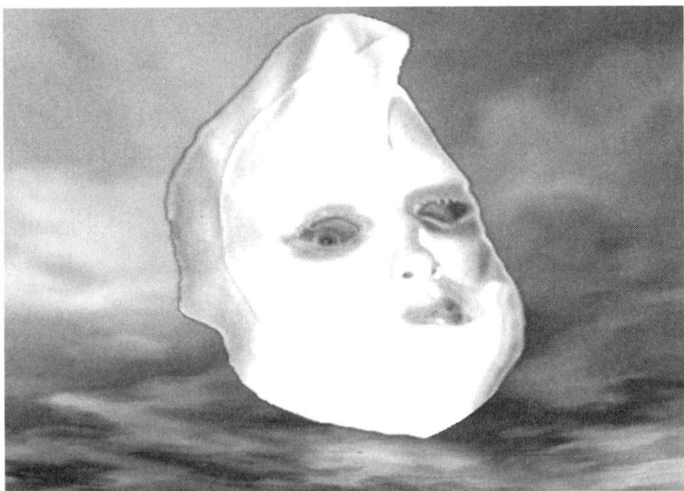

FIGURE 11.7 The finished picture is composited against a Bryce sky.

BITMAPS AS TEXTURES

Bitmaps can be used instead of (and in addition to) procedural materials. We all have favorite bitmap photos and images that we have collected over time and stored away. Bryce allows us to use our favorite bitmaps as textural components in a material. In reality, there is very little difference between a bitmap object and a bitmap texture. A bitmap object, in Bryce, is written to a 2D Picture Plane, and usually is not tiled or multiplied. A bitmap-based material, and a material that folds bitmaps in with procedural textures, uses the bitmap just like a procedural. Other than that, there are no differences in the ways that you access the bitmap data in the Picture Editor.

The only other use for bitmaps, one we already covered in Chapter 3, "Trees," is their use as topographical maps for Terrain data. Now that you have explored the use of the Picture Editor, it's worth noting that the color information that the bitmap contains, the image, can also obviously be mapped to Terrains. This means that a bitmap that is translated into a 3D object in the Terrain Editor can be mapped with its own color image from the Materials Lab Picture Editor output. This gives the bitmap dimension as well as an Image map (see Figure 11.8).

FIGURE 11.8 Unlike Figure 11.7, the sky face picture was mapped to a 3D Terrain object of the same face as topography, giving it dimension. The mountain face was mapped with the same material as the mountain.

Random Picture Maps

You can apply the Random Mapping Type to imported bitmaps as well as procedural materials. You might have to adjust the size of the image in the range of –2 to +2 to still be able to see identifiable parts of the bitmap, or simply use an abstracted version of the picture with larger or smaller sizes. Colorful bitmaps provide the richest texturing possibility with this technique, especially when Symmetrical Tiling is switched on. Here's how:

1. With an object selected on screen, open the Materials Lab and activate Channel 1 by placing buttons in Diffuse and Ambient (Color), Diffusion and Ambience (Value), and Transparency (Optics). Click the "P" (Picture) button, and then click the Edit button.
2. Load in a graphic or digital photograph. No Alpha channel is needed, so return to the Materials Lab.
3. Under Mapping Options, activate the Random option. This scatters your image across the object. Explore resizing it in the Transformations palette. Explore the Symmetrical Tiling function. Keep an eye on your Materials Nano Preview to see what your manipulations are

doing. When you achieve a satisfactory image, return to your Bryce world. Render, and save to disk (see Figures 11.9 and 11.10).

FIGURE 11.9 These six spheres were mapped with a digital photo of my neighbor's tree. The first one shows the image untouched except for a small amount of rotation. The last two in the first row display Symmetrical Tiling at various size alterations. The second row of materials was developed by using the Random mapping function with various sizes involved.

FIGURE 11.10 This terrain is mapped from World Top with the same digital picture that was used in Figure 11.9. Picture-based materials can generate intriguing and colorful Terrain maps.

Picture-based materials mapped to Terrain objects can take a very long time to render. Consider switching antialiasing off, unless you absolutely have to use it. Besides, a rougher look to a terrain image often looks more real.

MOVING ON

This chapter focused on both the Deep Texture Editor and the Picture Editor to create textures that are more complex. The next chapter continues our investigation of complex Bryce materials.

CHAPTER

12 Infinite Planes

This chapter explores Bryce Infinite Planes, and how to create some interesting projects and f/x through their use. In order to do the tutorials in this chapter, you need to know the following:

- How to locate the icons that trigger the placement of Infinite Ground, Water, and Cloud Planes in the Create toolbar.
- How to rotate Infinite Planes on any selected axis.
- How to choose between Surface and Volume Infinite Planes.
- Using Multi-Replicate.
- Placing a Stone in the scene with the Stone icon.

THE TUNNEL OF ETERNITY

In this tutorial, we will focus on the placement of multiple Infinite Ground Planes, and how they can be used to create a never-ending tunnel. No matter how far into the tunnel you place the camera, you will never get any closer to the end of the tunnel, which remains at infinity in the distance. Do the following:

A similar effect was used to great advantage in the 1960s Surrealist European film Last Night at Marianbad.

1. Place an Infinite Ground Plane (abbreviated as *IGP*) in the scene, and World Space map it with a Pitted Concrete material. Use a Bump Height of –888, and a Scale Size of 8.5% on the XYZ axes.
2. Duplicate the IGP twice, and rotate and move the duplicates to form a triangular opening at the end, as seen in the Camera view. Try to center the view on the opening, and rotate the camera so that it can see the "floor" of this tunnel as it recedes into the distance.
3. Add a sky (your choice). Add a light-blue haze of 10. This will add a ghosted effect to the triangular opening, blurring the distant edges, and adding to the eerieness of the scene.
4. Center a Sphere at the bottom of the tunnel. Map it with a Reflective material.
5. Multi-Replicate the Sphere so that 75 duplicates recede into the background. For this exercise, we used the following values in the Multi-Replicate dialog: Quantity = 35 and Z Offset = 75. To really "reach" the end of the infinite distanced opening, we would have had to create an infinite string of Spheres. This might be a bit much for anything but a system with an infinite amount of RAM (!).
6. Render to preview, and adjust as necessary (see Figure 12.1).

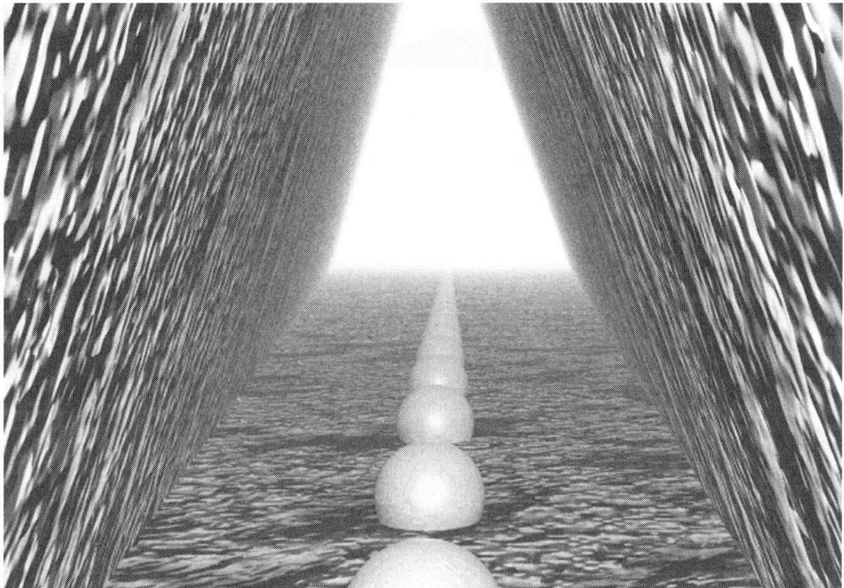

FIGURE 12.1 The finished tunnel. No matter how far in you place the camera, you will never get any closer to the opening at the end.

A standard illustration technique used to emphasize or "force" the appreciation of perspective in a 3D scene is to replicate the same object as many times as needed, and to make the replicates recede into the background or toward the horizon. This was why the sphere was added to this scene.

DAWN BEACH

There are times when you will not want the Infinite Planes to define the horizon line. This exercise is a case in point. Do the following:

1. Create the Terrain Editor form shown in Figure 12.2 from a Symmetrical Lattice.
2. Reduce the Vertical scale of this object when it appears in your scene until it is very thin.
3. Work in the Top view. Duplicate two more, and layer and overlap them, rotating the duplicates so they appear to have some randomness as seen by the camera.
4. Place a Water Material on them with Object Space mapping. Set Reflectivity to around 40%. Place a button in the Channel A Transparency spot, so the Material takes its transparency cue from the procedural Material.

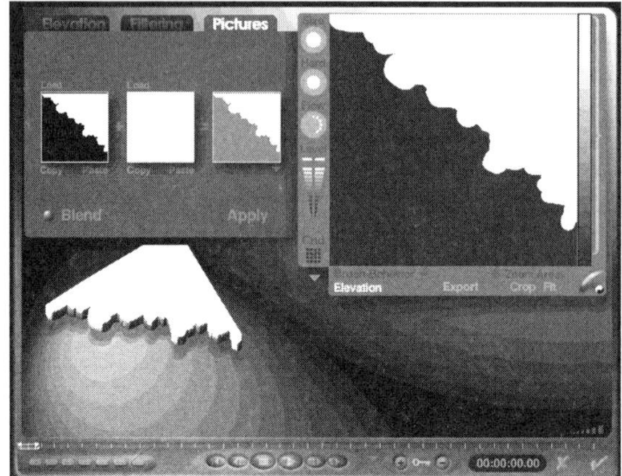

FIGURE 12.2 Create this form.

5. Create an elongated Cube, and squash it. This will be the "water" horizon in the distance.
6. Now for the beach. We could use another Primitive object, like a Cube, but we want to demonstrate how an Infinite Ground Plane can be used here. Place an IGP in the scene, and set its height just below the "water" level. If you render a test view from the camera, a strange effect occurs. Beyond the water-mapped Cube, the Ground Plane continues to another horizon line. We do not want this. Go to the Right view and tilt the IGP down about 2 degrees. That way, it will not be seen in the Camera view beyond the water-mapped Cube, since it will be covered by the Water objects (see Figure 12.3).

FIGURE 12.3 The initial beach scene.

7. It looks OK for a start, but a little bland. Click the Stone icon in the Create toolbar to place a rock in the foreground, and another different one farther into the water. Texture, and render. See Figure 12.4.

FIGURE 12.4 The finished Dawn Beach scene.

CANALS

Here's a way to create straight cuts in an IGP that are also infinite:

1. Place a Volume IGP in the scene, and make it a Positive Boolean.
2. Duplicate it twice, and rotate the duplicates 90 degrees on the X-axis. Make them Negative Booleans.
3. From the Top view, adjust the sizes of the Negative Boolean planes so that they equal the width of the canals to be cut. Move and/or Rotate them into position.
4. Group all three volumetric IGPs (see Figure 12.5).
5. Place a Surface Infinite Water Plane at the level you want the water to be in the canal, and use a suitable material to texture it. Render (see Figure 12.6).

This has the look of an artificial and manicured cut, so do not use it for rivers. This technique can also be used to create sunken roadways.

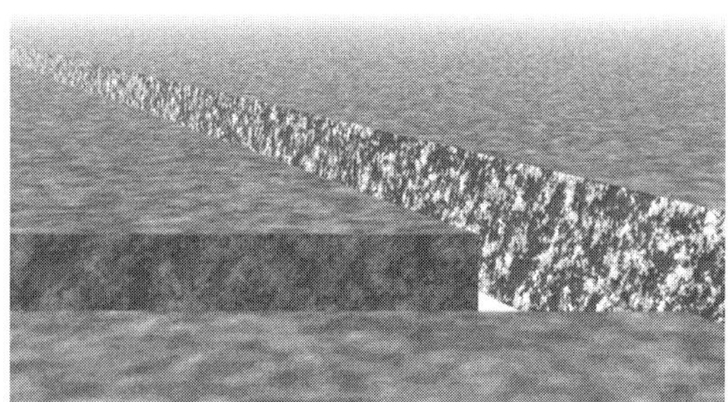

FIGURE 12.5 The canals are cut.

FIGURE 12.6 The canals are ready to irrigate the land, or to act as causeways for boats. The tree was created in the Tree Lab.

FIRE LAKE

Do the following:

1. Infinite Planes of any type look fake if left flat. Create an IGP. Place low-scaled Symmetrical Lattice terrains on the IGP, duplicated and rotated for variety. Place them near the camera. Map the Symmetrical Lattices and IGP with the same material texture so they match.
2. In the Sky Lab, configure a sky that shows a large Moon object shining on the scene, and explore the cloud settings until you develop a picture that has a yellowish cast. Render for preview (see Figure 12.7).
3. Select all of the Symmetrical Lattices and the IGP, and make them Positive Booleans.

FIGURE 12.7 The initial scene takes shape.

4. Create another Symmetrical Lattice, and open the Terrain Editor.
5. Click New. Create a solid-white Block.
6. Select Round Hills from the Fractals list, and apply the Fractals modifier. Select Round Edges and apply it. Your Terrain Editor should resemble Figure 12.8.
7. Accept the object. Place it so that it intersects the foreground Symmetrical Lattice in the group, and make it a Negative Boolean. Group everything. Edit the position and size so that a crater is formed in the foreground. Place an appropriate Rocky material on it (see Figure 12.9).

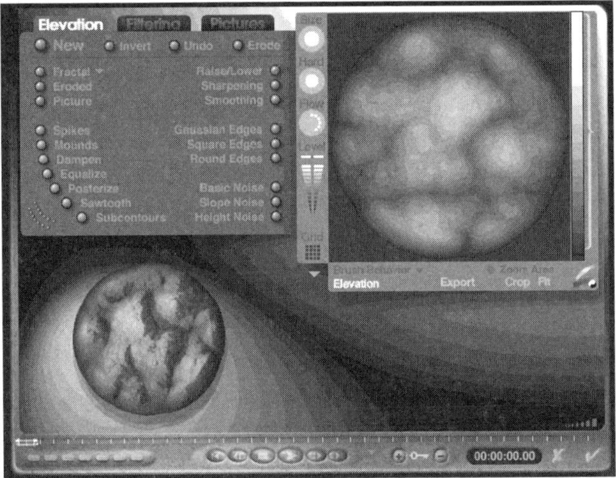

FIGURE 12.8 Your Terrain Editor should resemble this.

8. Place a Cylinder in the crater to emulate the contents. Map the cylinder with the Santraginus V selection from the Water & Liquids

FIGURE 12.9 Create a crater.

Library. Enter the Deep Texture Editor, and change the colors of the material to reds and yellows.

9. Place a large Sphere in the crater, with a diameter that covers the crater's diameter. Enlarge its vertical scale by 200%. Go to the Materials Lab, and select the Volume Library. Apply the Fire Material. Use the parameters shown in Figure 12.10.

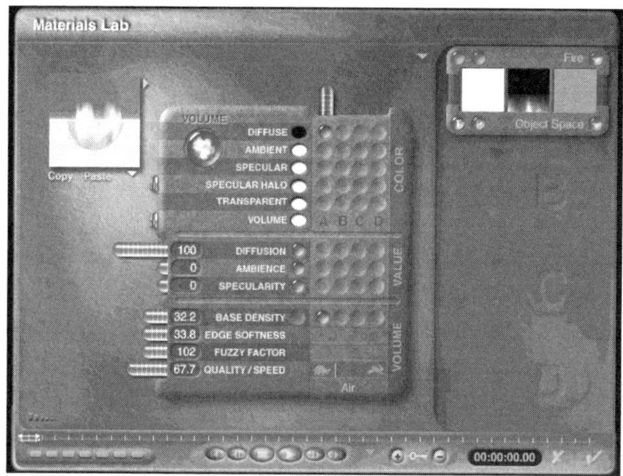

FIGURE 12.10 Use these parameters for the Volume/Fire Material.

10. When the render is complete, you will see flames rising from a lava-like lake (see Figure 12.11).

FIGURE 12.11 The finished image.

Be aware that all large Volumetric mapped objects take an inordinate amount of render time, so use them sparsely. We used volumetric fire instead of surface fire here because it looks better.

THE WATER SANDWICH

There is one important alternative to consider when you need to create water (or any other alternative liquid component) in a scene: your ability to layer different strata of mapped planes together. You rarely call upon this option for Infinite Ground Planes, given that most ground attributes require only one surface. You can use this technique with Infinite Sky Planes (abbreviated as ISP), although it is not usually required. When it comes to water, it is a different matter. That's because water, even more so than air, has a personality based on degrees of transparency. In a shallow stream, water is transparent enough to allow you to see through to the underlying bed of pebbles and stones. In deeper water, you might see down to the tops of a bed of seaweed or coral, or even further to some dark hint of an ancient ruin.

When you apply an Infinite Water Plane (abbreviated as IWP), always consider using two or three layers to achieve more realism.

WATER OVER ROCKS

You can adapt this tutorial to any situation that requires the viewer to appreciate that the water exists over a more solid surface. Do the following:

1. Create an IGP, and map it with a Rocky material (Gilliam's Barnacles from the Miscellaneous Library works well) that has a high level of Bump mapping. Angle the camera so it is looking down at the surface by about 45 degrees. You won't see the horizon (see Figure 12.12).
2. Embed five or six Stone objects in the plane to give it some variance. One should be large enough to rise above the water surface (see Figure 12.13).
3. Add an IWP over the IGP. The closer you can place it without revealing too many hidden rocks, the better. Add a Water material to it (the Caribbean Resort material from the Liquids Library works well when the transparency is increased to 100%) (see Figure 12.14).

The more you rotate the camera to look straight down on the water, the more the underlying content will be revealed.

FIGURE 12.12 A Rocky material applied to an IGP.

FIGURE 12.13 Add some Stone objects.

FIGURE 12.14 The streambed.

FIGURE 12.15 The textured sphere is seen through the surface, and includes the underlying textured plane.

Adjusting the transparency of a water surface and the angle of the camera can produce some interesting results (see Figure 12.15).

Avoid using volumetric IWPs in your composition. They take an eternity to render, and have no real use. You can always use tints to colorize underwater scenes.

SKY OPTIONS

When it comes to creating ground for your scene, you have three options: using a very large object (like a huge resized Cube or Terrain), a Surface Infinite Ground Plane, or a Volumetric Infinite Ground Plane. The material you use determines the look of the ground primarily by the content (color or procedural/bitmap material) in the Diffuse and Bump channels. The same three options hold for Infinite Water Planes. When it comes to Infinite Sky Planes, however, it's a different matter. ISPs can incorporate Surface and Volumetric materials. There is another option that is addressed when you select a preset sky from the Sky & Fog Library. The ISP that is addressed from these presets cannot be rotated or otherwise transformed. It is, in fact, unreachable. To prove this, open the Camera & 2D Projection window, and change the Y position value to 99,999 (the maximum). Make sure the camera is pointing straight down at an object. Make sure a sky preset is loaded, one with a high quantity of clouds and Cloud Quantity set to 100%. Render the Camera view. You will not see any clouds below the camera, just the IGP and any included object.

When you create an ISP Surface or Volume plane, it can be placed at any set level in the scene. In that case, you can place the camera above it and actually look down through breaks in the clouds. You can use a Volumetric ISP (also called a *slab*) and create an animation that allows you to fly through 3D clouds. Like water volumes, however, this is cautioned against because of extremely slow rendering, no matter how fast your system is.

Procedural Image Content for the Default Sky Plane

The Default Sky in Bryce takes its appearance cues from the material mapped to it. This material is usually Procedural material based, but it can also be bitmap-image based. It is also possible, as with any material, to mix procedural and image data in different channels, or even in the same channel. What we are concerned with here is your ability to draw upon your own procedural libraries for inclusion in the sky look. You do this by default when you select a preset sky from the Sky&Fog Library (see Figure 12.16).

FIGURE 12.16 When you select a sky preset from the Sky&Fog Library, you are really selecting a Procedural-based image to be mapped to the sky.

What we want to do is configure our own sky image data, so we can create unique cloud patterns and save them out as presets that we can draw upon at any time. Here are two ways to do it:

1. Go to the Sky&Fog window, and select the Simple White Background preset. Accept it.
2. Open the Sky Lab, and click on Cloud Cover at the top. Activate Stratus. Clouds will appear in your preview window. Note that the Clouds controls configure the Diffuse and Alpha channels of the Cumulous and Stratus cloud patterns, along with the quantity, height, and other controls (see Figure 12.17).

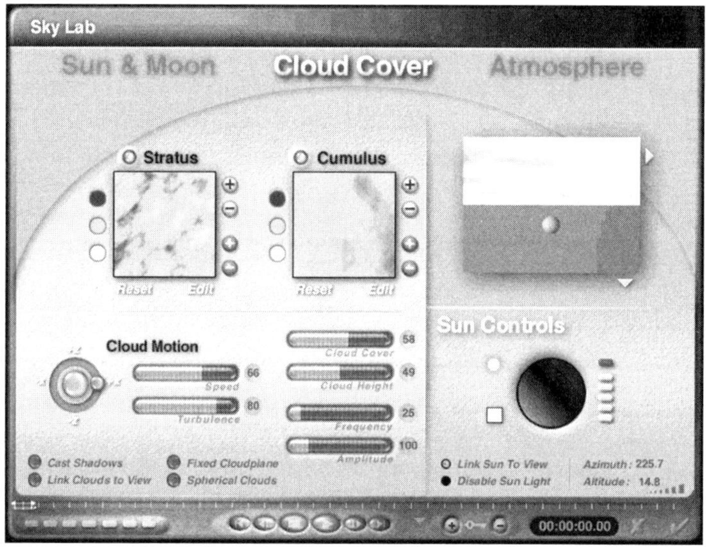

FIGURE 12.17 Activate both Cumulous and Stratus components.

3. The next control you will activate is the most important step in configuring your own sky and cloud patterns. Note that there is a small Edit control at the lower right of both the Stratus and Cumulous preview windows. Click Edit beneath the Strata preview window. It takes you directly to a mode in Bryce that you should already be quite familiar with: the Deep Texture Editor! (See Figure 12.18).
4. In the Deep Texture Editor, you will see that your sky and clouds are presently made from a one-component Alpha image. Color is taken from Component 4, the Combination image data window. Click the button that protrudes from the top right of the Combination data window. A Textures Library window appears. This is where Deep

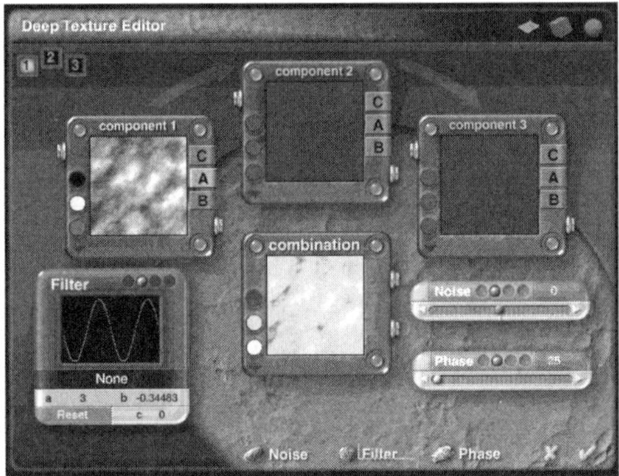

FIGURE 12.18 You are transported to the familiar Deep Texture Editor.

Textures are saved and loaded from. Select the Cloud Textures option (see Figure 12.19).

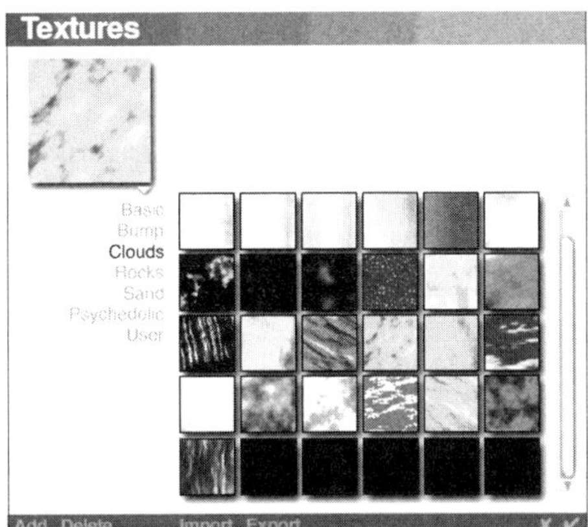

FIGURE 12.19 The Cloud Textures option in the Texture Library window, accessed from the Combination window in the Deep Texture Editor.

5. We could select any of the texture presets displayed here, and use it to configure a new cloudy sky, but let's get a bit more creatively risky than that. Open the Psychedelic Library option, and select the Electronic pattern (see Figure 12.20).
6. Back in the Deep Texture Editor, note that the pattern now resides in the Component 1 window and in the Combination window (see Figure 12.21).
7. Click the C button in the Component 1 window, because a sky needs only the Alpha channel data ("A" should still be selected). Color is applied back in the scene.

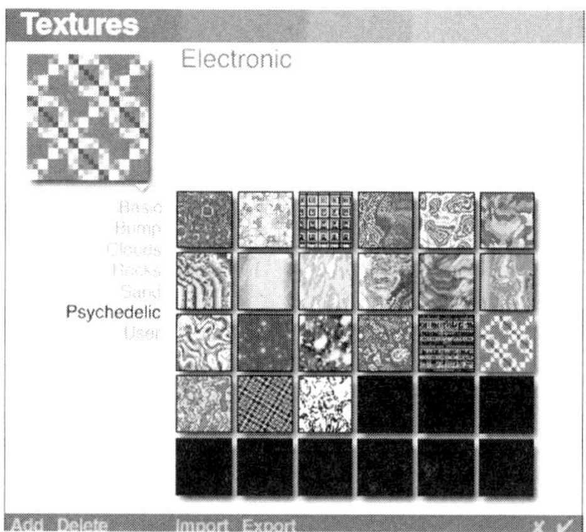

FIGURE 12.20 Select the Electronic pattern.

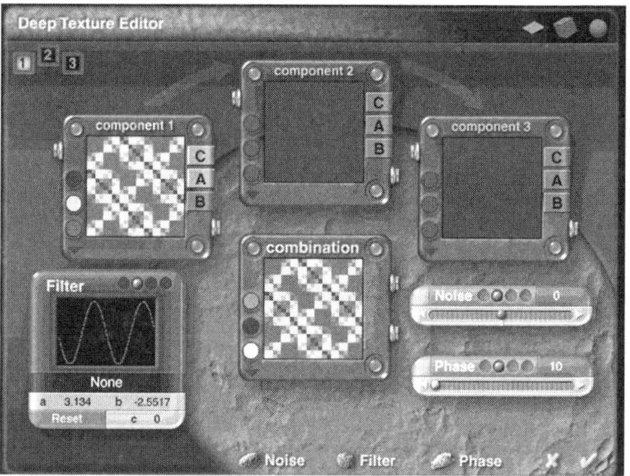

FIGURE 12.21 The Electronic pattern as seen in the Deep Texture Editor.

8. Accept this pattern, which returns you to the Sky Lab. In the Stratus window, click on the Plus sign at the upper right three times to add chaos to the pattern. Accept this Stratus setting, and return to the scene.
9. Click Cumulous off in the Sky&Fog Options list. Set the Sky Color to dark blue, and the Horizon Color to purple. Set a light-blue Haze of 3, a Cloud Height of 50, and a Cloud Cover of 12. Render to preview, and edit in any way that pleases you. If you like this sky, save it to the Sky&Fog Presets Library (see Figure 12.22).
10. Now for a variation. This time, open the Sky Lab/Clouds window, and activate Cumulous. Leave Stratus off. Click Edit to alter the Cumulous pattern. Select IceBump from the Bump Library as the pattern, and make sure that it appears as an Alpha ("A") only image in Components 1 and 2 (see Figure 12.23).

FIGURE 12.22 This sky has a strange, quilted appearance.

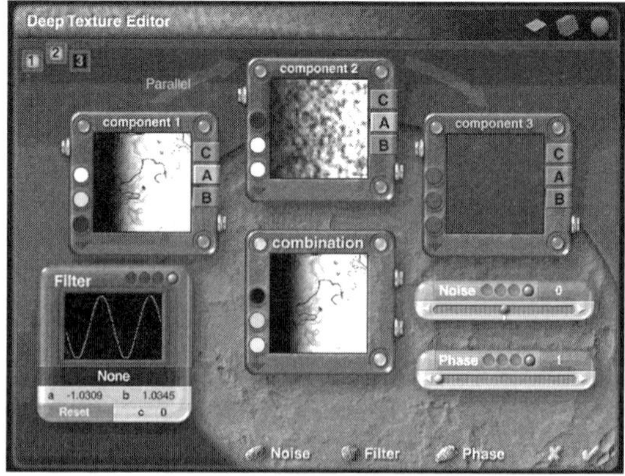

FIGURE 12.23 IceBump uses Components 1 and 2, so they should be Alpha only for a sky configuration.

11. Tweak the color and other parameters to your liking back in the scene (see Figure 12.24).

By saving the same texture, this time with color ("C") on in both Components 1 and 2, to the Textures Library, you can call on it to map any object in addition to the sky. Procedural sky textures appear very differently when mapped to other scene components (see Figure 12.25).

FIGURE 12.24 The IceBump patterned sky.

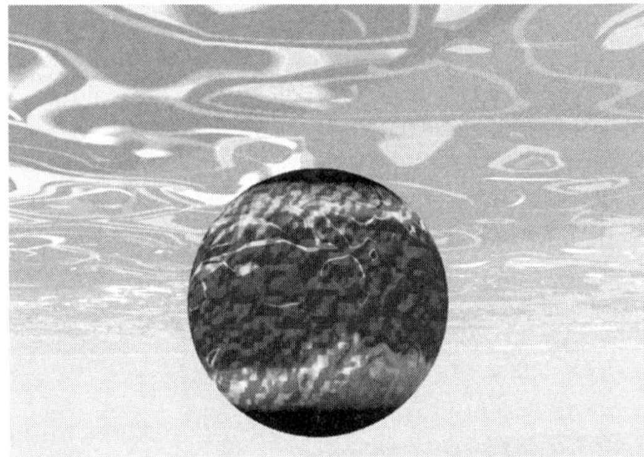

FIGURE 12.25 Believe it or not, the same texture was used to map the sphere and the sky, although the results appear very different.

Tweaking Procedural and Bitmap Image Content for an Infinite Sky Plane

What about placing bitmap image content on the default Sky Plane? Sorry. The default Sky Plane cannot accept bitmaps, only procedurals. Well, then, how can you create a sky/cloud pattern that makes use of bitmap content? Easy—just use an Infinite Sky Plane (Surface or Volume, although Volumes are not recommended). Do the following exercises.

ADDRESSING PROCEDURAL CONTENT

The Infinite Sky Plane is a special object, but an object nevertheless. As with any object, it can be addressed with textures configured from Materials in the Materials Lab—any materials. Your creative options for placing textures on an Infinite Sky Plane far outweigh those allowed by addressing the default sky plane. Do the following to prove it:

1. Place a Surface ISP in your scene. Open the Materials Lab and map it with a Plank Wood Material, using World Top mapping (see Figure 12.26).

FIGURE 12.26 An ISP mapped with a Wood material. Unlike the default sky plane, materials mapped to ISP objects use all channel data, including color.

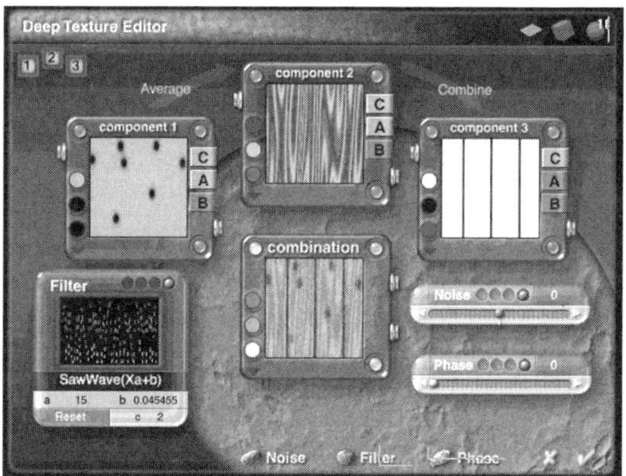

FIGURE 12.27 Plank Wood's Deep Texture Editor.

2. Go to the Deep Texture Editor for the Plank Wood Material (see Figure 12.27).
3. Open the Noise dialog for Component 1 by clicking the green button at the left of the dialog. A configuration window opens (see Figure 12.28).

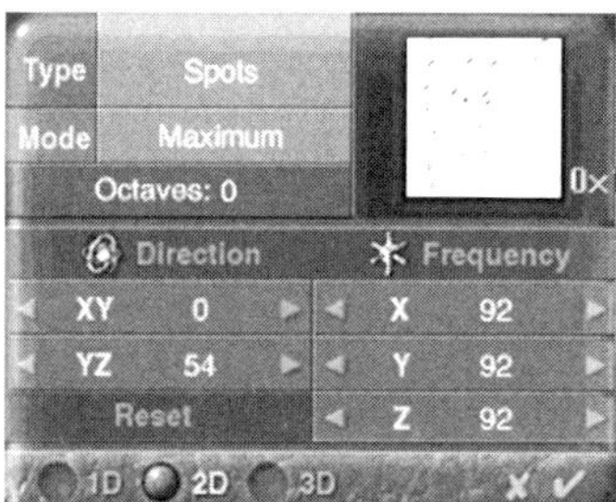

FIGURE 12.28 A configuration window opens.

4. Right now, the Type option is Spots, which creates the knots in the wood. Click and hold on the word *Spots* to bring up the options list. Select Techno from the list. Now, instead of spots, the wood texture has an embedded Techno pattern. Use the Noise dialog's configuration controls to alter the structural patterns in Components 2 and 3 in the same way, selecting whatever options you like. Keep an eye on the Combination window to see the results of your explorations (see Figure 12.29).

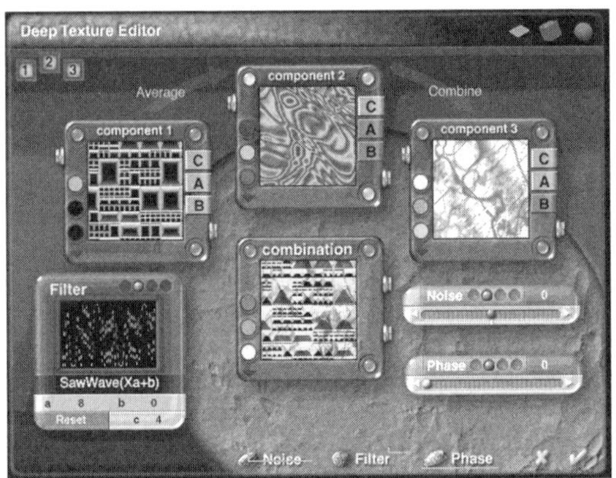

FIGURE 12.29 Alter the patterns in all three Component areas.

FIGURE 12.30 The same material is mapped to an ISP and a pyramid.

5. Place an object on the ground in the scene, and use the same material on it. Render the scene (see Figure 12.30).

ISPs usually take World and World Top mapping best, while an object might look best with Object or Parametric mapping. This is one reason why the same material can appear so different when mapped to a Sky Plane and an object.

ADDRESSING BITMAP CONTENT

Addressing an ISP with a bitmap image material is simple; it's just a matter of selecting the bitmap and configuring it in the Picture Editor of the Materials Lab. From there, however, complexities can be added. Do the following:

Bitmap image content in the Materials Lab usually prefers Parametric or Parametric Scaled mapping types.

1. Place an ISP in the scene and open the Materials Lab. Use the default Hermetic Man as the Diffuse and Ambient image for it, with Procedural mapping and the scale set to 0 (see Figure 12.31).
2. Change the mapping type to Random (see Figure 12.32).
3. Now we will explore a unique way to configure an ISP texture by using both bitmap and procedural components. Leave the image at its present settings in the Texture A slot in the Materials Lab. Activate channels A and B for the Diffuse component. For Texture B, use the

FIGURE 12.31 The ISP mapped with the default Hermetic Man bitmap image.

FIGURE 12.32 Random mapping the ISP creates a golden web effect in the sky.

RedLayers texture from the Textures Library in the Deep Texture Editor. Render, and tweak as needed (see Figure 12.33).

FIGURE 12.33 Unique skies are best created with bitmap/procedural mixes.

MOVING ON

In this chapter, we detailed a number of ways you can customize and use Infinite Planes. In the next chapter, we'll explore the use of the Sky Lab further.

CHAPTER

13 Atmospherics

This chapter covers atmospheric operations that are connected to Sky Plane customization. You can address these operations using the Sky Lab, or from the tools at the top of Sky&Fog mode.

GLOBAL REALITY

What makes Bryce users come back time and time again to sculpt and shape their creations? Bryce users are drawn into the wonder and mystery of world creating, of transforming the elements like a new-age alchemist, and watching as endless new worlds evolve out of the mist. Working in Bryce has all the lure of a challenging adventure. More than just spreading out new tools on the table in front of you, Bryce invites you to pick them up and discover what you can do.

The way that Bryce goes about this is to provide you with a number of one-stroke pathways to the virtual environment, and letting the environment that results influence your options from that point onward. The dominant and most immediate pathway presented in Bryce centers on atmospherics and the default Sky Plane look, so much so that an entire toolbar is provided for that singular purpose.

The Sky&Fog toolbar, shown in Figure 13.1, is usually your first stop when customizing an atmosphere or the default Sky Plane. This is the place of atmospheric activity, where the sun, moon, clouds, and fog hold sway. The key numbers in Figure 13.1 outline the important features of this toolbar, so let's take a quick look at what's involved and why these features and tools are so important. Refer to the callouts in Figure 13.1 for the text that follows.

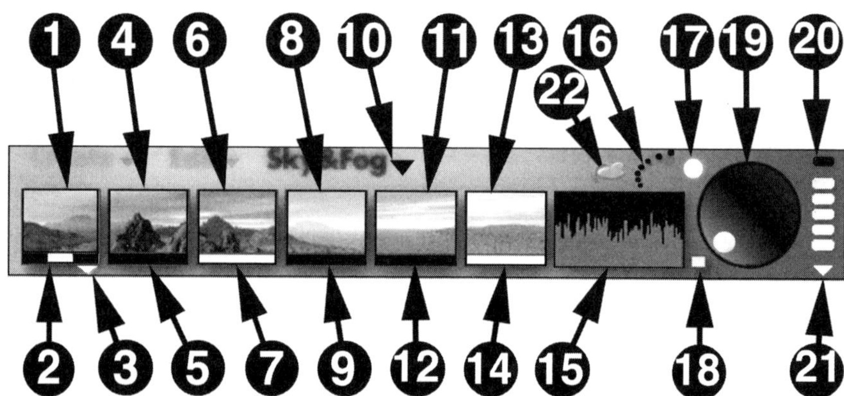

FIGURE 13.1 The Sky&Fog toolbar.

The Sky&Fog Toolbar

Looking at Figure 13.1, here are some things to pay attention to as you navigate the Sky&Fog toolbar. The numbers indicate callouts on the figure.

CALLOUT #1

This is the Sky Mode controller. You can click and drag the mouse, or access one of the four specific modes from the list (#3): Softer, Darker, Custom, and Atmosphere Off). Clicking and dragging moves you through the four modes interactively.

CALLOUT #2

This is an Eyedropper control that allows you to select any color from either a pop-up palette or from anywhere in a picture. It works only when you're in Custom Sky or Atmosphere Off modes.

CALLOUT #3

This arrow brings up the Modes list: Softer Sky, Darker Sky, Custom Sky, and Atmosphere Off. Custom Sky and Atmosphere Off are the most important features for creating original sky elements, with Softer and Darker used as customizing options once you have a sky n the screen. Using the Custom Sky option, you can use the associated palettes and their Sky&Fog tools to create an original sky. Using Atmosphere Off (and manually moving any Haze and Fog settings to 0, as well as deleting any Infinite Planes), you can create one-color backdrops.

Solid-color backdrops are important for both compositing your Bryce images for video (blue-screen/green-screen work) and for developing text slides and overhead transparencies. Solid-color backdrops also foster the ability to cut the image out in a paint application for 2D compositing.

To develop a solid-color backdrop, do the following:

1. Delete all Infinite Planes, and make sure Fog and Haze settings are at 0.
2. Select The Atmosphere Off option, or select the black or white backdrop from the Sky Presets palette, which automatically gives you a solid black or white backdrop. Stop here if either black or white is your goal.
3. Select the color of your choice from the Eyedropper color palette (#2 in the figure).

CALLOUTS #4 AND #5

This is where you set the Ambient Shadow intensity and color of the atmosphere. This color sets a general emotional and atmospheric tone to the scene.

Use a black color to have little or no effect on the scene, and a white to wash out the atmosphere. Other colors tint the elements in the scene, as if the air was that specific hue. As colors get darker, the effect is moderated and lessened.

CALLOUTS #6 AND #7

Allows you to set the Fog intensity (click and drag the mouse right to increase from 0 to 100%) and height (click and drag the mouse vertically to increase from 0 to 100%). To see these modifications in the Nano Preview, you must be in either Camera or Director's view.

In the Sky&Fog palette (accessed by clicking on item #21 in Figure 13.1, you can blend the fog intensity with the sun. Doing this allows the fog to "burn off" as the day progresses.

A Fog Experiment

Do the following:

1. After having placed an object in your scene and deleted the Ground Plane, create a Sphere and sink it halfway in the Underground. Turn the Underground option off (right-hand toolbar).
2. Set the Fog intensity to 50% and the Height to 3. Color it a medium green. Render the scene.
3. Increase the Fog Height to 50 and render the scene. You should see the Fog creep up over part of your object. Doing animations with this basic technique allows you to cause the Fog to wash over objects.

CALLOUTS #8 AND #9

This is the Haze control. You should always have Haze set to some amount (a good standard is 50) when you are developing a scene that shows the horizon line where the sky and ground meet. If you don't, that line will be far too evident and unreal. Haze also adjusts LOD (level of Detail), so that objects farther away from the camera are rendered more blurry than those close up. In selecting the color of the haze, opt for a color that matches the sky at its lowest point.

CALLOUT #10

This triangle triggers the appearance of the Sky&Fog Presets Library (see Figure 13.2). It's called Sky and Fog because the sky thumbnails you see come with Fog and Haze settings as well. Use the presets as they are, or as basic elements that can be customized. Remember to add (save) your own customized skies here for later use, or to export them to other directories for storage and sharing with other Bryce users.

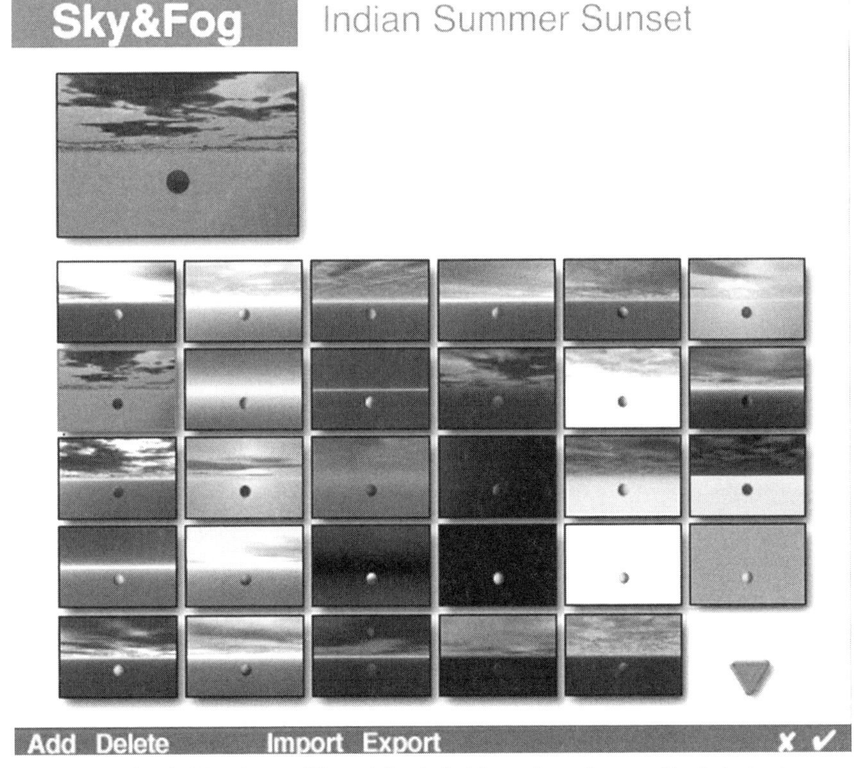

FIGURE 13.2 The Sky&Fog Presets Library is loaded with a variety of preset skies for instant addition to your world.

CALLOUTS #11 AND #12

Cloud Height and Sky Dome Color can be modified from here. Alterations in Cloud Height cause radical changes in the look of your sky, and also affect the light in a scene. If Cumulous Clouds are not switched on, the Stratus clouds will create different gradient washes when the Sky Height is altered, but still based on the color of the Cumulous Cloud setting. Sky Dome Color tints objects in the scene to simulate twilight and dawn lighting, but the effect is very subtle.

A Cloud Height of 0 and a Cloud Coverage of 100 creates a solid-color sky. Color is referenced to the Cumulous Color (#14). Coupled with the middle palette bar in the Custom Sky option of the Sky Mode controller (#1), a solid color is also added to the ground (as long as there is no Terrain Plane and no Haze or Fog). This gives you a solid two-color backdrop.

CALLOUTS #13 AND #14

Cloud Coverage and Cumulous Color are set here. A Coverage of 0, with Cumulous Clouds Off, produces gradient wash skies. With Cumulous Clouds switched On, the higher the coverage, the darker the sky, which is great for an impending storm. A gradual change in solid colors from light to dark takes place as you move upward in Cloud Coverage, as long as the frequency/amplitude settings are flatlined.

CALLOUT #15

Although you can watch the numbers at the bottom of the left-hand palette change as you drag the mouse horizontally and vertically in this interactive controller for clouds, it's far better to watch the waveforms so you can get an intuitive feel for how they influence cloud creation. Flatlining the waveform creates solid colors in the sky.

CALLOUT #16

Don't miss the chance to at least explore the use of the Randomizing features in the toolbar. Clicking on these dots produces some very bizarre skies, which can be accepted or customized.

CALLOUT #17

This icon switches between sun and moon, telling you instantly if it's night or day. Instead of just working within this clock system, you are free to mix and match effects. For example, you can create a daytime look with a night sky by simply adding a light source to illuminate the scene, even when this icon is showing the moon.

CALLOUT #18

Clicking and holding here gives you access to the Color palette for the sun. Turning the sun black allows you to be in the Bryce "day" with all of the effects of the night.

CALLOUT #19

This is the control you will use most in this toolbar, if not in Bryce itself—the sun/moon positioning trackball. The moon is always on the opposite side as the sun. Make sure Link Sun to View is selected in the Sky&Fog options list, and make doubly sure that you have configured your camera so that it faces the top of the screen in the top view, in order to orient yourself properly.

CALLOUT #20

These are the sky Memory Dots, allowing you to save and instantly recall your skies. They are especially useful in animating skies, since you can target specific keyframes with a saved sky setting.

CALLOUT #21

It is vital that you understand all of the items and implications listed in this menu when you click on this arrow. Listed here are a number of Sky&Fog options, with the all important Sky Lab option at the bottom of the list.

CALLOUT #22

Trigger for bringing up the Sky Lab.

Auto Update

Every time you alter the sky with this option checked, it will begin a rendering. Your work habits might differ from ours, but we suggest leaving it off. You should use the Nano Preview instead of this annoying and time-consuming alternative.

Link to View

Yes! Always leave this checked so you can orient yourself properly in your Bryce world.

Stratus Clouds/Cumulous Clouds

As you create your customized skies, explore switching one and/or both of these options on and off. You can only appreciate the creative options Bryce offers you when you explore them thoroughly and constantly.

Reset Sky

If you get totally lost and confused, use this option to return you to the beginning of the session.

Sky Lab

Clicking on the Sky Lab option brings up a three-tabbed settings dialog. The tabs are named Sun & Moon, Cloud Cover, and Atmosphere. Here are a few things to pay attention to in the options presented.

SUN & MOON

The following settings are recommended (see Figure 13.3):

- Leave Horizon Illusion checked. The default value of 40 is OK, although you might want to enlarge this later to create larger suns when they are visible on the horizon.
- We prefer leaving this checked because rings of light look nice around the sun (they are too vague around the moon image). If you check this On, also check Secondary Rings. Explore what this looks like by placing a sun on the horizon in front of the camera.
- Moon Phase/Use Moon Image should also be checked On. Use an Earthshine of 100% for sharper moons, and lower settings for moons with blurry edges.
- Link Sun to View should always be On.

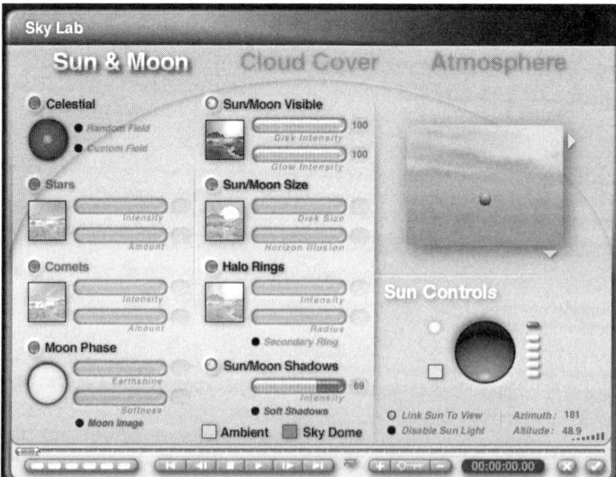

FIGURE 13.3 The Sun and Moon tab in the Environmental Attributes dialog.

- Stars and Comets are not worth checking, since they are far too washed out. There are better ways to create them, as we shall explore later in this chapter.

CLOUD COVER

Clicking on the Edit option under either or both the Stratus and/or Cumulus cloud previews will take you guess where? Of course! To the Deep Texture Editor, where you can use the by-now familiar controls to create all kinds of unique clouds. After developing an interesting customized cloud material, return to the scene to preview what it really looks like, although you can also get a miniature preview in the image area under this tab (see Figure 13.4).

FIGURE 13.4 The Cloud Cover tab in the Environmental Attributes dialog.

ATMOSPHERE

Volumetric World is definitely a *Do Not Check* in most circumstances. Bryce renders volumetrics slow enough; you don't have to punish yourself by making it render even slower. Blending Fog and Haze with the Sun is an option you should explore on a project-by-project basis, since there are too many possible variables to set any hard-and-fast rules for its use (see Figure 13.5).

Creating Sky Types

There are so many variables to consider when creating a sky that laying out rules for all of the possibilities and variations is impossible. What we

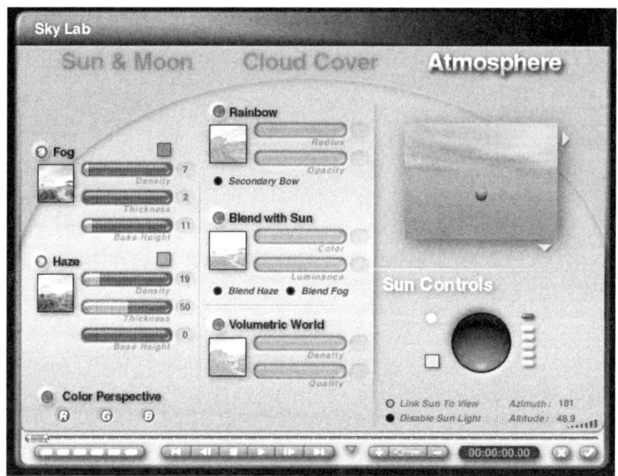

FIGURE 13.5 The Atmosphere tab in the Environmental Attributes dialog.

can do, however, is delineate a handful of examples that take some of the possible parameters into consideration. Table 13.1 lists some basic custom sky types and how they can be created by using the associated settings. All use the Custom Sky mode. Strata and Cumulous is switched On for all examples unless otherwise noted. The Sun is positioned at the top center of the trackball, and a "Horizon Illusion" number of 70 is used throughout. You can use these examples as is, or as starting points for your own modifications (see Figure 13.6, page 292).

TABLE 13.1 Basic Custom Sky Types

SKY TYPE	FOG & HAZE	HEIGHT	COVERAGE & CUMULOUS COVER	FREQUENCY & AMPLITUDE	COMMENTS
Mellow	Fog: 1/0 and Lt. Gray Haze: 12	Height: 24	Cover: 17 Orange	119 / 156	This is a peaceful sky, allowing you to breathe easy.
Murky	Fog: 22/30 Blue Gray Haze: 15	Height: 47	Cover: 50 Dark Green	9 / 322	You can almost feel the humidity.
Breakup	Fog: 0 / 0 Haze: 3	Height: 53	Cover: 42 Light Yellow	137 / 309	A sign of hope.
Doom	Fog: 3 / 9 Dark Red Haze: 10 Dark Red	Height: 0	Cover: 36 Dark Green	200 / 141 Black Sun	This sky uses a black sun. Don't go outside!

TABLE 13.1 Basic Custom Sky Types (Continued)

SKY TYPE	FOG & HAZE	HEIGHT	COVERAGE & CUMULOUS COVER	FREQUENCY & AMPLITUDE	COMMENTS
Yawn	Fog: 0 / 0 Haze: 4	Height: 70	Cover: 31 Pink	32 / 101 Light Blue Sun	We don't know why, but this one makes us want to go back to sleep.
Dream	Fog: 0 Haze: 100 Pink	Height: 0	Cover: 0	Flatlined White Sun	A walk in the dream world withStratus and Cumulousswitched Off.
Heat	Fog: 0 Haze: 50 Peach Color	Height: 0 Stratus and Cumulous switched Off	Cover: 0	Flatlined Yellow Sun with Horizon Illusion Off	Loosen your shirt, it's going to be a scorcher! Shadows made yellow to emphasize the effect.
Blue Swoon	Fog: 0 Haze: 0	Cover: 0 Stratus On, Cumulous switched Off	Height: 11 Dark Blue Shadows set to White	58 / 72	A blue sun and lavender sky assure us that we are not on Earth.
Aura	Fog: 0 Haze: 0	Height: 100 Red Purple	Cover: 12 Turquoise	4 / -125	A sky meant for prophetic visions.
Sol Etude	Fog: 0 Haze: 0	Height: 100 Dark Blue	Cover: 42 Turquoise	9 / -132	Dark, but not threatening. Violet shadows.

BETTER MOONS AND STARS

The Moons and Stars that Bryce allows you to add to your world from the Sky Lab are in many cases less than optimal. Compared to the Sun, which can be positioned and colorized so that it becomes an integral part of the scene, the Moon often appears much too dim, and the image of its surface is not at all well defined. The "stars" are far too dim, and just about disappear when printed out. These two natural elements do not tend to mix well with the startling content of a Bryce scene, so we have to look for other alternatives for their creation.

MOONS

The best way to add a moon to a Bryce world is to map a specific material to either a disk or a sphere, and manually place it in the sky where you need it. Using a sphere is suggested if the moon is a place you want to visit, or to actually fly around. The problem with a sphere is that when placed at great distances from the camera (which might be a necessity with Moon objects), it tends to distort. Two-dimensional disks do not

FIGURE 13.6 These images refer to the Sky Types in Table 13.1 (from upper left): Mellow, Murky, Breakup, Doom, Yawn, Dream, Heat, Blue Swoon, Aura, and Sol Etude.

distort, but might take the material in a way that doesn't look too convincing on first inspection. If the Moon object is to be seen from the surface of a planet, whether you use the 2D or 3D object, make sure to turn Shadows Off for both Casting and Receiving. In addition, make sure you don't have a local light in the scene with "no falloff" selected, since that might illuminate the moon too. If the Moon object is far enough away, linear falloff on a local light should be OK (see Figures 13.7 and 13.8).

Two-dimensional disks to be used as moons should be mapped with Object Front. Note that you could use a Boolean Cylinder to cut the moon into the familiar quarter-moon shape.

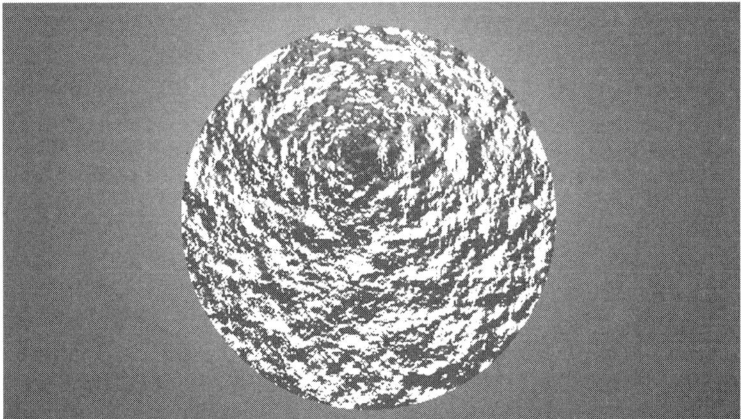

FIGURE 13.7 Here is a 2D disk moon ready to place in your sky at a far distance. It has a Volume Visible Radial Light behind it, sized at 3X the object, to give the moon an aura.

FIGURE 13.8 Using a 3D Sphere for a moon is a better idea, and gives it 3D shadowing, but watch out for distortion when the moon is placed too far in the distance.

2D MOONS FROM 3D MOONS

How about the best of both worlds? Since a 2D moon can be placed in the far distance without distortion, and a 3D moon has better shading, why not combine the two? Here's how:

1. Create a 3D moon. Use the Planet material to map it, and use Parametric mapping. Render the moon on a solid white background, and Save it out (Export it) as a picture.
2. Create a Picture Plane disk. Go to the Materials Lab, and map the 2D disk with the 3D moon graphic you just saved. Now you have the 3D moon's quality, with the 2D moon's usefulness.

STARS

Creating a field of stars is simple in Bryce. Just do the following:

1. Point the camera upward, so that the stars are created at the vault of the heavens. Set the Frequency/Amplitude of clouds to 0 for both, and uncheck Strata and Cumulous. Set the Sky mode to Atmosphere Off, and color the sky dark blue.
2. Place a horizontal Disk primitive in the scene. Move it up to the sky, and resize it so that it is very tiny. Assign a light-blue material to it with a 100% Specularity.
3. With the disk selected, Multi-Replicate it 60 times in place.
4. Select the entire group of Multi-Replicated copies by extending a Selection marquee around them. Go to the Randomize tool in the Edit toolbar, and with 2D Disperse Size selected, click and drag the mouse right to spatter the skies across the sky. Preview for a look (see Figure 13.9).

You can repeat this procedure several times, and then select some individual stars for color alterations. This makes a stunning and more realistic starry sky.

COMETS AND METEORS

When creating comets and meteors, we draw upon the same skills used thus far to create moons. There are only two differences. The first is that we have to find the proper material(s) for the tasks, and the second is that we might want to add some trail fire or debris. Comets are large balls of ice and rocks that trail vapor and ice chunks, while meteors are large chunks of stone that glow once they hit the friction of the atmosphere.

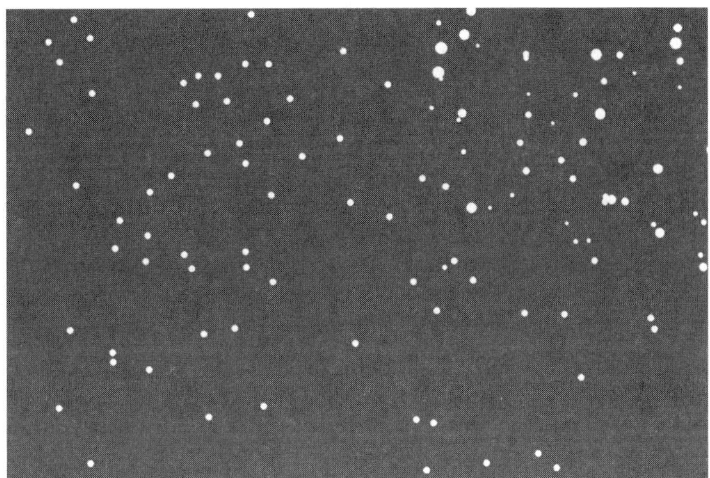

FIGURE 13.9 A starry sky, created with 2D circular planes, Multi-Replication, and the Randomize process.

Comet

1. Place a Bryce Stone object on the screen from the Create toolbar. Use the Rocky Planet texture from the Rocks presets in the Materials Lab. Use a light-blue specular color. Set the specular value to the texture, and set the slider at 10. This makes the Comet ice glow.
2. Attach (Link) a stretched-out Cone to the comet for the tail. In reality, the tail can be millions of miles long, but you don't have to try that in Bryce for now. Make the tail about three times as long as the comet, with the small end of the cone stuck in the comet itself.
3. Now for the material of the tail. Open the Materials Lab with the tail section selected. Use a Marble texture from the Rocks list, and make it a Volumetric texture. Place a channel marker for the marble texture next to Diffuse Color, Diffusion value, and Base Density. Set the sliders as follows: Diffusion and Ambience Value to 100, Base Density to 13, Edge Softness and Fuzzy Factor to 0, and Quality/Speed to 30.5. Render, and Save the project to disk (see Figure 13.10).

Meteor

The meteor would just look like a rock if it were traveling in space, so we'll make this one appear as if it was interacting with the friction of an atmosphere.

1. Place a Bryce Stone object on the screen from the Create toolbar. Use the Rocky Planet texture from the Rocks presets in the Materials Lab.

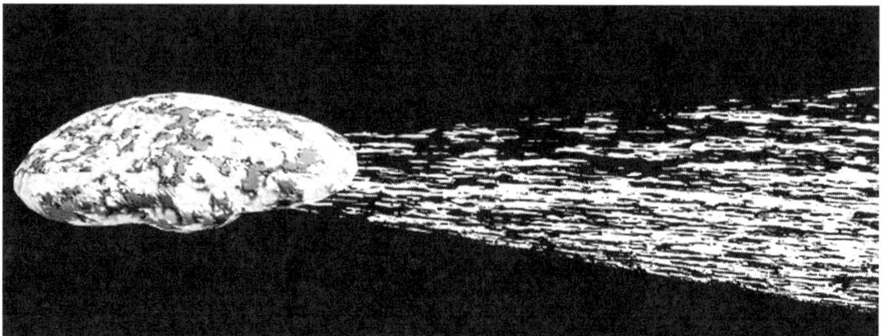

FIGURE 13.10 The comet streaks along as its tail marks its path.

Use a yellow-orange specular color. Set the Specular Value to the texture, and set the slider at 10. This makes the meteor glow.

2. Duplicate the meteor, and without repositioning it, enlarge it by 10%. There is now a shell around the meteor that matches its form.
3. In the Materials Lab, set a Volumetric material for the enlarged duplicate form. Use the Rainbow texture from the Psychedelics folder. In the A channel, set the texture for Transparent Color, Ambient Value (100), and Base Density (40). Set Diffusion value to 100, Edge Softness to 24, Fuzzy Factor to 30, and Quality/Speed to 40.

The duplicate form provides the meteor with flames that flicker across its surface. Render, and Save to disk (see Figure 13.11).

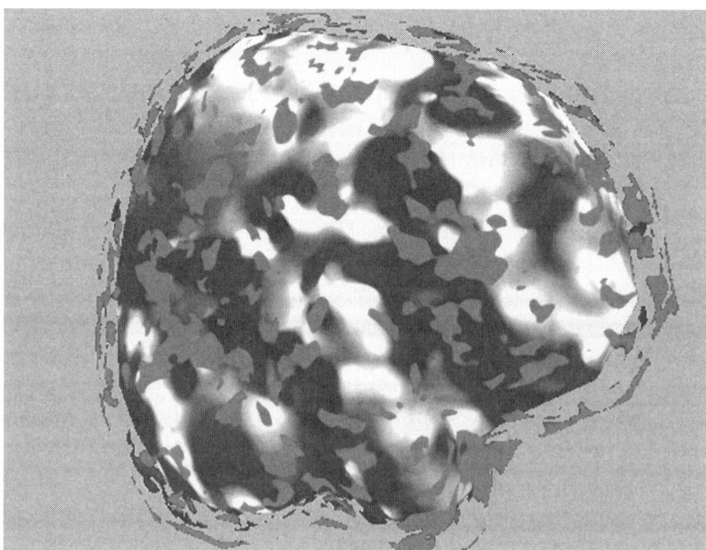

FIGURE 13.11 The meteor glows as flames flicker across its surface.

DOUBLE SUNS AND DISTANT PLANETS

Using the same process we detailed for creating moons, we can also create additional suns for the sky, or even large planets. Bryce is set to an earthly environment, but most users at least explore the possibility of developing alien worlds. We know from astronomy that double suns and multitudes of moons are not uncommon features in the galaxy, and most probably are familiar structures in other galaxies as well. All it takes is the right texture and material, or bitmap, to evoke a multitude of otherworld features. We might not be able to travel to these places in our lifetime, but Bryce and our own creative explorations can bring us as virtually close as possible (see Figure 13.12).

FIGURE 13.12 What place is this with double moons while in the sky a planet looms?

OTHER SKY PLANE MODIFICATIONS

Remember that Bryce offers us two different ways to create skies. The first is the sky that can be created from modifying the parameters set in the Sky&Fog toolbar, which we have delved into quite a bit in this chapter. The other way we can create a sky in Bryce is by using an Infinite Cloud Plane. Cloud Planes are useful for more than sky attributes, however. One of the best uses around is to use them to mist out terrain.

There are two ways to add a mist around mountains. One is to use a 3D object, like a squashed Sphere, and map it with a Volumetric or Surface material. This is good for very localized effects, like a fiery cloud around a volcano, or a cloud around the mythic Mount Sinai while the Ten Commandments are being sculpted. The problem with Volumetrics is rendering time, and the problem with both is that you can always tell what the 3D form is, no matter how fuzzy. Using interleaved Cloud Planes for the same purpose leads to much more realistic results. The only drawback to using a Cloud Plane to mist out terrain is that the plane is infinite, and panning the camera will reveal the Cloud Plane in all directions. Therefore, when you use this technique, don't pan the camera. You can also compound the effect by adding haze and ground fog.

Misty Mountains

Here's one way to add mist to a mountain or an entire range.

1. Create a mountain that fills your Camera view, and use a Terrain material of your choosing to map it (Object Space).
2. Add four Surface Cloud Planes. Place three of them at different heights so that they intersect the summit of the mountain, and one so that it is raised a little above the mountain's base.
3. Use varying Cloud Presets on each plane to randomize the look, and use different levels of transparency on each. Render, and Save to disk (see Figure 13.13).

As an alternate method to using three Surface Cloud Planes to mask the summit, you could use one Volumetric Cloud Plane to do the same task. Rendering proceeds faster with Surface Planes, but if you want to fly through the mist, Volumetrics are the best choice.

SKY ROTATION

You are already aware that Infinite Planes can be rotated, but what about the sky itself? At first glance, this seems impossible. But is it? First, remember that you are looking at the Bryce world through a camera, which represents your eye. The camera has controls, and one of those controls is banking. In any view, you can use the rotation tools to turn the camera on its side. When you couple this with your ability to rotate the camera so it's looking at the sky alone, you have the possibility for creating images that show the sky painted from the bottom to the top of your screen, instead of from left to right.

FIGURE 13.13 The mountain range rises into the clouds, while a ground fog hovers near its base.

OK, but what good does this do? What use could you possibly have for this capability? There are two uses that come to mind immediately. This is one way to generate "portrait" aspect work, as differentiated from Bryce's standard "landscape" aspect graphics. Portrait aspect is often in demand for print output, and this is one way to generate it. That's the more conservative reason you might want to explore this technique, but there's a more creative answer as well. Since you can bank the camera at any angle, and since skies (like everything else in Bryce) can be animated, you can create animations that show the sky moving at whatever angles you desire across the screen. The only challenge is that you will have to set your scene up at angles too. Here's how to do it:

1. Create a scene, complete with Ground Plane and objects.
2. Select the Camera and everything else (including the Ground Plane), and Group them.
3. Go to the Left or Right view, and point the camera toward the sky. Everything else will also rotate.
4. Go to the Front view and bank the camera by rotating it on an angle left or right. Render a preview in the Nano Editor, and you will see an angled sky behind your scene. If you want a true portrait aspect image, the camera must be banked 90 degrees left or right (see Figure 13.14).

FIGURE 13.14 Even this simple composition takes on a heightened interest level with the clouds running vertically as opposed to their default horizontal orientation.

THE VORTEXTRON

Never allow the *rules* to dissuade you from exploring the impossible. Just as we discovered that the impossible can be done by rotating the sky, so impossible and unsuspected visuals can be created by resizing bitmap textures on a Cloud Plane. Since Infinite Planes go on forever, mapping a bitmap picture to an Infinite Plane at a 1:1 ratio results in an infinite tile of the image, as shown in Figure 13.15.

FIGURE 13.15 Resizing a bitmap texture mapped to an Infinite Plane at 1000% or more results in a series of interference patterns that look like energy fluctuations.

When you resize the bitmap, however, strange things begin to occur. In addition to the image getting smaller to accommodate more samples, as the numbers increase you start to see patterns instead of just reduced copies of the original image. If you push the resizing to 500 or more, moiré type patterns emerge. These patterns become their own image, transparent sheets of energy that can suffice for simulating wave effects in a Bryce project. Various percentages of resized bitmaps are shown in Figure 13.16.

The pattern is always dependent on the Alpha transparency of the bitmap, so every bitmap will necessarily display its own interference pattern when more bitmaps are forced onto the Infinite Plane.

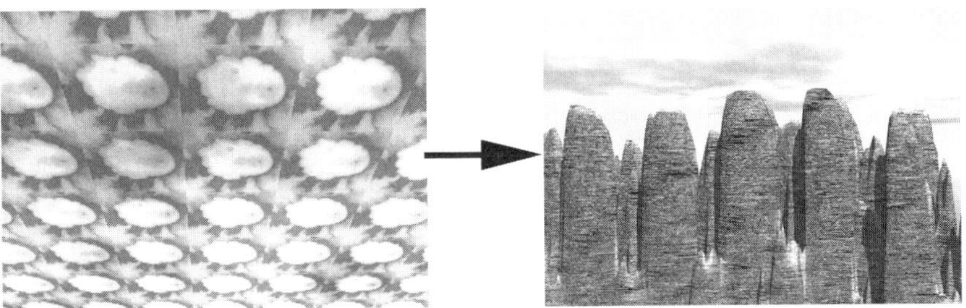

FIGURE 13.16 At a 1:1 ratio, bitmapped graphics tile themselves forever on an Infinite Cloud Plane (left), and can be used to create mountains in the Terrain Editor (right).

RAINBOWS

Somewhere deep within ourselves, we all hold a special reverence for rainbows, whether from Dorothy's visit to Oz or from some archaic unconscious source. Rainbows have always been a sign of hope that tomorrow will be better than today. Bryce has a wonderful rainbow generator, and it functions in accordance with the laws of optics. In our everyday world, the sun must be coming from the opposite direction from our perception of the rainbow. If we see a rainbow in the west, the sun must be in the east. This is exactly the way rainbows are configured in Bryce. If you positioned your camera correctly, and if you checked the Link Sun to View option in the Sky&Fog toolbar menu, then we are ready to explore rainbow creation. To create a rainbow, do the following:

1. Create a suitable scene for the rainbow to be placed in. Make sure the sun is at your back.
2. Open up the Sky Lab, and go to the Atmosphere tab. Check Rainbow, and if you want, Secondary rainbow. Input the radius and intensity.

A good default is a Radius of 60 and an Intensity of 70, but you might want to explore other settings.

3. Look at the Nano Preview, and render when you have a good mix. Save to disk (see Figure 13.17).

To make rainbows more visible, try turning off Stratus and Cumulous clouds. In addition, try raising the sun a little to move the rainbow lower to the horizon.

FIGURE 13.17 Creating rainbows in Bryce is a snap, and the results can be quite alluring.

FOREGROUND PLANES

In a picture or an animation, the way target subjects are framed by other elements often becomes the major part of a composition. If you look at the Disney Studios' work over the years, you can appreciate this technique. Often, a black silhouetted foreground acts as a frame for color targets in a picture. Bryce allows you to easily introduce these framing components into your work. Here's how:

1. In a paint application, set your palette to work in two colors, black and white. Paint a silhouetted scene with black, allowing the drop-out color to be white. One of the most common subjects of a foreground painting like this is a jungle scene, a silhouetted image of a group of trees, vines, and associated elements.

2. Save the image to disk in a format that Bryce can read.
3. In the Picture Editor of the Materials Lab, import the image. You shouldn't have to do anything about the Alpha channel, since the white areas will be set for dropout automatically.
4. Map this picture to a Picture Plane that covers your screen. Make sure there are no lights in back of the scene, including sunlight, so the foreground picture remains totally black except for the transparent cutouts. Place 3D elements in the scene in back of this Picture Plane. The final rendering should show your 3D world as framed by this 2D graphic. If the graphic is large enough, you'll be able to pan the camera to see different parts of the 3D scene showing through (see Figure 13.18).

Another common Foreground Plane picture would be a window cutout, making it seem as if you were in a darkened room looking out on a colorful Bryce world.

FIGURE 13.18 Using a 2D graphic to frame a 3D scene.

MOVING ON

In this chapter, we explored the use of the Sky Lab, and increased our knowledge of using and customizing the look of the Sky Planes. In the next chapter, we'll investigate Bryce lights.

CHAPTER

14 Lights

Light not only illuminates worlds, light also creates its opposite: shadows and darkness. For any visual artist, darkness and shadow are the defining principles of 3D perception. Shadow causes us to imagine that we are seeing 3D shapes on what remains only a 2D screen. All of the information we have covered thus far concerning the application of materials to objects, especially materials that look three dimensional because of Bump-mapped elements, take light and lighting, shade and shadowing, into consideration. With the right lighting, materials and textures jump off the screen. With the wrong lighting, materials and textures look flat and washed out, erasing all of your long hours of effort. Lighting also lends emotional content to what we see. This can be best appreciated by looking at a model of the human face with different lighting methods applied, as seen in Figure 14.1.

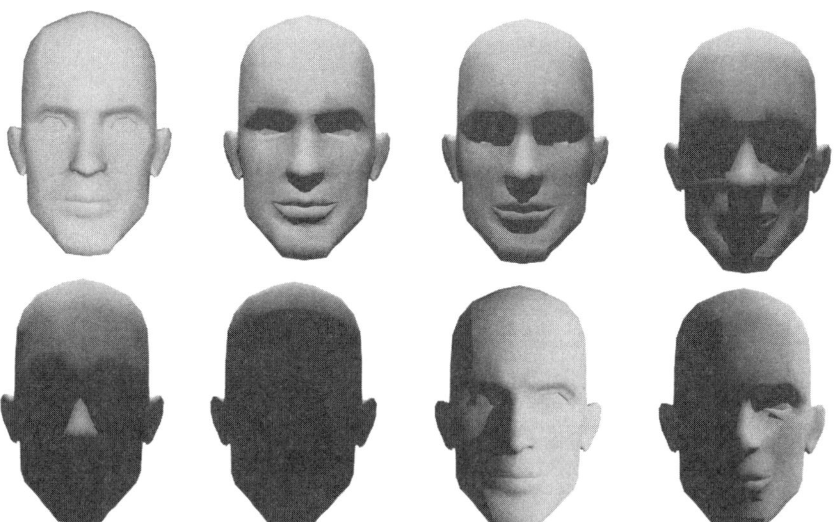

FIGURE 14.1 For 3D interest, a face with full front lighting looks flat when compared to lighting that casts partial shadows. Lighting also influences our perception of the actor and the story being told.

THE BRYCE LIGHTING TECHNICIAN

You have all of the tools you need to become a master lighting technician in Bryce, for both setting and modifying light sources for your worlds. Bryce handles nature-oriented light sources, the Sun and the Moon, and also an array of other lighting types at your disposal. The four light types in Bryce are *Radial, Spotlight, Square Spotlight,* and *Parallel Light*. Each has its uses, and each affects a scene in a different way.

Radial Light

The Radial Light is represented by the spherical Light icon in the Create toolbar. The Radial Light is spherical, and throws its illumination in all directions equally. It's perfect for use as a light in a lamp. When you need light that illuminates everything in a scene equally from a light source, use a Radial Light. Radial Lights also throw illumination on the Ground Plane, something no other light does. You might describe a Radial Light as one that is constructed from an infinite number of Spotlights, since the illumination it throws off is represented by a circular patch on the objects that receive the light. Here are some ideas for using Radial lights:

- If you place a Radial Light in a cubic room, you will see a circular patch of light on each wall, the ceiling, and the floor.
- Drop a Radial Light in the crater of a volcano to illuminate the crater edges and anything that might be ejected out of it.
- Use a Radial Light as a placed sun in your sky.
- Use a Radial Light as a lamp. Place it inside of a Lightbulb object, and Link it to that object. The lamp can also be a street lamp.
- Use a Radial Light. reduced in size, inside of a candle flame.
- Use a Radial Light inside of any fire material, useful for campfires or larger conflagrations.

CREATE A STREET LAMP

To create a street lamp that uses a Radial Light, do the following:

1. Create a series of objects in your scene that will be illuminated by the lamp. Leave room in their collective center for the lamp.
2. Create a pole from a stretched Cylinder primitive, and place it on the ground in the center of your objects. Place a Sphere on top of the pole. Use a Gold material on the pole, and a light-blue material for the globe. Make the globe 65% transparent. Move the globe to the top of the pole.
3. Place a Radial Light in the center of the globe. Make the Radial Light a Volumetric light in its Edit dialog, so you can see it (see Figure 14.2).

Spotlight

Spotlights illuminate the scene from a specific direction (see Figure 14.3).

Spotlights are used for two main purposes. The first is to target a specific element in your scene, perhaps by moving across it to reveal it in steps. Second, use the Spotlight to emulate various light sources, including

FIGURE 14.2 A street lamp globe example.

FIGURE 14.3 The Spotlight illuminates a scene from a specific direction; in this case, from the camera position.

vehicles headlights, searchlights that move across the sky, mysterious light sources emanating from an ET ship, for the eyes of a robot to add extra excitement, and inside the nozzle of a rocket, adding extra punch to the exhaust.

Square Spotlight

Square Spotlights work very well when you need to render a light streaming through a window (see Figure 14.4).

FIGURE 14.4 The Square Spotlight is the best light to choose when you need light to stream through a window into a darkened room to illuminate the contents.

Square Spotlights are good for global illumination. They cast a squarish illumination, but not as defined as Parallel Lights. The beam tends to smear and be somewhat rounded. Its best use is for general scene illumination from a specific direction. If you wanted to have light streaming through a window to light all of the objects in its direction, the Square Spotlight would be a wise choice.

Parallel Light

Parallel Lights are perfect for projecting *Gel* images onto a scene. Although you can do this with any of the four light types, Gels projected through a Parallel Light look like square-edged slides from a slide projector.

EDITING LIGHTS

Use the Light Lab (new in Bryce 5) to edit and customize your lights. The controls are self explanatory (see Figure 14.5).

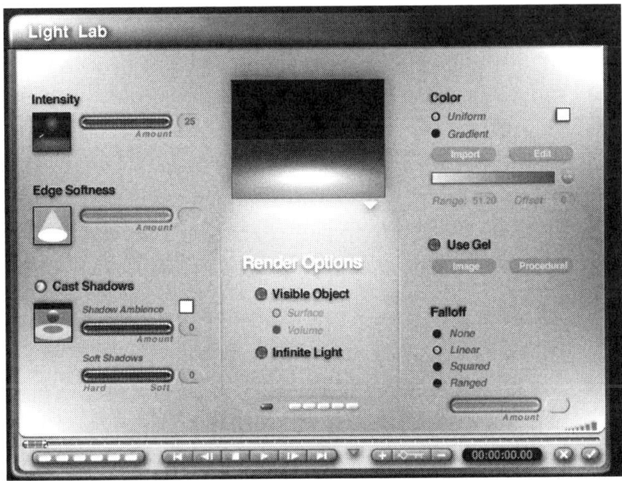

FIGURE 14.5 The Light Lab contains all of the controls for editing and customizing lights.

Access the Light Lab by clicking on the Editor icon in the Edit toolbar with the light selected, or by clicking on the E control in the light's attributes list.

Here are some tips to think about when using the Light Lab:

- Keep the Light Intensity to 50 or below if you want to see the light color (as long as it is anything but white, which is always visible).

- Setting the Light Intensity at 100 or above, and the Color to black, produces some interesting dark light effects. Use the effects to add subtle mystery to a scene.
- Preview with the Render in Scene option if you're not sure about the parameters you're setting. This takes a little time, but it shows you how your intensity and other changes are affecting the scene itself. Most of the time, you will use the default Render Against Neutral, especially when you are experienced enough with light settings to intuit what the results of your tweaking will be.
- Only in rare circumstances would you push the light intensity above 100%. This is because it causes a hot spot on objects that washes out their materials. When this occurs, move the light back some distance from the object(s).
- Never leave the color white when using the softened light aura. Always apply a color, even if only a subtle pastel.

VOLUMETRIC LIGHTS

Volumetric Lights have 3D volume as compared with surface lights. They can be made to take on 3D materials just like any other object. Normally, the materials they accept are provided by the Volume Library in the Materials Lab; however, this is not a hard-and-fast rule or limitation. You can also explore adding textured materials to a Volumetric Light, or any volumetric, within the framework of the Surface environment of the Materials Lab. When applying textured materials to lights, there are a few cautions to observe so that you can avoid long rendering times.

- Avoid super close-ups (larger than 1/4 screen) of Volumetric Lights that display a textured material.
- Make alterations in the light's Edit dialog before you do anything in the Materials Lab. Never return to the Edit dialog after you have customized material in the Materials Lab, or you will undo the Materials Lab customization.
- The highest rendering time cost applies to transparent textured materials. You don't have to avoid them; just be aware of this fact.

The Falloff attributes are listed in the light's Light Lab settings. The most common option is Linear Falloff. Linear Falloff is based on distance from the intended light target. The more distance between the light and target, the less illumination. Sometimes, depending on the lighting effect you want to create in a scene, selecting No Falloff becomes necessary. Using No Falloff will cause the light to illuminate everything in its projection beam evenly, so that objects in the far distance are illuminated the same as objects close to the light. Use No Falloff for effects such as explosion flares, pseudo sun or moon elements, and surrealistic effects.

GELS

A Gel is an image that can be projected by any light source. Bryce differentiates between bitmap-based Gels and procedural-based Gels. A bitmap Gel is defined as any graphic that Bryce can import, which can then be used as a Gel. When you access a bitmap Gel, you are presented with the Picture Editor from the Materials Lab, so that you can manipulate the Alpha channel as necessary. Procedural texture-based Gels use elements you configure from procedural materials. These can be either presets from the Materials Library or your own customized materials. Gels are accessed and loaded in the light's Light Lab controls.

Preset Gels

The Gel Folder in the Bryce Directory contains a number of ready-to-assign image Gels, although you can also use any of your own bitmap images. The unique thing about the Gels in the Bryce folder is that they are all two-color silhouettes, perfect for emulating shadows from invisible objects such as trees or venetian blinds. This allows you to get the benefit of the presence of objects in a scene by their shadow, with the actual object not having to be present (see Figures 14.6 and 14.7).

FIGURE 14.6 Here, a Spotlight uses a Gel to cast the Horizontal Slats pattern on everything in its illumination path.

FIGURE 14.7 The type of light casting the PICT Gel makes a difference; in this case, a Square Spotlight was used.

Procedural Texture Gels

The entire Material Presets Library is at your disposal for using Procedural Texture Gel Patterns, as are your own customized textures. The benefit of using procedural textures as Gel data includes the ability to resize the Gel information in the Materials Lab. All of your Deep Texture Editing skills can also be incorporated when customizing Gels (see Figures 14.8 and 14.9).

FIGURE 14.8 A Spotlight with an Object Front mapped Yellow Noise Texture Gel casts patterns on objects and ground.

FIGURE 14.9 The same Spotlight using the same Texture Gel as in Figure 14.8. The difference is that Spherical mapping and a higher size setting were configured in the Materials Lab.

Silhouetted Gels work best on objects that are mapped with color alone, while Procedural and Image Gels work well on objects that have Material content already mapped to them, resulting in a blended Material look. Turn Ambience off and Diffusion down on objects that are to receive Gel targeting. Keep in mind that rotating the light will also rotate the Gel.

Parallel Light Gel Projections

Parallel Lights are used to project Gel data that is meant to be perceived as a slide on a screen (see Figure 14.10).

Parallel Lights are perfect when you need to keep the illuminated area square. This is the light type to select for projecting window lights, or for creating pseudo slide shows and movies within your scenes.

FIGURE 14.10 The Parallel Light casts a rectangular projection, and throws its illumination in a specific direction. The edges of the illuminated area can be customized to remain completely square, perfect for projecting images like this Crosshatch Window Gel.

MATERIALS AND LIGHTS: AN ALTERNATE METHOD

You can use an alternate method to place a material texture on a light. Simply click the Material button ("M") in the light's Attributes list to bring up the Materials Lab, and select a material preset or design your own, just as you would for any other object.

If you use this method, do not use Volumetric options, or your system might crash.

The best light type to use for this method is the Radial Light. The material will be transmitted to objects in the vicinity as expected. This way of applying a Texture Gel is more direct than going through the Light Lab. The best materials to use are those with drop-out Alpha textures, since this will project symmetrical patterns on objects. If you increase the size of the texture in the Transformations dialog of the Materials Lab, you will start to see interference patterns being projected. This can be very effective for emulating energy waves on material, such as a pebble being cast into a pond, and is a great animation effect, too. Set the light intensity to 100, and the blur to 50 (see Figure 14.11).

FIGURE 14.11 The materials used to achieve these Radial Light interference patterns are (upper left to lower right): Gilded Cage, Gilded Cage resized to 3x, Peeling Paint, Carnival Tent, Rainbow, and Volcano Heart.

The color of the plane you map your interference patterns on should not be too light. A red color darkened to a reddish black looks good. This technique does not work with textures in the material, only color. Choose lighter colors to tint the Radial Light. Try using "No Falloff" if the projected texture is too light, and if moving the light closer to the material has little or no effect. Moving the Radial Light closer to the object sharpens the projected image.

RADIAL LIGHT F/X SAMPLES

Let's look at a few visual examples of radial light F/X. Under each graphic is a detailed description of how the effect was created. Note that the Gilded Cage material was used on all examples. You can select another preset textured material, or create your own (see Figures 14.12 through 14.17).

Work in the Edit dialog first, followed by the Materials Lab. Do not return to the Edit dialog, because all of the Materials Lab settings will be undone if you do.

To achieve the effect shown in Figure 14.12, do the following:

1. In the Edit dialog: Set Intensity and Fuzziness to 100. Make it a Volume Light with Linear Falloff.

FIGURE 14.12 This is our first example. The Radial Light has a textured material applied, but the beam casts only a normal light.

FIGURE 14.13 In this example, the Radial Light is wrapped with the material and projects the same material.

2. In the Materials Lab: Assign the Gilded Cage material. Use the Channel 1 marker only in the Transparent Color row and the Transparency Optics row. Select the Blend Transparency type. Wrap the material to the light in Object Space.

To achieve the effect shown in Figure 14.13, do the following:

1. In the Edit dialog: Set Intensity and Fuzziness to 100. Make it a Surface Light and Infinite.
2. In the Materials Lab: Assign the Gilded Cage material. Use the Channel 1 marker only in the Diffuse and Ambient Color rows (with slider settings of 80 and 30, respectively), in the Bump Height Value row, and in the Transparency Optics row. Select the Blend Transparency type. Wrap the material to the light in Object Space.

To achieve the effect shown in Figure 14.14, do the following:

1. In the Edit dialog: Set Intensity and Fuzziness to 100. Make it a Volume Light and Infinite.
2. In the Materials Lab: Go to the Volume controls, and assign the Gilded Cage material. Use the Channel 1 marker in the Diffuse Color and Base Density rows only. Input the following settings: Diffuse Value = 80, Ambient Value = 30, Specular Value = 22, Base Density = 55, Edge = 100, Fuzzy factor = 300, Quality/Speed = 30. Select the Flat Shaded type. Use Spherical mapping, and wrap the material to the light in Object Space.

To achieve the effect shown in Figure 14.15, do the following:

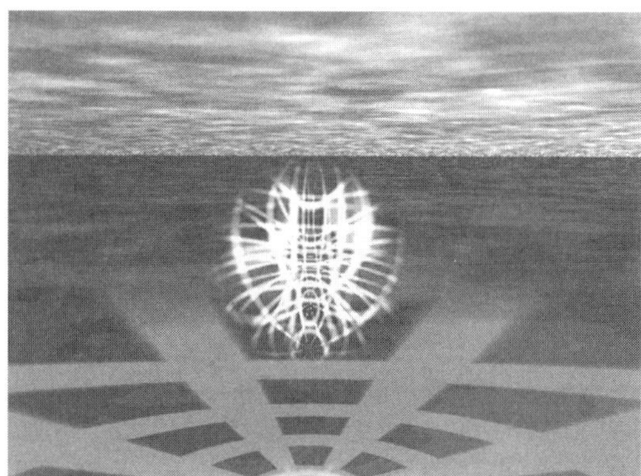

FIGURE 14.14 In this example, the Radial Light is wrapped with the material and projects the same material. It is also fuzzed out and soft in appearance

FIGURE 14.15 In this example, the Radial Light is a standard Volumetric with no material wrapped to it. Note that using a solid black sky emphasizes the light's contrast.

1. In the Edit dialog: Set Intensity and Fuzziness to 100. Make it a Volume Light and Infinite.
2. No need to do anything in the Materials Lab.

To achieve the effect shown in Figure 14.16, do the following:

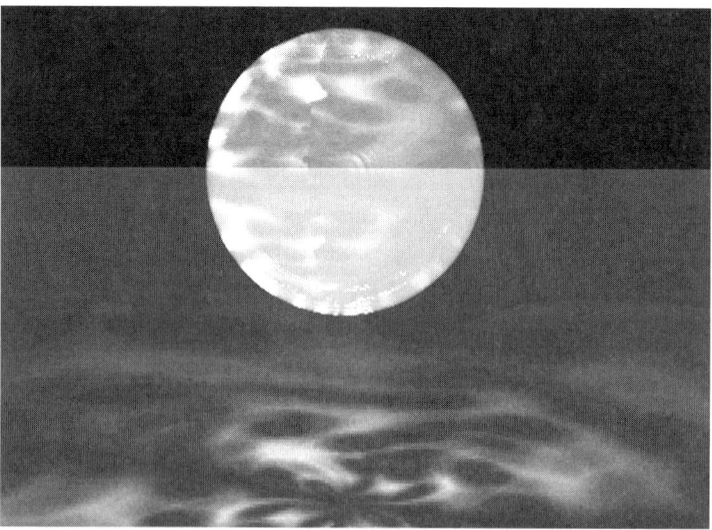

FIGURE 14.16 In this example, the Radial Light is a Volumetric with a Pict Gel, Watery Reflections, mapped to it. Some settings were altered in the Materials Lab.

1. In the Edit dialog: Set Intensity and Fuzziness to 100. Make it a Volume Light and Infinite. Click on Gel, and load the Watery Reflections item from the Gel folder on your Bryce CD.
2. In the Materials Lab, do the following: Make it a Volume material with Full Shading. Place the texture marker in the Diffuse Color row and in the Diffusion Value row (setting = 100). Set Ambience Value to 50. Give it a Base Density of 16, and a Fuzzy Factor of 100. Set Quality/Speed to the center (Air).

Normally, you would not see the light itself, just the fractal Watery Reflections. The customization we did in the Materials Lab made the light visible. Turning Atmosphere Off in the Sky Lab enhances all projected light effects. If you need clouds, add them on a separate Infinite Cloud Plane.

FIGURE 14.17 Four customized street lamps provide all of the light in this scene, using the same method detailed from Figure 14.16.

Which Light Type Is Best to Use with a Gel?

There is no hard-and-fast answer to this question, because it depends on what the project demands and how you configure the nearly infinite variables involved. There are a few guidelines, however:

- Use Radial Lights when you want the Gel to influence objects that surround the light source, and the other types for targeted objects.
- Use Parallel Lights when you want to emulate slide and movie projectors in your scene.
- If you want to apply silhouetted light/dark images to objects, use Silhouetted Gels. If you want to apply color washes, use Texture Gels.
- Consider the use of Alpha channel data when using Silhouetted Gels when the image contains more than two colors (black and white).
- Use colorful materials when opting for Procedural Gels, because that will enhance your targeted objects more.

ADDENDUM LIGHT TOPICS

Here are a few more points concerning lights: Preset Lights, Object Lights, and Grouping Lights to false Light objects.

Material Preset Lights

There are two Material presets that we use constantly for spheres to create stars or false Sun objects (the term *false* is used to distinguish these objects from the Bryce default Sun). These are the *GreenLit* and *Marley's Ghost* presets in the Complex Materials Library folder. GreenLit can be easily customized and colored. Bring it up on your system now, and explore how it is put together in the Materials Lab.

Object Lights

Any object in Bryce can be made into a light, or at least an element that has some of the attributes we expect from lights. This does not include illuminating other objects directly, but through a perceptual trick. What is the trick? Transparent objects that cause everything that we see through them to look brighter, fooling the eye into thinking they are lights. The three most common objects used for these pseudo-lights are spheres, cones, and very thin cylinders.

FALSE SPHERICAL LIGHTS

These objects can be used effectively as suns, and mapped with plain color or more evocative materials for use as background planets. Used for this purpose, they are not usually transparent, but just fuzzy around the edges. If they are made transparent, they can be used as ghostly lights that can be placed anywhere in the scene. When you create a false spherical light, make sure you do the following (see Figure 14.18):

- Make them Volumetric objects. This gives them more dimension.
- Use Flat Shading on them, which allows you to pay more attention to their color than their contents.
- Play with the Base Density slider to achieve the opacity or transparency you need.
- Set the Diffuse Color slider to whatever color you want, and the Diffusion value to 100%. Set Ambience to 0.
- Resize and place the object as needed in your scene.

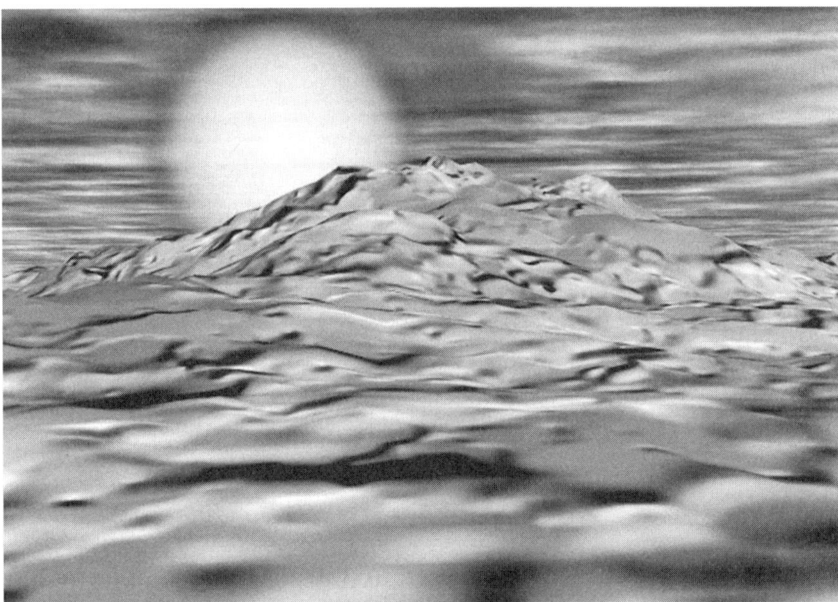

FIGURE 14.18 False spherical lights can act as effective stand-ins for suns and planets.

FALSE CONIC LIGHTS

Simply use a cone for this option and select the Light Shading option in the Materials Lab (Surface Material). Turn down Ambience on all objects that the false conic light will seem to touch, or the image will lose contrast and the effect will be lost. Place the cones at an angle, so they appear to be emanating from the same source. In the Materials Lab, the Volume Color determines the color of the rays, and Transparency Optics controls density. Move the Transparency slider to at least 65%, and even higher for more subtle effects. Make sure to pay attention to light directions and specular highlights in your scene, so the rays are coming from the same direction. This same effect can work for rays streaming from a globe, or even a Radial Light source. It can also be used for searchlights and spotlights, as long as true lights are grouped with the false ones (see Figure 14.19).

FIGURE 14.19 Rays from a false sun illuminate a landscape.

FALSE LASER LIGHTS

Bryce can be used to create perfect laser beams. In the Imported Objects folder of the Objects Library is a screw that can be used as a light. Its threads act to give a Light object just the right touch or variance and randomness. When stretched out, you can no longer tell what the object is, because the threads are stretched into flowing curves. Look at Figure 14.20. There is a lot going on here with different lights—we'll describe some of the elements involved.

In Figure 14.20, because the Bryce sun is illuminating this scene from the back, objects tend to be on the dark side. This being the case, the Ambience channel value was raised to 100%. This allows various parts of the material to literally glow in the dark. The Specularity of the simple color material used on the ship was raised as well, to pop it out of the dark. The internal glow emanating from the bottom of the ship is a Radial Light. It is toned down by the Torus that surrounds it, shielding the buildings from the light. A Screw object is used as the beam. The beam is textured with the Volumetric Red Laser Beam as a Volume Material. Additive Shading with a Volume Altitude Blend is used. The sliders are set to 100 for Diffusion, 17 for Ambient Value, a Base Density of 17, an Edge Softness of 50, a Fuzzy Factor of 142, and Quality/Speed at 5. Two volumetric flames rise up from the target, while the ground is mapped with the fiery material (see Figure 14.20).

FIGURE 14.20 A cosmic laser blast.

Grouping Lights to Objects

When you use false lighting of any kind, it usually helps to place a "real" light at the point from which the beam seems to be coming. This allows you to use the false light at its maximum effectiveness, while using the real light to cast shadows in the mix. The light coming from the bottom of the space ship in Figure 14.20 has a Radial Light grouped with the laser light.

MOVING ON

In this chapter, we explored Bryce light types, and how to modify what lights do in some unique ways. In the next chapter, our focus will be on the camera.

CHAPTER

15 The Camera

The Bryce camera acts as your eye in the scene, and is an object that can be manipulated in a number of ways (see Figure 15.1).

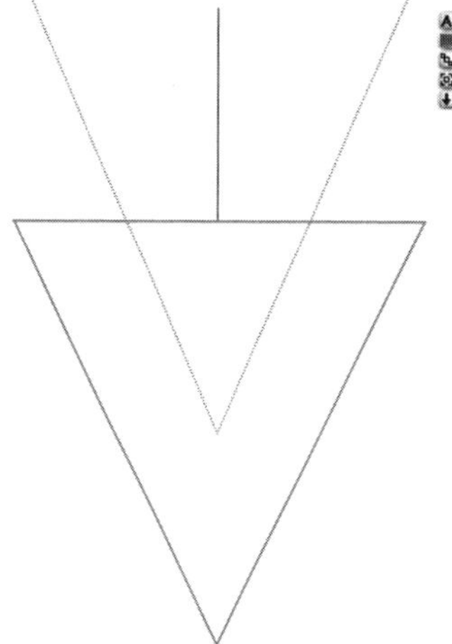

FIGURE 15.1 The camera is represented on screen by this symbolic icon. It can be moved and rotated like any other object. The camera cannot be scaled.

Through the camera, you witness the stunning beauty of Bryce landscapes and the actions of animated actors in your play. The camera is the bridge that spans the reality of two realities, your everyday world and the virtual world on your screen Bryce creates on your computer monitor. What you do to control and manipulate the camera reshapes the content of your Bryce scenes so you can appreciate and be awed by what is taking place in the Bryce worlds you create.

The First Step

The first and most important action you can take, before any elements are configured for a Bryce scene, is to orient the position of the camera. This is no small matter, because it will affect everything you do on screen, your comfortability in maneuvering and selecting objects, and the way in which you think about light sources. Machiavelli said that a society can be brought down if you alter the way that its citizens relate to their measurement and orientation systems, and in Bryce, the ease with which you set up a level of comfort and maneuverability with these systems is similarly essential.

The default position of the camera in Bryce, the position and orientation it is placed at when you first open the program, is not very suitable for art or animation work. The camera is placed so that it is looking at the scene from the Northwest corner of the world. The sun, your main source of orientation (controlled by the trackball), is situated so that it looks like it functions from a Bottom to Top view. You can force the sun to orient itself to the camera by selecting the command "Link Sun to View" from the Sky & Fog options menu, but all this does is to add immeasurable confusion to the issue, the same type of confusion that Machiavelli cautioned against. In order not to bring down your virtual society before you even start to build it, and in order to work in a clearer and more logical fashion, here is what you should do. Go to the Top view, and orient the camera so that it is pointing from the bottom of the screen upward toward the top of your monitor, as illustrated in Figure 15.2. To get the camera rotated the correct amount from the Top view, select the Camera icon and use the "A" button in its Attributes list . Set the Rotation amounts to X=0, Y=0, and Z=0.

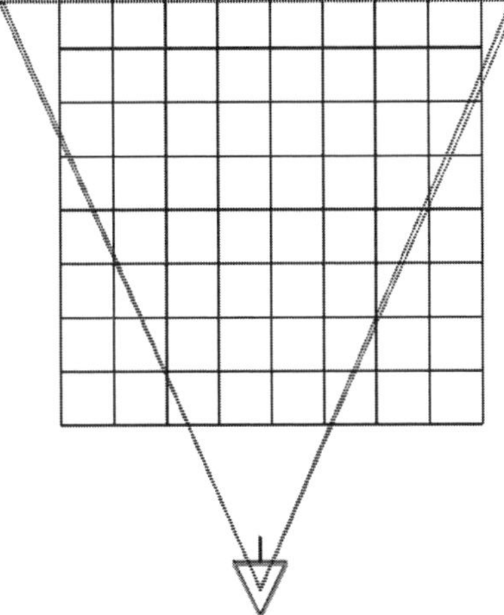

FIGURE 15.2 This is how your initial camera position should look when seen from the Top view.

Unfortunately, Bryce has no memory of where you place your camera when you shutdown the application, so it will reboot with the camera in the same confusing default position. It is strongly suggested that you save your new default to a convenient file, best located in the Bryce folder. Name the file something like MyCam.br3, or something similar. That way, after you boot up, all you have to do is load this scene, and everything will be in position.

The Camera Attributes List

We've already spoken about the Attributes list for the camera in our discussions about changing its orientation. The camera functions like a special object in Bryce, so it has an Attributes list of modification possibilities. There are several very important items to point out in the Camera Attributes list, although it is assumed that your reading of the Bryce documentation has already alerted you to the Camera Attributes basics. It might be a good idea to open the Camera Attributes list now, so you can see the items we will mention. There are five associated icons involved, and important points associated with each.

ATTRIBUTES (THE "A" ICON)

Clicking on the A icon brings up the Attributes dialog (see Figure 15.3).

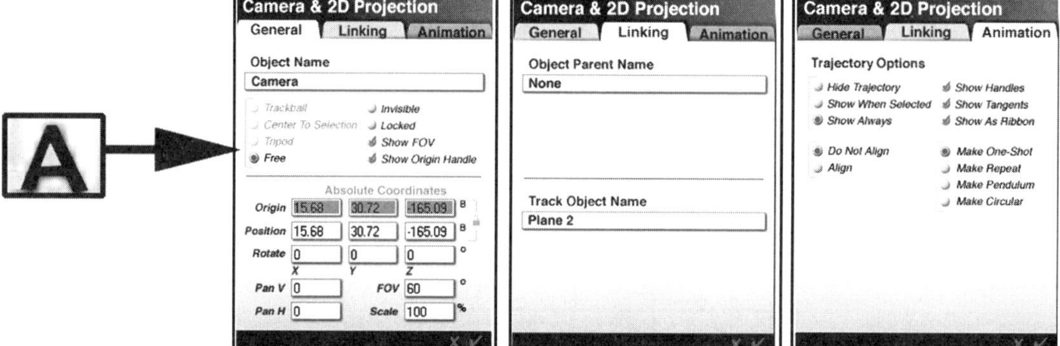

FIGURE 15.3 The Camera Attributes dialog.

Although the camera is treated like any other object in many ways, the contents of its Attributes dialog shows it to be a special type of object.

The General Tab

You cannot rename the camera, although this might change in future versions of Bryce if multiple cameras are allowed. "Free" is marked by default, allowing you to move it anywhere, except when you have checked "Locked." Instead of "Hidden," an option given for other objects, you have the camera option "Invisible." Hidden objects can still be seen on screen because they can be assigned special powers. Invisible objects do not appear. Check "Invisible" if the camera is getting in your way, and you continue to select it by mistake. Show FOV (Field of Vision) should always be

On, so you can see what objects in the scene are in view. Origin Handle should also always be On, since it allows you to positions the camera's center anywhere on the scene for rotation around selected objects.

Let's skip down to the FOV and Size controls, which not only determine the parameters of what the camera sees, but are also vital in creating camera-based animations. Decreasing FOV to 40 gives you the same initial view of the scene as increasing Camera Size to 160, but one does not really equate with the other. FOV sets the Field of Vision of the camera, how much of the scene the camera takes in, with 60 being the Bryce norm. Taking in more of the scene widens your view and makes everything in it appear smaller at the same time. Size, on the other hand, is a Zoom mechanism. You can zoom out or in, but there are depth anomalies associated with pushing this tool to the extreme. Objects in your scene, especially those that move when the camera is zoomed, seem to warp as they approach or recede from the camera with either setting. However, starting from what looks like a similar view, radical size alterations produce more exaggerated warping effects. Try this exercise.

1. Place a Sphere in front of the camera, making it about 1/4 of the screen size. Create an animation that moves the screen from in front of the camera to the right of it in 30 frames.
2. Open the Attributes dialog with the Camera selected, and set the FOV to 180 for the length of the animation. Preview the animation from the Camera view. Notice that the sphere elongates in the direction of its path the closer it gets to the camera. This would be an interesting but mind-bending way to see a train moving from the distance to the right of your position. This happens because your FOV is so wide, it allows you to see clearly what we normally see in a blurred fashion in our peripheral vision.
3. Set the FOV back to its defaulted position of 60, and set the Size in the Camera Attributes dialog to 20. Run a preview of the animation. The sphere still warps, but a little more evenly.

The Links Tab

Be careful about Linking the camera from a distance to an object being followed, since whatever convolutions the object goes through (bouncing, sudden jolts), the camera will go through as well. Use Link when the camera is closer to an object, as for example, when the camera is in a car looking ahead at the road. Targeting objects with the camera requires fewer cautions. Targeting the camera is the single most important procedure that shows your capabilities as a director. In general, follow these simple rules when targeting objects with the camera:

- Try to stay away from targeting the camera from one camera position, because it's likely that intervening objects will pop into view, and it is really boring.
- Make sure to move the Origin Point on the object to an interesting location, so the object can be targeted by the camera at a place on the object that is both interesting and central to its identification.
- Allow the camera to have its own path as it targets an object, so it can draw closer and farther at different points. The reason for this is to excite viewer interest. Watch films of car chases for excellent examples of camera tracking and movement.

The Animation Tab

Camera animation techniques, and the use of the items in this tab, are covered in the next few chapters.

FAMILY COLOR (THE COLOR BOX ICON)

Select a color for the camera that stands out in your scene, since it is the most used object. The defaulted color (blue) is not satisfactory in our opinion, because it gets lost in other wireframe colors. Whatever color you select, do not use it for any other objects (see Figure 15.4).

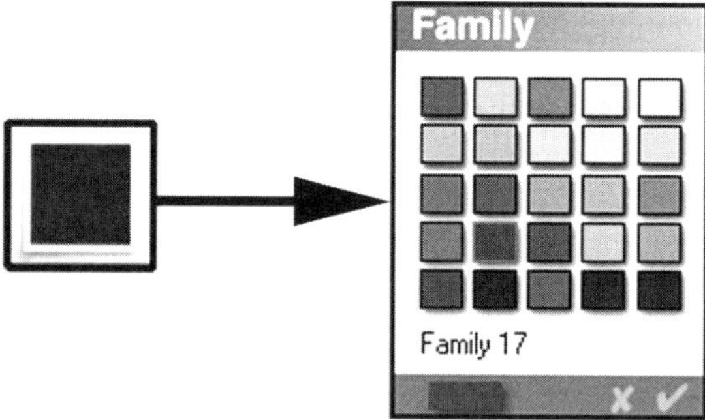

FIGURE 15.4 The Family Color dialog.

LINK (THE CHAIN ICON)

The Icon that resembles a chain is the Link tool.
See Figure 15.5.

TARGET (THE TARGET ICON)

See Figure 15.6.

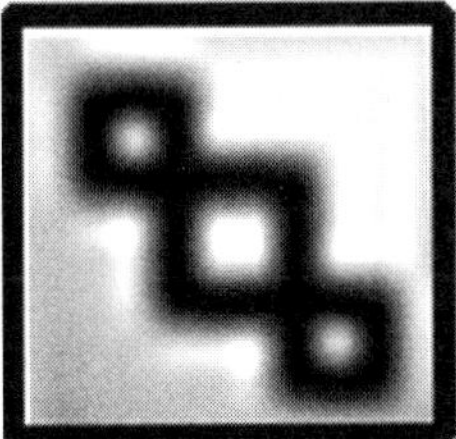

FIGURE 15.5 The Link icon. See the section on Linking under the General Tab information covered earlier.

FIGURE 15.6 The Target icon. See the section on Targeting under the General Tab information covered earlier.

GRAVITY (THE ARROW ICON)

See Figure 15.7.

FIGURE 15.7 The Gravity icon.

The camera can be placed in positions you didn't intend in a time-consuming session, so the Gravity Arrow can be a useful aid in getting it literally "down to earth" again. As seen from the Front, Left, Right, or Back views, the camera will drop down to the next item below it when the Arrow icon is clicked. Although Infinite Planes go on forever and are only represented by limited grids in Bryce, the camera has to be over the grid in order to notice that it exists when applying the Gravity Arrow.

From the Director's View

Producing a large animation project requires the use of storyboards, so that the director and animators can see the scene from whatever perspective is needed for location planning and action sequences. Use the Director's view and the other alternate camera modes to rotate and position the scene as needed for storyboarding and choreographic planning. The three alternate Director-only modes in the Camera Attributes dialog (accessible only when Director's view is selected) are Trackball, Center to

Selection, and Tripod. Explore these three options to see how they affect the placement and movement of the camera.

Camera Sky Shots

There are times when you want your actors to be photographed against the sky alone. After all, sky art is one of Bryce's major strong points. When you have scenes with a good number of separate objects involved, this can present a problem. Ground and Water Planes are infinite, so it is sometimes difficult to shoot your objects against the sky only unless you delete all of the Infinite Planes. Even when you do that, and try to shoot against the sky alone, you are presented with a banded horizon line. Here's how to proceed when you run up against this challenge:

1. Set up your scene, with all of the items in place. Adjust the Camera view so that you see everything in the right frame and perspective.
2. Create or import a sky from the Sky presets, and adjust the light so that the objects in your scene appear as you would like them to. Since the Ground Plane, or any other Infinite planes, will not be needed, you can delete them.
3. Select all of the items in your scene, including the camera (drag a marquee around them), so that they are all included. Group them.
4. Rotate this grouped selection by going to the Right or Left views. Make the Rotation about 35 degrees tilted upward. Do a preview render to make sure you see nothing in the background but the sky. Ungroup, and adjust as necessary.

The difference between this technique and simply turning the camera upward is that you can control the perspective better. Turning the camera upward enough to negate the Infinite Planes or the horizon line often forces you to accept perspectives that you do not want. A liability exists with this method if you plan to resize or rotate elements after they are rotated, since this might produce warping. It's best to do that when they are in the initial position (see Figure 15.8).

Creating Textures with the Camera

The camera has a very close focus. In fact, the minimum distance that you can get from a targeted object is limited only by the material that the object is composed of. If the material is made from bitmapped components, then you might see a good amount of pixelization up close. If the material is procedurally based, however, then the laws of fractals intervene, and closeness just reveals more detail. The only other influence

FIGURE 15.8 Camera shots that include only the sky are very useful for product advertisements, as well as dreamlike graphics.

that might intervene is light. You'll have to make sure the procedurally textured material is being lit strongly enough and from the correct angle, so you can see what is there to be revealed.

Why would you want to take a close-up shot of a procedurally textured material? The answer is, to make another material, this one bitmapped based. Here's how it works:

1. With an object selected, open the Materials Lab, and create an original material that uses one or more channels. Work in the Deep Texture Editor to achieve something unique. Make sure it has elements of interest that draw upon layered effects (Altitude effects are good because you get an automatic blend of the three composite ingredients). Refer to Chapter 11 if these instructions seem indecipherable to you.
2. Leave the Materials Lab when you're done. The material is now wrapped to your selected object. Make sure the object is lit well enough so that the material can be seen.
3. Move the camera as close as you would like to the object on which the material has been placed. Make sure that the material fills your viewscreen from whatever view you select (Camera or Front views are the best to use).

Make sure Reflection and Specularity are Off to prevent unwanted highlights.

4. Render the image with normal antialiasing on (never use fine antialiasing unless you are going on vacation, and don't need to see the finished render until you return, if then).
5. When the rendering is complete, Export (save) the image to disk.
6. Create an object and select it. Open the Materials Lab and go to the Picture Editor after clicking "P" on one of the channels. In the Picture Editor, load in the graphic of the material you saved, and keep its Alpha channel solid black. Alternatively, if you like, you might explore Copying the image and Pasting it into the Alpha channel. In the Materials Lab, explore various mapping options and other controls until you achieve a bitmap material you like.

You will find that the bitmapped material acts very differently from the procedural material when mapped to your selected object. This technique is based on an informed use of the camera (see Figures 15.9 and 15.10).

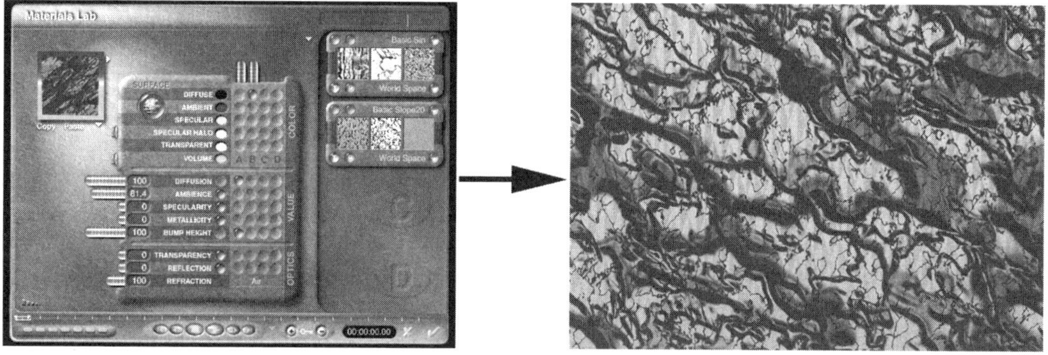

FIGURE 15.9 From the original procedurally developed material textures created in the Materials Lab and Deep Texture Editor, the camera is used to take a picture of the applied material.

Panoramic Vistas

You can develop panoramic Vistas in Bryce that can be translated as Web panoramas for use on your homepage, with the display help of Apple's QuickTime VR technology, or other applications. Visitors will be able to stand in the center of your Bryce world and turn the camera around to appreciate the view. This is all made possible by understanding how to place and manipulate the camera. Here's how:

1. Click on Default in your Document Setup dialog, and on the QTVR Panorama rendering option.

FIGURE 15.10 From there, a Terrain map and Bitmap material are used to construct a scene. Outrageous materials can be developed in this manner, using your knowledge of the camera as a way to develop bitmaps from procedurals.

2. Set up your objects, with the Camera at the center.
3. Select Render to Disk, and choose a folder on your hard drive.
4. Load the finished rendering into Apple's QuickTime VR or another suitable panorama application for viewing (see Figure 15.11).

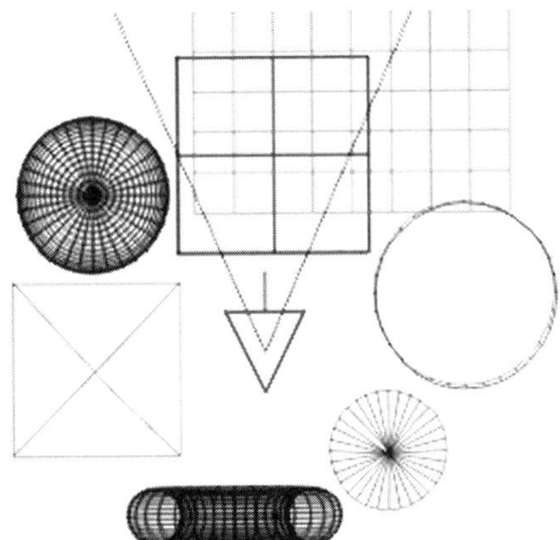

FIGURE 15.11 On the left is a view of the camera placed in the center of the objects (Bryce Top view), while the illustration on the right shows the resulting Panorama rendering. A panoramic image is rendered so that the left and right sides stitch together perfectly.

Enhancing 3D Depth

There is a problem when looking at Infinite Planes through the camera: they are infinite. The other problem is that the computer sees too clearly. Reality is neither perceptually infinite nor very clear. In the real world, we can take a plane or a car and move around the visible curve of the horizon to where not even your most powerful telescope can see us. We can also take advantage of the thickness of the atmosphere, so that as we move a certain distance from you, even though we have not moved past the horizon's curve, we will still be invisible to your eyes. Both of these problems, and their solutions, can be emulated in Bryce. They are basically camera-associated challenges because they involve optics; that is, how the Bryce world is seen through the camera's eye. Here are some steps to take to help the camera take a picture of a more "real" Bryce world:

- Explore the use of a larger FOV setting in the Camera's Attributes dialog. A setting of 80 seems to enhance the depth well.
- Place an object close to the camera that has detailed material.
- Make sure objects in the far distance are blurred as compared to foreground objects. Use the Fuzzy option in the Materials Lab when applying materials to background objects.
- Use the Resize operation to make objects smaller than they are when used in the background. This enhances the perspective.
- Color objects in the background with a bluish tint. The farther away they are, drop their complex materials in favor of a light grayish blue.
- Always use the Distance Blur option, in the Materials Lab, on Infinite Planes.
- Always consider a Haze setting of at least 10. Color the haze based on the sky at the horizon.

If you consider all of these suggestions, the view through your Bryce camera will look all the more believable (see Figure 15.12).

If you were to do just one picture like Figure 15.12, and not an animation, you could render a Distance Render map in addition to the color render. Then, you could bring both into a suitable paint application, with the Distance Render used as an Alpha overlay. This would allow you to achieve a blurring of objects farther from the camera just by marrying the two layers.

FIGURE 15.12 Helping the camera transform computerized 3D depth into a surrealistic landscape means using every Bryce function at your disposal, as suggested in the preceding text.

YOU CAN CREATE F/X LENSES FOR THE CAMERA!

This Bryce capability is not detailed in the documentation. You have already seen that the camera has many of the features of a real camera, including the possibility for modifying the focus and zoom. Professional photographers often bring a collection of special lenses when they go out on an assignment. These lenses distort reality by their form (convex, concave, and other forms) and by their refractive index, their ability to bend light.

You can create your own f/x lenses for your Bryce camera. It's best to start with a spherical form in your explorations. Just make sure it is placed so that it covers the cone of view from the camera. You can alter the object's refractive index in the Materials Lab, after mapping it with a Glass material. These explorations are up to you, but you can see some of what is possible by looking at Figures 15.13 through 15.18.

FIGURE 15.13 Start off with any scene you like. Here's a scene with no extra lens applied yet.

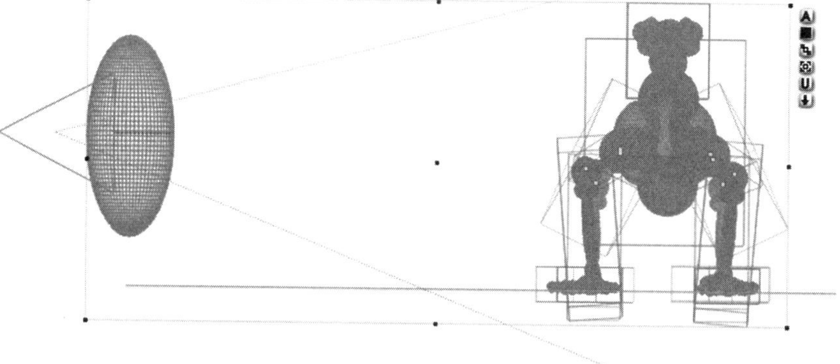

FIGURE 15.14 A flattened sphere is used as a lens, and mapped with a Glass material.

FIGURE 15.15 Setting Transparency to 100 and Specularity to 0, a refractive index of 22 creates this scene within a scene.

FIGURE 15.16 Altering the Refraction Index and distorting the form further changes the effect.

FIGURE 15.17 The view through a toroidal lens creates another effect.

FIGURE 15.18 Adding a high Bump component to the material adds a pixelated effect.

MOVING ON

In this chapter, we investigated the camera.

CHAPTER

16 Animation Basics

THE ROOTS OF ANIMATION

Movement is the first seduction of the eye. The most primitive creatures that possess some form of visual perception see movement as the play of light and shadow, which tells them either to run from being eaten or that dinner is on the table. Our eyes are fine-tuned to notice movement for the same initial reasons, although the "fight or flight" reaction has now been enhanced to include new possibilities through the development of our consciousness. To the human eye, the detection of movement also includes the possibility that something interesting, or even awe inspiring, might be occurring. Movement to the human eye, and perhaps even to some animal's eyes, also means life. We intuit that anything that moves has a life of its own. This includes trees that sway in the breeze, as well as creatures that swim and fly. This is why cartoons and animated features of all kinds are so hypnotic and alluring. Everything is given the potential for life and a suspected consciousness. Just look at the magical visions communicated by the world of advertising, where frogs sing the praises of beer, and all manner of inanimate objects dance and talk back. Anthropologists have given the name "animism" to the primal view that everything in the world, from rocks and trees to all of the animals, is conscious and alive, and "animism" is the root word and the motivating principle for "animation."

As far as perception goes, we are able to trick the eye into believing that a series of projected images that change at the rate of 10 times a second or more represent animated movement. Below that rate, movements look jerky, disbelief is fostered, and the magic is lost. This is the secret of creating animations. Animations, whether produced in Hollywood by a bevy of professional animators or by someone on a home computer, are nothing more than a stack of single frames played back at a frame rate that tricks the eye into seeing movement. This activity is enhanced by the fact that the single frames have some content that looks like it is not moving (or not moving much), and some elements that are displaced a good deal from frame to frame. We call the content that is not moving or moving very little the "background," and the elements that are doing the most movement the "foreground" or even the "actors."

In animation, the actors are alive (or some form of consciousness is at least suspected of being in the driver's seat), no matter what form they take. The planning that goes into bringing the actors in an animation to life is called *scripting* and *storyboarding*. Scripting refers to the verbal descriptions of what is going on from frame to frame, and storyboarding is the layout of the choreography, from one important nexus of movement (called a *keyframe*) to the next. With the computer, you choreograph the keyframes, the important points in the movement, and the computer figures out or interpolates the intervening frames, called *in-betweens*. This is different from creating an animation in the traditional manner with a series of drawings done by a collection or artists, where the in-betweens have to be manually drawn along with the keyframes. This is one reason for the explosion of computer animation, since being responsible for only the keyframes cuts the production time of an animation by at least 90 percent.

THE BRYCE ANIMATOR

In Bryce versions 1 and 2, you could create wonderful and startling pictures. If you wanted to create an animation, you had to do it one frame at a time, a tedious and frustrating time-consuming process. There were no tools to automate the process, and all of the in-betweens had to be created manually. This all changed with the release of Bryce 3, and remains so in version 5. Unlike other applications that start out as graphics oriented and gradually make the jump to animation over several releases, Bryce has bridged the gap from images to moving pictures in one tremendous leap. Not satisfied to simply include a few nominal animation tools and options, the Bryce developers have included tools found in no other animation application on the market. The development of Bryce's animation tools was fostered by the release of Jan Nickman's stunning science fiction film, *Planetary Traveler*, done with a customized version of Bryce prior to the release of version 3. This fully animated feature film, rendered with commercially available desktop computers, ignited worldwide interest in Bryce as a software platform for animated storytelling.

In this chapter, our focus centers on a collection of basic tools and processes you must familiarize yourself with in order to feel comfortable in getting your animated story across in a timely manner. Experienced Bryce users might want to skim this chapter and move on.

THE ANIMATION CONTROLS PALETTE

The Animation Controls palette is where all of the decisions you make regarding the movement of the selected elements in your Bryce world are put in place. Please refer to Figure 16.1 and the Keys as we detail some important animation tools and features.

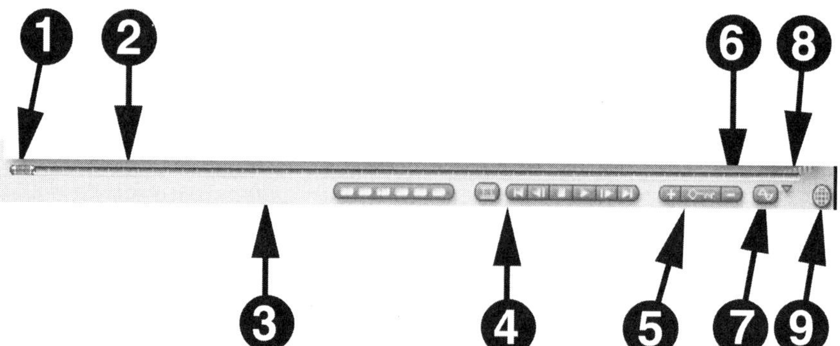

FIGURE 16.1 The Animation Controls palette, with Keys indicating its elements.

KEY #1

Clicking and dragging this lozenge along the Timeline indicates the frame number you are interested in keyframing, or the place in the animation where some work needs to be done. Always pay attention to the data display at the left, which tells you the exact frame number and time the sliding lozenge is at.

KEY #2

This is the Timeline. It is marked with tickers that indicate all of the separate frames in your animation, or the time involved. The lozenge relates to these ticks as places in the animation you want to add a keyframe, or stop for additional editing of the selected object(s).

KEY #3

This is the Memory Dot area, allowing you to store selected frame numbers from the Timeline, so you can instantly snap to that position. Although useful, it makes more sense to use the VCR keyframe buttons to get to keyframe positions quickly.

KEY #4

This is the VCR controller, with buttons for Start Frame, Previous Keyframe, Stop, Play, Next Keyframe, and Last Frame as placed on the Timeline. When designing and choreographing an animation, this where you will spend the majority of your time. The animation can be played back as either wireframe objects or boxed areas. When the scene gets very complex, use boxes, unless you absolutely have to see the outline of specific objects.

KEY #5

The Plus and Minus signs indicate Add and Delete keyframes. The Key Symbol is there just so you can locate the Plus and Minus signs quickly. Holding on the Plus or Minus signs allows you access to specific parameters for the camera, sky, sun, or a selected object. These options allow you to control the specified parameters of the item, as opposed to the global controls that come into play when you simply press the Plus keyframe button. Since these advanced controls are so important to your animation in Bryce, it is important that they be more specifically detailed.

The Auto-Key Option should be checked when you use the Advanced control options. You should also try to use as few Advanced controls as possible in a single keyframe, as it's very easy to forget where you are and what actions you have taken.

It is suggested that you use global controls for animating these items; that is, with Auto Select checked On, move or manipulate the camera however you desire in its present keyframe. Then use the Advanced controls to delete those specific actions in the selected keyframe that are not wanted. For example, holding the Minus sign down and accessing the Advanced controls, you could selectively delete just the rotation for the camera or any of the other items for the specific keyframe you are at, without bothering any repositioning that has been activated for that keyframe. Using the Advanced controls in the Add Keyframe mode (the Plus sign) complicates matters more than needed.

Advanced Camera Controls

The options are Position, Origin, Banking, Focal Length, Pan X or Y, and Zoom X or Y. Pans and zooms are covered later in this chapter concerning camera animations. There is also an "ALL Timelines" selection, but that is rather redundant, since under global alterations, you already affect all of the Timeline elements. You do not have to have the camera selected to use the Advanced controls to delete a specific camera function in the keyframe you are at. Here is an example of how to use the Advanced controls to affect an animation:

1. Set the camera at frame 1 as a keyframe.
2. Move the Lozenge to frame 30, and rotate and reposition the camera.

3. Using the Advanced control with the Delete keyframe button, hold and select the Camera Rotation item.

The result will be that in frame 30, you will have removed the new rotation, and have left the new position in place. If you did this globally by simply selecting the Minus sign (Remove keyframe), you would have removed both the new rotation and position from frame 30.

Advanced Sky Controls

The Sky Advanced controls work exactly the same as the Camera Advanced controls, with the difference being that you have more options in this list. Every sky parameter can be individually selected, although they can also be accessed through the Sky&Fog toolbar or the associated Sky Lab dialog discussed previously. Unless you enjoy applying effects from a list rather than individually and interactively from the Sky&Fog toolbar or the Sky Lab dialog, it is suggested that you dispense with the use of this list.

Advanced Sun Controls

Here again, you have all of these controls offered in a more interactive manner in the Sky&Fog toolbar and the Sky Lab, so why complicate your life and access them in this manner?

Advanced Selected Object Controls

These Advanced controls work on whatever object, or group, is selected in your scene. The options include Position, Rotation, Scale, Shear, and Origin. These controls are useful, especially when it comes to deleting one or more of these options from a keyframe. Otherwise, deleting the entire keyframe with the global Minus sign might not give you the more delicate result you are looking for.

KEY #6

This is the trigger for accessing the Advanced Motion Lab, a topic fully detailed in a chapter 19.

KEY #7

This arrow triggers the Timeline Options menu. There are two options involved: Auto-Key on and off, and what the tick marks on the Timeline indicate. Tick marks can delineate either frames or various time markers in seconds. The time options include .25. .5, 1, 2, and 5 seconds. At the start of your animation, use the Frames option. Later, when the animation gets long and consumes more time, switch to whatever time marker allows you to see all of the ticks on screen at once.

KEY #8

This is the almost invisible Scale Timeline controller. Clicking and dragging the mouse over it allows you to stretch out or squash how much of the Timeline can be seen at one time.

KEY #9

This Globe symbol toggles you between the Timeline and Selection palettes. In an editing session, it is often necessary to switch to the Selection palette in order to locate a specific object in your scene.

The Animation Setup Dialog

It's a good idea to access this dialog from the File menu before you start to design your animation. That's because there are items here that will affect how your Timeline behaves (see Figure 16.2).

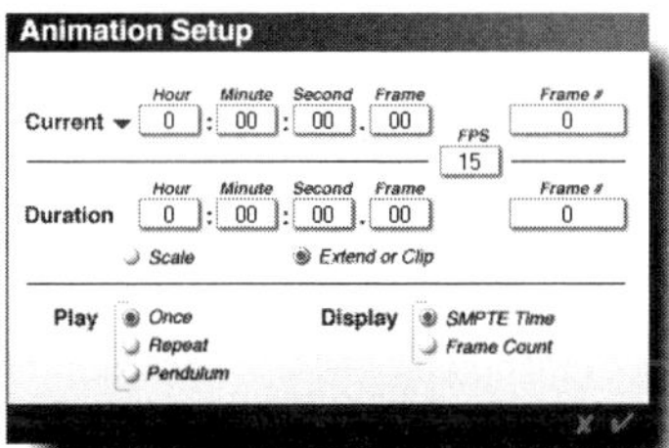

FIGURE 16.2 The Animation Setup dialog gives you global control over specific parameters of the animation.

The first item to configure here is the FPS (frames per second) input. Never enter a number less than 10 or more than 30. The most common FPS rates are 15, 24, 29.97 (and other SMPTE rates), and 30. Bryce does not offer interleaved 60 FPS Field rendering, commonly used in broadcast video productions. The best video choice for NTSC (25 FPS for PAL) is 30

FPS, except for SMPTE work (called "drop frame"), which involves the capacity to add and edit synchronized audio with specific hardware and editing applications.

Under the Play list are three options that have an important effect on your animations: *Once, Repeat,* and *Pendulum*. These options affect how the animated objects in your scene will be displayed when previewed, and also how they will act in a rendered animation if the sequence is long enough. Play Once is the default, allowing your animation to move from start to finish as expected. Repeat plays the animation from start to finish over and over again until you press the Stop button. Pendulum (called "Ping-Pong" in the trade) plays the animation from start to finish, and then from finish to start, continuously until you press the Stop button. These preview options are important because some multimedia and Web designers need their animations to play in a looping manner, and this allows a preview of those motions.

TO ASSIGN REPEATS AND PENDULUMS TO A RENDERED ANIMATION

If you want an object to either repeat its actions or to act as a pendulum in an animation, do the following:

1. Set up an object movement over 10 frames that has keyframes at frames 1 and 10.
2. With the object selected, go to its Attributes dialog and the Animation tab, and click on Repeat or Pendulum as desired.
3. Go back to the Timeline, deselect the object, and move the Lozenge to frame 30. Preview the animation, and you will see the object either repeating its 10-frame action, or moving back and forth, in direct response to your selection of either Repeat or Pendulum in the Animation Setup dialog.

CIRCLE

On an object's Animation tab in the Attributes dialog, you will see one more option that has an effect on the way the object moves along its path: *Make Circular*. This command creates a closed loop, so that the first frame of the animated object on its path will equal the last frame as far as position is concerned. Every time you move the object, it expands the circle (it's really a warped oval). Expanding the duration of the animation would show the object racing madly around, over and over again. This is one way you might create one object orbiting another.

Use the Make Circular option on standard paths, or rather with the object that is creating the path selected. If you turn this into a Ribbon Path, you will see two nodes close together if you zoom in (the first and last frame) instead of one smooth closed path. This is OK if you want to break the path, but it loses the unbreakable coherence of a closed path. If the first and last node are split on a Ribbon Path and you use the Make Circular option, the object will suddenly appear again at the first node when the action repeats. Of course, this might be an effect you want.

PATHS, LINKS, TARGETS, AND THE ANIMATED CAMERA

OK, having covered all of the important preparatory material, we are ready to begin a detailed investigation of Bryce's animation tools and techniques. We will center on four integrated topics for the balance of this chapter: *Paths, Links, Targets,* and *Animating the Camera.*

Paths

Think for a moment about the word and meaning of a "path." A path is usually defined as a nonmovable access way that is tied to the larger environment. A path is also associated with the elements that construct it by their movements. For example, the path that exists in the great North that marks the way of the migration of the elk was made by the elk themselves over hundreds, perhaps thousands, of years of repeated movement. If the elk become influenced by constructs (pipelines, for example) in their way as they traverse the path, they have two options. The first is to create another path around the disturbance, and the second is to bully their way through the potential barriers, and try to stick to the path created over time. Of course, there is always the possibility that they will become so confused that they will simply stay where they are. It is thinking about natural occurrences like these that gives the animator an insight into the tools she uses.

If a path is glued to specific geography, it is immovable. It is then defined not primarily by its shape, but by what surrounding elements it traverses over time. An East-West path across a bridge, for example, is not defined so much by its orientation as it is by the fact that there might be only one bridge across a river. The fact that the river might bend so that the way across is North-South is of no consequence to those who must use a bridge to get across the river, unless there is another bridge at the North-South point. This is called an *immovable path,* because to get across the river, you must use specific items located in the geography; in this case, the bridge. Bryce has immovable paths.

If, on the other hand, your primary aim is to get from South to North no matter what, then it doesn't matter if there is a bridge or not. Swimming or flying across the river is just as viable an option as traversing the bridge, as long as it doesn't lead to your demise. You could start anywhere in the South and simply select the shortest point to your Northern destination. If you had to take a train, then you might build your track with South-North as your primary focus, and decide later where the South-North tracks should be laid. In a sense, you have defined a movable path, because the options are open where it will interact with the geography, and there will be many options. Movable paths can have control nodes so that when a mountain or river is encountered, simply stretching the node will give you a more suitable path to go around or over the obstruction. Movable paths are more like objects than paths in that they can be modified and customized, and remain separate from the elements that travel on them. Bryce has movable paths, called *Ribbon paths*.

BASIC PATH CREATION

The standard paths that are simply the result of an object moving in space over time in Bryce cannot be moved or otherwise modified, unless you reposition or rotate the object, camera, light, or other element that has created them. As standalone entities, they are immovable in every sense of the word. They are not objects at all, but rather the results of the actions of objects. Have you ever seen the cartoon character that is able to move a hole in the ground to a new place? The reason that this is impossible is that the hole, under Earth physics circumstances anyway, is not a thing as such. It is rather the result of an action of a thing or being who dug the hole. The hole can only be manipulated by actions of actors, who can cover it up, fill it in, or enlarge it. The hole, in a sense, is an immovable result of an action. In the same way, standard paths in Bryce are the results of objects' actions.

If you set a keyframe for a sphere at frame 1 of an animation, and then set another at frame 30 after moving it, you will see a blue line that indicates its path, a Timeline that stretches from frame 1 to its new position at frame 30. Previewing this animation with the VCR controls will show the object moving from its position at frame 1 to its new position at frame 30 over 30 frames of time. The time it takes will depend on how you set the fps rate. If it was set at 15 fps, then the object will travel from frame 1 to frame 30 in two seconds (30/15=2). If you set the frame rate at 30 fps, then the journey will take only one second (30/30=1).

But, what if you wanted the path to be a curve instead of a straight line? Clicking on the path to adjust its shape would do nothing. The path does not exist as a separate entity. Only the object exists at specific points on the Timeline. To make the path a curve, you would have to do the following:

1. Go to the frame where the maximum point on the curve should exist; for example, frame 15.
2. Click on the object to select it, and then move it to its new position for that frame.
3. Make that position a new keyframe for the object.

Having done this, and without ever touching the path directly, you would see that the path now has a new shape. This was caused by your actions on the object that made the path in the first place. The path cannot even be seen until the object that made it is selected (see Figure 16.3).

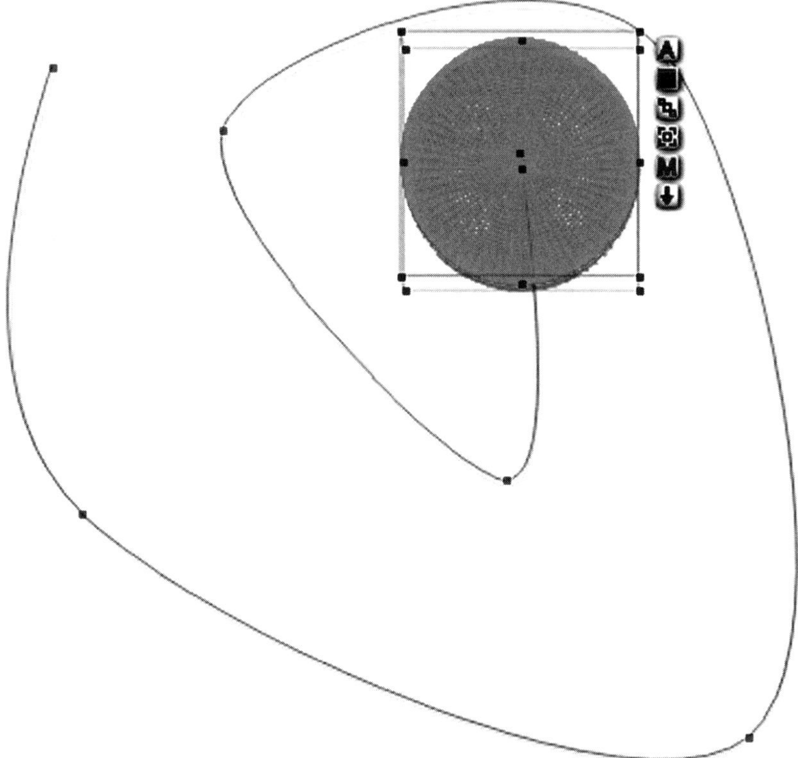

FIGURE 16.3 With an object selected, you can see exactly how it will move over time in the animation.

Note that the distance between keyframes on a path is an indication of the speed of an object. An object between two keyframes that are 10 frames apart has to travel that distance in the exact number of frames. Setting the same keyframes apart over a longer distance will result in the object speeding up to make it to the next keyframe. Setting a shorter distance between the same two keyframes will slow the object down. If this is new information to you, explore the results by actually doing it.

RIBBON PATH CREATION

Ribbon paths represent a new concept and way of editing paths in computer graphics. Unlike standard paths, which are not things but only the result of the action of things, Ribbon paths are full-fledged objects. As an object, you can edit a Ribbon path directly, without selecting any object(s) assigned to it. Ribbon paths can be created in two ways: by loading them from the Create Objects Library, or by transforming a standard path into a Ribbon path.

To Create a Ribbon Path Separate from Any Object

1. Go to the Create toolbar, and access the Objects Library.
2. Activate the Paths folder, and select a Ribbon path from one of the thumbnails. Click on the check mark to place it on the screen (see Figure 16.4).

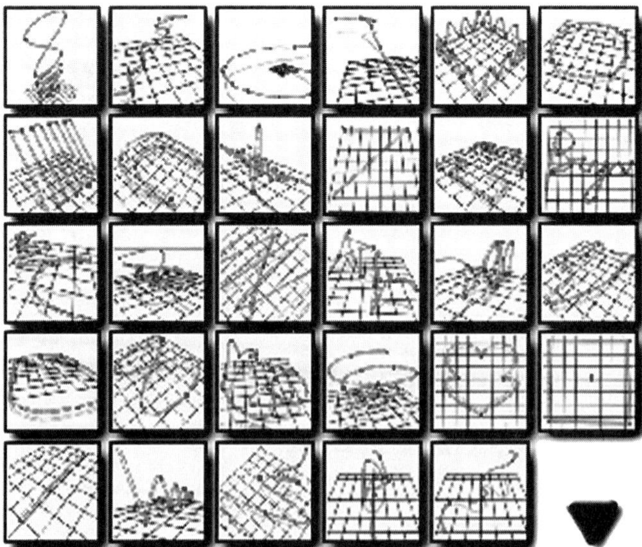

FIGURE 16.4 Ribbon paths can be added directly from the Paths folder in the Create/Objects Library.

To Create a Ribbon Path from a Selected Object Path

1. Select the object whose path you want to become a Ribbon path.
2. Go to the Objects menu and select Create Path. The object's path has now become a Ribbon path (see Figure 16.5).

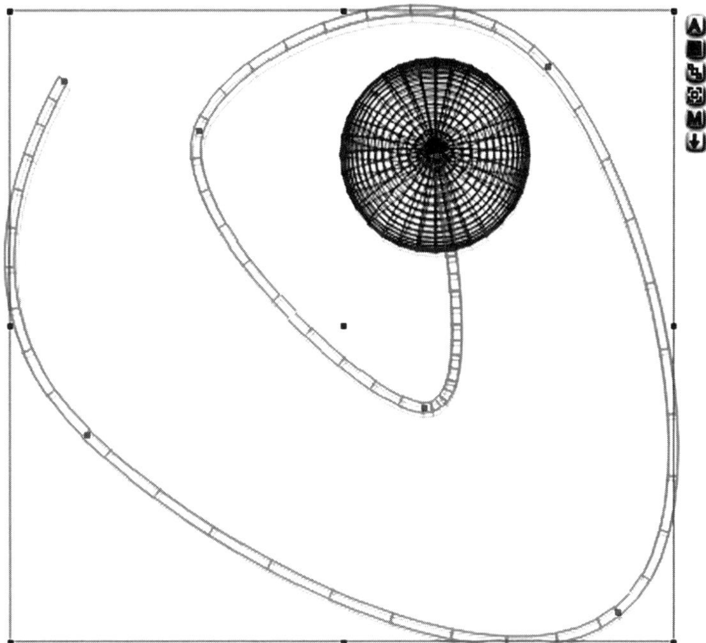

FIGURE 16.5 The object's path has now become a Ribbon path.

DESIGNING, EDITING, AND ANIMATING RIBBON PATHS

Ribbon paths have interesting properties. To begin with, they are full-fledged objects, and can be resized, rotated, or repositioned like any other object. Until and unless you take specific actions (defined later under *Links*), they are not related directly to the objects whose paths gave them birth. Moving the Ribbon path, for example, will not move the object whose path created it. However, deleting the original object will also delete the new Ribbon path. They are grouped in a strange relationship, and cannot be ungrouped in the standard fashion.

To delete the original object from the new Ribbon path, find and select it from the Selection toolbar. It will become highlighted. From there, it can be cleared *without effecting the Ribbon path.*

Designing a Ribbon Path

To design an original Ribbon path, do the following:

1. Place any object in your scene.
2. Keyframe it at frame 1. Move the Timeline lozenge to frame 30, move the object, and keyframe it again. You will see its path in blue, indicating the distance it moved from frame 1 to frame 30.
3. With the object selected, go to the Objects menu and select Create Path. Your new Ribbon path appears on screen.

You can select the Ribbon path and Add it to the Objects Library in the Paths folder. Make sure, however, that you delete the original object first, as detailed previously.

Editing a Ribbon Path

You can edit your own Ribbon paths, or any that you load from the Paths folder in the Objects Library. Ribbon paths have visible nodes that can be pushed and pulled just like a Bezier curve. In fact, Ribbon paths are a form of Bezier curve, familiar to those who have worked in vector drawing applications such as Illustrator, FreeHand, CorelDraw, or Canvas.

There are two types of nodes on a Ribbon path. *Resizing nodes* allow you to resize the Ribbon path along an axis indicated by the node when your mouse cursor is over that node. If the node reads "Z," for example, dragging the mouse left or right will resize the path along the Z-axis. If the node reads "X," then you can resize along the X-axis. To resize it along all axes simultaneously, use the Resize tool in the Edit toolbar.

The other node is the *Reshape* type. These nodes are placed at keyframe intervals. Reshape allows you to alter the perimeter of the path, squashing it or stretching it at that point. A circle can become a heart, or you might decide to raise the point along the Y-axis, creating a roller coaster path. To add or delete keyframe Reshape points from any path, standard or Ribbon, add or delete keyframes themselves. This adds and/or deletes associated points from the path.

In the Attributes dialog of any selected object is the command Show as Ribbon Path. This allows you to see the standard path as if it were a Ribbon path, but does not allow you to interact with the path as you could with a real Ribbon path. The reason for this command, since it does nothing useful, is questionable.

All paths have the Reshape nodes, placed at points where keyframes exist. The difference between standard and Ribbon paths is that Ribbon paths can be moved and resized independently of any object (see Figure 16.6).

Importing a Ribbon path from the Objects Library always places the path so that it is parallel to the ground. Work in the Top view first to resize and reshape the path.

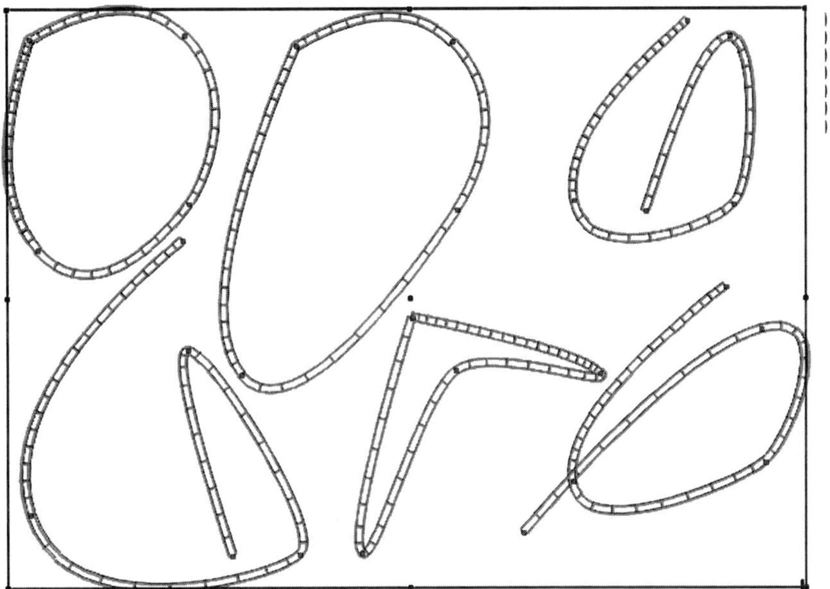

FIGURE 16.6 Ribbon paths can be reshaped at any point in an infinite number of ways. These examples started out as circular paths.

Animating Ribbon Paths

Aside from the objects that can be attached to a Ribbon path (see the *Linking* section later in this chapter), you can also animate the path itself. Here are some examples:

- Resize the path over time. Any objects traveling along the path will also be resized automatically.
- Rotate the path. Objects traveling along the path will also be rotated. This will result in an orbiting object whose path was spinning, like the old models of electrons around a nucleus.
- Reposition the path in an animation. This will foster things such as a planet orbiting a sun, while the whole system moved through space.

Remember that Repeat, Pendulum, and Make Circular can also be applied in the Attributes dialog of a selected Ribbon path, so that repetitive patterns can also occur over time.

If you need a Ribbon path to consume a determined amount of time, create it first with an object that you manipulate in the standard fashion. Then, go to the Animation Setup dialog, and under Duration, enter that time in seconds and frames. The path is now active, and will contain the time element you configured.

PLACING PATHS BEFORE OBJECTS

Here is a novel way to work with Ribbon paths. Design the elements of a scene, but leave out the main actors. Instead, use an object to design a path that moves through the places in the scene you are interested in. Save the scene as you would any other scene. Now you have a scene with an active path, which can be used over and over again with many different actors assigned to that path.

ALIGNING OBJECTS TO A PATH

Selecting the Align function in an objects Attributes dialog is not always the wisest thing to do. For the most consistent results, it's better to deselect this option, and align the object by hand in selected keyframes. *Do not* rotate the object in World Space, but in its own Object Space.

Links

Links are represented by the small chain-shaped icon in any selected object's Attributes list. By clicking on this icon and dragging the mouse to any other object, causing the target object to turn blue, a Link is established between the two objects. You can also Link objects by going to any object's Attributes dialog and to the Linking tab. Under Parent Object, find the name of the object you want to Link the selected object to. The object you Link to does indeed become the Parent object, so that it leads the Child object by the hand. If the Parent object is resized, rotated, or moved, the Child object follows along. However, all Children have independence as well, and the same is true with Linked objects. Child objects can be resized, rotated, and repositioned on their own. There is always an invisible umbilical attached to the parent, however, no matter how far removed the Child object might be.

A good example would be a moon linked to a planet, which itself is linked to a sun. As the sun rotates, the planet and its moon also rotate (think of the sun as the Grandparent object). The Planet, however, can also have its own rotation, which would cause its Child, the moon to rotate. The moon also has independence for its own actions, and can be rotating as well. We could even complicate matters further by making a satellite the Child of the Parent moon. A rule of thumb for complex animations like this is to set up the individual elements first, and then do the Child/Parent Links.

If you want to animate trains on a track, or any other object that has elongated dimensions along one axis, do not do this on a Ribbon path. Instead, arrange and rotate the objects manually in a step-by-step fashion, and then transform the path into a Ribbon path if you want to. Elongated objects on a Ribbon path distort as they go around curves.

WHAT CAN BE LINKED?

Any object can be Linked to any other object in Bryce. Objects can also be multilinked, so that any Parent object can have multiple Children. A Child object, however, can have only one Parent. You could have a figure, for example, with two hands linked to one Parent arm, but you could not have one hand linked to two Parent arms. You could, however, group the two arms, so that linking one hand to them would really be Linking to one Parent.

BODY PART MULTILINKS

Whether you are animating a robot, a spider, or a human model, you can (and should) Link all of the parts together in a chain. This allows you to animate the objects one part at a time, so they can walk, sit, jump, and perform other feats.

Try not to import DXF models for Linking. DXFs often come in with their groups mixed up, so that ungrouping the object to get to the parts can lead to unpredictable results. Import OBJ, 3DS, or LWO objects instead. DXFs are OK to use, but not for ungrouping and Linking parts.

WHAT IS THE DIFFERENCE BETWEEN LINKED OBJECTS AND GROUPED OBJECTS?

Attaching objects by grouping them is different from linking them. There are important considerations for both operations.

- Grouped objects have no Parental hierarchies, so selecting one object for any transformation selects all in the group equally. There is one way around this. Using the Control key (Mac and PC) after selecting the group allows you to select an individual member for transformation, but that transformation is associated only with the selected object, and not any others in a chain.

- Grouped objects can accept a material as one object, which usually results in a far different textured look than mapping each object individually. The only way to address this same situation in a Linked hierarchy is by multi-selecting each object and then applying the material. The results, however, will not be the same, since the Linked objects will retain their individuality.
- Boolean objects that are assigned Negative, Positive, or Intersect qualities must be grouped and not linked (see Chapter 18, Boolean Animations.)

If you use the Control key to select an individual object in a group, and then Link it to one of the others in the group, it will no longer be part of the group.

THE PROPELLER PROBLEM SOLVED!

There are times when all of the logic and planning built into an application just isn't enough to tackle a persistent problem. If you take an elongated cylinder as a stand-in for a propeller, and try to get it spinning, you will find that most of the ways you thought you could easily pull this off evaporate into a cloud of frustration. This is a problem that consumed another Bryce whiz and me for several hours each week for a period of months. We sent e-mail back and forth, evidencing the blind alleys we ran into. Using the Repeat function does no good at all, since it seems Repeat doesn't appreciate rotations much. Just rotating the propeller didn't help either, as more than a 180-degree rotation just wouldn't take. Then, while writing this chapter on Links, the solution came. Here's how to do it:

1. Create a Sphere, and center it on your screen as seen from the Front view.
2. Create the propeller from an elongated Cylinder, or import a Propeller object if you have one.
3. Place the propeller against the mid-front of the Sphere, as seen in the Front view. Link the propeller to the Sphere. The Sphere is now the Parent object.
4. Keyframe this arrangement for frame 1, and go to the last frame in your animation duration (move the lozenge).
5. Select the Sphere, and using the Rotation tool in the Edit toolbar, Rotate the Sphere on the Z World axis as many times as you like by dragging the mouse without letting up on the mouse button. A good number of rotations is 10 for a five-second animation at 15 fps.

When you play this back, you will have a rotating propeller. A three- or four-bladed propeller looks nicer than a two-bladed one when animated.

Targets

What are the differences between Targets and Links?

- You cannot Link a Targeted object back to the object that is tracking it. This would lead to an impossible loop, so that as the Targeted object moved, it would move the Targeting object, which would then move the original object. If you could do this, the computer would crash, since the computations would go on forever.
- When a Child object also Targets the Parent object in a Link, much more useful orbits can be created. This is because as the Child object orbits the Linked parent, it also automatically rotates in position. This is an absolute must technique when the Child object is to emulate our moon, which always turns the same face toward us as it orbits.

Animating the Camera

No matter what actors move in your Bryce worlds, the way that you look at their actions is the difference between a boring ho-hum animation and one that will startle your audience. To create state-of-the-art animations, you have to know what the camera is capable of, and how to control it. The camera has a close and creative relationship with everything we have discussed so far in this chapter, especially with Paths, Links, and Targets.

When creating camera animations, there are a few things to keep in mind:

- If you want the animation to loop, to return to the place it started, set the last keyframe at the start to be the same as the first keyframe. It's easy to mistakenly alter keyframes without knowing it, so take care to do this at the start. This is also necessary to do with the camera when you are looking at objects on a circular path.
- If something goes amiss, and the camera moves when you don't want it to, use the Undo command immediately. Do not attempt to reset the camera manually. Chances are that 99.999% of the time, you won't get it exact, and the render will show a jump. Sometimes, using the Delete keyframe operation will fix it, too.
- Check to make sure you are at the first frame on the Timeline as a habit. Often, we forget to do this, and throw a whole animation out of whack.

- Remember to make the camera invisible when working on a complex scene as seen from the Front view. This can save a lot of time because you won't be selecting the camera by mistake, and will be able to see more clearly. You could also Lock it in its Attributes dialog. When you need it unlocked, select it from the Selections palette by clicking the Globe symbol, and then going to the Selections list.

CAMERA ANIMATION EXAMPLES

There are infinite ways to create animations based on camera movements alone. The following are some important examples.

Rotate Around a Selected Object

To rotate the camera around a selected object, do the following:

1. Select the camera.
2. Click and Drag on the Target icon in the camera's Attributes list, until you are over the Target object, and the object's display box turns blue.
3. Set the frame 1 position of the camera as a keyframe. Go to the camera's Attributes dialog, and under the Animation tab, select Make Circular.
4. Go to the Top view, and by moving the camera (which will always point to the Target automatically), describe a circular path of keyframes (which will also be drawn automatically in accordance with your camera moves).
5. You might want to alter the height of the camera at various keyframes, so your targeted object can be seen from other perspectives.

Repositioning the Camera

We could just as well call this example "investigation," because it allows you to view the intended subject from every possible angle and perspective. The intention is to give the viewer the best sense of the 3D nature of an object. It consists of creating keyframes that look at the object from any angle or distance that looks interesting. When doing an animation like this, make sure you extend the duration long enough so the view doesn't go by too quickly. One way to do this is to stay awhile at particular viewpoints, by moving the lozenge on the Timeline from one keyframe to another, and setting another keyframe without moving the camera. This allows the viewer to linger before moving on.

There are two rules for getting the most out of a camera investigation:

- Make the object different and interesting, even as a silhouette.
- Darken the lighting so that the object appears mysterious, so the audience has some heightened anticipation.

A Camera Light

One way to make the investigative camera even more useful is to Link it to a Spotlight. Don't make the Spotlight too bright, and make sure the edges of the beam are fuzzed out. Perhaps, even give the light a mysterious color, like light blue or green. The light should not illuminate everything in the field of view, but just enough to whet the viewer's appetite for more clarity (see Figure 16.7).

A rule of thumb for camera lingering is not to overstay your welcome. A couple of seconds is usually enough time in one place. Doing this three times in an animation is also a suggested limit.

FIGURE 16.7 The investigative camera is Linked to a Spotlight. A Cloud Plane was used as the ground, adding even more mystery to the scene.

A Moving Target

Whether it's a cannon tracking a flying behemoth, or the eyes in a figure tracking an insect, the ability of objects to track other objects is a well-used technique in computer animation. However, the camera can also track objects, and since the camera is a stand-in for your eyes in Bryce, the effect is like that experienced when you watch anything with care. There are two camera tracking modes: Stand and Track, and Follow and Track.

- **Stand and Track.** In this mode, the camera is placed in an optimum position, where it can see most of the actions of the targeted object. It might not see it when it goes into a tunnel, but keeps tracking anyway. The camera never moves from its position. Unless there are times when the targeted object is hidden from the camera, this technique can produce animations that instantly cure insomnia.
- **Follow and Track.** Follow and Track is best used when the camera is at a fairly close range from the object. The object might be a ball traveling through a series of openings. The camera becomes a ghost that follows the ball through the openings, giving the impression that the audience is to identify with the ball itself, like the personality of the ball. This is the mode used when the camera is placed in a car or on a roller coaster. The camera becomes a hitchhiker, and in some cases, the invisible personality behind the wheel.

Linking to an Object

Be very careful when Linking the camera to an object. Targeting an object is one thing, since the FOV (field of view) can take care of any erratic motions the object might display. When you Link the camera, however, every motion the object makes will be duplicated by the camera. If you are going to Link the camera to the object, it is better Linked close to the object than at a distance. It's also better if the object doesn't display too much bouncing or wiggling motion, because the camera will imitate the motion and the viewer might get seasick.

Camera as Parent

This is a situation that has limited use because of the unexpected nature of the actions. If you make the camera a Parent Link to an object (when the object is in center view of the camera), then no matter where the camera looks, the object will be center stage. The camera actually becomes the puppet master of the object. The object itself will look like it is being tracked. You can actually emulate a sometimes-used Hollywood effect by doing this. It is similar to the effect displayed when the camera is watching two people dance, and the room seems to be twirling around them. If you explore this option, create an animation that surveys the panorama of the scene, and takes in a section of the sky. At the very least, it's an option you should be aware of. The best thing about it is that the

Child object really defines no path at all, but just acts in accordance with camera moves.

Linking to a Ribbon Path

This is a great way to get more use out of the paths stored in the Objects Library. Besides controlling objects placed on them, they can also act as tracks for the camera. This capability is especially useful in Follow and Track animations, since both an object and the camera can be Linked on the same Ribbon path.

A better way to accomplish more interesting results than just camera and object Linked to the same path is to duplicate the path first. Set the object to one path, and the camera to the other. The camera path can then follow the same general curve as the object path, but can do so from the side, top, bottom, or even from changing angles. Sometimes it will outrun the object and look at it from ahead, and sometimes it might lag behind. This is a method that is extremely useful when tracking vehicles in a race.

FOV Animations

The larger the camera's FOV setting, the smaller all of the objects in the scene will become. If you alter the FOV over time, resizing it in the camera's Attributes dialog, you will notice radical distortions near the edge of your visual plane. FOV animations look like zooms with distortion applied (see Figure 16.8).

FIGURE 16.8 The frame on the left features the FOV animation about 40% of the way through, with the objects appearing to be at a somewhat standard distance from the camera. On the right is the last frame, with the FOV at 179. Because the sky is also centered, the zoom effect is enhanced.

If you are looking for some great sky renderings, use the maximum FOV settings with the camera pointed at the sky. The renderings will look like big sky country in the American West.

Camera Scale Factor Animations

Playing with the FOV settings gives you distortions on both ends of the spectrum. On a scale of 1 to 180, 60 is the normal setting. Settings less and more than 60 result in distorted perspectives. The scale factor is different in that the highest setting, 100%, presents you with what you would expect the scene to look like, with no distortion applied to objects. A setting of 1%, however, is a radical zoom out. If all you want to do is to zoom in or out of a scene with a standard view as your starting or end point, alter the Scale setting of the camera. If you want radical distortions on both ends of a zoom, use the FOV animation method (see Figure 16.9).

FIGURE 16.9 The zoom effect when the scale of the camera is altered is even more radical. here. The Scale is set to 10%, with 100% being the standard default setting. Compare the perspective look of the sky with this 10% Scale setting with the sky as depicted in the right half of **FIGURE** 16.8.

Panning a Scene

You can do an animated pan of a scene by altering the Camera Pan settings in the Attributes dialog. Pans can be horizontal or vertical. There are two types of Panning operations: general and targeted. In general Panning, all that you are interested in doing is to give the audience a feel for the panoramic environment on an incremental basis. With targeted Panning, the object is to Pan to an object of interest, like a special feature in the foreground on the left, or a vehicle traversing the sky. You should explore both types.

Repeat, Pendulum, Make Circular

In the Animation tab of the camera's Attributes dialog, you will find the same options for applying these three animation types as with any other selected object. The same rules that we discussed previously regarding the uses of these options apply to the camera. The difference is, since the camera represents your eyes in the scene, you will feel that you are personally swinging your vision around and creating these effects.

MOVING ON

In this chapter, we began our exploration for creating Bryce animations. In the next chapter, we'll continue this process by investigating animated Earth, Air, Water, and Fire f/x.

CHAPTER

17 Earth, Air, Water, and Fire

In the archaic alchemical and astrological traditions of the western world, Earth, Water, Air, and Fire were considered to be the four basic elements. Everything was said to be composed of a mixture of these four forces. In the East, especially in China, Wood was considered to be a separate fifth element. For our purposes in this chapter, we will stick with four, placing Wood with Earth, detailing 40 elemental effects.

EARTH F/X

There are four categories in Bryce that relate to the element Earth: the *Infinite Ground Plane, Terrain objects, Stones,* and *Materials* associated with Earth-related textures. We will explore 10 different Earth-associated f/x that look at all of these categories.

Emergence

In this animation, earthen objects emerge from the Ground Plane. Do the following:

1. Place a series of random objects below the Ground Plane. Everything is mapped with the same material in Global Space (including the Ground Plane), so the objects that emerge really look like parts of the terrain are bulging up.

To use different materials would distinguish the objects from the plane, which is another possible effect altogether from the same saved Bryce file. There are dozens of variations on this theme, of course. The idea of something appearing out of the ground could be applied to a graveyard mystery, for example, with semitransparent Poser skeletons rising slowly upward. Not all animations that play upon this theme need to be that dire. In fact, generated in reverse, you could also show raindrops falling to the ground. You could also use this animation method to show the geological evolution of a specified terrain, the emergence of the Himalayas, for instance. Just so you know what to expect, using Global Space mapping on all of the elements will make it look as if the material is expanding and stretching to accommodate the rising objects. You can always use Object Space mapping on the objects if you don't want this (see Figure 17.1).

2. Keyframe frame 1 with everything below the Ground Plane.
3. Keyframe the last frame of you animation with all objects moved upward so that they display about 75% of their forms above the Ground Plane.

The task of the animator is to do the unexpected, even with a fairly basic animation technique. When you develop an emergence animation, make sure that the elements that move are staggered in time, so they don't all move at once. It's also a good idea to vary their shapes, subtly or radically.

FIGURE 17.1 In the Emergence example, the very ground looks like it is surging upward, since everything is mapped with the same material.

Wall Evolver

This is a method for causing a wall to build itself from a collection of stones. Here's how:

1. Create a Stone from the Create toolbar, or import one from the Rocks and Trees folder in the Objects Library.
2. Multi-Replicate the stone 15 times. Move each stone into position as part of a vertical wall, varying the length of some of the stones. Select all of the stones by surrounding them with a dragged-out marquee, and Group the wall into one object. Assign an Object Space mapped material to the wall (this makes the texturing of each stone a little different).
3. Create a 60-frame animation, and make sure the last frame is a keyframe. This is very important, because we are going to work backwards.
4. Go to frame 1, and select half of the stones randomly, and each stone in succession (by holding down the Control key as you click on the separate stones). As each stone is selected, move it to some random position above or below the Ground Plane, and out of the view.

5. Now, go to frame 20, and repeat the same movement on the remaining stones. If you set the keyframe for the last frame correctly, the last frame will show the wall built in place, and the first frame will show just the Ground Plane. If you render an animation from this project, it will show the rocks magically rising from the Ground Plane to assume their position in the wall.
6. To add more believable randomness to the animation, go to various random frames in the sequence, and reposition and rotate selected stones (see Figure 17.2).

FIGURE 17.2 The stones gradually fly up and create the wall.

Crack of Doom

Open up the Earth on a fault line with this effect, creating a rift valley. This is your first opportunity in this book to work with animation in the Terrain Editor. Here's how:

1. Create a 60-frame animation. Place a Terrain object in your world, and with it selected, open up the Terrain Editor.
2. Lower the Terrain so it looks like gently rolling hills instead of a mountain. In the animation Timeline at the bottom of the Terrain Editor, make a keyframe of the terrain at the first frame.

3. Go to the last frame. With the Elevation brush enabled, select a pure black color and a medium-thin brush size. Paint a jagged line from the bottom of the topographical view to the top. As you look at the preview model, you will see that a valley has been cut through the model. Return to the workscreen.
4. Place a mountain behind the animated Terrain to add some interest, and render the animation. You will see the rift valley created before your eyes as the animation plays back (see Figure 17.3).

FIGURE 17.3 This rift valley is created while you watch. Just for effect, the Material is also animated.

Volumetric Evaporation

The Base Density control in the Volumetric Materials Lab is a magic wand that can create some startling animation effects. Here's one example of its use:

1. Create a 60-frame animation. Place an egg-shaped object (an elongated Sphere) on the Ground Plane so it can be seen clearly in the Camera view.
2. Create a Symmetrical Lattice, and map it with whatever material you like. Place it inside of the egg-shaped object.
3. In the Materials Lab, assign a volumetric texture to the egg-shaped object. Set the Base Density to 100%, making it opaque.
4. Go to the last frame, and set the Base Density to 0, so that the egg-shaped object disappears.

Always use Full Shading on volumetric textures that are set to evaporate, since that creates the most interesting patterns. Although there is a high rendering cost for volumetric materials, there is nothing quite like them for unusual effects. You might also think of this as the "beam-me-up-Scotty" effect (see Figure 17.4).

FIGURE 17.4 As the egg shape evaporates, a Symmetrical Lattice object is revealed inside. Volumetric Base Density controls it all.

Volumetric textures do not map to a Terrain object in Bryce, but can be used on any primitive. There is other great news, however. Imported objects do *take on volumetric materials. If you need to evaporate Terrain, design the Terrain object in another 3D application, and save it out in a 3D object format that Bryce can read. Import it, and evaporate away!*

Terramorphs

Terramorphs are animations created in the Terrain Editor. The rift valley we created in the "Crack of Doom" example is a basic Terramorph. Complex Terramorphs, however, take advantage of the full range of features and tools in the Terrain Editor. Creating a Terramorph means using the Terrain Editor tools in reference to the timeline, so that your painted elevations and effects are set to various keyframes in an animation. You can accomplish absolute magic by morphing terrain over time. Here are some basic guidelines:

- Plan ahead by doing a rough storyboard of what you want to accomplish, especially as far as what your keyframes should look like.

- Make sure there are at least three seconds (at 30 fps) between keyframes of a Terramorph. This allows the audience to appreciate a smooth transition.
- Try to design an intermediate keyframe, so that the audience is surprised by the final outcome. For example, if you want to transform a sharp peaked mountain into a volcano, show an intermediate keyframe that assigns maximum erosion to the mountain first. Then assign the crater to the last keyframe.
- Always preview the animation in the Terrain Editor, which shows you a full shaded rendering, and is much faster than rendering it first.
- It is suggested that you use only one Terramorph as the center of attention in your finished animation. More than one is, in most cases, overkill.

ON THE CD

Make sure you view the four Terramorph animations (TM1 to TM4) included on the CD-ROM. They are short, but magical.

A/B Impacts

A number of things can happen when Object A is hurtling through space, and meets Object B, all depending on the mass of either object.

- Object A can bounce away from Object B, with B remaining in place, or Objects A and B can both bounce away from each other after the impact.
- Object A can break up, Object B can break up, or they both can break up.
- In computer graphics worlds, Object A can pass without notice right through Object B.

In the following two animated scenarios, we take a look at two A/B interactions.

SLAM HAMMER

In this scenario, Object A meets Object B while Object B is on the ground. The resulting impact causes Object A to bounce off Object B, but not without acting as a hammer that drives Object B further into the ground. Do the following:

1. Create a 60-frame animation at 15 fps. Create two rocks. The moving one will be called Rock A, and the stable one Rock B.
2. Plant Rock B in the ground about one-third of the way. Move Rock A out of the scene and above Rock B.

3. Set a keyframe at the beginning of the animation for Rock A. Move Rock A so that it touches Rock B at frame 20 of the animation. Set a keyframe for both Rocks A and B at this point. From frame 21 to 60, Rock A should bounce off Rock B and bounce out of the scene. Rock B should be driven vertically into the ground about two-thirds of the way from frames 21 to frame 45.

Solving the Horizon/Distance Problem

Commonly, your Ground Planes have horizons that are in the infinite distance. You cannot place anything at or beyond the observed horizon line in Bryce, using an Infinite Ground Plane. Unless you move objects a huge distance from the camera from the Top view, you can't even come close to object placement near the horizon. However, like every other problem you might face in Bryce, there is a solution. To place an object near the horizon without moving it very far from the camera, do the following:

1. Place a Ground Plane and a primitive Sphere in your scene.
2. Multiselect the Camera, Ground Plane, and the Sphere, and Group them.
3. Move the group upward, about three screen inches away from the Underground boundary, and tilt the group 15 degrees on the X-axis (see Figure 17.5).
4. Use a 75% Haze setting, and turn Cast Shadows Off on the object in the Materials Lab.

You can achieve close to the same result just by rotating the camera so its FOV skims the ground, but the horizon line is usually too apparent.

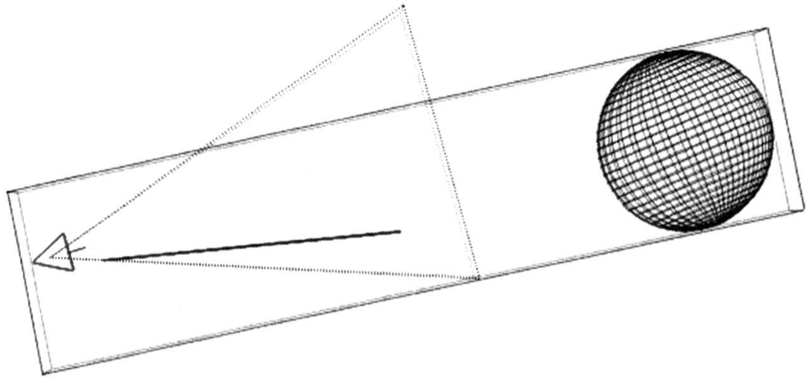

FIGURE 17.5 This figure shows the placement of the elements in the scene.

If you must show an object rising from below the horizon line to above it, a false sun or a more esoteric object, replace the Infinite Ground Plane with a flattened Terrain object (give it a Y size of 2). Elevating and tilting the components as in the previous example should still be followed, although some exploration of the variables is important for each project. This time, however, you can place objects so they are totally or partially hidden by the false horizon line, and animate them to interact with it (see Figure 17.6).

If you elongate Terrain Plane substitutes far enough on their Z-axis, they can also show Haze and Fog effects. You can also use an intervening Infinite Cloud Plane placed vertically between the end of the Terrain Plane and the object to show clouds passing in front of the object, which adds to the believability of the depth and distance involved. If you do this, explore the use of the Tea Kettle Steam material (see Figure 17.6).

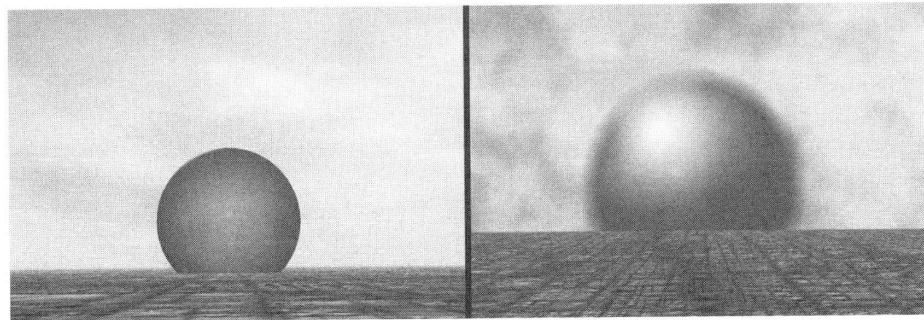

FIGURE 17.6 On the left is the tilted Infinite Ground Plane method, and on the right is the Terrain object substitution, with an intervening vertical Cloud Plane (50% transparent). The right-hand object is also a Fuzzy object, emphasizing the distance.

AIR F/X

Air f/x center on everything we can do to customize or affect the look of the sky in Bryce. This includes Haze and Fog effects, since the sky is not just something "up there," but takes in general atmospherics.

Deep Sky Editing

When you simply have to have a sky that you can't create from the preset components, and the random generator isn't providing you with what you need, there is another more personal alternative. The same Deep Texture Editing process that allows you to get to the very roots of texture generation when it comes to customizing materials is also available for creating sky textures. There are no limits to the unique looks available, as long a you are conversant with the Deep Texture Editing process (see Chapter 11).

If your Deep Sky textures are not rendering, try the following:

- Turn Cumulous Off. Stratus clouds often take better advantage of this procedure.
- Try setting Cloud Height to 10 and Cover to 5. This seems to clarify the new patterns.
- Try altering the Custom Colors. More contrasted colors seem to show the patterns better.
- Make sure the material you assign to the sky has an Alpha channel in the Deep Texture Editor. If it doesn't, create one. This allows "holes" in the Sky Plane (see Figure 17.7).

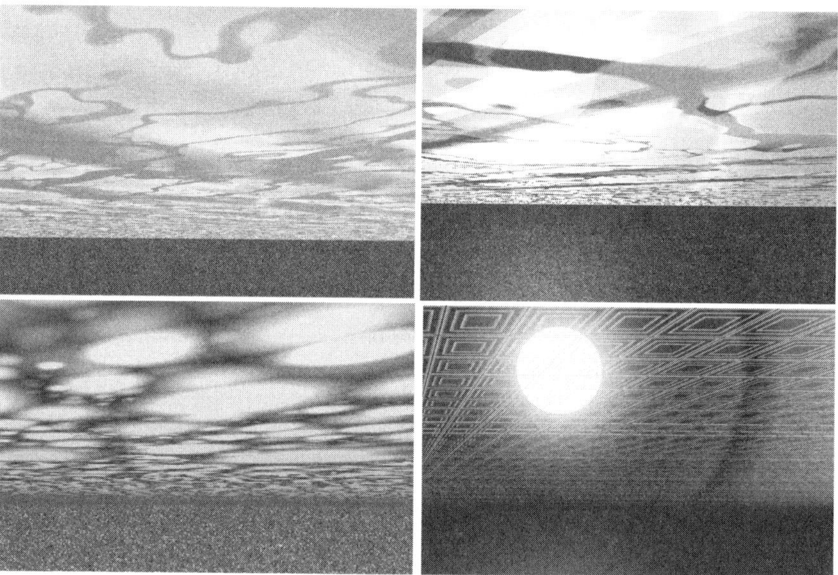

FIGURE 17.7 A collection of skies created by Deep Texture Editing explorations displays unusual and unfamiliar precincts of the air.

De-Fogger

Using fog settings, we can generate animations that reveal things that were previously hidden in a progressive manner. A very effective, yet simple to create Fog effect is to watch the Fog burn off in front of our eyes, going from 100% to 0%. If you plan on using this effect, make sure there is something interesting that gets revealed.

Haze Lighter

Using a 75% Haze, alter the Haze color over time. Haze adds a strange glow to objects in the distance, and altering the Haze color accentuates this effect. You can also explore different Haze percentages for more subtle or enhanced variations.

Stone Sky

This effect is best applied to an intervening Cloud Plane, leaving the background sky set to No Atmosphere and a solid color, or a gradient (by switching Cumulous off, and using Custom Sky).

Sky Stack Trip

This animation is similar to the effect at the end of Stanley Kubrick's *2001: A Space Oddessy*, when the spacecraft moves through a series of Infinite Planes. The difference is, this effect moves you vertically through the planes. Here's what to do:

1. Create a stack of six Infinite Cloud Planes, separated by the height of the camera on your screen.
2. Map each of the planes with a different Cloud material, making sure that about 35% to 50% of the materials show transparent areas.
3. In the first frame of a 120-frame 15-fps animation, place the camera at the bottom of the lowest Cloud Plane, facing straight ahead, and keyframe it. In the last frame of the animation, move the camera vertically, so it is above the top Cloud Plane. Render and save.

Aurora Borealis with Shimmer

This one's a real beauty. It should be composited against a dark sky. Here in the North, we consider the Aurora a sign of hope, although it often indicates very cold weather for the coming winter. Here's how to do it:

1. Create a scene with a few mountains and a dark-blue sky.
2. Place a 2D Vertical Plane in the scene in back of the mountains. Make it large enough so you can't see any edges when viewed from the camera.
3. With the 2D Plane selected, open the Materials Lab. Load the Waves2 texture from the list into channel A. Activate Diffuse, Specular, Specular Halo, and Transparent Colors; Diffusion (100), Ambience (82), and Specularity (53) Values; Transparency Optics (22). Notice that

we leave the Specular button in the Color palette mode, because this allows us to alter the color of the Aurora over time, and to see that color against a dark sky.

4. Create a 120-frame animation at 30 fps. At random places on the Timeline, alter the Specular color and the size of the Aurora. Render and save to disk (see Figure 17.8).

FIGURE 17.8 The beauty of the Aurora Borealis is captured by Bryce.

Clearing

This effect is easy to understand and apply, but the results can be spectacular. Switch Cumulous On and create an animation that moves from 100% Cloud Cover at the first frame to 0% at the last frame. Turn Stratus Off. The best version of this effect is the one that displays an enlarged sun shining behind the clouds, with halos turned on. If your scene has some interesting terrain and objects, you will be amazed by the results. Work with a 30-fps 240-frame animation as a minimum, to allow the effect to take place slowly.

24 Hours

This is another easy-to-understand-and-apply effect. It emulates day passing into night and again into day. All that it takes is an interesting scene, so shadows get cast as the sun moves. Water is nice to add to the scene, because there are different reflections that occur as the sun moves.

Pulsar

A Pulsar is a star that revolves in a steady repetitive cycle, so that it produces radiation "noise" that can be picked up by radio telescopes here on Earth. In our Bryce Pulsar example, we will change the size and color of the Sun object to emulate this effect. Do the following:

1. Create a 120-frame animation at 30 fps.
2. Create an alien landscape, and make the sky color red with either no clouds, or a few bizarre clouds created by using the Deep Sky Edit dialog (activated by clicking on the Edit button in the Sky&Fog palette).
3. Move the Sun so that it is on the horizon in front of the camera. Go to the Sky&Fog Edit dialog and switch the Horizon Enlargement option on, with a percentage of 100 for the first frame. Select a yellow color for the sun.
4. At frames 20, 40, 60, 80, 100, and the last frame, alter the size and color of the sun, so that it gets larger and smaller and exhibits different colors. Render the animation, and save it to disk (see Figure 17.9).

FIGURE 17.9 A Pulsar reigns over an alien landscape.

Alien Storm

Bryce not only offers you the capacity to animate Sky Planes by manipulating the light and patterns, but in addition, you can create animations that use completely different skies on separate keyframes. The result is that one sky type gradually washes over another. The Randomize buttons at the upper right of the Sky&Fog toolbar allow you to march through a series of unexpected sky parameters and patterns. Adding these two capacities together, the ability to keyframe different skies and the ability to generate random skies results in strange animations that show one unique sky morphing into another. All you need to do is to click the Randomize button and watch the Nano Preview. When you find interesting skies, add them to the Sky&Fog Presets Library. When you have half a dozen favorites, select each one in turn, and keyframe it as part of an animated sequence.

WATER F/X

Water is the elixir of life. As far as we know, life cannot exist in any form comparable to ours without it, although off-planet explorations await. Water effects in Bryce offer some of the most stunning renderings and animations. There's something about reflections and transparencies at the same time that makes us dream. Here are 10 suggestions for using Water f/x in your Bryce projects.

Agua Terra

When you think of water in Bryce, do not confine your thoughts to Infinite Water Planes alone. As we have seen in the Mud project detailed earlier, Terrain objects are great objects for a host of needs. Water is no exception. Referring to the Terramorph examples we looked at previously, it's just as easy to sculpt Terrain to look like water f/x. Here's how:

1. Create a 120-frame animation at 30 fps. Place a Terrain object on the screen, and go to the Terrain Editor.
2. In the Terrain Editor, first create a solid block by clicking New and then Invert. Lower the block to about one-tenth of its size by dragging right over the Raise/Lower control.
3. This time, we'll create animated ripples. Use the Elevation brush to paint concentric rings at frame 60 on the Terrain. Alternate between black (low elevation) and medium gray (higher elevation) until you have a series of concentric rings.
4. Allow the last keyframe to return to the flat surface you started with. Preview the animation in the Terrain Editor. After you quit the Terrain Editor, map the Swimming Pool material to the terrain slab, and set the Camera view. Render the animation, and save it to disk (see Figure 17.10).

FIGURE 17.10 This is a close-up of the Terrain Ripple effect.

Fog Water

You don't need water to achieve a water effect. Under the right circumstances, with the right environmental look in your scene, you can generate water by using low-altitude Fog. Off the Maine coast in the early morning, there are times when the ocean is subject to large patches of low-level fog, and the water as such is completely obliterated. Fantasizing oceans in faraway worlds, there might be seas of ammonia or other nonwater elements that rise and fall with the tides created by more than one moon. In both of these situations, our appreciation of a liquid surface might be enhanced not so much by the constituent components of the sea, as by its actions. Seas that we are familiar with have specific motions, waves, and rising-falling actions. You can use Fog in Bryce to emulate a sea, one that is either covered over with Fog, or a nonwater liquid (see Figure 17.11).

One reason to use Symmetrical Lattice objects in a water scene is that they are symmetrical on their vertical axis, so placing them in a transparent or partially transparent material makes it seem as if they always have a reflection. It takes less time to render a Symmetrical Lattice than it does to compute and render a reflective surface, so you get the same effect without the cost.

Radial Reflections

Radial Lights can be mapped with procedural textures. As long as the texture has an Alpha channel, the Radial Light will project eerie fractal pat-

FIGURE 17.11 In some compositions, Fog can substitute for Water, and renders faster.

terns on the surrounding area. When using this method, attend to the following:

- Place the Radial Light over a water surface, causing the water to glow as if under its own power.
- Create a scene that has thoughtfully placed and interesting objects in the vicinity, so the reflections will play on all of the surfaces.
- Always use Linear Falloff.
- Do not apply this texture as a Gel in the Radial Light's Edit dialog, but instead apply it as a procedural texture in the Materials Lab. Make sure the Alpha channel for the texture is activated in the Deep Texture Editor.
- The best way to animate these reflections is to rotate the Radial Light over time.
- Always use moonlight to enhance the power of textures projected through a Radial Light., as the Sun will tend to dilute and wash out the effect (see Figure 17.12).

Seasick

The rocking motion of the sea is solace to some, and nauseating to others. Bryce allows you to simulate this motion by tilting the Infinite Water Plane from side to side, as seen through the Camera view. To emphasize this effect, build a small boat and place it in the water. Bon voyage! (See Figure 17.13.)

FIGURE 17.12 As if radiating energy, the pool seems to reflect patterns on everything in the vicinity. It's really the hidden Radial Light causing this fractal water effect, projecting the Wavy procedural texture.

FIGURE 17.13 By tilting the Infinite Water Plane from side to side, you can simulate a rolling sea.

When your Water Plane tilts one way, rotate any craft on the surface the opposite way to enhance the rocking motion. See the Seasick1.br3 project on the CD-ROM if you want the elements necessary to create an animation displaying this effect, including a small boat. Warning—Don't watch the animation too long after you render it, unless you've brought along some seasick remedies.

THROWN ROCKS AND RAIN

Use an Infinite Water Plane as the target for the following effects, which are based on the previously described Square Light Pict Gel projections. To mimic a pebble being thrown in the water, move the Square Light with the concentric rings projection Gel as close as possible in frame 1 of an animation, and then move it far enough away vertically, at the last frame, that the Linear Falloff causes the projection to disappear. As the light moves to the last frame, decrease its intensity and increase the fuzziness. The result will be an expanding ripple that fades at the end. Do this with 10 or more randomly placed Square Lights on a Water Plane, and you have Rain.

You can control the density of Square Light projections by altering the intensity of the light, while adding fuzzy edges to the light will make the projected images fade at their extremities.

Waterfall

Waterfall simulations are some of the most sought-after effects in computer graphics. This water effect is usually added in a post-production phase of the animation by another application, such as Adobe After Effects. You can, however, create an interesting, although basic, waterfall effect in Bryce. Do the following:

1. Create a 240-frame animation at 30 fps. Create a scene that has a rocky cliff, which will be the home of your waterfall. Create a pool at the bottom of the cliff, a reservoir for the tons of falling water.
2. Create a Cylinder object, set on its side as facing the Camera view, and place it in the area of the cliff that is to evidence falling water.
3. Map it with a Volumetric water material. The Polluted Waterfall material is a good choice. You can go into its Deep Texture Editor and recolor the yellow-brown texture a light blue, instantly correcting the pollution.
4. At the base, where the water meets the pond, place a Sphere. Map the Sphere with a Volumetric cloud texture, which will be the spray evaporating as the water hits.
5. There are two components of this scene that you will want to animate, the waterfall and the spray cloud. Animate the waterfall itself by simply revolving the cylinder, and altering the Base Density of the texture over time. Animate the spray cloud by altering its Base Density over time (see Figure 17.14).

If the waterfall is very high, consider using a series of cylinders, so it looks like the water is cascading from one to the next.

FIGURE 17.14 A Bryce waterfall pours its water into a waiting pond.

Tap Water

Here's a water effect that's small by comparison to oceans and waterfalls. It's simple to set up, with perhaps the most challenging part being the modeling of the faucet. If you load the project, tapwtr1.br3, from the CD-ROM, you can take the faucet object apart to see how basic Bryce Primitive objects were used in its construction.

What about the water? A Screw object, included in the Bryce Imported Objects Library folder, was used. It was mapped with a 96% transparent Swimming Pool Water material in the Materials Lab.

Animation Suggestions

If you want to animate this scene, what should you target for movement, and how?

- Animate the faucet handle turning. It is a separate group from the rest of the faucet, and can be rotated by using the Rotation tool on the Y World axis.
- Animate the "water" coming out. This can be accomplished by simply reducing the vertical height of the "water" until it disappears into the faucet, and then elongating that length over time. You should also rotate the water on the Y World axis as it leaves the faucet (see Figure 17.15).

FIGURE 17.15 A close-up shot of the faucet reveals its structure, and the usefulness of the inverted screw as a stream of water.

See to Bottom

This project uses a volumetric transparent water block with a sandy bottom and moving "fish." Here's how the project was created:

1. The Valley Terrain Map, from the Bryce Terrain Maps folder, was imported in the Terrain Editor. It was resized to about one-fourth of its height, and placed in the scene. It was mapped with the Rainforest Rock material, which was sized to 1000% to make the textures smaller and more numerous.
2. A rectangular block was added for the water, and mapped with a 85% transparent Aqua Glass material, with a Bump map channel added (Waves Bump texture).
3. A sandy bottom with pebbles was added at the lowest level of the water, using another Rectangular object embedded in the Terrain "river." It was mapped with the Riverbed textured material from the Sand Materials Folder. It was resized to 625%, and turned 35 degrees on the Y World axis, so that mechanical symmetry could be broken. The texture was darkened in the Deep Texture Editor to give it a wetter look, although it is only visible at the bottom of the rendering.
4. Stones were added to the composition to give it more viewer interest.
5. A public domain DXF "Fish" object was added and duplicated for a school, and the camera and lighting were adjusted for filming.

The "water" you place in your scene need not be derived from a standard water material. As in this case, you can use a transparent glass, and perhaps add a Bump channel. You can, in fact, use a mirror (see Figures 17.16 and 17.17).

FIGURE 17.16 A DXF public domain model of a shark was reconfigured as this somewhat unique fish.

FIGURE 17.17 A school of fish swims near the sandy bottom of a stream.

Splash

You can use the same process that was presented in the Earth section in this chapter on dispersal explosions to explode water as well. The difference is that this is not called an explosion, but a splash. All you have to do is to embed small spheres mapped with a transparent water material under your watery surface. Multi-Replicate the spherical particles 30 times or so. Throw a virtual pebble in the water, and at the very moment it hits the surface, begin the dispersion of the spheres. You can move any by hand later that don't meet your visual requirements. All you have to remember is to map the spheres with a very high transparency level, and perhaps to elongate them into more teardrop shapes as well. Use the 3D Move, Rotate, Resize dispersion method.

Extra! TV Rain and Snow

Before the dawn of computer graphics and animation, TV productions would simulate rain and snow mechanically. They would place a cylindrical roll with white or black markings and a drop-out blue background in front of a second camera, and superimpose the markings over a scene shot by camera 1 as the cylinder was turned. In computer animation, this is called Alpha Channel Compositing, so it's something learned from the historical tradition of animation. We can certainly accomplish this same process in Bryce. Here's how:

1. Create a 320 × 480 grayscale graphic in a paint application. On a white backdrop, add black antialiased streaks that are randomly placed and randomly sized, and that are on an approximate 15-degree angle. This will be our Rain map.
2. Create a Cylinder that is laying on its side as seen in the Camera view. Resize it so that it covers the whole scene, and move it so that the camera is inside of it (as seen in the Top view).
3. In the 2D Picture Editor in the Materials Lab, import the rain graphic and wrap it on the Cylinder (cylindrical mapping). If anything looks disoriented, use the Rotation tool to correct it. The image should come in with white acting as an Alpha dropout. If not, simply copy the graphic to the Alpha channel in the 2D Picture Editor.
4. You can map it a multiple number of times, which will create repetitive sheets of rain (a monsoon?). When you create the animation, simply keyframe the starting position at the start and end of the animation, and make sure the cylinder rotates 360 degrees (on the X World axis) to make the streaks look like falling rain.

To create a gentle snowstorm, use snow-flake designs instead of streaks in the bitmap, making sure they are randomly placed and sized. To create a blizzard, use white dots instead of designed flakes. To create a meteorite storm, use red-orange streaks with a somewhat bulbous end. To create a cats-and-dogs rain, use cat and dog graphics as the Image map.

FIRE F/X

Fire, like water, has a dual personality. It can be life giving when it resides in a stove or a candle, and life threatening when it is the heat and power of an explosion. Fire f/x are a mainstay of computer animations, since they allow the sudden removal of objects from the scene, and can also display lighting factors not possible with artificial lighting components. There are many more ways to use Fire f/x than the examples presented here, but these should give you a good overall view of what is possible with Fire designs in Bryce, and how to create it.

Sparky

Glance one flinty stone off another, and the friction causes sparks. Campfires also release sparks into the air, as do electrical mishaps. You already have the technique for creating sparks down pat if you have worked through the Doom and Splash examples earlier in this chapter. All that's new is to create the initial Spark object itself.

The Spark object, unlike stars placed in the sky, should be a 3D object. If you are going to create it in Bryce, use three crossed elongated squares grouped together and very tiny. Map them with a very high Specular Red-Orange color, so they appear no matter how dark it is. Also use a high Red-Orange Diffuse color. The rest of the operation is the same as those already mentioned. Just select the object and Multi-Replicate it in place, and use the dispersion 3D/Move/Rotate operation on them. There might be some occasions, like an exploding rocket, that demands a Resized Dispersion as well. Use your judgment to fit the project you're working on (see Figure 17.18).

Candle

Candles have been used for millennia, both to light the darkness, and as symbols of hope and faith. Candles in Bryce can be constructed so that their flame casts light on receptive objects in the surrounding scene. Here's how to do it:

FIGURE 17.18 Evolution of a Spark.

1. A candle starts with a Cylinder. Attach six or so elongated Spheres to the sides of the cylinder to represent melted wax, and Group everything. Place a black cylindrical wick in the candle.
2. Assign a Psychoactive Christmas Ball material to the candle body with the following settings: Object Front mapping; Ambient color alone is activated for the channel; Diffusion value(100), Ambience Value(28), Specularity Value(75); transparency Optics (35).
3. Design a Candle Holder from two flattened Cylinders to make a plate, and use a Polished Bronze material on it (Metals folder).
4. For the flame's gases, place an elongated Sphere on the wick. Map it with a clear Glass material with the following settings: Fuzzy, Object Space mapping,
5. Use a small Radial Light on top of the wick for the flame itself. Color it light blue, and make it volume visible. Set Intensity to 50, and Fuzziness to 35 in the Light's Edit dialog.

Group everything as one Candle object when it's done. Place it in a scene on a table with some objects around it. To animate the flame, elongate and shorten the gases at various keyframe points along the Timeline, and allow the flame itself to pulse with less and more intensity (see Figure 17.19).

Glowing Coals

Glowing coals, whether experienced as the remnants of a campfire or as the main actors in a barbecue pit, can be easily created in Bryce. All that you need is a suitable Rock material with a high deep-red Specularity. To make the glowing coal a more esoteric object, like a recently landed Cosmic object, just make sure that the Specular Color channel relates to only one texture in a mix of two or more. This gives you patches of light, as opposed to having an entire object that glows.

FIGURE 17.19 The candle glows in a composition because of the embedded Radial Light.

Fireplace

Computer greetings cards, whether printed out and sent through the mail, or used as part of a Web page, are very popular ways of displaying your expertise as a 3D artist and animator. If used as an animation element, the flame has to be moving. Let's look at how a fireplace with burning logs can be created in Bryce:

1. Use a Boolean Negative Cube to cut away a Boolean Positive Cube to construct a basic fireplace. You can place a mantle on top, made from another Cubic primitive. Set a wall behind it.
2. Use Cylinders mapped with a Wood material and a very high Bump map channel for stacked logs.
3. Place a Sphere over the logs for the fire. Map a Wood material to the Sphere.
4. Place a yellow Radial Light in the flames so the light will be cast into the surrounding room, and whatever artifacts you decide to place near the fireplace (see Figure 17.20).

Lightning

Lightning is the ultimate spark. Usually, we associate it with a sky occurrence, but varieties of lightning can also be useful to science and fantasy scenes, like the power surges that brought the Frankenstein monster to life in an underground laboratory. You can create some pretty realistic lightning in Bryce. Here's how:

1. Open your favorite paint application, and draw a lightning bolt. Use whatever copy you need if you are unaccustomed to drawing. Draw it as a bright blue graphic on a white backdrop. Save it to disk.

FIGURE 17.20 The warmth and light of a fireplace casts a spell on everything in the vicinity.

2. Now, use your paint application's Magic Wand tool to select the background, and inverse it. The bolt should now be outlined. Paint it solid black. Save it as the graphic's Alpha channel.
3. Configure a scene in Bryce appropriate for lightning, with a darkened sky. Place a 2D Picture Plane in the background where you want the lightning to occur. Select it, and in the Materials Lab, map the bolt to the 2D Picture Plane.

If you want to animate this effect, make sure the 2D Picture Plane is in view for two or three frames when the lightning is to be seen. The rest of the time, make sure it is out of the view. You don't want it to slide into view, but to suddenly appear. This means that you should keyframe it as not in the frame on either side of the keyframes that show it as present. It will suddenly appear, and seem to flash. Do this two or three times in an animation (see Figure 17.21).

If you see a Picture Plane border around your image, and you can't get rid of it, then you are not using the 2D Picture Plane, but another 2D Plane. Make sure you are using the 2D Picture Plane.

Fireball Disintegrator

How about creating a fireball that reacts to altitude, so that as it gets closer to the Earth, it burns more intensely. You can do it in Bryce, and here's how:

FIGURE 17.21 Lightning has always been a symbol of power.

1. Create your Fire object. Commonly this is a Rock, but it can be anything you desire (a rocket, a cube a Poser head, etc.). Map it with a material that has a Specular channel, because we want it to glow against a dark backdrop.
2. Place a Cone primitive on the screen. Resize its larger end to be as large as the back end of the Fireball object, and rotate it into place over the Fireball object.
3. Use the following Volumetric Material map on the Cone: Channel A—the Fading texture, with markers for Ambient Color, Diffusion (80) and Ambient (60) Value; Channel B—the Fire texture, Diffuse Color and Base Density Volume (75). Other settings not tied to channel markers are Specularity value of 80, Edge Softness and Fuzzy factor at 40, and Quality/Speed at 5 (see Figure 17.22).

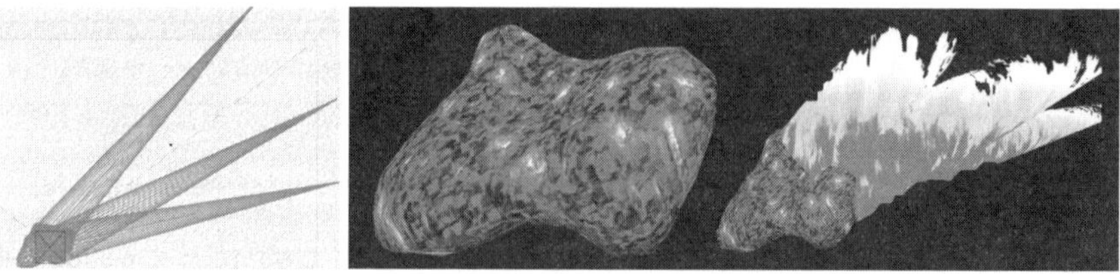

FIGURE 17.22 A cosmic fireball streaks across the night sky, burning more reddish as it gets closer to impact.

Lava Flow

Our final Fire f/x might also be listed under Earth f/x, since lava is a mixture of the temperaments of both Earth and Fire. Our concern here is twofold. First, to use a suitable material to wrap a surface that simulates lava, and second to move a series of these surfaces to emulate the flow. By the way, using the same procedure that was detailed for the Waterfall project, we could also create a river of lava. For simulating moving lava surfaces, here's what to do:

1. Create seven 2D disks, and elongate them on their X-axis so they are all a little different.
2. Use the Lava Rock texture in channel A to map the ovals, and set channel markers in Diffuse and Ambient Color. Set the Diffusion and Ambience values to 100, and do the same for Bump map value. The XYZ texture size should be set at 10%.
3. Create a volcano in the Terrain Editor, and use the Elevation brush to slice away part of the slope, so it can "leak" lava. Place the volcano in your scene, and stack the lava mapped ovals under it. You might need to resize them smaller to do this.

Make sure all of the lava ovals have a name, so you can locate them easily (such as lava1, lava2, etc.).

4. Place a Cylinder of "lava" inside the volcano, and create a Radial Light at the top, over the Cylinder, to light it up (Linear Falloff, and no Surface or Volumetric options).
5. Create the rest of the elements in your scene. You should use a reddish sky to emphasize the fiery nature of the environment.
6. Make sure your Ground Plane is beneath the sliding lava flows. Set an animation length, and get ready to set keyframes for an animation.

A LAVA FLOW ANIMATION

When you animate this scene, attend to the following procedures:

- As the animation progresses, the lava cylinder inside of the volcano should move up and down about 10% each way. This gives the illusion that the lava is active.
- The intensity of the Radial Light inside of the volcano should vary in intensity. It can flash or throb, depending on what you want to show.
- A 2D Disk mapped with surface reddish clouds should be set above the calendra of the volcano, to catch the variations in the Radial Light.

- If you like, you can add exploding sparks and lightning flashes, as detailed in previous examples.
- The Lava Planes beneath the volcano should gradually move across the Ground Plane, from the direction that shows the split in the volcano. One by one they should creep out, with some overlapping each other as they move. Given enough frames to take advantage of the slow movement of the lava (no less than a 10-second animation will do), this will create a startling scene (see Figure 17.23).

FIGURE 17.23 Lava spreads across the landscape from an active volcano.

MOVING ON

In this chapter, we covered some interesting animated f/x. In the next chapter, we'll take a look at *Object Animations*.

CHAPTER

18 Object Animation

Animation brings your Bryce objects to life. Although it's interesting to animate the camera and fly around a scenic Bryce world, appreciating the textured landscape as it comes into view, depending upon this alone for sustained audience excitement is not enough. We are storytellers and story-listeners, and we demand empathy with the actors in the stories we tell, not with their environments alone. The actors can be human or animal, robotic, or even basic geometric forms. What they must do, however, is to somehow navigate within the confines of the world in which they live. They must be seen to move on their own, because we intuit that their movement indicates life. There are different classes of object types that can be animated in Bryce. In this chapter, we investigate three general animated object categories: *Singular, Composite,* and *Boolean*.

SINGULAR OBJECT ANIMATIONS

A Singular object is defined as one that cannot be ungrouped to form more than one object element. No matter if primitive-based or imported, Singular objects are the most basic forms that can be animated in Bryce. It's strongly suggested that you keep your use of Primitive objects for structures, and that you use imported objects in your animations. Primitive objects tend to warp and skew more than imported ones, although this is more the case for Composite objects than for noncomposited ones. You can use basic Primitive objects for simple animation tasks, however, and they offer the best way to explore the Bryce animation functions when you are at the start of the learning curve.

The Bryce Primitives

All of the Bryce primitives are Singular objects. Aside from all of the primitives we have already identified as such in Bryce, we should also add the Symmetrical Lattice to this list, because it, too, is a Singular object. Even Terrain objects themselves are Singular objects, and can be used as such (set on an animation path) when they are reconfigured in the Terrain Editor. As standard terrain, however (hills, valleys, and mountains), there is no known need to race them along paths, although even this strange result is allowed. As Singular objects in an animation, Terrain and Symmetrical Lattice objects are usually given a new shape personality in the Terrain Editor first (see Figure 18.1).

FIGURE 18.1 Some examples of a Terrain object and a Symmetrical Lattice object transformed into a suitable form for object animating.

The best Terrain to use for designing a customized object in Bryce is the Symmetrical Lattice, because it appears in the Terrain Editor without a base. This makes it perfect for sculpting into customized shapes.

Linking and Grouping Singular Objects

Linking and Grouping can be used interchangeably if all you are interested in is moving objects around to get a better single shot. However, when used as animation methods, they produce very different results. For more on Grouped and Linked objects, see the section on *Composite Objects* that follows in this chapter. In general, here are the suggested rules:

- If you want the object to act as one unit, Group all of its separate parts. To select any single element in a Grouped object, hold down the Control key when selecting with the mouse.
- When Linking objects together, pay strict attention to hierarchies, and what is a Child of a specific Parent in the chain. Moving, Resizing, or Rotating a Parent always is applied to all of the Children and other offspring (Grandchildren, Great Grandchildren, etc.) in a chain. Moving, Resizing, or Rotating a Child that does not have Children of its own just acts on that Child.
- You can always Link any Singular or Composite object to a stable element in the scene, even if that element is hidden. This element then acts as a global control over the object. For example, Linking an orbiting sphere to a central sphere, and rotating the central sphere, can produce perfect circular orbits. Perfect circular orbits are now possible just by using keyframes to move an object.

- Link a Light to an object if you want the object lit in the same manner no matter where it is or what the global lighting is doing (see Figure 18.2).

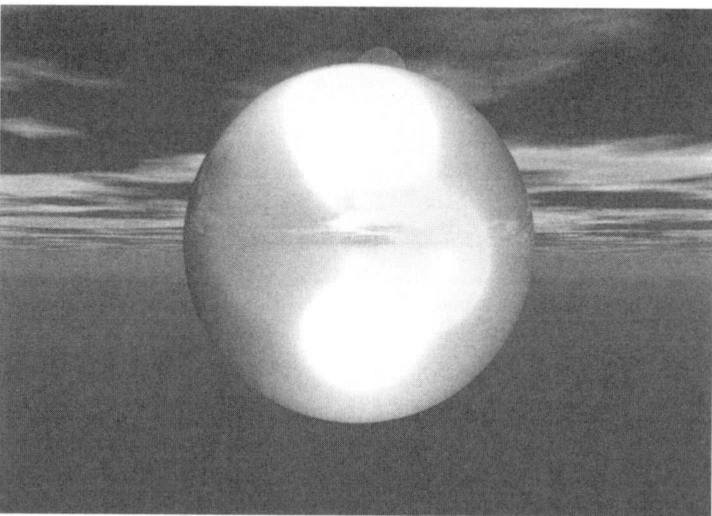

FIGURE 18.2 This globe is illuminated by six separate Spotlights, and each is Linked to the globe. No matter where it moves in the scene, or how dark the scene gets, the Spotlights will remain illuminating the same orientation of the globe.

Singular Objects and Standard Paths

Standard animations paths are created by selecting a new position on the Timeline and rotating, moving, or resizing an object. This automatically creates a new keyframe at that point. This is done automatically with *Auto-Key* switched On. With Auto-Key Off, you must press the Plus Keyframe button to create the new Keyframe. Standard paths are not objects, so they cannot be moved by themselves, nor can they be resized or rotated. They are merely indicators of how the object that created them moves over time.

You can, however, alter the shape of a standard animation path: simply move its control point, the point that creating a keyframe generates. This is useful when you need to alter the path to get around or through other elements in a scene.

MAKING SHARP CORNERS ON A STANDARD ANIMATION PATH

Normally, the shape of a path from one keyframe to the next is either a straight line or a smooth curve. What about creating a sharp corner in an animated movement, however? This can be done very simply: just set two keyframes for the object while it is in the same place. You might have to straighten out a little loop that forms on the path, but you will see that it produces a square corner.

Singular Objects and Ribbon Paths

You do not have to create a path with an object only to make the object move in an animation. Your purpose might be quite different, because the object itself might be dispensable. You might want only the path itself. If this is the case, then create the path by moving the object, and select Create Path from the Object menu while the object is still selected. A new Ribbon path will be created over the standard path. Then, all you have to do is to select the object separately, and select Clear from the Edit menu. Now you have only the path, and as a Ribbon path, it can be manipulated like any other object.

ANIMATING SINGULAR OBJECTS ON RIBBON PATHS

To assign a Singular object to a Ribbon path, simply Link it to the path. You will see it snap to a position on the path. If you move it, it will only move to another position on the path, unless unlinked. It will not, however, use the path as an animation path unless you first set it for specific keyframes on the path. The easiest thing to do is to set its beginning keyframe at the start of the path, and a second keyframe at the path's end. This makes it follow the path from beginning to end in an animation.

In animation, farther equals faster. The farther you move something between two keyframes, the faster the object must go in order to make its targeted destination at that moment. The rule of thumb in noncomputer animations is to move an object only a small amount at a time if you want it to move smoothly, while movements that cover larger distances produce more erratic and jerky movements. This same rule is true when creating computer-based animations. Also remember that on a Ribbon path, an object can reverse or bounce back and forth between any two keyframes, without affecting the path one bit.

The Importance of Origin Points in Animations

There is no more important placement to understand when animating objects (Singular or Boolean), than that of their Origin Point. By now, you are aware that an object's Origin Point can be viewed by toggling it on in the object's Attributes dialog. Doing so turns it green so you can move it. Any Child object Linked to a Parent object is Linked to the parent's Origin Point, so if you move the Origin Point, the Child object points to the new Origin Point's position. It is actually an object's Origin Point that is used to place points on a path when you move the object in a keyframe sequence.

ANIMATING WITH A SINGULAR OBJECT'S ORIGIN POINT

There are two ways to use Origin Point movements on an object to create animations. The first is to animate the object, and the second is to animate any Linked Children.

Origin Point Animation on the Object

An object's Origin Point is its center of rotation, so moving its Origin Point allows it to revolve and be resized from the new placement. You can place the Origin Point inside any other object, and the initial object will then orbit the second object like a planet around a sun. Moving the Origin Point again will give the object a new center of rotation. For example, setting a planet's Origin Point at the center of one "sun" and then moving it to the center of another "sun" would make it orbit first one and then the other in an animation.

Origin Point Animation on an Object's Children

A Linked Child points to a Parent object's Origin Point, so it is that Origin Point that controls the placement of the Child object. Although the Parent object might not manifest movement of its own (like a mountainous terrain), it can be controlled by Child objects by the mere displacement of its Origin Point over time.

If the object is a Terrain object, you can only move its Origin Point once, producing a linear movement in an animation.

Singular Object Animation Tips

When animating Singular objects in Bryce, consider the following:

- Create your initial animation path by keyframing just the start and end first. Then, go back and create keyframes at points where the path has to move around objects, and move the resulting points of the path into place. This usually saves a lot of time, and makes the process clearer to customize.

- Use as few keyframes as possible to prevent jerky jumps in the animation.
- If you want the object to make a sudden or angular move, place two keyframes at the same point on the Timeline and adjust them afterward to remove unwanted loops in the path.
- When adding keyframes to adjust and fine-tune the animation, work with Auto-Key Off. The only time not to do this is when animating the camera, since Auto-Key usually needs to be on to track all of the camera moves and turns.
- Remember that as objects, Ribbon paths can also be linked to other Ribbon paths or objects, and that extremely complex movements can be generated in this manner.
- You must select *Constrain to Path* in the Objects Attributes dialog if you want the Linked object to be on the Parent path. Otherwise, it will relate to the path from whatever distance it is at.
- In the object's Attributes dialog, next to the Constrain to Path check item, is a percentage input area. This tells the object what part of the path it is to be attached to at that keyframe—0% is the start of the path, and 100% is the end. At the start of an animation, when the object is Constrain-Linked to a path, it is common to use a 0% keyframe at the beginning and a 100% keyframe at the end of the animation. This allows the object to make one complete revolution on the path.
- When you Link multiple Singular objects, their Child/Parent hierarchy is all important. For example, you can Link a satellite to a moon, so that rotating the moon rotates the satellite. Link the moon to a planet, so that rotating the planet rotates moon and satellite. Link the planet to a sun, so that rotating the sun rotates the rest of the hierarchy. Then, Link the sun to a proscribed Ribbon path so that everything moves through space while maintaining its own motion.

Solving the Multiple Orbit Speed Problem

Linking multiple children to a central object and rotating that Parent object will cause all of the Children to orbit the parent at the same keyframe rate. Objects further out from the Parent will orbit faster, because they have a longer distance to cover between the start and end of the animation, and objects closer to the Parent will orbit slower for the same reason. But what about planets around a sun? Most times, the rate of their orbits should vary radically, so that some planets orbit a few times while others orbit just once. How can we solve this problem?

Actually, there is more than one way to do it.

- You could just Link everything to appropriate Parent objects, and rotate the Parent as necessary. That, however, would not give you any variance in the orbital speeds of Child objects (planets) positioned around a common Parent.
- You might select to place invisible spheres inside of the Parent (sun) object, and name them as controllers for each Child (planet). That would work to give you specific control over each Child (planet), but it would be a bit cumbersome.
- You could also select to import a circular Ribbon path for each Child (planet). That would work OK, but again, it would be a bit cumbersome. You would also have to make sure that you set the repeats as needed for each Child (planet).
- The best way is to use a combination of Origin Point moves and Links. Use Origin Point moves in every Parent/Child relationship, so that the Child's Origin Point is placed in the center of the Parent object. Then, Link the Child to the Parent. Nothing has to be Linked to the central sun, since moving a Child's Origin Point will do the trick by itself (see Figure 18.3).

FIGURE 18.3 This is a single frame from a Solar System animation, which uses the Origin Point/Link collaboration method.

If an object needs to revolve around its own center as well as around another object, moving the Origin Point might not be the best method. In that case, use another control sphere at the Child object's center, and simply Link it to the Parent.

COMPOSITE OBJECT ANIMATIONS

A Composite object is one made up of grouped elements, which can be ungrouped and relinked in Bryce. The best thing about composite objects is that they can have their own movements, aside from path associated animation. A Composite Spider object, for example, can show all of its legs and antennae moving, while it is also moving on an assigned path. Composite objects are those that we identify most with living forms. You must be knowledgeable concerning Linking methods in Bryce to make full use of Composite objects.

Stay away from composited primitives if possible, because they tend to do strange things when used as animated objects, like flipping object parts around on their own. The best Composite objects you can work with in an animation are those that have been imported as either 3D Studio or WaveFront (OBJ) formats. DXFs work well as animated objects, too, aside from their uncorrectable faceted look (which you might like), but there are sometimes problems in the way that DXF objects are grouped when they are imported. This leads to problems with ungrouping and animated links. If you have a composite DXF object you really like and need in a scene, the best thing to do is to import it into an application that can save it out again in a 3DS, LWO, or OBJ object file format.

Composite Symmetrical Lattice Objects

These objects represent the most complex objects that can be created inside of Bryce. Unlike Terrain objects, Symmetrical Lattice objects have no Base Plane to worry about or erase. Their top and bottom sections are perfectly matched. Using Elevation and Effects brushes in the Terrain Editor, you can create extremely convoluted shapes for compositing into larger objects. The results are rather mechanical, so they work best when used to glue together parts for robotic figures and vehicles. The best thing about using the Terrain Editor and Symmetrical Lattice objects as elements for 3D animated actors is that there is no need to use Boolean operations to shape holes (unless you want to do that in addition to what the Elevation brush offers). It is more common to Group parts of a Symmetrical Lattice composite together than to Link them, as long as no animation is needed within the object itself. If you do require animated parts (flapping wings or moving appendages), then select to Link the parts (see Figure 18.4).

To create Symmetrical Lattice objects with organic folded skin, use the Erode operation on them.

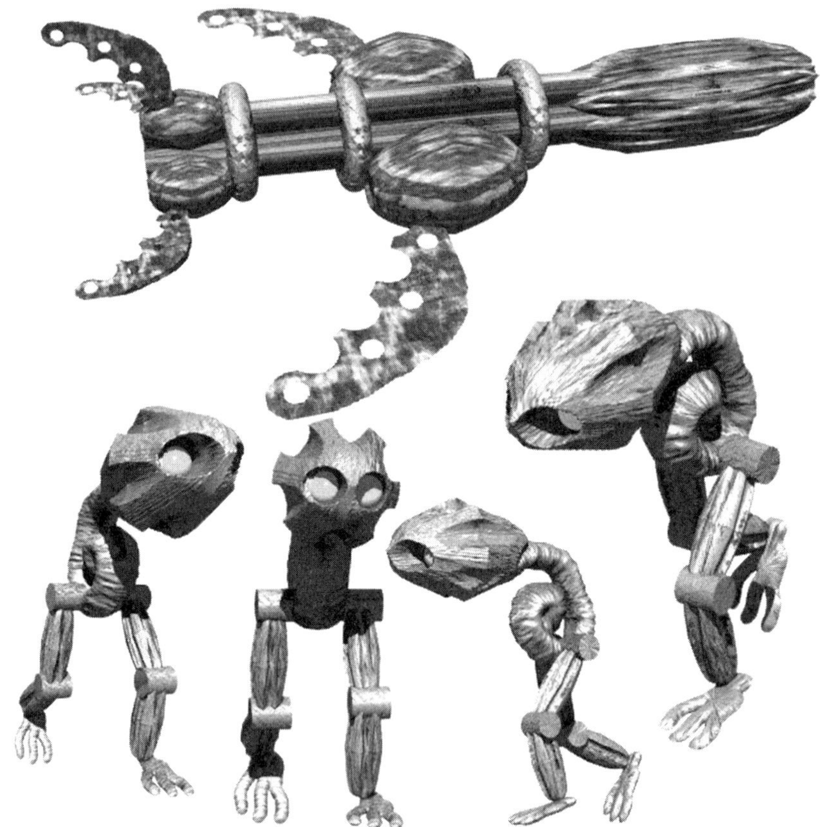

FIGURE 18.4 On the top is a Symmetrical Lattice grouped object, and on the bottom is a Linked object in several views, composed of Symmetrical Lattice parts.

Linking and Grouping Composites

The rule, as previously stated, is simple: If the composite object is to have moving parts, then use Linking to attach the moving elements. All non-moving parts can be Grouped. In general, Grouped objects have more stable behavior than Linked objects, but each Composite object has to be judged on its own. The placement of the Origin Point is absolutely vital for Linking, since that determines the fulcrum point to which the moving element relates.

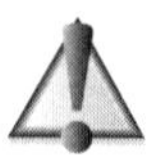

This is extremely important! When you need to clone a Linked chain of objects, select just the main Parent, and use Copy/Paste. Then, you can rename the cloned parts to keep everything clear. Using other methods to clone Linked hierarchies might result in skewed and distorted elements.

Note that grouped elements have no accessible Origin Points. To move a grouped element in a Composite object, first Link it to a sphere as Parent to act as a ball joint, and then rotate the sphere.

Composite Objects and Standard Paths

There are few special rules that apply to Composite objects that don't apply as well to Singular objects. The only caution is that Composite objects can have their own moving parts that have nothing to do with the path of the composited whole. One of the best ways to handle this is to create the animated Composite object first, and save it out as a complete object, including the necessary Timeline information that tells the object what to move and when. When you load it in and alter its rotation, size, or position in the standard path creation manner, you can increase the size of the animation and use the Repeat or Pendulum functions to make the animated object repeat its internal movement while also moving on a path (a common procedure for walking and other motions).

Composite Objects and Ribbon Paths

There are no special rules for Linking a Composite object to a Ribbon path that are not covered in the Standard Path concerns discussed previously.

Composite Object Animation Tips

- Group the parts together when you are designing a Composite object that has no moving parts, like a spaceship. If the object does have moving parts (like the tires of a pickup truck), Link those parts to the whole.
- Pay attention to where you place the Origin Point when Linking one element of a Composite object to the whole.
- Choose one main Parent as the central element when designing a Composite object with moving parts. This is normally the torso on humanoid and most animal forms. This is the element that must be keyframed when the object is to be rotated, scaled, or repositioned on a path. It controls the global rotation, global resizing, and global repositioning of the object and all Linked Child objects.
- When Linking elements of a Composite object together, it is essential that you use spheres or cylinders as ball joint Parents between the moving elements. Linking these elements directly is guaranteed to cause unwanted shearing and warping of the elements.

BOOLEAN OBJECT ANIMATIONS

Boolean animations are f/x-oriented animations, and stand out as a completely separate animation category. In a Boolean animation, an invisible force seems to be present in the animation, causing objects to magically disappear and reappear. There are two types of Boolean animations in Bryce: Negative/Positive, and Intersecting. Each creates a unique effect.

There is one major rule for configuring all Boolean objects and animation elements: Create all of the separate elements first, and tag them as Booleans in the object's Attributes dialog, and following that, group all of the items together that will participate as either object or animation elements.

Negative/Positive Boolean Animations

A typical Negative/Positive Boolean animation shows a Negative Boolean drilling a hole in a Positive Boolean object. This is interesting, but like any f/x, it grows tiring and anticipated after one or two showings. In order to spice up your Negative/Positive Boolean animations, here are some suggestions for creating variations on the theme:

- Use a variety of forms as negative components. Cubes, Cones, Spheres, Rods, and other forms add interest because the holes they drill change size and shape as the animation progresses.
- Stagger a group of Negative Booleans so that as one hole is part way through, another is just beginning.
- Use multiple Negative and Positive Booleans in more complex choreographies, so that unexpected interactions take place.
- Rotate the Positive element(s) so that the viewer sees a hole being started on one end of an object, and also sees the exiting negative on the other end afterward.

Intersecting Boolean Animations

Intersecting Boolean animations do the opposite of Negative/Positive types. They, too, require a Positive Boolean partner or partners, but the Positive object(s) remains hidden until the Intersecting object displays all or part of them. The animated result is stranger, because it reveals something in the 3D world not visible before.

Linking and Grouping Booleans

All of the components that are to take part in a Boolean animation have to be grouped, just as they are in a Boolean object. In fact, you can take any Boolean object and instantly make it into an animation. Simply move the parts closer or farther from each other over time, or rotate or resize them, keyframing as you go.

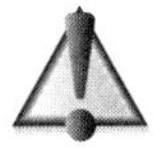

Do not Link elements in a Boolean group to each other, as it will ungroup elements in the group, and destroy the Boolean construct. If you do this by mistake, you might have to clear the screen and start over, since the elements might not be reconfigurable. You can Link the entire group to an object not in the group, however.

Boolean Objects and Standard Paths

There are no special rules for creating animation paths with Boolean objects. Any member of a Boolean group can be repositioned, resized, or rotated over time and keyframed to form an animated sequence. It is only the interactions of the members within the Boolean group that will cause Boolean interactions to be displayed as the animation progresses.

Boolean Objects and Ribbon Paths

As stated previously, no special considerations are needed when using Boolean groups on a Ribbon path.

When to Use Boolean Animation Techniques

Here are some project ideas that give you some sense of where Boolean animations might be useful.

- **Beam-me-up/Beam-me-down.** Using a light source with a visible beam pointed at an object that sits on the ground, you can use a Negative/Positive Boolean animation to make the object seem to be vaporized in the beam. Using an Intersect Boolean method would work to make an object suddenly materialize out of thin air.
- **Laser-cutter.** Shine a column light on an area of an object, and use a Negative/Positive Boolean to cut a hole where the beam makes contact.
- **Set the table.** Design a dishes and utensils setting that sits on a table. Group each place setting as Positive Booleans, along with a Negative Boolean object large enough to cover each. In an animation, slowly move the Negative Booleans to reveal the settings slowly materializing.
- **Flicker-flames.** Wherever you use flames that need to be animated, whether from a candle wick or the nozzle of a rocket engine, think

about using Boolean interactions. If you make the flame object Positive and group it with a Negative Boolean, you can control the size and seeming flicker of the flame over time.

The strangest animated results can be generated when you use all three Boolean types in one group: Positive, Negative, and Intersecting. Imagine, the computer is calculating that the Positive object can only be seen when it is covered by the Intersecting object, but the Negative object wants to hide it at the same time. You will find that size wins out. If the Intersecting or Negative shell is larger than the other, it will affect the Positive object in a dominant manner at those junctures. Experiment with this technique. At the very least, your animation will be unique.

The Camera Drill

Here is a perfect use for Negative/Positive Boolean techniques. Do the following.

1. Create a series of five Cubes that are lined up in front of the camera, so that the closest one hides the rest. Color all of the Cubes with a different hue. Reshape each of them so they are wider and longer than they are deep, and separate them by a space equal to their depth. Make each of them Positive Booleans.
2. Place a Cone primitive in the scene so that its apex faces in the same direction as the camera. Make it a Negative Boolean, and Group it with all of the resized rectangles. This cone is our drill.
3. As seen from the Top view, place the camera just inside of the base of the Cone. Do not Link or otherwise Group it. Place a Spotlight in front of the camera (100% intensity and fade, with Linear drop-off, and colored as you like). Link the Spotlight to the camera. This is like the lamp on a miner's hat, lighting the hole that the Cone drills.
4. This is very important. If you were to Link the camera to the Cone drill, it would warp, due to the rotation and resizing of the Cone. From the Top view (or the Right or Left view), select just the Cone from the Group (Control/Click after selecting the Group). With the Cone selected, shift-select the camera. Now the camera, Cone drill, and Spotlight will move as one, as long as you use the position controls and not the mouse to move this group of objects.
5. Place some sort of treasure scene beyond the walls, so that when the hole breaks through, the camera has something to look at. Start the animation with the camera behind all of the walls, and end it at a point where the camera drill breaks through, and you can only see the treasure. This same technique can be used to drill through a

mountain or any other "solid" object. If you want to see textures as the drill goes along, it is best used with Volumetric objects, as long as you are aware that this takes up a lot of rendering time (see Figures 18.5 and 18.6).

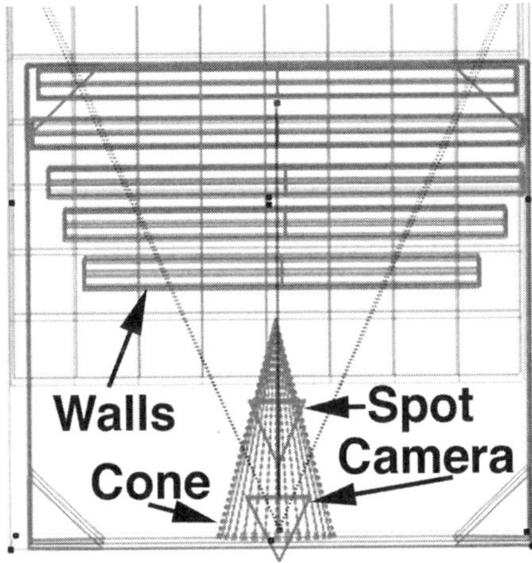

FIGURE 18.5 This is a Top view of the Camera Drill project.

FIGURE 18.6 The Camera Drill moves through a series of walls to reveal the treasure on the other side.

The Moving Pen

The "Moving pen" animation shows a moving pen, pencil, chalk, or brush that seems to be magically writing as it moves with no hand attached. This animation is a perfect place to use Boolean Intersections in Bryce, since what is displayed is at first hidden. Simply create the "message" first, and make it a Positive Boolean object. Next, create your writing implement. As it passes over selected parts of the message, use an Intersection Boolean, grouped with the message, to display the text.

MOVING ON

In this chapter, we explored some of the ways to think about animating various objects. In the next chapter, we'll delve into the intricacies of the Motion Lab.

CHAPTER

19 The Advanced Motion Lab

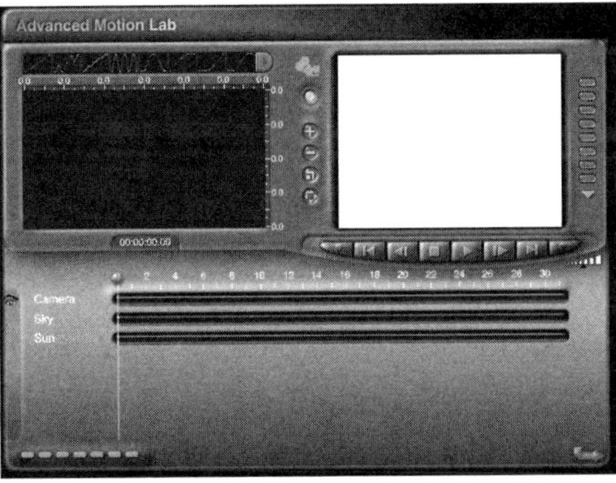

The Advanced Motion Lab is another of the special editing interfaces in Bryce. It allows you to customize animations much like the Materials Lab and the Editor allow you to alter materials and terrains. The Advanced Motion Lab has animation controls for every aspect of your Bryce world. The Advanced Motion Lab represents the final step in customizing your Bryce animations. Although you can input some parameters for controlling your animations under the Animation tab in an object's Attributes dialog, and also by selective keyframing (accessed by holding down the Plus or Minus buttons), it is far better to do all of your animation fine-tuning in the Advanced Motion Lab. This is because everything is at your fingertips, and you are presented with an instant preview of any alterations made. It's also because there are animation tools here that can be found nowhere else.

MASTERING THE INTERFACE

The Advanced Motion Lab is activated when you click on its icon in the Animation palette (see Figure 19.1).

It is important for both experienced and new Bryce users to spend some time getting acclimated to the new options presented in the Advanced Motion Lab interface, as shown in Figure 19.2.

FIGURE 19.1 The Advanced Motion Lab icon.

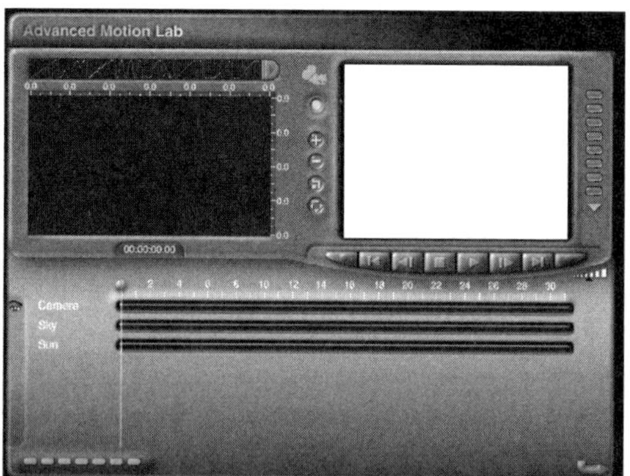

FIGURE 19.2 The Advanced Motion Lab interface has three basic sections: Motion Wave Assignments, Preview/Playback Screen, and Object/Item Selection.

Motion Wave Assignments

This is the central control feature, the heart of the Advanced Motion Lab. By clicking on any of the wave thumbnails, that particular wave shape is placed on the screen below. From there, you can move the shape's control points to reshape it, or use the Pencil tool that appears when the mouse is over a nonshape area to draw your own wave. All customized wave shapes can be saved to an empty slot in the thumbnail section simply by clicking on that empty slot.

Each wave shape determines the movement of the selected object or item over time. The bottom border of the shape shows the selected item's attribute at the start of the animation, while the top border is the last frame of the animation. The left-right parameter shows the time from the first to last frame. A noncustomized wave shape would be a straight diagonal line that travels from bottom left to upper right. This would cause the selected object or item attribute to move from whatever setting you dictated at the start of the animation smoothly to its targeted attribute at the end of the animation. If, for example, an object's color was set as red at the start of the animation and blue at the end, setting this default wave shape would show a steady movement from red to blue as the animation progressed.

Understanding at a glance what different wave shapes force an attribute to do is necessary for the mastery of Motion Wave Assignments. Let's take our previous example. What if you wanted an object's color to move evenly from red to blue and back to red in an animation, although you only assigned it red at the start and blue at the end? Do you have to reassign the colors all over again? No. You simply have to apply the appropriate motion wave in the object's Color Attributes channel. In this case, the proper motion wave would be a smooth curve that started at the lower left (the object's Color channel assigned to red), moved at the middle of the animation to the top (the object's Color channel equated with the assigned blue color), and finished at the lower right (back to red again). Any attribute listed in the object's Attributes channels could be played with in the same manner.

UNDERSTANDING MOTION WAVE SHAPES

Remember that Motion Waves can only customize attributes that have at least two set keyframes in an animation, assigned normally while you are creating the animation. The Advanced Motion Lab can therefore be thought of as a secondary or post-creation process.

With a little exploration and time spent in the Advanced Motion Lab, you will begin to see exactly how the shape you import or create will affect the selected object or item attribute. Starting with the default assignment, the straight diagonal line that moves from lower left to upper right, you can learn to "see" time. Here are some pointers to observe:

- If lowest points assign starting attribute conditions to the selected object or item, and the topmost point assigns a targeted state, then points in the middle of any line or curve indicate a blend of the two conditions. In our previous example of color animation, a mid-point would force the object to be a blend of red and blue.
- Vertical lines force the object to move very quickly between the assigned attributes. In the case of colors, for example, straight vertical lines in your wave shape will cause them to flash. Many vertical lines in the wave shape will cause the attributes to change quickly and repeatedly.
- Straight horizontal lines in your wave shape will cause the selected attribute to remain stable at that state. In our color example, a horizontal line at the middle of the wave would cause the object to remain at a set red-blue color for the amount of time indicated by the length of the horizontal line.
- Small fluctuations in a motion wave will cause the selected object attribute to fluctuate between the lower and upper points of the smaller curve. Assigned to a color attribute, an object or light would flash just a bit. Assigned to a brightness attribute, a light would dim and brighten. Assigned to a position attribute, an object or item would take steps back and forth, although moving gradually toward a targeted position. All other attributes would be treated in a similar manner.
- If you go past the vertical when moving control points, the curve will be reshaped as a smooth curve containing the points of the vertical line. This prevents a non-allowed time reversal.

Preview/Playback Screen

The Preview/Playback screen allows you to preview whatever adjustments you are making to the animation. The VCR controls below are the same as those you have grown accustomed to in the Animation palette, and in the Terrain Editor and Materials Lab.

Object/Item Selection Options

There are three categories listed here for selected objects, Sky, and Sun. Each of the three can be expanded by simply clicking on their name in the list. Object options are included for every animated object in your scene, including the camera and any lights. The parameters of a selected item must be animated, so that the way the animation unfolds can be tweaked in the Advanced Motion Lab. If an object's position, for example, is not animated over time, but its rotation is, then you can only customize its animated rotation in the Advanced Motion Lab. All animated attributes can be reconfigured in the Advanced Motion Lab.

OBJECT ATTRIBUTE OPTIONS

Using the Advanced Motion Lab Motion Curves, you can alter the selected object's Position, Rotation, Scale, Shear, Origin, or Material, by selecting that attribute in the Object/Item list.

Material Attribute Options

When you need to alter an object's Material, a separate Attribute list becomes available. You can alter every item in the material's Color, Value, and Optics channel attributes. As you might expect, all of the attributes in a volumetric material's attributes can be customized as well.

CAMERA ATTRIBUTE OPTIONS

The camera attributes that can be Motion Graph influenced in the Advanced Motion Lab include Position, Origin, Rotation, Banking, Focal Length, Pan XY, and Zoom XY.

LIGHT ATTRIBUTE OPTIONS

If your selected object is a light, the following attributes can be animation tweaked in the Advanced Motion Lab: Position, Rotation, Scale, Shear, Origin, Color, and Intensity.

Sky Options

Remember that Sky options are keyframed when nothing else is selected in your scene. There are 34 sky attributes that can be animation customized in the Advanced Motion Lab by applying or creating a Motion Graph. You could also do this by assigning multiple keyframes from the Sky&Fog palette, but it would take a lot longer. All you need to access these parameters in the Advanced Motion Lab is to have assigned a beginning and ending keyframe in the animation

Sun Options

Using the Advanced Motion lab and a Motion Wave, you can alter the Sun's color, intensity, Disc and Halo colors, and direction.

Complicated Motion Sandwiches

This is one of the most important methods that you can use three different animation setting options in Bryce to cooperatively alter the movements of your animated objects, camera, and/or lights. It involves the Animation Setup dialog, the Animation tab settings from the Attributes dialog, and the Advanced Motion Lab. All three of these setup areas can work together to influence how selected objects move in your Bryce world. The order in which you do things however, is vital. Your priority should be:

1. Length of animation setting in the Animation Setup dialog .
2. Animation tab of the object's Attributes dialog.
3. Return to length of animation setting in the Animation Setup dialog .
4. Advanced Motion Lab settings

Here's why this order of operation is important. Let's say you have a sphere on the screen that is to be animated. The movement it goes through is determined to be one second long at 15 fps. You would first set that animation length in the Animation Setup dialog. Next, the sphere would be moved on whatever path you create from its initial frame to the last frame.

Following that, with the object selected, you would open its Attributes dialog, and go to the Animation tab. There, you might click on Make Pendulum. If it takes one second for the sphere to traverse from its initial position to its end position, Make Pendulum means that it will take two seconds for it to travel from the target position back to the source. But with only one second as the length of the animation so far, the sphere has just enough time to travel only once from source to target, so we have to lengthen the animation.

Therefore, we open the Animation Setup dialog again, and this time make the animation eight seconds long. How will this affect the sphere? Well, since we have Make Pendulum checked, and since it will take the sphere two seconds to make one pendulum swing from source to target and back again, it will repeat this process four times (8/2) for the length of the animation.

Now, to complicate the issue even more. With all of the preceding done, we bring the lozenge on the Timeline back to the start of the animation, and open the Advanced Motion Lab. The sphere is listed there as whatever name you have given it. Clicking on that name opens up all of the sphere's attributes for animation. Since all we have done is to change the sphere's position, we click on the sphere's Position tab. In the Motion Graph Display, a straight diagonal line is shown. This means that the sphere is set to move from its initial position to its end position over the length of the animation, even though the Make Pendulum option is not indicated on the graph.

Selecting the triple sine wave graph will force the chosen attribute of the sphere, its position, to move from initial to target position back and forth six times in the animation. Since Pendulum is already indicated in the object's own Attributes dialog, this means the pendulum effect will also be multiplied. This makes the object move faster between the initial and target points 18 times during the animation, or 3 × 6. Why 18? The first number 3 is the number of times it would have moved anyway, due to the Pendulum setting. The 6 used as a multiplier comes from the Motion Graph applied to whatever is happening on the sphere's path during the animation; in this case, three sine waves. Each sine wave, however, will move the sphere twice, once on the upward curve and once on the downward curve.

If you read this and remain confused, the only (and best) way to get a clear idea of what is going on is to explore the possibilities by doing the project in Bryce. There are infinite variations, dependent upon the length of the animation, an object's Animation Attributes, and the quality of the Motion Graph applied in the Advanced Motion Lab.

If you have multiple objects in your animated scene that need to be targeted for more complex movements as in the preceding example, their initial movements should be set before the final animation length is set so they repeat according to the final Advanced Motion lab settings.

SUGGESTED PROJECTS TO EXPLORE

The following project ideas are left up to you to consider and explore. All make use of the options made possible in the Advanced Motion Lab that you learned about previously. Using your learned skills in the Advanced Motion Lab, see how you can complete the following project ideas.

Pulsar

A Pulsar is a star that pulses in brightness and sometimes in color as well. The solution is based on altering the Sun's color and brightness attributes.

Piston

A piston is an object that moves up and down on an attached rod. The solution in creating a piston motion cycle is in the application of the piston's position attribute.

Pendulum

A pendulum swings back and forth on an attached line. Over time, the pendulum's swing deteriorates because of friction and other forces. The pendulum can be made to deteriorate by adjusting the shape of the curve used to address the line's rotation in the Advanced Motion Lab.

Canon Ball

A projectile shot from a muzzle has a trajectory that is defined by the force of ejection and the way that gravity pulls on the mass of the projectile. This changes the projectile's path in space. The force works to fire the projectile in a straight line at its maximum height, but gravity seeks to bring it to the ground. By adjusting the projectile's position over time in the Advanced Motion Lab, you can alter its animated motion curve.

Start the motion curve as a horizontal straight line to represent the minimal lack of gravity.

Putt-Putt

A vehicle might exhibit a start and stop motion when it's running out of gas or in other trouble, although it might eventually reach its destination. By programming stop points in an animation in the Advanced Motion Lab, you can achieve this effect.

Using short, horizontal, straight lines in the motion curve stops motion-intermittently.

Dual State

Some objects look good as a blend of two diverse materials, remaining that way over time. Create an object that is a blend of wood and glass, without blending the materials in the Materials Lab.

Schizo-Clouds

For a strange effect, clouds can reverse their movement across the sky a number of times in an animation. Use the Sky item in the Advanced Motion Lab to create this effect.

MOVING ON

In this chapter, we explored the Advanced Motion Lab. The next chapter is the last one in the Animation part of the book: *Advanced Animation Techniques*.

CHAPTER

20 Advanced Animation Techniques

ANIMATING APPENDAGES

Whether you build creatures in Bryce using available object primitives, import them from CD-ROM collections, or bring in Poser figures, you are going to be faced with linking the parts so you can develop animated characters. Unless you link the parts of an animated figure together in the correct fashion, all sorts of unpleasant warping and skewing of the parts will occur.

Mastering Animated Links

There is a new term that you should become familiar with, in order to optimize your animation work in Bryce: *Appendage Control*. An Appendage Control is an object, most commonly a sphere, inserted between the moving Child object in a linked hierarchy and its Parent (see Figures 20.1 and 20.2).

It is advisable to remove the "neck" from a Poser figure, and substitute a visible spherical Appendage Control in its place.

If the spherical Appendage Controls are visible, they should be resized so that they are not obvious on the finished model.

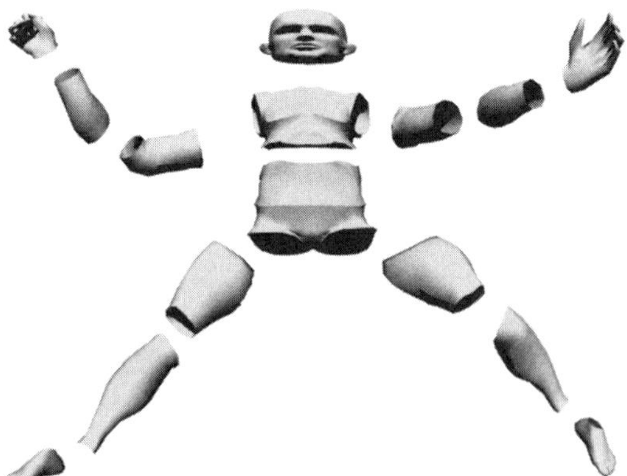

FIGURE 20.1 Here is an imported Poser figure with all of its parts ungrouped and ready for linking.

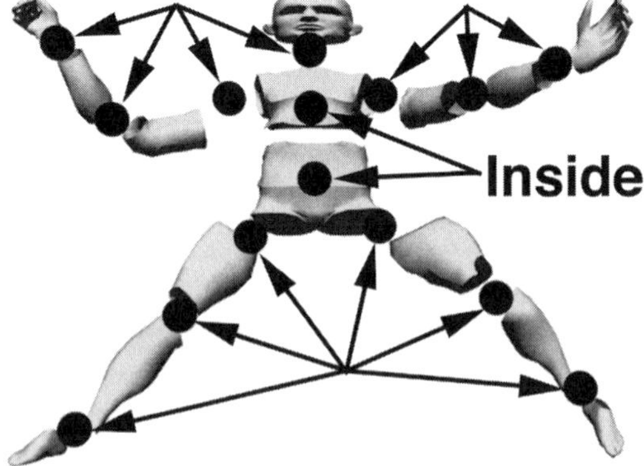

FIGURE 20.2 Spherical Appendage Controls are inserted in the Poser figure as indicated, between the linked parts. In many cases, the spherical Appendage Controls are textured with the same material as the parts linked together, or they can even be made invisible.

HOW TO LINK APPENDAGE CONTROLS

This information is absolutely vital, and not even hinted at in the Bryce documentation.

When you link the parts of a model together that has Appendage Controls inserted, *do not* link the Appendage Controls to objects in the hierarchy. Let's take a hand-lower arm-upper arm example. Link the hand to the Appendage Control between the hand and the lower arm. Link the Appendage Control between the hand and lower arm to the Appendage Control between the lower and upper arm. Link the lower arm to the Appendage Control between the lower and upper arm. Link the Appendage Control between the lower and upper arm to the Appendage Control that is between the upper arm and the body. Finally, Link the upper arm to the Appendage Control that is between the upper arm and the body. When you are set to create keyframes based on the rotation of the parts, select the Appendage Controls for rotation, and not their associated body parts. This gives you smooth animated movement with no warping or skewing of the parts.

Name all of the Appendage Controls to fit their task. For example, "LhandC," "LowerLArmC," and so forth.

ALWAYS USE APPENDAGE CONTROLS

There are times when you can go without using Appendage Controls inserted between the hierarchical parts of your animated object, but they are rare. because Bryce does not have a "Bones" utility (a way of allowing you to move object parts without separating them first), and because in most cases rotated elements can warp and deform, it is necessary to insert intervening control elements.

Visible or Invisible

Appendage Controls are invisible most of the time (see the section on *Null Objects* later in this chapter). There might be times, however, when you want them to be visible. If they are objects that are part of a larger collection of objects for example, they can act as the master choreographer, so their movements visibly influence the movements of others in the collection or tribe. The advantage of making them invisible is that their shape need not have anything to do with the animated objects you want the audience to see. Usually, invisible Appendage Controls are spheres or cylinders, but any object will do.

Why would you make Appendage Controls visible? There are two reasons. First, you might notice that when a specific appendage, an arm or leg part, is rotated past about 20 degrees, an obvious split becomes apparent. It might look as if the part has separated from its Parent element. In this case, the Appendage Control (usually a sphere) can serve as a material fill-in object, so no split in the object takes place. The other reason for making the Appendage Control visible is when the rotating appendage is a grouped element, so no movement of the Origin Point is possible. In that case, the grouped element rotates around its center, which is usually not the place you want it to. An Appendage Control element is always desirable in this situation, and since without it an obvious split in the parts takes place, the Appendage Control element is made visible and textured with the same material as one or both of the connecting parts.

PROPAGATION: WHAT IT IS, AND WHEN TO USE IT

The Propagation toggles are the four options under the Linking member name in the Animation tab of the object's Attributes dialog. They appear when you set the linked Parent's name. They are Distance, Offset, Rotation, and Size. They take any or all of these attributes from what you do to the Parent. If you activate Rotation, for example, you will rotate the Linked child when the Parent of that Child is rotated. If Size is activated, then resizing the Parent will also resize the Child object accordingly. Propagation components are hereditary traits that tell the object what it will inherit from its Parent object.

Although each object can offer its own complications where animated parts are concerned, switching Size off on animated Child elements prevents warping of appendages in most instances.

It's always best to select the propagation features you want before moving an object into place in a hierarchical chain. If you do all sorts of moving and rotation first, the object will have to be resized and repositioned after it is Linked, because of propagation components.

Primitive Constructs

There is a way to animate Primitive objects that are not grouped to minimize potential problems later. This consists of turning Rotation and Size Propagation Off in all Child objects. Child objects can be rotated singly by moving their Origin Points to a fulcrum position, usually at the top center of the Child object. This makes it more effort to set the keyframes (since the Child objects of the rotated element do not automatically rotate), but results in a distortion-free animation.

This same method can be used on some imported objects that have been ungrouped, although each case might react differently.

Save the resizing of object primitives until after the Linking and positioning has been accomplished. Resizing a Parent will move the Child objects in the chain, however, as long as Distance and Offset propagations are switched On.

Origin Points can be animated to smooth over unwanted anomalies that result when object parts are rotated at different angles.

Imported Models

Try not to work with imported DXF models that are to be animated. There are dozens of DXF formats, and some cause strange relationships amongst their elements when they are ungrouped. Work with 3DS (3D Studio), OBJ (Alias WaveFront), or LWO (LightWave) models whenever possible in Bryce.

Some models that you import will not be open to ungrouping. Ungroupable models are not suitable for animation, because there is no way to move their elements separately. One solution is to take them apart in a separate 3D modeling application, and export them again to Bryce.

Conglomerate Objects

What is a Conglomerate object or model? It is any object or model made up of a mix of parts, either from separate models, or between Bryce object primitives and imported components. Because there are an infinite number of ways that Conglomerate objects can be stitched together, many problems can crop up when the object is animated. In general, here are some rules to keep in mind when creating a Conglomerate object whose parts are to be animated:

- Always use Appendage Controls between elements if either one of the elements is a Grouped object.
- Don't forget to move the Origin Point of selected elements so that rotation takes place around the correct axis fulcrum.

- Use the Advanced Motion Lab whenever possible to apply suitable and/or repetitive Motion Curves to the selected elements. This saves a lot of time and handwork.

The Conglomerate Linking and Modeling methods described here are also valuable when working with the animal models from Poser.

COLLECTING BODY PARTS

This sounds like a rather macabre practice at first hearing, but it is a rather benign activity. What it means is that in order to create interesting composite animated models, you have to have interesting parts. The most common parts to collect, and store in the Bryce Objects Library, are wings and heads, followed in order by anything else that interests you (see Figure 20.3).

FIGURE 20.3 These dove's wings were imported from a separate 3D model, ungrouped, and added to this sphere and animated.

Linked Material Shells

Just as clouds can be mapped to an outer sphere that revolves around a Planet object, any object can also have its own outer shell. Shells can be used for clothing on a human figure, or more esoteric looks. You can, for example, wrap a shell on a human, animal, or robotic figure and map it with a fuzzy light, giving the figure a perceptible aura as it moves in the scene (see Figures 20.4 and 20.5).

FIGURE 20.4 A Linked cloud shell revolves around a planet.

FIGURE 20.5 Steel Cage, Dali Bee Stripes, and Random Basic material shells are Linked as a shell over a Poser figure.

When building a shell for a Poser figure, it's best to select the parts in the grouped model one by one to enlarge them before apply a material. Otherwise, the parts will not fit correctly over the entire figure.

USING NULL OBJECTS

A Null object might be a brand new concept to you; besides being a word you've never heard before, you are sure you haven't used them in Bryce. However, if you worked through the previous section in this chapter concerning Appendage Controls, you have already begun using one type of Null object: Appendage Controls. A Null object is any object in a scene that has power over other objects or facets of an animation without itself having to be rendered. Null objects are usually invisible, and vital for certain animation actions and effects.

Types of Null Objects

There can be an infinite array of Null objects, but for our purposes in Bryce, let's classify five important ones: Appendage Controls, Gravity Wells, Negative and Intersecting Booleans, Camera Targets, and Propagation Engines.

APPENDAGE CONTROLS

We have already investigated Appendage Controls in the first part of this chapter. Appendage Controls, especially when they are made invisible in their Attributes dialog, are perfect examples of a Null object. They control every aspect of an animated figure without being noticed in the rendering.

GRAVITY WELLS

A Gravity Well Null is an object, usually not rendered, that controls a number of moving object in a scene. A Gravity Well Null can simulate the power of a black hole or a super-magnet, attracting and influencing objects that are Linked to it. As a core Parent object, its effects can be seen, while the Null object itself remains hidden.

A Gravity Well Experiment

Here is a basic Null Gravity Well animation that you can create to study this effect: Do the following:

1. Create a Positive Boolean Cube, drilled from the top by a Negative Boolean Cylinder to create the well. Use a Stone material on the Cube, and a basic red on the Cylinder.
2. Place a Radial Light at the bottom of the well, tinted yellow at a 50% intensity, to give the well some depth character.
3. Make the project a 150-frame animation, 30 for at 5 seconds.
4. In frame 1, create a sphere that sits in the air above the well. Create a Cube, which will be our Null object, at the mid-point of the well. Link the Sphere to the Cube. Note that this Null cube can be visible because it is hidden in the well.

5. Move the Null cube from the mid-point of the well at frame 1 to the bottom of the well at the last frame. This will pull the sphere along with it.
6. On the last frame, make sure the Sphere is in the well so it cannot be seen by the camera. Stretch the Sphere in the last frame to four times its vertical height. This makes the Sphere look like it is being distorted by the pull of the well as it is being drawn into it.

   Render the animation, and save it to disk.

NEGATIVE AND INTERSECTING BOOLEANS

By their very nature and actions, Boolean Negative and Intersecting objects are Null objects. They are invisible, but their influence on the Positive objects grouped with them is readily apparent in a rendering.

INVISIBLE TARGETS

Objects, lights, or the camera can be Linked to a Null object to control their movement, rotation, and other animation factors. In addition, a Null object can be used as a target for the camera, so that instead of moving the camera itself to create an animation path, you can move the target. This forces the camera to follow along, and many times, it's easier to do than moving the actual camera. This is especially useful if you have a scene, perhaps a room, full of objects that you want to focus on one at a time. By using an invisible Null object as a target for the camera, you can pause on different objects as long as necessary, before moving on to the next one. This would be extremely complicated to do by moving the camera itself.

DISPERSION ENGINES

We already investigated the Dispersion tool in the Edit toolbar. You know that by using the Dispersion routines, you can act on any number of selected objects. Why use a Null object to control dispersed objects?

If you select a number of objects and disperse them, they remain single objects if they are not grouped. As single objects, using the Rotation tool on them rotates them in place, around their own Origin Points. Grouping them and using the Rotation tool rotates them around a common Origin Point (see the Disnull animation on the CD-ROM). Using a Null object that every member of the group is Linked to gives you both options. With the Null object selected, using the Rotation tool rotates all of the objects around the Null's Origin Point. Because the objects remain

ON THE CD

ungrouped, however, Marquee-selecting all of the objects also allows you to rotate the objects individually around their own Origin Points. This gives you the best of both options (see Figure 20.6).

FIGURE 20.6 This collection of dispersed floating cubes is rotation controlled by a hidden Null object.

NULL MATERIAL PALETTES

Here's a novel use for Null objects. You might have the occasion to need to copy a selection of materials already used in your scene to more than one additional object. You can find the object that has the required material, Select it, Copy its material, Select the Target object, and Paste the material. All of that is doable, but it takes time. Using a Null palette method, you can accomplish this task much quicker. Just use a portion of your workspace that is not included in the rendering to set up as many Null objects as you need, naming them according to their materials. Select them by name when you need to Copy/Paste materials, and proceed with the Copy/Paste operations. You can save them out with the scene for future reference.

PARTIALLY AND TOTALLY VISIBLE NULLS

Null objects can be rendered along with your other objects in a scene if you want them to be. Just turn off the "Hidden" item in the Null object's

Attributes dialog, and treat them the way you would treat any other object (making them display a material and other light-sensitive attributes). This is especially effective when the Null object is of a different type than the objects linked to it. A Null cloud, for example, can be used to control the rotation and path movements of a flock of birds. The viewer is less likely to suspect the cloud as having this power than he would a bird leading the pack. When you do make a Null object visible in the render, try to shape it into an object that the viewer does not suspect as the controlling influence.

THE CANNON

The concept that "a strong defense initiates the creation of a stronger offense" has proven itself out in wars for millennia. Let's use Bryce to create a cannon that can knock down barriers in an animated scene. Open Bryce, and do the following:

Creating the Cannon

1. Create the wooden part of the base of the cannon by stacking three rectangular Blocks on each other as shown in Figure 20.7. Map with your choice of a Wood material. Duplicate for the other side.
2. Add the rectangular metal part of the base, mapped with a darker metal and a Bump mapped texture to make it look a bit scratchy and worn (see Figure 20.8).
3. In 3D design, you can do something that is very difficult using simple elements. We had an inkling of an idea that we could build a very realistic cannon barrel out of Tori primitives. The entire plan centered on the way that the Edit Object window addresses the Torus in Bryce (see Figure 20.9).
4. You can slide the mouse cursor back and forth in this window to alter the separation between the two radii that make up the Torus, creating

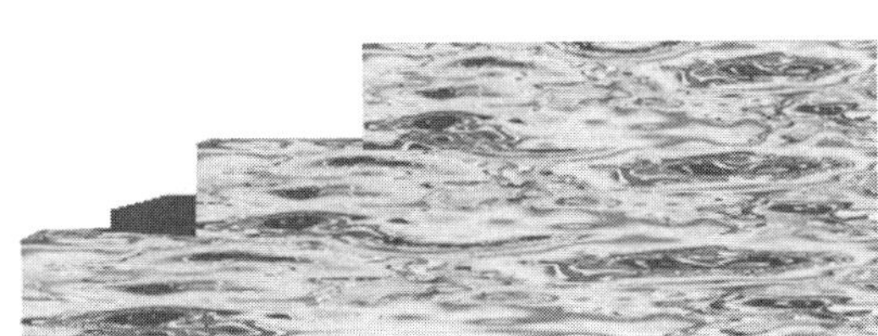

FIGURE 20.7 The wood base.

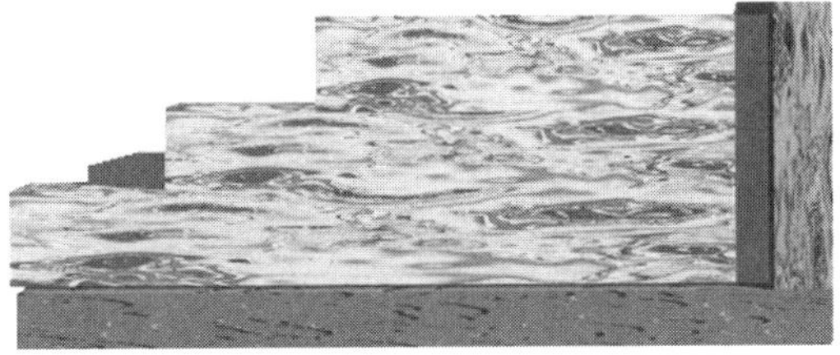

FIGURE 20.8 Add a darker metalized part of the base.

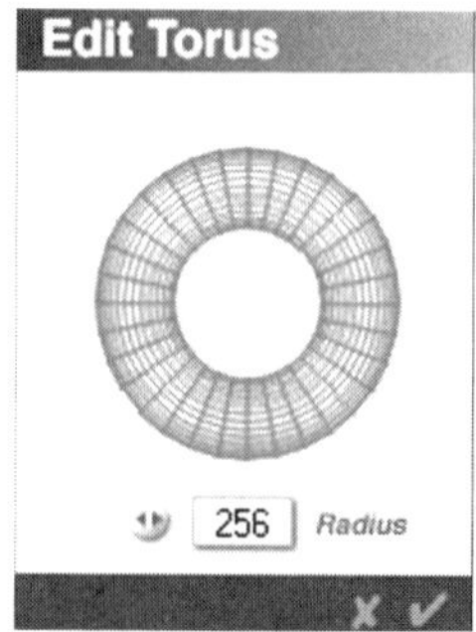

FIGURE 20.9 The Edit Object window for a Torus.

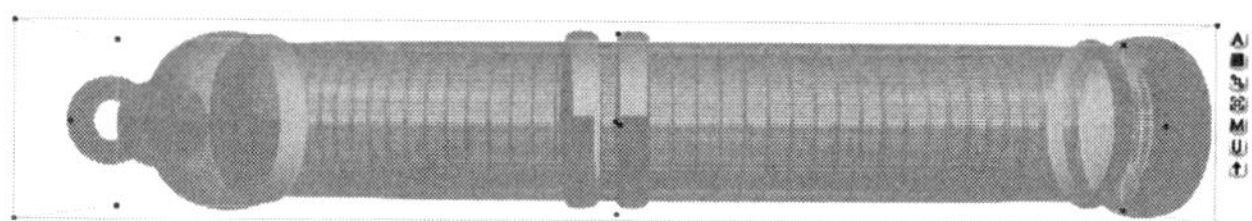

FIGURE 20.10 Create this form, composed of nothing but primitive and scaled Tori.

object from thin "O" rings to squashed spheroids. Explore that process with multiple Tori to create the form shown in Figure 20.10, a grouped model built entirely from Bryce Tori.

5. When set in place on the base and rendered, the cannon will look much better! (See Figure 20.11.)
6. Place a Symmetrical Lattice in the workspace and go to the Terrain Editor. Select New, and create the form shown in Figure 20.12, which is one-half of the frame at the back of the gun carriage.
7. Duplicate, Flip on the X-axis, and Group the two sides of the frame (name it "Frame"). Place as shown in Figure 20.13.
8. Add two cylindrical pivots and an axle as shown in Figure 20.14.
9. Create a wheel in the Terrain Editor from a Symmetrical Lattice. Create a wheel with spokes from another one (see Figure 20.15).

FIGURE 20.11 Place the new barrel on the base.

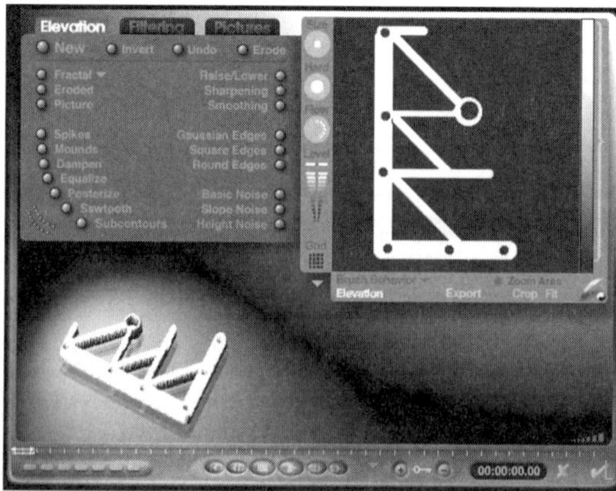

FIGURE 20.12 Create this form.

FIGURE 20.13 The frame is placed on the back of the carriage.

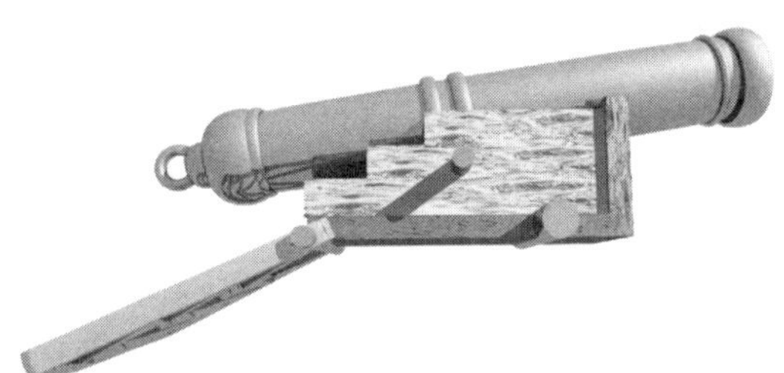

FIGURE 20.14 Add two pivots and an axle.

10. Make the spoked wheel a bit less deep than the second wheel, and place the spoked wheel inside the other wheel. This creates a composite wheel. Group, naming it *wheel*. Use small yellow spheres at the end of the spokes for studs. Group the studs to the wheel. Position, and duplicate for the other side (see Figure 20.16).

FIGURE 20.15 Create two wheels with spokes.

FIGURE 20.16 Views of the finished cannon.

11. Create an Infinite Ground Plane, and use a Grassy Plane material on it (World Space mapping). Create something in the background for the cannon to target. We used a walled fortress, created inside Bryce from primitives. Place a suitable material on your target. If you prefer, place a character near the cannon. We used an Amorphium character, but a riousLabs' Poser character will work, too. Create a sky backdrop. Place some suitably sized cannon balls on the ground (see Figure 20.17).

Animating this Project

There are four animated elements that are used to give life to this scene, and all start as primitive spheres. They are the Cannon Muzzle Flash, the animated Cannon Ball, the Explosion Flash, and a Negative Boolean Sphere that cuts away at the distant object (in this case, the wall around the tower). When you create explosions and flashes in Bryce, give your object a 0-0-0 dimension all the way up to the explosion of the flash frame, and then drop it to 0 again after the first flash frame. Keyframe animate the cannon ball on its path to the target. Just as it strikes the target, give it a 0 dimension in the next frame so it disappears. Make the target (in this case, the wall) a Positive Boolean, and create a Negative Boolean from a sphere sized to represent the hole in the wall. Group them. Move the Negative Boolean into position after the explosion (see Figure 20.18).

FIGURE 20.17 The finished scene.

FIGURE 20.18 A series of frames from the animation, showing the muzzle flash, travelling ball, explosion, and the resulting hole in the fortress wall.

MOVING ON

In this chapter, we explored some advanced techniques for Linking animations and using Null objects. The next chapter includes two more projects you can explore.

CHAPTER

21 Two Projects

A KPT FRAXFLAME PROJECT

To work along with this tutorial, you will need Bryce (obviously), and the Corel KPT5 plug-in filters installed with Photoshop, Painter, or another compatible 2D painting application. You can substitute KPT Effects for KPT5, since they both have the plug-in we'll reference here. The *FraxFlame* plug-in we refer to in this chapter can result in the creation of some very unusual and stunning Bryce objects. If you have all of the applications installed and at your fingertips, please proceed.

Using 2D Plug-Ins in Bryce

Many plug-in filters can be accessed directly, or internally, from Bryce. If you have never done this, then you will have to tell Bryce where to look for your plug-in filter folder. If you have already done that, you can skip the following walkthrough. To install the path to your plug-in filters into Bryce, do the following:

1. Open Bryce. Place a Sphere on the screen from the Create toolbar.
2. Open the Sphere's Material Lab by clicking on the "M" that appears on the side of the Sphere. The Material Lab for the Sphere appears (see Figure 21.1).
3. Place a bead in the Transparency Value row for Texture A. This means that the object—in this case, a Sphere—will refer to whatever

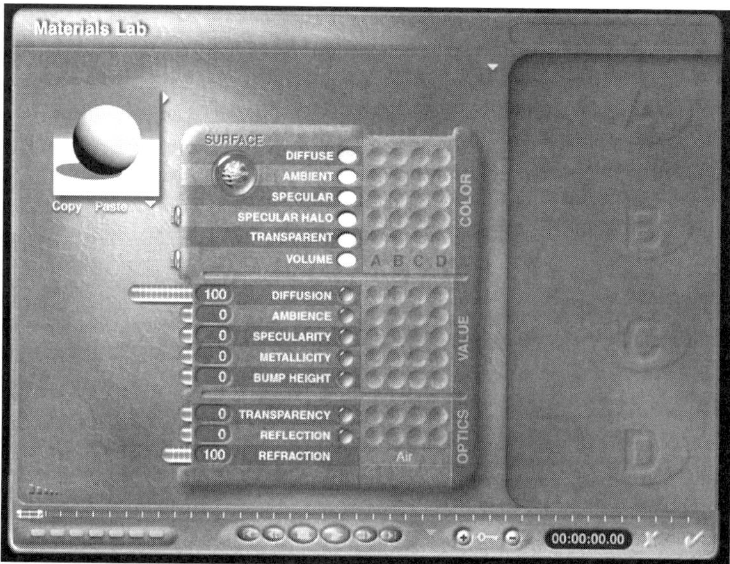

FIGURE 21.1 The Materials Lab for the Sphere appears.

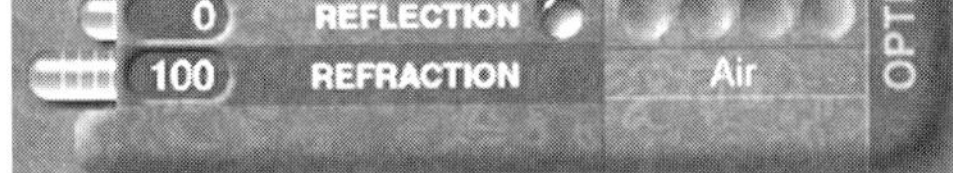

FIGURE 21.2 Place a bead as shown here.

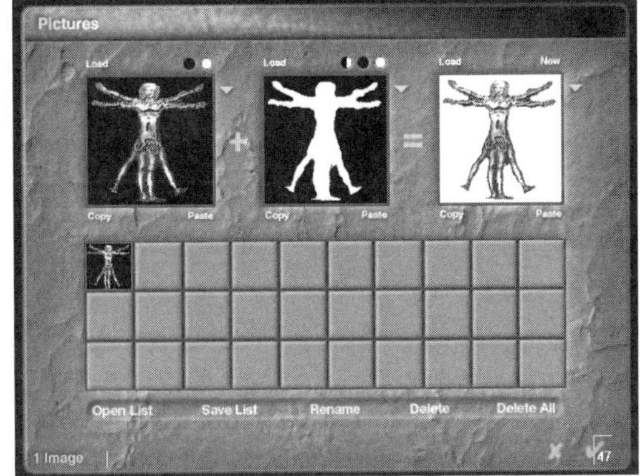

FIGURE 21.3 The Pictures Editor.

is referred to in this Texture A slot for its opacity/transparency (see Figure 21.2).

4. The Texture Mapping Mode controls will appear at the upper right. Configuring the parameters addressed by these controls will create the Transparency Map content for the sphere. Click the "P" for Picture at the bottom left of the Texture Mapping Mode controls. Then, click the Texture Source Editor at the top left of the Texture Mapping Mode controls. This transports you to the Pictures Editor(see Figure 21.3).
5. As you are by now well aware, Bryce allows you to create texturing data in two ways: from Procedural (mathematical) textures or from bitmap images (pictures). We will create a texture from Picture data. Make sure the default Hermetic Man image is selected. At the upper right of the first preview box, you'll see a downward-pointing arrow. Click on it to open the plug-ins list. If you haven't told Bryce where your plug-ins are, or if you want to change where Bryce looks for them, select the item in the list that reads "Select Plugins Folder." A window appears called "Browse for Folder." Use the path data in the folder to select the plug-ins folder where your KPT plug-ins are located. After this folder is selected, all of the plug-ins in that folder, including those for Bryce 5, will be accessible in Bryce.

TIME FOR FRAXFLAME

The plug-in filter that this tutorial will center on is FraxFlame in either the KPT5 or KPT Effects collection, but we have to prepare for that first. Filters can only be applied to existing images. The only image that appears by default in the Pictures Editor is the Hermetic Man. However, we do not want a texture that includes the Hermetic Man, so we have to delete him. If we just press the Delete key, however, and delete this figure, and then attempt to select a plug-in, Bryce might crash. That's because there will be no image to relate the plug-in to. Therefore, we have to find another way to maintain some image content, but to delete the Hermetic Man from it. Do the following to accomplish this:

1. Above the first and second preview areas in the Picture Editor, you will see a black circle. Click on each of these black circles in turn, and answer Delete when the message reads "Are you sure you want to delete?" Now you have two black preview areas, followed by an area with nothing in it (see Figure 21.4).
2. Now you can return to the plug-in list activated from the top-right arrow next to the first preview area. Select KPT5 or KPT Effects from the list, and then select the FraxFlame plug-in filter. The FraxFlame filter's interface appears (see Figure 21.5).
3. Make sure you have read the FraxFlame documentation before proceeding, so that you know what the terms we will use mean. If you need to refresh your memory of how FraxFlame works, click on the Torus Knot symbol at the upper right of the FraxFlame interface to bring up the docs in PDF format (see Figure 21.6).
4. Here are some tips for configuring FraxFlame parameters for this tutorial:

    - Because we are working with a sphere, select the Spherical option in the Style window. This will make the mapping conform to a sphere easier.

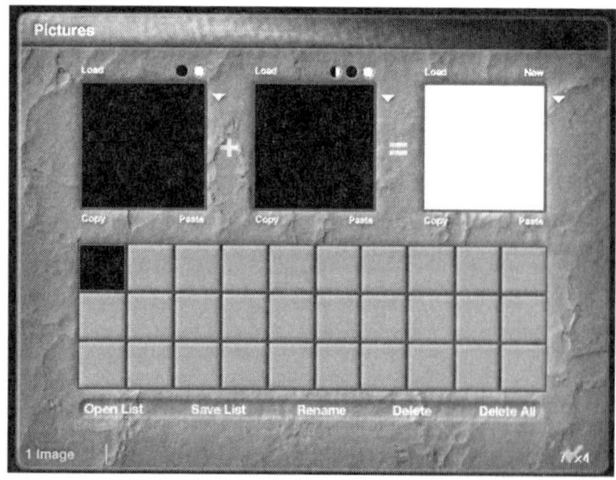

FIGURE 21.4 This is what your Picture Editor should look like now.

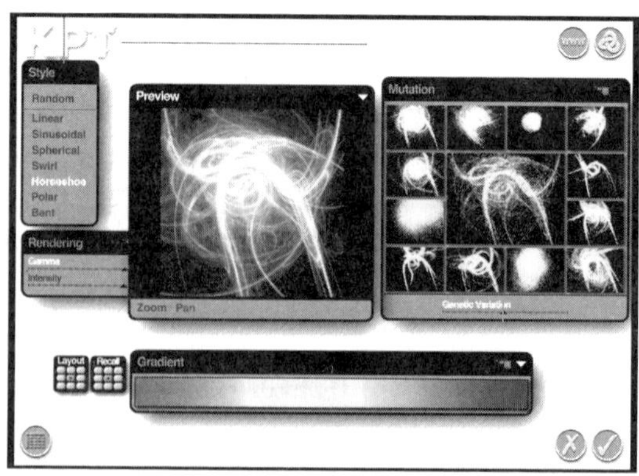

FIGURE 21.5 The FraxFlame filter's interface.

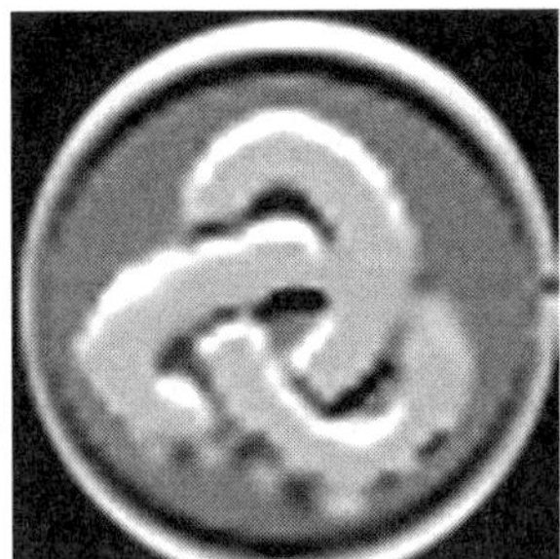

FIGURE 21.6 Click on this symbol on the FraxFlame interface to bring up the docs in PDF form.

- In the Rendering window, set the Gamma slider to about one-third of the way to the right. Gamma settings determine the way that the light "bleeds" over the entire Image map. We are addressing the Transparency channel, so having too much light bleed means that areas of the Image map will not cause 100% transparency. We would not want that.
- In the Rendering window, set the Intensity slider to about two-thirds of the way to the right. Higher intensities create very contrasted images, meaning that there would be less blending between the image content and the edge of that content. Two-thirds is high enough.
- Select a FraxFlame image that is fairly "stringy," so that you are creating a transparent object with linear streaks (see Figure 21.7).

5. Back in the Picture Editor, Copy the new content of preview area 1 to preview area 2. The screen should look like Figure 21.8.
6. Accept these changes and return to the Picture Editor. Place a bead in the Diffuse channel for Texture B, and select the Procedural texture

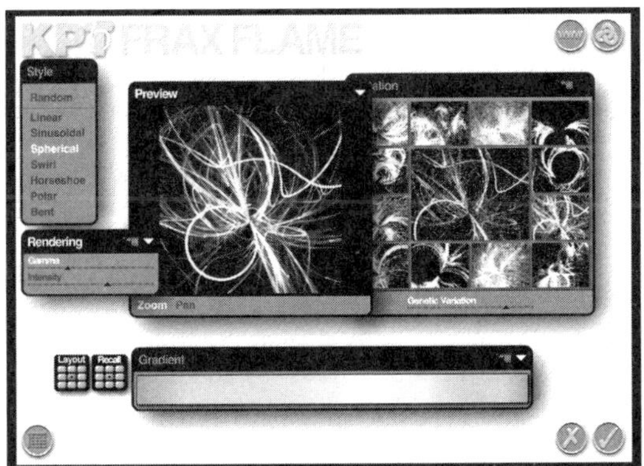

FIGURE 21.7 Select a fairly stringy image as shown here.

FIGURE 21.8 Your screen should resemble this example.

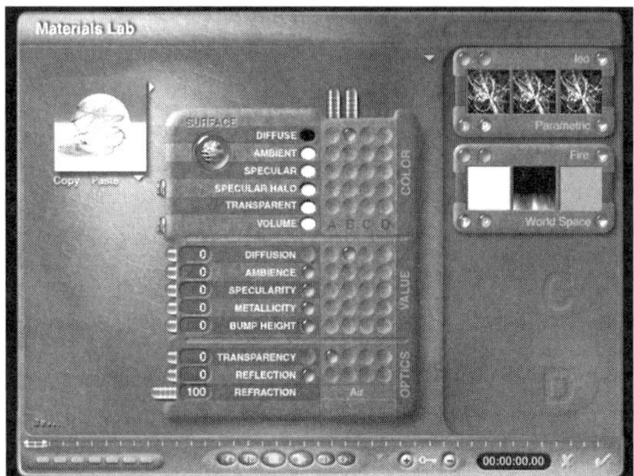

FIGURE 21.9 The Materials Lab window should now look like this.

FIGURE 21.10 The FraxFlame sphere creates an interesting sky effect.

called "Fire." Your Materials Lab should now look like that in Figure 21.9.

7. Accept the settings. Back on the main Bryce document, enlarge the Sphere to about 30 times its original size. Create a plane. Mapped with any texture you like. Go to the Sky Presets and select a sky. Make sure the sphere is cut in half by the Ground Plane (use the Front view). Render for effect (see Figure 21.10).
8. You can rotate the Sphere on any axis in order to find an image that you like best. Obviously, you can also animate the rotation of the Sphere. Now for some experimentation: Duplicate the Sphere, and Scale the duplicate to 120%. Rotate the duplicate 20 degrees on any axis.
9. Place other Primitive objects in the scene of your own choice, and apply the same material to them. Place an anatomical figure in the scene if you have access to one, and apply the same material to it without any transparency, but with the FraxFlame material in its Diffuse and Ambient channels. Your image will be unique, based on your selection of objects. Our results can be seen in Figure 21.11.

Have fun exploring other Bryce uses for the FraxFlame textures.

CREATING A STILL LIFE

Still life studies have always served painters as a way to understand materials, color, form, and the way light behaves. This is as true in this age of electric art as it was when the artist placed items on a table, and with oil paint palette in one hand, began to apply paint to a canvas. The main dif-

FIGURE 21.11 In this image, the FraxFlame material was applied to everything but the Ground Plane. The beings you see lurking in the scene were created with Amorphium Pro, and imported into Bryce, where they were also mapped with the FraxFlame material, but with no transparency. The Ground Plane is 100% reflective to create an even eerier effect.

ference lies in how the final rendering is displayed. When displayed on a computer monitor or TV screen, the color and light are projected directly into your eyes, as opposed to being appreciated as reflective light being bounced off of a paper or canvas surface. No matter the media, you can learn a lot by setting up and painting or rendering a 3D still life.

We will use two of Bryce 5's new features in this tutorial: Metaball modeling and Tree objects. Open Bryce 5, and let's begin.

1. Set your screen size to 640 × 480. Delete the default Ground Plane. Turn Ground Shadows and Underground Off, using their respective icons on the right side of the display.
2. Go to the Sky & Fog mode, and under the Sky Options thumbnail at the top, select Atmosphere Off. Use the Eyedropper to select a white hue. This allows us to work on a solid white canvas.
3. Go to the Create mode. Click on a Cube icon to place a Cube in the scene. Scale the Cube so that it looks like a table top, which is what it will be (see Figure 21.12).
4. Click on the "M" icon next to the table top to bring up the Materials Editor. Select a Plank Wood material from the Simple & Fast folder.

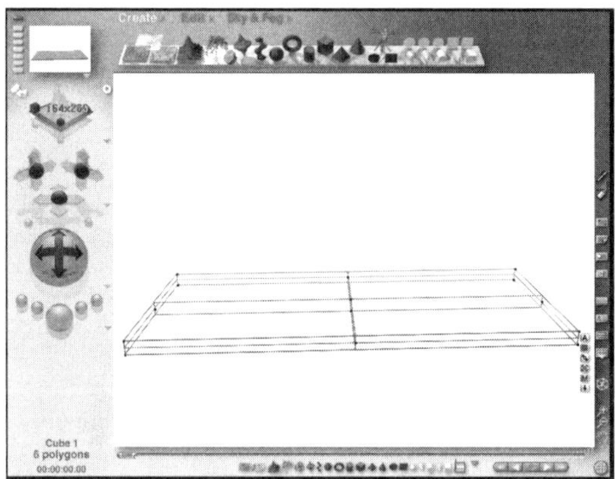

FIGURE 21.12 Create a table top from a Cube.

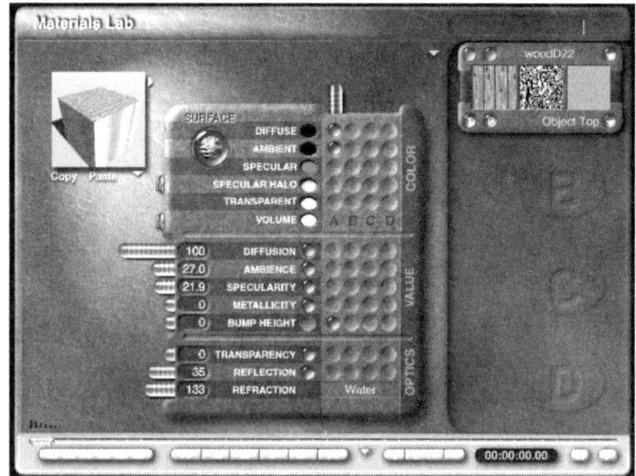

FIGURE 21.13 Configure a Plank Wood material for the table top.

Set the XYZ Scale of the material to 60%, and use Object Top mapping. Set Reflection to 35% (see Figure 21.13).

5. Do a test render of the scene so far. It should resemble Figure 21.14.
6. Open the Imported Objects folder in the Objects Library, and select the Slotted Screw. This makes a nice table leg. Click on the check mark to place it in the scene (see Figure 21.15).
7. Apply a Polished Walnut material to the Screw from the Simple & Fast folder in the Materials Library.
8. Scale the Screw so that it is sized for a table leg. Place it in position at one of the corners, using a Front and Top view to position it cor-

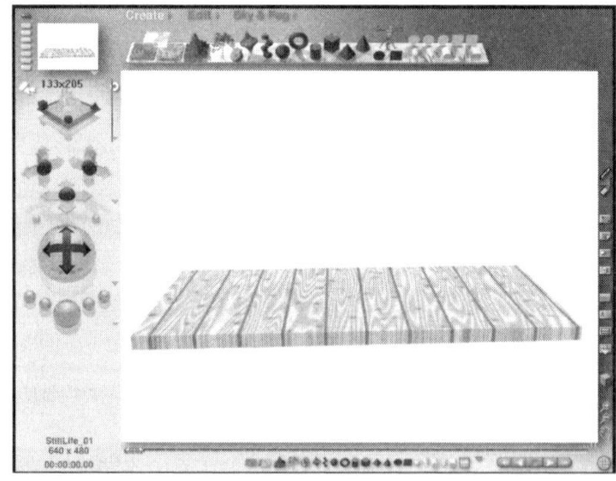

FIGURE 21.14 Do a test render.

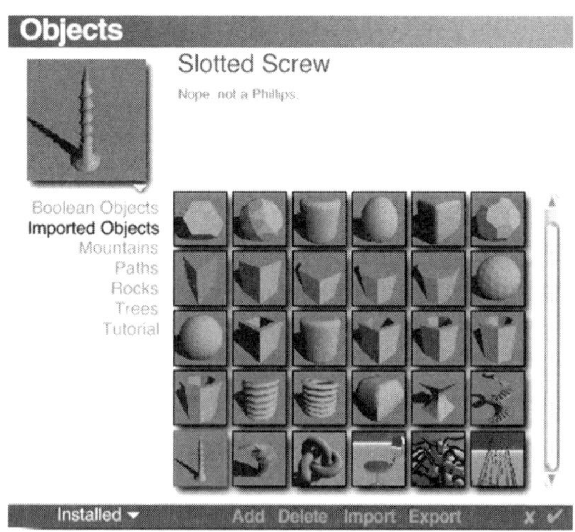

FIGURE 21.15 Select the Slotted Screw.

FIGURE 21.16 The table as it looks so far.

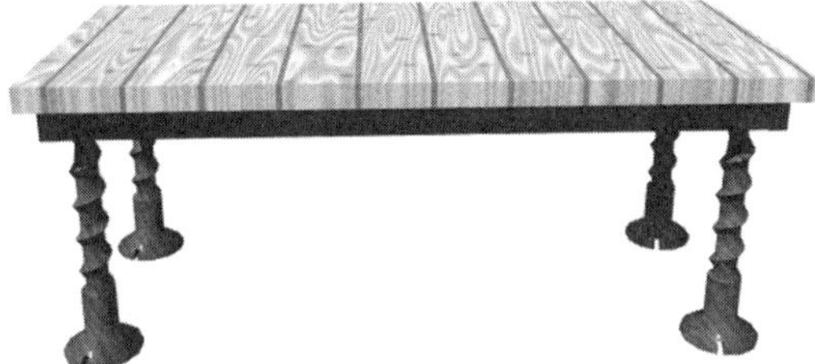

FIGURE 21.17 Create the table frame.

rectly. Edit>Duplicate three times, and move the duplicates into position for the other three legs (see Figure 21.16).

9. Create a Polished Walnut frame from duplicated Cube primitives, and place under the table top to finish the table, as shown in Figure 21.17.
10. The table is complete, but the top looks a bit out of place. The wood is too light. Darken the wood by opening the Materials Editor for the table top Plank Wood, and going to the Deep Texture Editor. Reset the colors as shown in Figure 21.18.
11. Group all of the table parts. Open the Objects Library, and save the table in the Tutorial or another folder (see Figure 21.19).

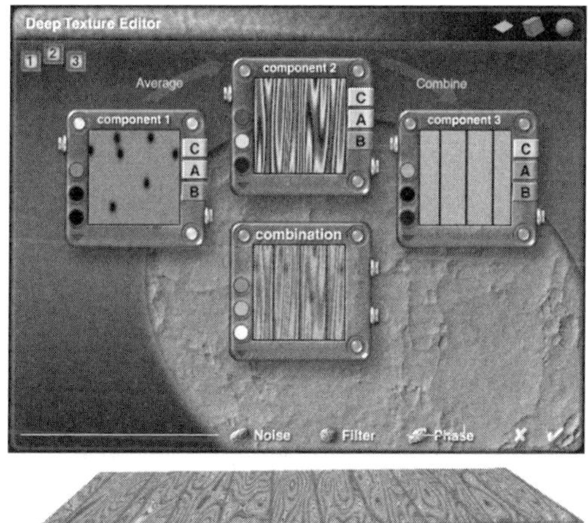

FIGURE 21.18 Reset the colors in the Deep Texture Editor.

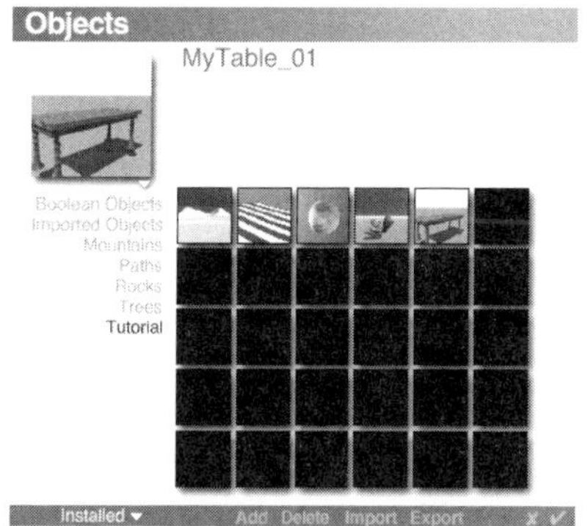

FIGURE 21.19 Save the model of the table.

It's always a good idea to save each object separately in a complex scene, so separate objects can be used in other projects later on.

12. Since you saved the table to the Objects Library, you can delete it from the scene for now.
13. Place a Metaball in the scene, and reduce its X-axis scale to create the form shown in Figure 21.20.
14. By Duplicating and Rotating, create a five-petaled flower from the squashed Metaball. Group all as Flower_1 (see Figure 21.21).

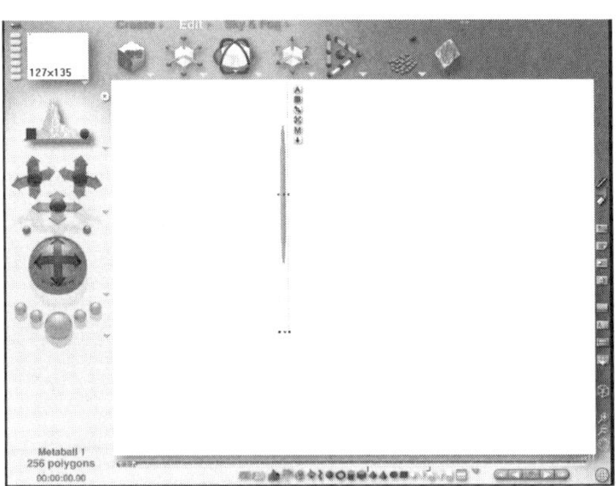

FIGURE 21.20 Create this Metaball form, as seen from the Front view.

FIGURE 21.21 Create an arrangement of five grouped petals.

15. Duplicate the five-petaled flower, and flip the duplicate vertically. Make it about one-third the size of the original, and group it with the original. This will serve as the finished flower. It doesn't need a stem for this project (see Figure 21.22).
16. Color the top cluster yellow, and the bottom one red. Save the completed two-clustered flower as Big_Flower to the Objects Library, and then delete it from the scene.
17. Go to the Imported Objects folder in the Objects Library, and place the Eight-Sides_Hollow object in the scene. This will serve as a vase (see Figure 21.23).
18. Map the vase with a Green Glass material from the Glass folder in the Materials Editor.
19. Place a Tree object in the vase, and open the Tree Editor from Edit mode. Use the settings shown in Figure 21.24.

FIGURE 21.22 The finished flower.

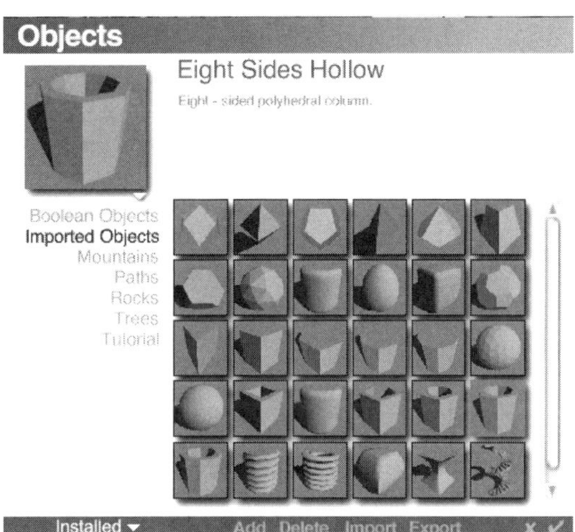

FIGURE 21.23 Place the Eight-Sides_Hollow object in the scene.

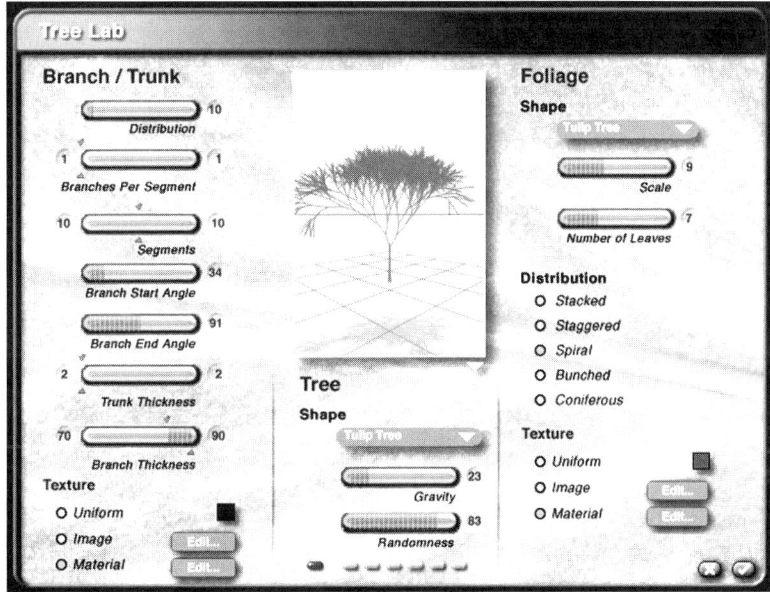

FIGURE 21.24 Use these Tree settings.

20. Load the finished flower that you saved previously from the Objects Library. Scale to size, and place duplicates of the flower in a random arrangement over the tree (see Figure 21.25).
21. OK. Let's add the table back in the scene, and place the vase of flowers on the table (see Figure 21.26).

FIGURE 21.25 Place flowers on the Tree object, which now serves as a plant placed in the vase.

FIGURE 21.26 Place the vase on the table.

22. Create a floor and background wall from squashed Cubes, and map them with whatever materials you prefer. We used a light wood paneling for the wall, and the Archeological Find material for the floor. Use an interesting camera angle. Do a test render (see Figure 21.27).

FIGURE 21.27 Create and place a floor and wall in the scene. Notice the subtle reflections from the green glass vase on the tabletop.

23. Use any bowl-like object from the Boolean Folder in the Objects Library. Change the bowl color to red, which is the complimentary color of the green vase, leading to more viewer interest and interesting reflections. Fill it with reflective gold spheres. Group with the bowl, and place on the table for more object and color interest (see Figure 21.28).

FIGURE 21.28 Add a bowl of golden reflective spheres to the composition. Just to break up the symmetry, we placed one sphere outside of the bowl on the table.

24. When it comes to creating great-looking pools of liquid, you can't beat Metaballs. Flatten a Metaball and Duplicate it, placing the Duplicates at a distance from the original in the top view so that they all run together. Use a material with a 75% transparency and a 45% reflection. Set Diffusion to 10% or less, and use a gray-blue color. If you like, place a tipped-over cup at one end. This adds some random chaos to an otherwise too-mechanical scene (see Figure 21.29).
25. When your 3D rendering is complete, you can port the finished image to Corel Painter or Adobe Photoshop, and use an appropriate filter to give the image a more traditional painterly look (see Figure 21.30).

FIGURE 21.29 Add a Metaball "liquid spill" and a cup.

FIGURE 21.30 These images of the still life have been altered with a selection of Photoshop filters.

IT'S JUST THE BEGINNING

Although you've reached the end of this book, your Bryce adventures will continue on. Hopefully, you discovered some new creative options in this book and on its companion CD-ROM that will enhance your future Bryce efforts.

APPENDIX

A About the CD-ROM

The CD-ROM that accompanies this book is full of all sorts of goodies for your use and exploration. The contents include the following Bryce associated material:

Anims folder: Here you'll find a collection of Bryce animation examples, all in QuickTime format. You can download QuickTime from www.apple.com if you don't have it.

Color Plates folder (ColPlts): All of the color plates in the gallery are included in this folder in TIF format.

Images: In this folder, you'll find dozens of images you can use for 2D Object maps and more.

Models folder: This folder contains dozens of 3D models that you can import into Bryce.

Materials (Mtls): Here's a variety of Bryce Materials that you can access from the Materials Lab to create new looks for your objects.

Projects folder (Proj): In this folder, you'll find a large selection of Bryce project files. Many reference the tutorials presented in the book, but there are also some extra ones included.

Textures Folder (Txtrs): This folder includes dozens of textures. The files are in TIF format, so they will work in Bryce on either a Mac or PC.

DEMOS

The CD-ROM also includes a variety of demos for you to explore. They are included in the Software folder in separate Mac and Win folders. This handshaking software can expand your Bryce creative options tremendously. Included are:

Amapi (Mac and Win): This is a full working version with no constraints. A demo of Amapi version 6.1 is also included, allowing you to distinguish the new features of the higher version in case you want to upgrade from version 4.15. Use Amapi as an alternate modeling system to create Bryce models, or as a 3D conversion system to export other modeling formats into models that can be exported to Bryce.

BodyPaint 3D demo (Mac and Win): Use this demo of Maxon Software's BodyPaint to paint in 3D in real time on your exported Bryce Terrain models, creating textures not possible using other methods.

Illusion demo (Win): Impulse's Illusion is the best and easiest way to create post-production pyrotechnic effects on a Bryce image or animation.

Poser and PoserProPak demo (Mac and Win): Demo versions of Poser 4 and the Poser ProPak are included here for both Mac and Windows users. Use Poser to create articulated poseable models for your Bryce scenes.

XFrog demo (Win): Use this demo of XFrog, from Greenworks, to create all manner of flora that can be exported as a WaveFront file for use in LightWave.

SYSTEM REQUIREMENTS

Windows® 98, Windows 2000, or Windows NT® (Service Pack 6 or higher) or Windows ME, Pentium® processor (or compatible processor), 64 MB RAM (128 MB recommended),100 MB hard disk space, 24-bit color display, CD drive, VGA monitor, and a mouse or tablet.

Macintosh® and Power Macintosh®, Mac® OS 8.6 or later, 64 MB RAM (128 MB recommended), 100 MB hard disk space, 24-bit color display, CD drive, VGA monitor, and a mouse or tablet. **Mac® OS X**, 128 MB RAM, 100 MB hard disk space, 24-bit color display, CD drive, VGA monitor, and a mouse or tablet. Both systems also require Bryce 5

APPENDIX

B Vendor Information

To create the detailed models and renderings required by high-end Bryce users demands other software applications whose output can be read by and imported into Bryce. We have mentioned quite a few of these applications in detail in this book, and additional applications continue to appear on the market. Although a wide selection of software applications have been mentioned in this book as valuable to your Bryce work (aside from a suitable professional 3D application that contains the necessary wide range of modeling tools Bryce lacks), the following are considered very valuable applications by the author for serious Bryce work. Check the Corel Web site regularly to remain aware of the latest updates:

COREL'S LIST

www.corel.com

These are the most important helper applications. Note that many of these applications are listed under the Corel subsidiary *ProCreate*. The list includes Painter, PhotoPaint, CorelDraw, all of the KPT plug-ins, as well as other plug-ins for Painter/PhotoPaint.

Painter

Painter has a long history as a supportive application for Bryce. Especially noteworthy is the Image Hose tool in Painter. Spraying graphic elements with the Image Hose allows you to create a huge array of valuable color and Alpha content to wrap on 3D objects in Bryce, making it possible to create highly complex and photorealistic scenes without the memory drain associated with adding loads of 3D objects to achieve the same effects.

PhotoPaint

Besides all of the internal effects and image processing found in PhotoPaint, this application includes versions of effects filters that have to be purchased as extras when you use other painting applications. There is a natural partnership between PhotoPaint and Bryce.

CorelDraw

CorelDraw offers the vector artist a wealth of drawing options, and it's easy to port CorelDraw images to your external 3D application. Once there, you can translate the vector art into 3D objects, and export the objects to Bryce.

KPT Plug-Ins

We can't imagine using Bryce without access to the KPT Bryce effects filters. Once installed in your Painter and/or PhotoPaint plug-ins folder, you can access any of the KPT filters directly from Bryce. With the KPT filters, you can create image-processed data for any channel in the Materials Lab, and use the KPT filters to augment your 3D elevation maps in the Bryce Terrain Editor.

Other Plugins for Painter/PhotoPaint

We could list 100 diverse plug-in applications here, but instead we'll point out a few of those that we have personally found extremely valuable for Bryce work.

ALIENSKIN XENOFEX AND ALIENSKIN EYECANDY 4000

These are two very hot collections of image effects from one of the best-known effects developers in the world. These effects filters are perfect for Bryce work (*www.alienskin.com*).

ENI OKEN ORNAMENTS COLLECTION

You have already spent a good deal of time seeing what the Eni Oken textures are capable of if you have worked through the eight tutorial projects in this book (*www.enioken.com*).

XAOS TOOLS TERRAZZO

When it comes to creating some of the most beautiful tiles for your Bryce palace floors imaginable, this plug-in does the trick (*www.xaostools.com*).

DIGIEFFECTS WEB EUPHORIA

This is a relatively new set of PhotoPaint/Painter effects filters, although they are based on filters marketed for Adobe AfterEffects by DigiEffects. The fire filter is worth the price of the entire package (*www.digieffects.com*).

ELECTRICIMAGE AMORPHIUM

In our opinion, Bryce without Amorphium is like a ice cream sundae without the topping. Amorphium give you the capability to create a huge array of unique objects, or to customize any Terrain Editor object with a wide array of deformation effects and tools (*www.electricimage.com*).

CURIOUSLABS POSER

When it comes to adding characters and anatomical figures to your Bryce worlds, either as full 3D objects or as renders for planar maps, Poser fills the bill (*www.curiouslabs.com*).

MAXON COMPUTER'S BODY PAINT

When it comes to high-end 3D painting applications, look no further than Maxon's BodyPaint. Using this software, you can intuitively paint color maps, reflection maps, bump maps, and other channel data directly to a imported 3D object. Use BodyPaint to place extremely detailed image maps on Bryce terrains (*www.maxon.net*).

OTHER BOOK MENTIONS

Appendix D, "Helpful Handshaking," covers other handshaking wares. Just so you can use this appendix to find the vendor you are looking for at a glance, although it is already listed in each separate chapter where appropriate, we'll repeat the vendor data here for your convenience:

BSmooth	www.kagi.com
DarkTree Textures	www.darksim.com
JewelSpace	www.caligari.com
Illusion/Organica	www.coolfun.com
ToonBoom Studio	www.toonboomstudio.com
Tree Professional	www.onyxtree.com
XFrog	www.greenworks.de
ZBrush	www.pixologic.com

APPENDIX

C Bryce Secrets Revealed!

As previously mentioned in various places in the book, Bryce Easter Eggs are hidden features in Bryce that can enhance your options. The problem is, you have to stumble upon the key combinations in order to use them. We have revealed a few in the course of your work through the tutorials, and here are some more.

Bryce Tree Object Files (Bryce 5.01 and later Updater). These files (.bto) fully describe a tree object without using the polygon count. The .bto files come in at 100 to 200 kb, instead of the 4 to 8MB a saved tree polygon model might consume. Here's what to do to access and save the .bto files:

1. Control/Click on the Tree icon in the Create toolbar. A window will open so that you can load a .bto object file. About 30 are included.
2. If you want to save your own trees as .bto files, Control/Alt Click on the Tree icon.

Exact Sun/Moon Placement. Control/Alt/Double-Click the Sun Control Trackball to enable the exact placement mode. Then, Control/Alt Click where you want the sun to be, or Shift/Control/Alt Click to place the moon.

Alternate Color Choosers. When selecting a color from one of the color bars in the Sky & Fog toolbar (which usually brings up the eyedropper), Alt/Click instead. This brings up a number of Chooser options. To access the System Color Picker, Control/Alt Click.

APPENDIX

D Helpful Handshaking

When you master Bryce, you might find that there are parts of a scene that you would like to create that can't be created in Bryce alone. Here are some applications that handshake in different ways with Bryce that you might want to consider adding to your digital toolset.

AMORPHIUM

Amorphium, from ElectricImage (*www.electricimage.com*), is a very valuable modeling application when it comes to customizing and deforming models to be used in Bryce scenes. There is no other 3D software quite like it. What makes Amorphium unique is its intuitive real-time clay modeling features and its array of deformation options. Bryce Terrain objects can be exported in several formats that Amorphium can read, and then imported back into Bryce once they have been customized.

ARTMATIC (MAC ONLY)

Here's one of the best creative solutions a Mac user can explore for generating unique bitmap textures for Bryce objects. The interface and tools allow you a maximum of hands-on interaction, and the textures range from fractal based to tiled. You can even use the images as sound templates. Go to U&ISoftware.com to learn more.

THE BAUMENT COLLECTIONS

Of all of the model commercial pre-constructed collections ready to import to Bryce worlds, the Baument CD volumes offer the best bang for the buck. As of the writing of this book, Baument (Baumgarten Enterprises) markets five separate CDs of modeled content, and each of the CD volumes contains a different set of model categories. Meshes I and II contain a variety of diverse models. Meshes III contains unique flowers and plants. The forth volume contains low-polygon count figures in period dress, making it simple for you to place a entire company of infantry in a Bryce world. Volume 5 (Combo 5) is a compilation of models from the other sets, and some new ones, too. All of the models are in 3DS format, so they import easily into Bryce for smoothing and materials application.

www.baument.com

BSMOOTH

BSmooth is the closest thing to a Bryce plug-in. It is the perfect application for creating a wide array of diverse and unique terrain elevation maps, as well as complete terrain models.

BSmooth can be found at *www.bsmooth.de*, and can be purchased for around $25.00 US. You can also download a demo version, although its effectiveness is severely limited until you register. BSmooth is a Mac-only utility, but a Windows version is under construction and might be available by the time you read this. Once you purchase the software key (which is placed in the same folder as the application), it remains viable for all future versions of the software. At the time of this printing, BSmooth was at version 3.3b5.

BSmooth creates models or terrain maps by allowing you to combine various elements ("operators") in a hierarchical pipeline. The operators include terrain modeling options not present in Bryce 5: Extrude, Vertical Lathe, Horizontal Lathe, Sweep, Lines Per Curve Segment, Pixel Layer, GEOPO30 and 1 Degree DEM Options, Invert, Amplify, Polar, Condensation, Mandelbrot, Wave, Gaussian Blur, and Mirror.

DARKTREE TEXTURES 2.0

DarkTree Textures, from Darkling Simulations (*www.darksim.com*), is a Windows-only application used to design procedural and bitmap textures. Procedural textures are designed for a number of 3D applications (3ds max, LightWave, AnimationMaster, Cinema 4D, and a few more), although Bryce is not among the procedurally supported group yet. The textures, however, can readily be saved a bitmaps, including a selection of wrapping options, which you can use in Bryce. Because even the bitmaps stem from procedural algorithms (formulas), the bitmaps retain the look of a procedural texture.

DarkTree procedural textures either can be built from algorithmic components, or can be constructed from one or more layers of texture presets. Any preset can also be edited on its own for more customized variety.

GROBOTO

GroBoto is a Mac-only application that features a large array of 3D modeled components that can be glued together intuitively to create some fantastic and bizarre models that can be exported to formats that Bryce can read. Although you can create some interesting organic forms in GroBoto, its modeled content is more suitable for "hard" objects such as mechanical parts and urban environments (*www.groboto.com*).

ILLUSION

Impulse *Illusion* (*www.coolfun.com*) is one of the most magical f/x applications available for computer graphics animators. With Illusion, a Windows-only application (a Mac version is in the works), you can quickly create hundreds of unique pyrotechnic and other effects. Illusion is a post-production product, meaning that you have to create the Bryce animation first and then apply the effects in Illusion.

If you need to create pyrotechnic effects for your Bryce animation (fire, explosions, smoke, or other particle-based effects), you soon realize that Bryce itself is not the place to do it. Bryce renderings are slow, and if you have reflective or transparent surfaces in the animation, the process can be very, very slow. Illusion is very fast, and provides the quality and breadth of effects that have only been available for major film production up to this point. Indeed, Illusion continues to be used for broadcast TV and Hollywood films.

JEWELSPACE

JewelSpace is from Caligari Corporation (www.caligari.com), the same developer that markets trueSpace, a classy Windows-only 3D application.

Caligari's new JewelSpace *software makes the design of jewelry very friendly. The interface of JewelSpace is exactly like that of the vintage trueSpace software, so users familiar with trueSpace will have a much more friendly learning curve when creating models in JewelSpace.*

What's different about JewelSpace when compared to trueSpace are the model and material libraries to which you have access. The model presets include ornaments, shanks, bracelets, earrings, pendants, pins, anniversary rings, bands, bezel rings, bridal rings, gemstone rings, gold rings, men's rings, and stackable rings. A new light setting called Jewelry is also included. In addition to the preset models, you also have access to a huge library of components that you can use to create customized jewelry. This includes every gemstone geometry you can imagine, and some you can't. The Paths library contains path elements that can be used as lofting paths for chains and other jewelry components. The preset Materials library includes over 170 new materials that you can use to create very realistic gemstones and other things such as pearls. A wealth of standard objects and materials round out the selections that you can use to build just about anything, in addition to jewelry objects—all for Bryce import.

KPT PLUG-IN FILTERS

You are strongly advised to purchase and install KPT 3, 5, 6, and KPT Effects in your 2D painting application's folder if you haven't already done so. As a Bryce user, you should definitely own and become working familiar with these plug-ins. Each KPT plug-in collection offers you a variety of options not available anywhere else as far as creating and enhancing Bryce content. The plug-ins can be installed in your Plug-ins folder inside your favorite 2D image application (e.g., PhotoPaint, Photoshop, or Painter), or directly within the Bryce 5 Plug-ins folder. Either way, the plug-ins can be accessed from Bryce. *www.corel.com*

ORGANICA

You already know about the metaball operations in Bryce, having worked through the early chapters in this book. There are also many external standalone applications and plug-ins capable of metaball modeling, whose results can be exported to Bryce.

The most full-featured metaball application around is *Organica* from Impulse Software (*www.coolfun.com*). Organica includes over a dozen metaball primitive forms, in addition to the common metaball sphere. If you enjoy working with metaballs in Bryce and want to push your metaball modeling into a more complex arena, investigate Organica.

PAINTER'S IMAGE HOSE

If you are a Procreate's Painter user (*Procreate* is a division of Corel, Inc.), you are no doubt familiar with the Image Hose tool in Painter. The Image Hose literally sprays image content based on a selection of "nozzles." The nozzles in Painter include dozens of unique brushes that reference all types of data, from abstract patterns to flora and fauna. Image Hose influenced paintings are best used in Bryce on a 2D Picture Plane object, cutting down on the memory required when you need to fill a scene with background components that look photorealistic, without the content having to be 3D model based.

Although you can use any of the nozzles that ship with Painter, we highly recommend the Jungle 3D CD from DigiArts Software. This heavy collection of Image Hose nozzles is made especially for Bryce work, and should not be overlooked by any Bryce/Painter user. Jungle 3D has over 1000 nozzles, with 50 different plants and trees. They're perfect for Bryce because the Alpha channel data is built in. Find out more at www.gardenhose.com.

POSER

Your Bryce worlds, no matter how unique, can always benefit from human, animal, and perhaps even fantasy characters. When it comes to adding anatomical models in Bryce, CuriousLabs' Poser (*www.curiouslabs.com*) is a vital handshaking application. No matter how well crafted and authentic a Bryce terrain might be, it becomes much more alive when you add a character or two to it. Poser 4 was the current edition of the software at the time this book was written, but it might well be in a later version by the time you read this. Poser has a huge array of anatomical models that ship with the software. In addition, there are models constantly being developed for Poser by other parties, the chief among which is Daz3D (*www.daz3d.com*)

Although CuriousLabs has developed a number of translation applications for porting fully animated project files from Poser to 3ds max, LightWave, Cinema 4D, and other 3D applications, it has not addressed Bryce as a target application for

*porting Poser animated content. Don't be discouraged, however, because someone else has taken the opportunity to do it! S&J Soft Systems Ltd. of Finland (*www.datamike.com/susu.htm*) has developed an application called Susanna that allows you to port fully animated Poser characters to your Bryce worlds.*

TREE PROFESSIONAL

OK. Answer this question: Can you ever have enough trees for Bryce worlds? If your answer is "no," then you will be interested in exploring Tree Professional from Onyx Software (www.onyxtree.com). Although Bryce features its own awesome tree generator with its own library of presets and control options, there might be times when the tree that your imagination is picturing just can't be generated inside Bryce. If and when that time arrives, consider purchasing TreePro, a valuable add-on for your Bryce work. TreePro allows you to alter the parameters of any of its preset tree forms, or to create your own tree and/or bush model from scratch. The TreePro presets include both real-world trees and fantasy models, any of which can be customized to any extent you need. Models can be saved out in a number of 3D formats for Bryce incorporation, including LightWave, Wavefront, and DXF.

TOONBOOM STUDIO

Imagine that in addition to singular images, you could map animated frames to a 2D picture plane in Bryce. Wouldn't that be great? If you could do that, you could easily show animated figures and objects going through their motions against your spectacular Bryce backdrops. ToonBoom Studio (*www.toonboomstudio.com*) for both Windows and the Mac systems is a superlative professional 2D animation application that allows you to manipulate your Bryce data in a post-production environment to create exactly these types of animations.

ToonBoom Studio (*www.toonboom.com*) was developed explicitly for the creation of animations that have the "flat" traditional cartoon look. If you are unfamiliar with what this indicates, just tune into the Saturday morning cartoon shows to see what this means. ToonBoom Studio was designed as a production tool for all animators wishing to post their works to the Web, and boasts the following features: complete Animation Path controls, a large set of Ink and Paint tools, sound track incorporation, global controls over sequencing and timing, multiple views for exact placement of 3D depth content, Light Table, exporting to Flash or Quick-

Time movie formats, multiple scenes with multiple Animation Sets in a single movie, and more.

XFROG

XFrog (*www.greenworks.de*) excels as a Bryce modeling application, especially when it comes to the creation of unique flora for your Bryce world. XFrog can also be used to generate all manner of tree models, and features a collection of preset libraries to emphasize that fact. In terms of 3D model creation for Bryce, however, some prefer to use XFrog to create other organic forms such as flowers and alien flora. XFrog uses an intricate pipeline of hierarchical elements to create organic models, most of which would either be impossible or extremely difficult and time consuming with any other application.

ZBRUSH

A good percentage of Bryce users are also fans and users of ZBrush from Pixologic (*www.pixologic.com*). One reason for this might be that Bryce users enjoy working with other software that is also on the creative cutting edge, and that certainly describes ZBrush. ZBrush is best described as an application that allows you to paint 2D images with 3D components, on either a Mac or a Windows system. You can also use it to create, deform, and export 3D objects that Bryce can easily import. ZBrush can address Bryce in three distinct ways: 2D image creation for placement on Bryce 2D picture object planes, 2D image creation for use as Bryce elevation map data, and 3D object creation for placement in a Bryce scene.

In addition to all of the aforementioned Bryce handshaking applications, you can use any of the professional 3D modeling and animation applications to develop 3D content for Bryce. This includes 3ds max, LightWave, Cinema 4D, Carrara, ElectricImage, and similar applications.

New, amazing software is in constant development that can be used to develop content for Bryce purposes, so stay aware of what is coming to the marketplace.

Index

B

C

U

V